CHILE:

Politics And Society

A quienes viven, imborrables, en nuestro recuerdo;
sus últimos suspiros inspirarán verdadero renacer.

A quiénes sufren, impotentes, la iniquidad y el tormento;
sus quebrantos abrirán porvenir de justicia y libertad.

Al Chile que fue, y aún más, (luego de este interludio amargo),
Al Chile que habrá de ser.

CHILE:
Politics And Society

Edited by

Arturo Valenzuela

and

J. Samuel Valenzuela

Transaction Books
New Brunswick, New Jersey

Transaction Books
Rutgers University
New Brunswick, New Jersey 08903

Library of Congress Catalog Card Number: 73-92814
ISBN:0-87855-087-9 (cloth)
ISBN:0-87855-579-X (paper)

Printed in the United States of America

Contents

Introduction

> As in the tragedies of Greek classical theater, all know what will happen, all do not wish it to occur, but each one does precisely what is necessary to provoke the unfortunate outcome everyone pretends to avoid.
>
> From a letter addressed to General Carlos Prats, retiring commander in chief of the Chilean armed forces, by Radomiro Tomic, a leader of the Christian Democratic party, a few days before the September 11, 1973 coup.

There was a profound sense of doom, of impending confrontation. The Chilean Left warned of a Fascist campaign organized in collusion with self-interested external forces, while the Right decried the imminent formation of a Marxist totalitarian state. Each event acquired an intricate political significance, and every fact had at least two totally divergent interpretations. The voices of conciliation and moderation were drowned out and dismissed as utopic and naive. It was no longer a matter of structuring an agreement but of imposing one's own solution.

The tense political climate engulfed everyone. Groups of opposing views skirmished daily in the streets of major cities. Essential services were interrupted or operated deficiently. Truck owners, shopkeepers, dentists, doctors and engineers went on

strike demanding President Salvador Allende's resignation. Sabo-
teurs wrecked pipelines, railways, high-tension cables. All inter-
urban transport was placed under armed protection. Long lines
formed in front of any store which opened its doors as consumers
rushed to replenish or increase stocks of essential items. Neighborhood committees in both upper- and lower-class sectors urged
residents to attend meetings for the purpose of organizing the
defense of their homes, each believing that an attack was
imminent from the other side. Throughout the country groups on
the Left urged unions and popular organizations to discuss
strategies for mobilization and resistance in case of a coup d'état.
Mass demonstrations were called as a show of force either in
support of or in opposition to the Popular Unity coalition government. Using recently acquired legal authority, military commanders pressed an indiscriminate and mostly fruitless search for
arms in factories taken over by the government or the workers.
While certain leaders of the Left and Center warned of the danger
of civil war and of the necessity to search for the means to avoid
it, quiet preparations for overthrowing the Allende administration
became the order of the day in military barracks. The tumultous
events of mid-1973 presaged the imminent collapse and failure of
the attempt to lead Chile toward socialism within its traditional
democratic and constitutional framework—an attempt which had
begun three years earlier with the victory of the Left in the 1970
presidential elections.

There are certain historical periods in which the tempo of
events quickens, in which a multiplicity of long-standing contradictions suddenly conflate to produce a particular result. The
short-lived Popular Unity administration was such a period. While
the Left's failure was not inevitable since it was partly a function
of contingent events, it cannot be understood without examining
the structural arrangements defining the broad outlines of
political choice and action. The difficulties the Allende government faced stemmed not only from the strong reaction it
encountered among the internal and external forces whose
position and privileges were threatened by policies of fundamental change; they also resulted from the constraints imposed
by the traditional parameters of Chilean politics and society.

The essays in this book are designed to describe some of the fundamental aspects of the Chilean sociopolitical system. They provide the necessary background for understanding not only Salvador Allende's accession to the presidency but also the principal constraints to his policies of basic social change within the nation's traditional constitutional framework. They underscore the fact that the Popular Unity's adherence to and participation within this basic framework constituted a basic source of its strength as well as a symptom of its weakness. It is important to note that these essays were all written before the right-wing September 11, 1973, military coup. Except for placing verbs in the past tense and other minor alterations, none have been changed since then. They are not, therefore, the product of *ex post facto* observations. While they do not incorporate recent changes, they provide an essential introduction to the nature of the system the present authorities are attempting to transform.

In the first chapter, Arturo Valenzuela analyzes the overall characteristics of the Chilean political and institutional system and reveals the sources of some of the impediments to the Left's success. The government was not able to deviate substantially from the incrementalist style of much of Chilean politics, with its overriding concern for wage readjustments and particularistic transactions. It was similarly unable to overcome the rivalries between the parties within its coalition, which produced time-consuming discussions and a lack of coordination in the executive. The administration's initiatives were questioned by the courts, stalled by the rambling state bureaucracy and blocked by the Congress. The extreme ideological polarization of the nation's political forces impeded the formation of the necessary consensus to permit the successful implementation of government programs and, as revealed by the failure of the last-minute talks between Allende and Christian Democratic leaders, to ultimately avoid the breakdown of the constitutional system. While this polarization had long been a characteristic of Chilean politics, its effects were exacerbated during the Popular Unity administration by the fact that for the first time in the nation's history the parties which sought a fundamental transformation of the socioeconomic order were the principal actors in a presidential coalition. As the commitment to—or the rejection of—basic change became the salient issue, the extremes in the ideological spectrum acquired inordinate weight and the various parties' adherence to the rules of the political game were relegated by varying degrees to a secondary position.

The next chapter focuses more specifically on the electoral constraints that the Left's strategy faced. Robert Ayres points out that the overall stability of electoral preferences made a sharp increase in support for the Popular Unity coalition improbable. Moreover, he shows that the parties of the Left could not expect to capture the votes of all lower strata.

Using a different data base, Prothro and Chaparro arrive at conclusions which closely complement Ayres's analysis. They convincingly show that the shift toward the Left in Chilean governments from 1952 to 1972 did not result from a corresponding shift in the Left-Right distribution of public opinion. It was, rather, a product of the various alternatives offered to the electorate in successive campaigns.

Paul Sigmund offers a glimpse into the extent of ideological differences in the Chilean political system. These differences played an important role in the ultimate collapse of its institutions. The public was exposed through a process of self-selection to mass media offering radically different interpretations of virtually every issue. This contributed to the division of opinion into blocks with dissimilar perceptions, reinforced the lines of ideological polarization and became a significant factor in the breakdown of cross-partisan communications. Sigmund's contribution is unfortunately weak in its presentation of the right-wing perspective, the importance of which has been magnified by recent events.

In the following chapter, Samuel Valenzuela analyzes the historical development of the Chilean labor movement and its pattern of conflictual integration into the overall political and institutional structures. This pattern combines an almost exclusive union concern with the pursuit of greater socioeconomic benefits with a multifaceted reliance upon the parties of the Left in order to obtain them. The characteristics of the labor movement made it virtually impossible for the Popular Unity government not to increase the worker's capacity to consume, which, in the absence of an effective system of rationing and/or dramatic increases in production, contributed to economic dislocations.

Various strata can be distinguished within the working class. James Petras's analysis focuses on the dissimilarity of their perceptions toward popular participation in the process of social change during the Allende government. Although his emphasis on some of the differences he uncovers is slightly overdrawn, he provides a useful view of the ideological and organizational complexity within working-class sectors.

The Chilean political system was traditionally characterized by a limited amount of popular participation. This situation began to change considerably during the last twenty years, complicating the politics of distribution. Electoral turnout underwent a three-fold increase, and a multiplicity of organizations was formed among the most excluded sectors of the population to press for their demands. Alejandro Portes' contribution examines the political orientations of a sample drawn from one of these sectors, the urban slum-dwellers. He shows that there was a wide variety of partisan preferences and ideological commitments among them; they were not, therefore, an exclusively leftist constituency. Portes further shows that the strongest predictor of a leftist inclination was not the degree of poverty but the work experience of the respondent. Support for the Left was highest among blue-collar workers employed in manufacturing and construction.

Brian Loveman focuses on the changes in the Chilean countryside during the last ten years. He examines the growth of unionization among rural workers who, like the urban slum-dwellers, traditionally lacked an effective means of presenting their demands for better living conditions. He also analyzes the process of agrarian reform, the attempts to organize new forms of production and the ambiguities and failures of government actions.

The next chapter examines the patterns of ownership and control within the mining, manufacturing and service sectors of the Chilean economy. Maurice Zeitlin and Earl Ratcliff emphasize the extent of capital concentration, the importance of foreign capital in mining and services, and the crucial role played by the state. They further show the preponderance of national private capital in manufacturing. This preponderance however, has been, tempered by the heavy reliance of private industry upon subsidies and tariff protections, as well as by the recent pattern of intermeshing between national and foreign capital. Moreover, foreign interests have the ability to exercise a high degree of control with a minority participation, in part due to the various forms of dependency of local industry on foreign concerns. This dependency is hard to measure, but it is reflected in such aspects as the control of technological procedures and necessary raw materials, as well as the greater availability of local and foreign credits. Aside from the nationalization of the copper industry, the Allende administration did not produce a lasting alteration of the ownership and control patterns which Zeitlin and Ratcliff describe.

Elisabeth Farnsworth, Richard Feinberg and Eric Leenson demonstrate that it is not possible to understand fully the difficulties the Popular Unity administration faced without examining the constraints imposed by external linkages. The United States' refusal to settle the renegotiation of Chile's staggering foreign debt and the challenges to the legality of the nationalization of copper in European courts created uncertainties which made long-term planning difficult. The credit restrictions disrupted foreign trade, blocked the realization of some investment programs and led to difficulties in the renovation of industrial equipment and in the acquisition of spare parts. These external constraints should not be construed as the only source of economic problems during the Allende government. They did, however, aggravate the situation. The expansion of the internal market due to the government's wage policies created shortages which had to be met through production increases and/or higher levels of imports. Either course required the availability of foreign exchange and normal external trade patterns.

In many ways, it is not the Allende administration but the present military government which represents the sharpest break with Chile's past. The new authorities are not only critical of the Popular Unity coalition period; they also blame the nation's ills on what they perceive as the "statist" and "Socialist" character of traditional administrative structures and on the policies of past administrations which reflected them. They have thus embarked on a course that marks a definite discontinuity in Chilean history. The smoldering ruins of the presidential palace, destroyed by air-force jets, symbolize more than the end of an unsuccessful attempt at fundamental change. They also represent the break-down of the traditional institutional system and of the constitutional machinery, which with few exceptions had yielded a regular succession of central political authorities for 140 years.

The political system has therefore undergone major changes. The Congress has been closed, thus eliminating the principal traditional arena of confrontation and compromise between opposing interests and ideological views. The political parties have been suppressed: those supporting the Allende administration have been outlawed and the rest have been forced to suspend their activities. They have consequently ceased to function as the main nexus between the multiplicity of different organizations and the centers of power. The politician no longer plays the key brokerage role. Petitions are now addressed directly to the central bureaucracy or are channeled through military commanders. The mass media no longer openly express views opposed to the government; the leftist organs were confiscated, and the rest are either censored or exercise self-censorship. The universities have lost their long-cherished autonomy. The potential political role of the church and of employer and professional organizations has been strengthened by the vacuum created through the abrogation of traditional institutions. An important explicit objective behind most of these changes has been the replacement of politics in favor of administration by technicians. The result has been the creation of that type of politics which equates it to administration by closely defining the range of what is permissible.

Labor and student unions and most types of popular organizations still exist, but they are reduced to little more than their relatively ineffective internal welfare and social security functions. Every type of election has been banned throughout the nation. Vacancies in the leadership of all kinds of associations are filled through appointment or by following seniority lines. The industrial relations system has been transformed. The *Juntas de Conciliación* and the right to strike have been suspended. The labor inspectorates have less to conciliate, more to control. As in other areas, the selective application of the legal system has decreased its value as an objective standard defining reciprocal expectations and granting a series of guarantees as well as obligations. The outlawing of the Central Labor Federation and of the leftist parties has eliminated the support structures that were an important component of most unions' capacities to obtain greater benefits.

In the economic sphere, the junta has reversed many policies which had been applied during the last forty years. The authorities have released price controls on all but a few items. This measure benefits particularly the agricultural sector, since food prices had been controlled since the 1930s to facilitate urban lower-class consumption. The relaxation of tariff protections and subsidies has undermined the conditions which permitted the development of the nation's highly diversified but relatively inefficient industrialization aimed at satisfying domestic demand for consumer foods. The objective is to restructure the economy around the production of those items in which Chilean enterprises can be competitive in international markets. Conditions of entry and profit remittances for foreign capital have been liberalized.

The junta has also reversed many of the changes which occurred during the Allende administration. Most enterprises and banks which had been taken over by the government or the workers have been returned to private hands. The new authorities have promised to review the issue of compensation for the American copper companies; however, it is, highly unlikely that the industry itself will be denationalized. Many agrarian reform centers have been dismantled. Some of the land has been distributed among the peasants; some has been returned to the former landowners. The flow of credits from United States public and private sources has resumed, and agreements have been reached with respect to the renegotiation of Chile's foreign debt.

Whether or not the junta will succeed in rendering permanent the many changes it has initiated is an open question. Carlos Ibáñez del Campo's first government (1927-31) constitutes the only precedent of a similar attempt in Chilean history. (It is not surprising that his name is presently invoked frequently.) Ibáñez's efforts ended in failure. Party politics reemerged, national elections were held and the subservient institutions he created collapsed. However, the extent of today's political repression--which has meant either death, imprisonment or exile to thousands—and the magnitude of present hostilities and polarization have no parallel. A rebirth of democratic politics requires certain reconciliation and a reinstitution of consensus over procedure. Is this possible within the present generation after the traumatic events of the past seven months?

1

Political Constraints to the Establishment of Socialism in Chile

Arturo Valenzuela

The election of Salvador Allende to the presidency of Chile in 1970 had significant implications far beyond that country's boundaries. For Chile, it marked the accession to power, after several previous and unsuccessful attempts, of a coalition dominated by the Communist and Socialist parties. In broader terms, it was the first free election anywhere of a Marxist head of government committed to a fundamental transformation of his nation's existing economic, social and political systems.

Not only the election, but also the new government's promise to institute its revolutionary changes in accord with Chilean constitutional and legal precepts, became a matter of international interest. Indeed, in his first message to the Congress on May 1, 1971, Allende argued that this process would constitute a historical challenge comparable to the Russian Revolution in 1917.[1] In a different historical context, his government was pioneering in attempting to conform to a second model for the construction of socialist society, a model based, not on the violent destruction of the old order, but on its peaceful replacement in accord with Chile's democratic, pluralist and libertarian traditions.

The overthrow of Salvador Allende in a bloody military coup on September 11, 1974, raises serious questions as to whether

An earlier version of this article appeared in *Proceedings of the Academy of Political Science* 30 (Summer 1972).

Author's note: The author wishes to express his appreciation to Julio Samuel Valenzuela for his indispensable assistance in the preparation of this essay and to Douglas Chalmers for his insightful suggestions.

fundamental transformations can be implemented within the framework of traditional institutions. From the very outset of his administration, important economic sectors such as industrialists, landowners, professional associations, small shop-keepers and even some white- and blue-collar unions resisted attempts to curtail their vested interests. At times they acted alone; at other times they acted in conjunction with parties of the Right and Center. Combined with U.S. economic retaliation and government mismanagement, this opposition contributed to create a serious economic crisis. At the same time, important governmental bodies, such as the Supreme Court and the comptroller general, challenged countless actions by administration officials. More seriously, the opposition-controlled Congress passed legislation which limited the executive's power to take over private enterprises and curtailed expropriations in the countryside. Through this action, the legislature blunted the major thrust of the Popular Unity government—its attempt to establish through legal means a dominant social sector in the economy.

When Regis DeBray asked Allende, in January 1971, how he would handle such an impasse, the president responded that he would resort to a national plebiscite, a tool provided by the Chilean constitution with which a popular government can overcome a recalcitrant legislature.[2] Ironically, when the impasse materialized, the opposition called for a plebiscite while the government argued that the matter should be settled by the Constitutional Tribunal. Apart from legal arguments on both sides, the administration's position constituted tacit recognition that it might not be able to win such a plebiscite.

The government was not only challenged by legal and institutional roadblocks and an opposition fearful of rapid change; it was also challenged by its partisans within and without the Popular Unity coalition who felt that Allende was too concerned with legal technicalities and with reaching accommodation with opposition moderates. This challenge was exemplified by events in the industrial city of Concepción during May 1972. Members of the Movimiento de Izquierda Revolucionaria (Revolutionary Left Movement—MIR), in alliance with regional members of Popular Unity, sought to prevent by force an authorized march by the opposition. They argued that such marches gave comfort to fascist elements and undermined the popular government. In the ensuing struggle, the police were forced to intervene; one student, a member of an extreme-Left group, was killed.

The reaction to the death of the student and to the confrontation in Concepción was immediate and widespread. With the exception of the Communist party, the regional organizations of the governing coalition called for an immediate dismissal of the intendant of the province, a Communist, and the dissolution of the police antiriot unit. Student and youth groups demonstrated in cities throughout the country, echoing these demands. Demonstrators in the capital expressed their anger by shouting slogans such as "Reformism opens the door to fascism" and "Down with politics of conciliation."

A few days later, Miguel Enríquez, the leader of the MIR, strongly attacked the reformist nature of government policies. He asserted that the government faced a clear choice. It could fall prey to the enemies of the people and follow the wishes of the bourgeoisie by instituting political settlements with the centrist Christian Democrats; or, it could declare itself, once and for all, against reformism and conciliation by adopting a genuine revolutionary strategy.

Less than a third of the way through his six-year term in office, President Allende found that his programs and methods were being challenged by an increasingly confident opposition on the Center and Right of the political spectrum. At the same time, he faced a growing and more determined challenge from the extreme Left, both outside and inside his government. Not only was the Left worried about the slower pace of government changes; it was even more concerned that the administration would condone bargaining and compromise with opposition parties.

In the absence of an overwhelming majority of the population on its side, the government found itself faced with two difficult alternatives. On the one hand, it could have sought an accommodation with the Christian Democrats to resolve the political impasse and assuage the opposition of key groups and institutions. On the other, it could have embarked on a rapid acceleration of its program even if it meant armed confrontation.

Both alternatives carried enormous costs. Because of the strength of the right in the Christian Democratic party and the power of traditional groups and institutions, the first alternative would have meant a substantial compromise of the Popular Unity program resulting in less than revolutionary policies. Allende would also have had to face increasingly violent opposition from the extreme Left, which he probably would have had to repress. The second alternative, based on a policy of arming the working class, would have provoked an early military coup or a violent confrontation leading to civil war. While the extreme Left argued that the working class could have won, given the initial disorganization of the opposition, such a course would have led to untold suffering. Allende, buffeted by both alternatives, was unable and appeared unwilling to follow either course. Instead, he adhered to his original goal of trying to bring about fundamental changes within Chile's traditional institutional framework. He did this by alternatively pushing for radical changes and then retreating in attempts at compromise. The key problem of the Allende strategy, however, was that the same political institutions which made his election possible also made it difficult for him to institute his basic program. They constituted a basic constraint to moving the nation toward socialism.

The purpose of this chapter is not to give a complete account of the Allende years, nor to provide a full analysis of the breakdown of constitutional democracy in Chile.[3] Rather, it proposes to analyze some of the key parameters of Chilean politics in an effort to illustrate how they provided important roadblocks to the adoption of fundamental societal transformations. First, however, some of the major events of Allende's tenure in office will be briefly reviewed.

ALLENDE'S YEARS

During its first months in office, the new government moved swiftly to implement its programs and met with considerable success. One of its primary objectives was to reactivate a stagnating economy. The economic growth rate was barely able to stay abreast of population increase and manufacturing indus-tries were operating at less than 70 percent capacity. To accomplish its objectives, the administration turned to a two-pronged strategy of income redistribution and state management of the economy.

Following the basic precepts of its program, the Popular Unity regime hoped for a major redistribution of income by allowing wages to increase 30 percent, while holding prices constant. Restrictions on price increases helped to curb inflation, and the wage increases contributed to an increment of the workers' share of the national income from 50 to 59 percent. Wage increases—together with a 100-percent increase of money in circulation—spurred demand and production. The gross national product (GNP) increased significantly during Allende's first year in office, producing one of Chile's best growth rates for a single year in decades.

The government also took the first steps in an effort to create a socialist economy. Major banks and industries were taken over by purchasing shares of their stock or by employing existing legislation permitting authorities to intervene in firms which for some reason did not provide essential services. Often workers, sympathetic to Popular Unity, struck or occupied a plant, forcing the enterprise to cease operations, thus opening the way for government take-over. A major accomplishment of the government was the nationalization of United States copper interests after the Congress, controlled by opposition Christian Democrats and Nationals, unanimously approved the necessary legislation. Though nationalization of the copper industry led to significant disputes between the government and the foreign enterprises, other foreign firms were taken over on mutually agreeable terms.

The take-over of urban banks and enterprises generally proceeded without much violence. The opposite was true in agricultural areas, where either landowners resisted government expropriation or farm workers took over the land on their own initiative. Members of the MIR made significant inroads in some rural areas, providing organizational support and, in some cases, arms for rural confrontations. The administration was reluctant to repress such activity and asserted that disputes occurred in only 0.5 percent of all agricultural properties. Spurred, in part, by the farm workers, the Allende government took over 1,300 properties during its first year, 300 more than the number expropriated in the six years of the preceding administration.

In the April 1971 municipal elections, held shortly after the inauguration of the new government, the Popular Unity coalition received a slightly larger percentage of the vote than all of the opposition parties combined. This tended to diminish the stigma of having received only 36.6 percent of the vote in the presidential election. The biggest gain in the contest was scored by the president's own Socialist party.

The early economic and political success of the government, however, was largely stalled by the end of 1971. Inflation during the first few months of 1972 was up again to pre-inauguration highs and, as the year advanced, the government was forced to authorize successive price increases on all price-controlled items (i.e., 50 percent for milk, 28 percent for bread and 60 percent for public transportation.) By the end of the year, inflation had climbed to over 160 percent. As members of the Allende coalition recognized, this rise in prices was due in large measure to excessive currency emissions and other fiscal policies, which, contrary to expectations of government economists, created demand pressures beyond the level that could be met by production increases.

Furthermore, despite a favorable overall economic growth rate, investments decreased by 8 percent. A 20 percent decline in private investments was attributed to the uncertainty of many private businessmen as to the government's intentions. Public investment also declined, partially because a considerable amount of money was being used to purchase stock in private enterprises and for nonproductive public projects.

A sizeable decrease in the price of copper and the shortage of new credits from international lending sources resulted in a critical dwindling of foreign exchange reserves. At the same time, it was necessary to import agricultural products at record levels to meet higher demand and to compensate for partial disruptions of production in the rural areas. Foreign exchange reserves decreased by more than 50 percent during the first eight months after the presidential election and were depleted by the end of 1971.

In the political sphere, the government experienced some erosion in popular support after the 1971 municipal elections.

Popular Unity candidates were defeated by a united opposition in three out of four congressional by-elections. In April 1972, the government's candidate was defeated in the crucial election for the rectorship of the University of Chile. The results showed that Popular Unity lost ground not only among the usually conservative sectors of the faculties, but also among segments of the university that had for years given majorities to Marxist candidates. Finally, in the first fully democratic popular elections of the Chilean labor federation, the Christian Democrats did surprisingly well, actually winning majorities in one of the large copper companies which traditionally selected leftist labor leaders.

The most serious political impasse continued to be the refusal of the Congress to approve constitutional legislation sanctioning the government's program of nationalization and expropriation of key areas of the economy. In the key showdown of Allende's regime, the Congress approved a proposed constitutional amendment requiring special laws to incorporate each private enterprise into the social sector. Because of retroactive provisions in the bill, the government faced the prospect of having to return some of the enterprises under its jurisdiction to private hands. The obvious recourse—an executive veto—failed to eliminate the challenge and the political storm became increasingly violent. A provision in the 1970 constitutional reform led the opposition to argue that only an absolute majority of the legislature was needed to override the executive's veto. Allende insisted that two-thirds majority was required. The government was in a difficult position and both the Right and the Left talked of a serious, possibly armed, confrontation.

It was clear that, in the political atmosphere which prevailed at the time, efforts to compromise were doomed to failure. This was especially true because both sides, particularly the opposition, held out hopes that the deadlock might be solved in the March 1973 congressional elections. The opposition hoped that it would be able to gain a two-thirds majority, enabling it to override presidential vetoes. Talks designed to find a solution to the impasse finally broke down in July 1972.

From that date until the election, the entire country lived in anticipation of the results of the congressional elections. Demonstrations and public marches escalated as each side attempted to prove that it commanded the allegiance of most Chileans. In October 1972, large and small businessmen and shopkeepers—with the support of private and public organizations identified with the opposition—brought the nation to a standstill with a crippling "employer's strike." Drawing from earlier instances in Chile's history, Allende responded by organizing a "neutral" cabinet with participation of the ranking officers of the armed forces. The highly respected military institution served as a buffer between the contending forces and an effective arbiter as the nation moved to the key electoral confrontation.

Contrary to expectations of the Right and Center and, in keeping with the relative stability of electoral patterns, the congressional election of 1973 did not resolve the impasse. The governing coalition obtained 43.4 percent of the popular vote compared to the opposition's 54.7 percent. In spite of astronomical inflation and a deteriorating economy, there were no dramatic shifts in the electorate. The government was actually able to slightly improve its position in the legislature—although it failed to command as much support as in the earlier municipal elections.

The failure of the elections to resolve the political impasse did not result in a successful attempt to compromise opposing views. Though Allende sought some accommodation, elements on the Left and Right moved for a final and decisive confrontation which they hoped would give victory to their cause. The MIR and some elements within the government argued that it was necessary to arm the workers. On the Right, politicians from several parties conspired with elements of the armed forces in the hope of staging a military coup. By June 1973 it was clear that the government could no longer maintain order and that the military was increasingly acting on its own. Constitutionalists in the officer corps, which had become more politicized after the incorporation of service commanders in the president's cabinet, rapidly lost ground to officers favoring a military solution to Chile's political crisis. Their position was strengthened by the calls of elements with Popular Unity for the formation of workers' militias and attempts by the Left to infiltrate the armed forces. Though Allende was apparently prepared to hold a plebiscite to determine the fate of his government, the armed forces—-encouraged by a new wave of strikes—led the violent coup which would inaugurate the longest period of direct military rule in Chilean history.

The problem with the Allende government was that it not only threatened a small group of wealthy individuals. It also threatened a host of middle and even working class groups that were in a relatively privileged position within an economy of scarce resources. Besides some of the material benefits they received, they feared the loss of a set of political and social arrangements that contributed to their position of strength. Previous incumbent governments, unable to meet the multiplicity of demands and expectations placed upon them, found that their support markedly diminished and their coalitions disintegrated by the end of the six-year presidential term. Allende, by attempting to go much further and by challenging more intensely the basic parameters of the Chilean system, encountered a strong reaction which ensured the premature end of his administration. In order to understand more fully the basic difficulties Allende faced, it is necessary to examine the main features of the Chilean political process; they constituted the fundamental constraints to the construction of socialism in Chile.

THE ELECTORAL ARENA

The dominant characteristic of Chilean politics has been the competitive party system which permeated all levels of the society, including the national congress and bureaucratic agencies—even the local high school. This party system was a legacy of Chile's nineteenth-century oligarchical democracy, in which the elite devised rules and procedures to fill positions of authority with a minimum degree of violence. Coups d'état and military rule, common in other Latin American countries, have been practically absent since the 1830s. By the second decade of the twentieth century, relatively stable party networks had developed, providing the republic with political structures which were instrumental in preventing a permanent breakdown of the regime in the late 1920s.

The adoption of liberal rules, dependent on suffrage and the development of strong parties, did not mean, however, that most Chileans were involved in the political process. On the contrary, a low level of political participation was an integral part of the system, and when suffrage threatened to expand rapidly in the early part of this century, political elites acted to keep it at a moderately low level. Only gradually were new groups allowed to enter the political process. Extensive suffrage is a very recent phenomenon; the enfranchised portion of the population, restricted to literate males over 21, fluctuated between 7 and 15 percent from the 1880s to the 1940s.[4]

The most striking feature of the Chilean party system has been its intense competitiveness. In the late 1930s, there were over 30 political parties. In the early 1970s there were ten, but, with the exception of the Christian Democratic party in the mid-1960s, no party has received more than 25 percent of the vote in congressional and municipal elections. This competitive system has remained markedly stable for decades. Though the Right wing gradually lost support, in general, the percentage of the vote commanded by different blocs spanning the ideological spectrum remained much the same. Only occasional surge-movements—such as those headed by President Carlos Ibáñez (1952-58) and, to a certain extent, President Eduardo Frei (1964-70)—temporarily eroded the strength of traditional party organizations. At the same time, it is clear that the distribution of opinion on basic political issues remained very stable from the early 1950s to the early 1970s. Differences in electoral outcomes in presidential contest were due more to shifting political coalitions than to broad shifts in public opinion.[5]

Salvador Allende was elected to the presidency of Chile because of the vicissitudes of the competitive party system. Since he gained office with a plurality of only 36.6 percent of the vote, he would probably have lost the election had groups of the Right and Center combined in a united opposition.[6] The fact that his election was not due to a marked increase in sentiment for the Left is underscored by the fact that this was a smaller percentage of the vote than the 38.9 percent he received in 1964 when he was backed by fewer political groups. The electoral system made it possible for him to achieve power with minority support. That minority position hindered his ability to exercise enough power to implement his programs.

The competitiveness of the Chilean party system has been as intense in local as in national contests. Party competition was not a mere by-product of the modernization resulting from socio-economic development. The fractionalization of the vote was as high in some of Chile's smaller and more backward communities as in the large industrial cities. While some social and economic cleavages were reflected in partisan alignments, organizational efforts by the parties themselves have produced significant divisions in the society. Although some parties, such as the Communist and the rightist nationals, were less likely to be found competing against each other in every district, most national parties faced one another uniformly across the country.[7]

The Communist and Socialist parties have been an integral part of the competitive game for several decades, having participated actively in congressional and municipal politics, as well as in the formation of governments. These parties, along with the traditional Radical party—the other major group in the Allende coalition—have accepted and, indeed, benefited from the electoral process. In fact, efforts to establish a single popular party from among those making up the Popular Unity coalition failed.[8] Failure was somewhat the result of ideological and leadership differences, but, just as important, it was an admission that the parties within the government coalition depended on the electoral process to measure their strength, not only in comparison to the opposition but also among themselves.[9] Indeed, an elaborate quota system was instituted by the government to distribute key leadership positions, and lesser patronage posts, to members of the coalition based largely on comparative electoral strength. On occasion, this competition for posts and positions led to bitter disputes within the coalition and to strong criticisms of sectarianism. Thus, for example, when a portion of the Radical party broke away from the government in April 1972, the Radical party claimed that it was entitled to appoint the new intendant of Valparaiso when the man occupying that post pledged allegiance to the defecting faction. Allende was forced to resolve the dispute by naming a neutral military officer to do the job. Anticipating the strategy he would follow later that year, he resolved a similar problem involving a cabinet post in the same way.

A second characteristic of the electoral arena was that each party had a cross-class basis of support, although certain sectors of society were more prone to identify with some parties than with others. The Christian Democrats and the Radicals appealed more to the middle sectors, the Communists and the Socialists to the working class, and the nationals to the more privileged groups. However, electoral analysis shows that, with the partial exception of the Communist party, all Chilean parties received some support from a wide range of social groups.[10] Among squatters in Santiago, many of whom voted for the first time in the 1960s, the Christian Democrats received about the same number of votes as the Communist and Socialists combined. Alejandro Portes has shown that radicalism, defined both in terms of support for the Communist and Socialist parties and by radical attitudes, was not correlated with marginality and despair. If anything, radicalism was more likely to be associated with higher educational and income levels.[11] Political organization and political education were more important variables in determining party preferences than the socioeconomic features of a given population group.

The cross-class party system posed difficulties to Allende since the large and disadvantaged majorities were not the coalition's exclusive electoral constituency.[12] In addition, the government depended on support from some middle-class elements which, though ideologically radical, would have been unwilling to let a confrontation threaten their way of life. At the same time, the government failed to increase significant headway in some marginal communities of Santiago. The radical activities of the MIR, according to the Communist party, further alienated certain middle-class groups from the government.

A third characteristic of the Chilean competitive party system has been its dual nature. The party system could be conceived as containing two distinct tiers. One was at the center in the capital city and included the party leadership and key political actors such as congressmen, ministers, government and university officials, labor leaders and so on affiliated with party structures. The national level was characterized by its highly ideological nature and its programmatic orientation. The top leadership of the parties, coming mainly from the universities, interacted primarily on an ideological level. This contrasted sharply with the local arena of neighborhoods, small towns and rural areas in which payoffs and political favors were more important, although ideology did play a role. Indeed, much of the Chilean style of electoral campaigning depended on face-to-face contacts and the delivery of particularistic favors. In small constituencies, candidates related directly to the voters; in larger ones, they communicated through an array of local brokers. This two-tier system, with a national ideological arena and a local electoral one, was bound together by vertical party networks of an essentially clientelistic nature. In exchange for votes, a congressman interceded with the bureaucracy to obtain necessary goods and services for individuals and communities. The existence of a local clientele system indicated that an enormous amount of the legislator's effort and time had to be expended in performing small favors. In a coalition government such as Allende's, elements of the coalition had to divide up the spoils for their electoral clientele.[13] Rivalries resulted not only over top ministerial appointments, but also over patronage at all levels of the bureaucracy and over the scarce resources available for new programming.

Communists and Socialists in many areas of the country mastered the clientelistic politics of the "small favor" and were often more skillful at it than their conservative counterparts. But, ironically, in winning supporters away from traditional rivals with the latter's own style of politics, they contributed to the maintenance of a political system based not on the genuine participation of lower sectors but on paternalistic cooptation. They also reinforced a pattern of political exchanges based on dependence on the central authorities and piecemeal distribution of benefits. Such a system may be quite functional to a society of scarce goods, but dependence on individualistic transactions inhibits new forms of popular participation.

The electoral arena was a legacy of Chile's past and the parties of the Popular Unity coalition reinforced this legacy by accepting the legitimacy of suffrage—both as a means to gain power and to demonstrate their own power capability. The basic characteristics of the electoral arena—high competitiveness, cross-class parties, and the two-tier system in which clientelistic transactions took place for particular goals—militated against the radical revolutionary process.

THE INSTITUTIONAL ARENA

Chile could be characterized not only as a highly competitive society but also as a highly organized one. It has a bewildering array of private and public organizations—each with its own goals and stakes, each attempting to assert its autonomy while trying to reap as many benefits as possible from an economy of very limited resources. This system has always favored the wealthy and the powerful, but it has also functioned to the benefit of the sizeable middle sectors of the country. However, urban and rural lower classes have not been marginal in the eyes of institutional arena. Their ties to these structures, however, generally resulted in domination and control, rather than representation and participation.

The Chilean institutional arena developed in part as a response to the exigencies of socioeconomic development and the complexity of modern life. Unlike many other countries, however, its emergence did not precede the development of electoral politics, a fact which allowed it to be shaped by the basic parameters of democratic procedures.

The institutional arena contained both private organizations and associations and public institutions.[14] Private-sector groups ranged from professional associations, business organizations, and student and youth groups to labor unions and church groups. During the 1960s and 1970s, the agrarian reform and the creation of neighborhood organizations added a whole new array of rural unions, cooperatives, *asentamientos*, mother's clubs, neighborhood councils, squatter's committees and so on to this vast institutional structure.

Many of these private sector groups are organized into national confederations.[15] For example, the Sociedad de Fomento Fabril (SOFOFA) includes many regional industrial groups as well as individual members and claims to represent a majority of Chilean private industrialists. The Sociedad Nacional de Agricultura (SNA) is a similar organization composed of private landowners. The Confederación Nacional de Sindicatos de Dueños de Camiones unites most local organizations of truck owners. The Confederación Nacional del Comercio Detallista includes many retail store owners of the principal cities. Professional associations are connected through the Confederación Nacional de Profesionales. The numerous national confederations of white- and blue-collar employees were affiliated to the Central Unica de Trabajadores (CUT). All of these organizations are mandated to defend the interests of their members before the government and the public at large. During the Allende administration SOFOFA leaders spent large sums of money for advertisements against state take-overs of private firms, and its leadership plotted against the government. The associations of truck owners, retailers and professionals declared crippling strikes in October 1972 and led the nation to virtual paralysis in August 1973. (The CUT, which attempted to mobilize its membership in support of the government, has been dissolved by the new military authorities.)

The Chilean Church suffered a decline in its political influence at an earlier date than its counterparts in most other Latin American societies.[16] Its strength was eroded by the growth of the secular state, the expansion of Protestant Pentecostal groups and the emergence of mass Marxist parties. After an initial period of conservative opposition to these new trends, the church responded with increasingly progressive stands aimed at insuring its relevance in a society undergoing rapid change. For the most part, the hierarchy of the Church supported the programs of the Popular Unity government and a prominent group of leftist clergymen provided Allende with strong backing. However, a major sector of the Church, which draws much of its strength from middle-class Catholics, was not prepared to go as far in supporting some of the far-reaching government measures. An indication of this sentiment was the objection of prominent Catholics, including the hierarchy, to implementation of a proposal to form a unified national educational system. The objections from the Church and other circles finally led to a postponement in the government's consideration of the proposal.

Although private organizations played a very important role in Chilean politics, the key to the institutional arena was the structurally differentiated public sector in which fundamental decisions were made. This is true not only because of the sector's size, but because most private groups and institutions relied on the state for favorable dispensation. The public sector, even before the Allende election, accounted for about 40 percent of the domestic product and 60 percent of all investments. It handled approximately 50 percent of the nation's short-term credits and employed about 13 percent of the active population. In no other Latin American country did the state play so prominent a role.[17]

Since the adoption of the constitution of 1925, the executive has been the dominant branch of government. However, in spite of the powerful resources at the president's disposition, other political structures also performed important functions and had considerable independence. Chile's legislature, which has now been closed by the military, was one of the strongest in the world, even though it no longer enjoyed the center of political life as it did at the turn of the century. The Congress retained final authority over the approval of laws. It created new programs, abolished old ones and reduced or modified budgets. As the Popular Unity government discovered, the Executive's attempt to increase its control over the economy could proceed only so long as the legislature approved or was unwilling to dissaprove. By majority vote, the Chilean Congress could also censure ministers and provincial intendants and force them out of office. As of June 1973, ten ministers and five intendants had been accused; six of these were removed from office, including two ministers of the interior. Censures and threats of censure affected the administrative continuity of several important government departments.

Since presidential elections did not coincide with congressional elections and coalitions that were formed for the presidential race usually disintegrated by the time of congressional contests, Chilean executives often found themselves confronted with a Congress which would cooperate only in exchange for important concessions. Often these concessions included a willingness to accommodate demands for special favors and benefits for groups or even individuals who depended on the legislators' brokerage abilities and may have had some control over his or her political future. A chief executive found, then, that he not only had to deal with the many ideological and programmatic stands of political parties to get his programs approved by Congress, but that he also had to accommodate a host of particular demands.

The Chilean court system was another government structure independent of presidential control, both in its functions and in the recruitment of its personnel. Some rulings of the Supreme Court were not to the liking of the Allende government. The court refused, for example, to remove the congressional immunity of a right-wing senator allegedly implicated in a plot to prevent Allende from taking office, a plot which led to the assassination of the commander in chief of the army, René Schneider. Later, it ruled against some of the procedures a government agency used in taking over private firms and it held the head of the agency in contempt of court. Attacks on the courts from the Left, interruptions of court proceedings in several communities and the refusal of some government officials to enforce court orders led to strong statements of support for the judiciary from magistrate associations and from the powerful association of Chilean lawyers. In June 1973, the Supreme Court, headed by a conservative judge, openly clashed with Allende over the question of law enforcement in a bitter exchange of public letters.

One of the most unusual branches of the Chilean government has been its independent Contraloría. An agency with a career staff composed of over 750 civil servants and a director appointed for life, the Contraloría has been charged with a variety of functions ranging from audits of public accounts to ruling on the legality of executive decrees and issuing advisory opinions on the constitutionality of proposed congressional legislation.[18] A prestigious organization, the Contraloría commands respect from most Chilean civil servants, who fear its scrupulous championship of legalism and frugality, sometimes at the expense of rationality and fairness. A public official who errs in the expenditure of public funds can be suspended by the Contraloría and asked to replace misapplied moneys. If there is criminal, as opposed to administrative, wrongdoing, the functionary can be prosecuted in the courts by the Contraloría.[19]

During Allende's tenure, the Contraloría ruled on whether compensation was owed to United States copper interests. In that case, it accepted most, though not all, of the government's arguments. The Contraloría also upheld some of the takeovers of private firms, but ruled that others were illegal. It also ruled on whether Popular Unity could restructure the University of Chile and once again rejected the government's position. After that, the Contraloría refused to process the government's decree implementing sections of the law regulating the economy, thus agreeing with the opposition's contention that the law could not be implemented without approval by a majority of Congress.

The president, with the concurrence of his cabinet, could insist on implementing any decree declared illegal by the Contraloría, except in matters of public expenditures. Although Allende had on occasion done so, he generally continued to respect the Contraloría.[20] When Allende was accused of involvement in the importation of some goods without the appropriate customs inspections, he asked the Contraloría to look into his personal affairs to clear up the matter. He was exonerated. In a society with numerous and complex laws, and sharp ideological divisions, an agency such as the Contraloría evolved as an interpreter of existing legislation as well as a guarantor of legalism. However, its concern for the most minute details of the law brought it under increasing criticism from the far Left.

The legislative and judicial branches of the government and the Contraloría could not be passed over lightly. Each of these institutions and their allies were jealous of their functions and prerogatives and did not hesitate to defend them when they were challenged.

Another important feature of the Chilean institutional arena was the marked autonomy of many public agencies, even within the executive bureaucracy. The bureaucracy's activities permeated all of society. Almost everything had to be done with the aid or at least the concurrence of a public agency. What was striking about the Chilean bureaucracy, however, was not how much power it gave the chief executive, but how difficult it was for him to control its day-to-day activities. This occurred because most public institutions lay outside the executive chain of command in the "decentralized agencies." Such entities determined much of their own budgets and controlled their own hiring practices, even though they were nominally under one of the 14 government ministries. Forty percent of all public employees in

Chile work for the more than 50 semiautonomous bureaus. They generally provide the bulk of economic and social services in areas such as agriculture, housing, social security and economic development. While they willingly accepted any administration efforts to increase their jurisdiction and functions, they strongly resisted attempts to decrease them or to change, in any dramatic way, the nature of programming and the style of action. Many of the Christian Democrats' innovative programs in housing and urban development were thwarted by the unwillingness of semiautonomous agencies to follow changed guidelines for programming and investments.

A president by law could not remove civil servants in order to replace them with a new cadre more congenial to his policy objectives. Indeed, in return for their support of his candidacy in the Congress, Allende promised the Christian Democrats that he would not attempt to dismiss any public employees. New presidents were thus forced to create new agencies to carry out their programs. Often a new agency would duplicate the tasks of an older one, further complicating the problem of coordination. And the more agencies, the more competition for the limited governmental budget.

Allende made ample use of the resources and jurisdiction of some of these semiautonomous agencies during his first year in office. Foremost among these was the Corporación de Fomento de la Producción (CORFO)—Association for the Promotion of Production—a public agency nominally dependent on the Ministry of Economics. Founded in 1939, it spearheaded much of Chile's postwar industrialization. Before the advent of the Allende government, it already owned stock in more than 80 enterprises and a majority of the shares in half that number. With the encouragement of the government, it became the majority partner in many more enterprises.[21]

But did these agencies and enterprises automatically fall in line with Allende's programs? They did, but they followed their own interpretation of those programs. Surveys of civil servants in Chile reveal that, in general, they favor state control rather than a strong private sector. At the same time, however, they are firm guardians of their own positions and prerogatives. They function with a set of norms and attitudes which do not differ substantially from the norms and attitudes of bureaucrats in the private sector. Bankers in the state bank use similar criteria in determining credit-worthiness and have similar relationships with their clientele as their counterparts in private banks. On many issues, civil servants are quite conservative, expressing less concern for land reform than for education or the cost of living.[22]

It can be argued that since more enterprises were brought into the public sector the Allende government underminded the strength of the private sector. A certain reorientation of the economic surplus took place. Nevertheless, the basic parameters of the Chilean political system were not substantially altered. The result was merely the reinforcement of one component of the institutional arena, a component that was difficult to mobilize to implement innovative and revolutionary programs.

Another fundamental characteristic of the Chilean institutional arena is that the highly organized private and public sectors of society are in many ways closely intertwined. Access by private institutions to public agencies charged with regulating them is highly formalized and key areas of the economy are dominated by essentially "private" governments. The boards of many government agencies include one-third representation from private interests, one-third from technical groups and one-third from the government. According to one study, in the period from 1958 to 1964 the four largest business organizations had voting membership in all major financial and policy institutions including the central bank, the state bank and CORFO. Each business group had voting power on the key government bureaus relevant to their particular economic sector. Before the agrarian reform law was passed in 1966, it was difficult to carry out any initiatives in rural reform because 30 percent of the vote in the key agencies was controlled by economic interests that would be adversely affected by reforms. Both the Frei and the Allende government moved to give more effective representation in these state agencies to organizations of the middle and working classes.

Broadening the base of representation brought new groups into positions of greater authority, thus diminishing the monopoly held by dominant economic interests over the policy process. This was a significant transformation. However, by incorporating new groups into the traditional bargaining process, the process itself was perpetuated. Since this system was intended to satisfy short-term demands and particular interests, its continuation made it more difficult to implement long-term strategies aimed at a fundamental restructuring of society.

The intermingling of private groups in the public sector is also reinforced by the existence of the strong professional associations and union organizations. In several important cases, professional groups have become influential in government agencies. Architects, for example, dominate the Ministry of Housing. The Ministry of Public Works is the almost exclusive fiefdom of civil engineers and the Ministry of Agriculture is staffed by agronomists and a few veterinarians. A university degree in a particular field is sometimes a prerequisite for appointment or advancement in a given agency, thus guaranteeing privileged employment opportunities for a small group of individuals.[23] The professional standards and outlook of a particular association, in addition to its vested interests, inhibited the execution of dynamic and innovative policies. This phenomenon was apparent in the nationalized copper industry where technicians demonstrated their power by calling 24-hour work stoppages when "outsiders" were appointed to positions in the mines.

Union organizations within the bureaucracy also guarded the interests of their members, particularly in pecuniary matters. Strikes over wage increases and welfare benefits became common as different sectors of the bureaucracy attempted to ensure that they did not fall behind other sectors. Strikes in the social security agencies, which were condemned by the government, are a case in point.

Finally, a discussion of the role of political parties is essential for understanding this intertwining of the public and private sectors in Chile. At first glance, parties may have seemed to be another layer of organizations, increasing the complexity of Chilean pluralism. In fact, the party structures which permeated the society were crucial linkage structures binding organizations and institutions at all levels to the political center. Local units of all parties were active within each level of the bureaucracy, each labor union, each student federation and each professional association, attempting to place its own members in leadership positions. Often parties succeeded in capturing a particular public agency. Once an issue affecting the organization arose, the party structure—with its congressmen, contacts in the central bureaucracy and any connections that it may have had with the executive—could be instrumental in conveying the organizations' demands to decision-makers. The party supported any action taken by the organization—such as work stoppage, strike or demonstration. Thus, the strategies of the different groups that form the basis of the Chilean institutional arena were interwoven with the activities of national parties and followed closely the general political life of the nation.

This intertwining of political parties with public and private institutions also influenced the extent of support which particular parties and the government received. Some organizations found it expedient to elect leadership cadres belonging to parties supporting the government, since they had greater potential for obtaining resources through regular channels. Others, however, found this to be a hindrance. A leadership partial to the government was more likely to accept its pleas for certain sacrifices and less likely to be forceful in presenting its demands. Often, then, many organizations turned to leaders with allegiances to opposition parties. This phenomenon accounted for some of the persistent erosion of support for incumbent governments in Chile. One example was the election of Christian Democratic union officials in the large copper mines during the second year of the Allende administration.

The vast number of interacting groups and institutions, both public and private, was a fundamental characteristic of the Chilean political process. While political parties provided a unifying force and direction to what would otherwise have been excessive pluralism, the weight of the institutionalized arena made it difficult to alter the basic structure of Chilean politics to adopt revolutionary economic and social policies.

In contrast to its neighbors on the American continent, the Chilean armed forces have not constituted a separate political branch of government. Under civilian control and imbued with the prestige provided by a tradition of clear-cut military victories, Chilean officers were content to develop their professional careers and reputations. There is no question that the military institutions fared relatively well. Within Latin America, Chile ranks sixth in per capita military expenditures and fifth in the size of armed forces relative to the size of the population.[24] Army officers were occasionally brought into presidential cabinets to provide a "neutral" administration or to break a political stalemate—but that role has been transitory and subject to the will of civilian executives. A former commander in chief of the Chilean army once summarized the role of the armed forces in the following terms: "Not only the army—I guarantee—but all of the armed forces have a clear doctrine: military power is consciously subordinated to the political power, the Constitution and the laws . . . never could we intervene on our own, because we are disciplined . . . . Furthermore, history demonstrated to us that never has that intervention been necessary, because our governors have a common sense and good judgement . . . ."[25]

The qualifier provided by the former army commander is instructive. Chilean officers stayed out of politics because they were relatively satisfied with the performance of civilian elites. When Allende came into office he went out of his way to accommodate the military. His administration encouraged salary increases for officers substantially above wage increases for other groups in society. At the same time it did not pose any objections to increased purchases of military material, particularly from the United States. But the officer corps was sharply divided over the Allende government and its reforms. When the economic situation worsened, polarization and violence escalated and, finally, the armed forces felt directly threatened. Those elements within each of the services who were hostile to the Popular United gained ascendancy.

INCREMENTALISM AND THE POLITICS OF CONCILIATION

The interplay between highly competitive electoral politics and the demands of numerous public and private institutions and groups resulted in a bargaining system which could be called the "politics of conciliation." Its main characteristic was that change could only be incremental, not radical.

The fundamental issue around which the politics of conciliation revolves is the demands by groups and individuals for their *reivindicaciones* (rightful demands).[26] For the most part, these involved wage readjustments. For decades Chile has had a high level of inflation, running as high as 30 percent in a normal year. Consequently, the main preoccupation of labor unions and other private and public groups has been an income readjustment commensurate with or above the estimated increase in the cost of living. Inflation, therefore, set the basic parameters for the bargaining system. Since the government and its agencies regulate both salary and price increases, the battle over *reajustes* was fought in the public arena.[27]

The battle did not end, however, with the approval of the budget. Government agencies, private institutions dependent on state support, labor unions and professional associations competed for their share of funds. The organizations tried to get a larger share of their funds from the treasury during the first quarter, since by the end of the year inflation would usually reduce the real value of their expected income. Bargaining, stoppages, strikes and demonstrations took place throughout the year as sectors of the society attempted to ensure that their benefits were not eroded. Often extraordinary *reajustes* and budget increments were sought to make up for unusual losses. The president and the top officials of the government spent much time mediating disputes and attempting to satisfy demands. The coalition nature of Chilean governments meant that many more disputes were brought directly to the president's desk for mediation than would be the case in a government dominated by a single party.[28] Allende, like his predecessors, was so bogged down with the day-to-day crises of government that he found it difficult to provide guidance for long-range programming and long-range political strategies.

Constant political demands for particular rewards with resources available for only a small number of new programs made it almost impossible to find adequate funding for long-range projects. Traditionally, Chilean governments have resorted to external credits for new projects. The Allende administration, which inherited a staggering foreign debt making Chile one of the highest per capita debtor nations in the world, was unable to renegotiate most of these external commitments and obtain new credit lines because of the United States government's retaliation for Chile's nationalization of the copper industry.[29] Not only did this deprive Allende of important credits to finance his new initiatives, but it also contributed to the deterioration of the country's economy.

The traditional bargaining style, with its incremental results, has contrasted sharply with the strong ideological postures of major parties and groups in the society. Key political groups have continually called for basic structural reforms and transformations. There has been a sharp discongruity betweeen an ideology of master planning and the incrementalist bargaining system.[30] This incongruity has probably contributed to the pervasive feeling of permanent crisis in Chilean politics. In the past, due to the acceptance of votes as the key currency of the system, the necessity of bargaining in a highly competitive atmosphere, and the weight of incrementalist decision-making itself, Chilean political elites were able to conciliate their differences when confrontation seemed imminent. But such an accommodation was often achieved at the expense of measures designed to bring about greater social justice. The Allende government's attempts to bring about basic changes, rather than merely consolidate gains, clashed with the basic constraints of the Chilean political system and eventually led to the breakdown of the regime. The overthrow of Allende and military rule may have a greater effect in changing the nature of the Chilean political system than the policies that Allende pursued.

NOTES

1. Allende's message is reprinted in Regis Debray, *The Chilean Revolution: Conversations with Allende* (New York: Random House, 1971).

2. Ibid., p. 53.

3. For an analysis of the breakdown see Arturo Valenzuela, "The Breakdown of Democracy in Chile," in *Breakdowns and Crisis of Democracy*, eds. Juan Linz and Alfred Stepan (New Haven: Yale University Press, forthcoming). An abridged version entitled "Il Crollo della Democrazia in Cile" appeared in the *Rivista Italiana di Scienza Politica*, No. 1, 1975.

4. For a detailed examination of the expansion of suffrage in Chile in the nineteenth century, which stresses the key role of conservative elites in enacting the suffrage laws see Julio Samuel Valenzuela, "Determinants of Suffrage Expansion in Chile: The 1874 Law," (New York: Columbia University, mimeo.). A general overview is Atilio Boron, "Movilización Política y Crisis Política en Chile," *Aportes*, April 1971, pp. 41-69.

5. See the analysis of survey data by James Prothro and Patricio Chaparro, "Public Opinion and the Movement of Chilean Government to the Left, 1952-1972," in this volume. In Chile every presidential election has been a "deviating" election, in which particular configurations of parties in different alliances determined the outcome. Coalitions lost support in the succeeding congressional or municipal elections partly because these contests reflected more closely the underlying partisan divisions of the vote, and involved different issues and personalities.

6. Allende almost won in the 1958 presidential election when he came within 33,400 votes of defeating Jorje Allessandri. He would have probably won if it had not been for the candidacy of an independent leftist, Antonio Zamorano, who received 41,300 votes.

7. See Arturo Valenzuela, "The Scope of the Chilean Party System" *Comparative Politics*, January 1972, pp. 179-99. Data from Chile leads one to reject an influential body of literature in the social sciences which suggests that underdeveloped communities divide less politically than developed communities. For example, see S.N. Eisenstadt, "Social Change, Differentiation and Evolution," *American Sociological Review*, June 1964, pp. 375-87; and Talcott Parsons, "Evolutionary Universals in Society," *American Sociological Review*, June 1964, pp. 339-57.

8. In the 1973 election parties in the government and opposition formed federations and instituted agreements on which candidates from which party would stand for election.

9. Even a few candidates associated with the MIR ran in 1973, demonstrating that elements on the extreme Left also see the value of obtaining elected representatives.

10. Multiple regression analysis with communal socioeconomic data reveals that at best only 37 percent of the variance in any party's vote can be explained.

11. See Alejandro Portes, "Urbanization and Politics in Latin America," *Social Science Quarterly*, December 1971, pp. 697-720; and the chapter by Portes, "Occupation and Lower Class Political Orientation in Chile," in this volume.

12. For a further elaboration of this point see the chapter by Robert Ayres, "Electoral Constraints and the Chilean Way to Socialism," in this volume.

13. With the exception of the government of Eduardo Frei, all Chilean governments have been coalition governments. Frei's attempt to govern as a single party, without paying heed to the bargaining aspects of the Chilean game, engendered much resentment in other political circles.

14. The best description of the Chilean institutional system is the standard work by Federico Gil, *The Political System of Chile* (New York: Houghton Mifflin, 1966).

15. A good description of political interest groups in Chile is David F. Cusack, "La Interacción entre el público y los agentes mediadores en el sistema político Chileno," Part 2 (Santiago: INSORA, mimeo, 1968).

16. The best discussion of the Chilean church can be found in Ivan Vallier, *Catholicism, Social Control and Modernization in Latin America* (Englewood Cliffs, N.J.: Prentice Hall, 1970).

17. Among the best treatments of the Chilean bureaucracy is Rafael López Pintor, "Development Administration in Chile: Structural, Normative and Behavioral Constraints to Performance" (Ph. D. diss., University of North Carolina, Chapel Hill, 1972). See also Germán Urzúa Valenzuela and Ana María García Barzelatto, *Diagnóstico de la Burocracia Chilena* (Santiago: Editorial Jurídica de Chile, 1971). Treatment of the role of the state in the Chilean economy can be found in the chapter by Maurice Zeitlin and Earl Ratcliff in this volume.

18. The comptroller general is subject to impeachment. Only one comptroller general (in 1945) has been removed from office.

19. For example, in 1969, several councilors and the mayor of the city of Aysen were jailed for having approved the transfer of funds from one budget item to another in order to give municipal employees a small Christmas bonus.

20. From 1959 to at least 1969, Chilean presidents did not issue "decretos de insistencia." See Alberto Silva Cimma, *Derecho Administrativo Chileno y Comparado*, vol. 2 (Santiago: Editorial Jurídica de Chile, 1969), p. 368.

21. A thorough study of public enterprises which details the role of CORFO in Chile is "Public Enterprises: Their Present Significance and their Potential in Development," *Economic Bulletin for Latin America*, vol. 15, 1971.

22. James Petras reports a survey of civil servants in his *Political and Social Forces in Chilean Development* (Berkeley: University of California Press, 1971), pp. 291-92.

23. See the remarks of Carmen Lazo, a popular Socialist deputy, criticizing the excessive technocracy in the Allende administration and arguing for a greater role for the nonspecialist in *Ercilla*, July 11, 1973, p. 11.

24. See Charles Lewis Taylor and Michael C. Hudson, *World Handbook of Political and Social Indicators* (New Haven: Yale University Press, 1972) for these statistics.

25. Quoted in *Ercilla*, September 15, 1965, p. 8. For some revealing attitudes of retired Chilean officers see Roy Allen Hanson, "Military Culture and Organizational Decline: A Study of the Chilean Army," Ph.D. diss., University of California, Los Angeles, 1967.

26. For this concept see Julio Samuel Valenzuela, "The Chilean Labor Movement: The Institutionalization of Conflict," in this volume.

27. The worst confrontation to date over *reajustes* was the large strike in the winter of 1973 at the El Teniente mine. Workers struck to obtain cost-of-living increases which were due by law. The strike cost Chile approximately $100 million.

28. As noted above, the Frei government was an exception.

29. Chileans are well aware that it is not enough to control production of copper—they have to maintain their marketing posture. This is difficult because of the highly integrated international copper market controlled by the same corporation that once owned Chilean copper. Diplomatic skill as well as a reputation for reliability is needed to maintain the crucial European markets and to open new ones elsewhere. For a discussion of these questions see Sergio Molina, "El Cobre: perspectivas y responsabilidades," *Mensaje* (Septiembre-Octubre 1971).

30. In the United States an ideology of "disjointed incrementalism" seems to be congruent with that of incrementalist decision-making. See Charles E. Lindbloom, *The Intelligence of Democracy* (New York: Free Press, 1965). The ideology of master planning in Chile and other Latin American countries is discussed in Albert O. Hirschman, *Journeys Toward Progress* (New York: Twentieth Century Fund, 1963).

2

Unidad Popular and the Chilean Electoral Process

Robert L. Ayres

The triumph of Salvador Allende and his leftist coalition in Chile brought to power a political elite pledged to revolution, to a profound transformation of economic, social and political relations in that country. For the bourgeois reformism of the pre-Allende past, the coalition proposed to substitute socialist revolution. Yet unlike other experiences with socialist revolution with which we are familiar, this revolution was not to occur through the rapid and violent destruction of the country's existing political values, political institutions and social structure. The implantation of socialism in Chile was to be electoral, parliamentary, peaceful, gradual, multiclass and multiparty. It was to occur, not through replacing existing institutions, but through their transcendence.

The peculiarities and uniqueness of the Chilean experiment raise numerous questions. One of the most important is the extent to which the coalition could have overcome those circumstances attendant upon its rise to power which seriously constrained its ability to effect a socialist revolution through electoral and parliamentary processes. These constraints were numerous and formidable. They included, for example, the fact that historical and structural conditions which ordinarily are conducive to the establishment of a revolutionary regime (such as

This chapter previously appeared in *Studies in Comparative International Development* 8 (Summer 1973).

widespread disintegration of the social system) were largely absent in the Chilean case. They included the difficulties of attempting to implant socialism by means of a coalition which manifested numerous heterogeneities of social base, organization and political style. And they also included constraints imposed by the country's institutional structure, such as the power of the Chilean Congress to obstruct presidential initiatives.

This chapter will deal with yet another set of constraints. These stem from the operation of the Chilean electoral process and past patterns of electoral behavior in Chile. Most scholarly observers of Latin American politics have not paid a great deal of attention to the electoral process. There is solid academic justification for this neglect, since the Latin American political process has historically not been characterized by the solvency of electoral politics. Chile, however, stands out as one of the few countries possessing a historically institutionalized political party system within which elections play an important part. The forces of Unidad Popular—UP (Popular Unity, the name given to the coalition which Allende headed)—came to power through the free electoral process. In view of the importance attributed to elections in the Chilean political process, the electoral emergence of UP and the openly proclaimed electoral nature of the transition to socialism in Chile, it becomes important to examine some aspects of the historical record of Chilean elections. Such an examination may help clarify the nature of the electoral constraints confronting the would-be revolutionaries and thus help to reevaluate the problems that blocked the successful implementation of their goals.

An attempt has been made to spell out at least three aspects of the historical record of Chilean elections which appeared as sources of electoral constraints for the success of the Allende experiment. Those aspects are: (1) the "noncriticality" of most modern elections and some perennial outcomes of the presidential electoral process in particular; (2) the electoral stability registered by several of the country's major political parties in modern elections; and (3) the voting behavior of an important social aggregate, the petite bourgeoisie. The conclusion assesses the constraints upon Allende and UP stemming from these electoral sources and gives a brief inventory of developments that conceivably could have overcome them.

HISTORICAL OUTCOMES OF PRESIDENTIAL ELECTIONS

Chilean presidential elections have seldom, if ever, been critical in the sense of contributing to an enduring realignment of political forces.[1] Observers of Chilean politics have tended to overlook this important point. After Eduardo Frei obtained 55.7 percent of the popular vote in 1964, for example, Gil and Parrish speculated about "the eclipse of the FRAP's [Frente de Acción Popular] political power and the future domination of Chilean politics by the Christian Democrats."[2] Similarly, after the 1970 election of Allende, some observers wondered if the Marxist triumph was irreversible. Speculations about such irreversibility increased after the April 1971 municipal elections in which UP forces obtained approximately 50 percent of the vote, compared to 36.2 percent in September 1970. This was not a unique historical occurrence, either. An election immediately subsequent to the presidential election generally produced gains for the political forces that supported the president elected in the preceding election—if not gains over the total obtained in the presidential election itself, at least substantial gains over the previous election of a similar type (i.e., congressional or municipal). Thus, in the 1961 congressional elections, the Christian Democrats received only 15.4 percent of the vote, but this jumped to 42.3 percent in the 1965 congressional elections, just six months after the election of Frei.

Although convincing time-series data are absent, it appears that longer-term electoral forces soon reassert themselves. In this regard, it is instructive to examine some trends in the Christian Democrat (Partido Demócrata Cristiano—PDC) vote. We have examined such trends from 1963 to 1969 (four elections: the municipal of 1963, the congressional of 1965, the municipal of 1967 and the congressional of 1969). Using various criteria for the location of a critical election by commune and with aggregate data, only a distinct minority of communes (out of a total of 286) could be found where it was appropriate to speak of secular realignment. From 1963 to 1965, there were 119 communes in which the PDC vote increased by more than 20 percent. The number of communes registering more than a 20 percent gain in 1963-69 was only 48, or 16.8 percent of all Chilean communes. The mean communal change in the PDC vote from 1963 to 1965 was +18.7 percent (i.e., in the "average" commune, the PDC vote increased by 18.7 percent in the electoral interval surrounding the 1964 election of Eduardo Frei). But this mean communal change for the 1963-69 period was only 10.6 percent. If the 1971 election results were to be included, it is highly likely that further PDC declines again reduced the mean communal change figure. (The change in the PDC vote at the national level for 1963 to 1971 was only +3.6 percent, a divergence from the mean communal change figure which demonstrates the importance of PDC vote declines in the communes of large population.) At the national level, the PDC vote total declined from 35.6 percent in 1967 to 29.8 percent in 1969 to 25.6 percent in 1971.

Whatever criterion is used in looking for secular changes in the PDC vote by commune, such changes largely occurred in communes of secondary importance in terms of population. They were overwhelmingly rural communes, in which either the Radical party or the forces of the Chilean Right (and especially the Radicals) were dominant prior to the occurrence of the critical election. The mean rural percentage of those communes— where the PDC vote increased during 1963-65 and also increased during 1967-67—was 71.3 percent. Only 5 of 48 communes which met a restrictive definition of a "critical election commune" could be considered urban.[3] In the 75 communes where the PDC vote increased in those same periods, the Radical party was the pre-1963 electoral leader in 32, the Conservatives in 11 and the Liberals in 11. In the ten largest communes (those with over 100,000 population in 1960), the substantial gains made during 1963-65 (with one exception) were not consolidated. In the commune of Santiago, for example, the PDC vote increased by 23.8 percent in the period 1963-65, but fell by 17.5 percent during 1965-69. This is a pattern of increase and decline characteristic of all the country's largest communes.

Chile, therefore, has not experienced a critical election at the national level in many years—in the sense of one which produced a durable realignment of party loyalties on behalf of change or innovation. This assertion is based on the large-scale reductions in the PDC vote in 1967 and 1969 (as well as in 1971) in the majority of the country's communes, reductions which in these communes effectively eliminated the gains made in the 1963-65 period.[4] Rather than the future domination of Chilean politics by the Christian Democrats, we predicted a return to past patterns of party politics in Chile. That meant (among other factors) that no single political force would be dominant, the forging of a prochange coalition would be extremely difficult, and the Chilean Right might reassert itself as a potent electoral force.

This phenomenon might be called the "social coalition disintegration thesis," according to which the social coalition electing a Chilean president disintegrates within several years of his election. Our impression gathered from a reading of the historical material is that this phenomenon was apparent in the case of the election of Carlos Ibáñez del Campo in 1952. The limited quantitative evidence indicates it was also present in the case of the 1964 election of Eduardo Frei. By means of correlational analysis employing provincial data, it is possible to define those social aggregates identified with the vote for Frei in 1964 but unidentified or identified with some other political force in the 1963 municipal elections preceding the election of Frei and the 1965 congressional elections following it. The following are the social aggregates identified with Frei in 1964, but unidentified with any party or identified with a non-Christian Democratic party in subsequent elections: urban middle class, urban middle- and upper-class managers, autonomous working class, autonomous lower-middle class and the work force in agriculture. Social aggregates identified with Frei in 1964 but unidentified with the Christian Democrats in 1963 included all of the foregoing plus independent professionals and upper administrative class.[5]

The fact that the right-wing forces departed from the coalition electing the Chilean president in 1964 constitutes partial evidence for the disintegration of that social coalition. This has frequently been cited as one of the factors contributing to the PDC's inability to carry through on some of their 1964 campaign promises for structural reforms. Right-wing obstructionism was renewed in earnest in 1965. From a different perspective, it could be argued that the loss of some social aggregates, whose interest and demands appeared most contradictory to those remaining with the Christian Democrats in 1965 or 1967, should have facilitated "ruling," in Kenworthy's sense of using government "to redistribute resources through contested decisions."[6] From one perspective, the social coalition disintegration phenomenon prevents ruling precisely because the departure of important forces from the coalition leaves it with a social base too tenuous to effect fundamental reforms. From another perspective the departure of certain social forces should facilitate ruling. A failure to rule in this case can be attributed to a weakness of political vision or will. The subsequent disintegration of the coalition electing a Chilean president has been one of two usual outcomes of the presidential-election process.

An alternative phenomenon regarding the presidential election is what might be called the "numerous and disparate interests theses," according to which the social coalition electing a Chilean president does not subsequently disintegrate but is nevertheless composed of such heterogeneous interests that meaningful ruling is proscribed. Such appears to have occurred in the case of the election of Jorge Alessandri in 1958. Correlation analysis reveals that the social coalition disintegration thesis did not hold in 1958, as it apparently did in 1964. Instead, a reverse phenomenon occurred. A number of social aggregates, unidentified in 1957 with the parties which later united in the Democratic Front (Frente Democrático) supporting Alessandri (Conservatives, Liberals and Radicals), were identified with the election of Alessandri in 1958 and remained identified with the Front through 1963. (These included the urban middle class, urban middle- and upper-class managers, independent professionals and the upper administrative class.)

The failure of the Front to act as a ruling coalition cannot be attributed to the disintegration of the social coalition electing Alessandri—it did not disintegrate until 1963-64. Three of the important social aggregates unidentified with Front parties in 1957, but subsequently identified throughout the life span, are three of the aggregates which deserted Frei in 1965 and whose desertion supposedly accounts for Frei's inability to rule (urban middle class, urban middle- and upper-class managers, and the upper administrative class). These aggregates were members of the coalition of the Democratic Front, but their incorporation in that coalition did not contribute to its ruling ability, due to the existence of an electoral formation composed of numerous and disparate social forces. (If there was ever an administration which did not use government to make hard redistributive decisions, it was certainly the administration of the Democratic Front.) Whichever thesis is accepted, it appears that Chilean presidential elections have in the past contained a built-in tension which has impeded major social change. Whether one takes the social coalition disintegration thesis or the numerous and disparate interests thesis, the phenomenon to be accounted for is the same: the relative absence of ruling coalitions, even following the important presidential election.

The coalition nature of the Chilean presidential electoral process constitutes a possible constraint for the coalition emerging victorious in that process. This constraint has in the past contributed to reigning rather than ruling coalitions in the sense that the coalitions have been unable to make hard redistributive decisions.[7]

The way around this constraint is clear enough, but difficult to implement. It would entail producing a coalition that constitutes a majority of the Chilean electorate but not at the expense of containing such disparate elements that ruling is thwarted. A look at the 1969 vote for the major parties constituting UP discloses the following percentages: 15.9 percent for the Communists, 13.0 percent for the Radicals and 12.2 percent for the Socialists. In the April 1971 municipal elections, these figures were dramatically changed: 22.4 percent for the Socialists, 17.0 percent for the Communists and only 8.0 percent for the Radicals. The narrow class-based alliance for which the Socialists in particular have long argued polled 39.4 percent of the total national vote. But it cannot be concluded that such a narrow class-based alliance was on the road to electoral irreversibility. The fact that the Socialist vote showed an extraordinary leap from 12.2 to 22.4 percent from 1969 to 1971 must be counterposed by the fact that the Christian Democratic vote showed a leap from 22.0 to 42.3 percent from 1963 to 1965. In each case, a dramatic presidential electoral victory for the nominees of the respective parties intervened. The fact that the PDC vote in 1971 was only 3.6 percent greater than its vote in the 1963 municipal elections hung like a cloud over projections of the likely future of the Socialist vote and of the total vote for UP. This was a crucial consideration because of the openly proclaimed electoral nature of the transition to socialism.

THE IMPLICATIONS OF ELECTORAL STABILITY

Closely related to the previously discussed items are some data concerning the recent stability of support for some major Chilean political parties. A simple statistical approach, involving correlations between communal party votes of successive years, has been used to arrive at some rough approximations of stability coefficients for each of the major political parties. For each major political party, all possible intercorrelations of that party's communal votes have been calculated over a ten-year period (1957-67).[8] To summarize the results of the various correlational analyses, a mean correlation coefficient for each party has been computed.

The results of this summarization procedure yielded one major party which easily outdistanced the others in terms of interelection stability. This was the Communist party with a mean correlation coefficient of .85. It was followed by the Radical party with a mean coefficient of .71. The parties that exhibited the next greatest stability were the Conservative and Liberal parties (later united in the National party). The mean coefficient for the Conservatives was .67 and for the Liberals .60 (by contrast, the mean coefficient for the Socialists was only .40 and for the Christian Democrats an even lower .37).

An alternative summarization procedure was also employed by simple regression analyses of party votes for the 1960s decade (the regression of the 1965 Communist vote on the 1967 Communist vote, the regression of the 1963 Communist vote on the 1967 Communist vote and so on). As an example of such an equation: the 1967 Communist vote = 1.7 + .83 Communist vote in 1965. The closer the approximation of b, the slope, to 1.0, the more perfect the relationship between the two variables under consideration. In terms of our analysis of electoral stability, the closer the slope to 1.0, the greater the stability in a party's vote between elections. Then the mean deviation from 1.0 for all such party slopes was calculated in an effort to rank the parties in terms of stability.[9] Again, the Communists, Radicals and Conservatives appeared the most stable. The mean deviation of Communist slopes from 1.0 was only .23; of Radical slopes, .40; of Conservative slopes, .46. By contrast, the mean deviation of Christian Democratic slopes was .61.

These data refer to areal or ecological stability, i.e., to stability in voting percentages using the commune as the unit of analysis. In themselves they say nothing about the stability of voting behavior on the part of social groups. Indirectly suggestive of such group voting stability are the correlations obtained between indicators of such groups and voting for some major Chilean political parties in elections of the 1960s. An analysis of provincial data, for example, reveals the following results.

Table 1

SOCIAL GROUPS AND VOTING FOR SOME MAJOR
CHILEAN POLITICAL PARTIES, 1960-67

Correlation

Dependent Working Class—Communist Vote, 1967	.63[a]
Dependent Working Class—Communist Vote, 1963	.65[a]
Dependent Working Class—Communist Vote, 1961	.78[a]
Dependent Working Class—Communist Vote, 1960	.72[a]
Mining Population—Communist Vote, 1967	.62[a]
Mining Population—Communist Vote, 1963	.74[a]
Mining Population—Communist Vote, 1961	.68[b]
Mining Population—Communist Vote, 1960	.64[c]
Rural Middle and Upper Class—Radical Vote, 1967	.32
Rural Middle and Upper Class—Radical Vote, 1963	.51[b]
Rural Middle and Upper Class—Radical Vote, 1961	.31
Rural Middle and Upper Class—Radical Vote, 1960	.33
Landowners—Radical Vote, 1967	.32
Landowners—Radical Vote, 1963	.50[c]
Landowners—Radical Vote, 1961	.25
Landowners—Radical Vote, 1960	.23
Work Force in Agriculture—Conservative Vote, 1965	.39
Work Force in Agriculture—Conservative Vote, 1963	.59[b]

Table 1 Continued

SOCIAL GROUPS AND VOTING FOR SOME MAJOR CHILEAN POLITICAL PARTIES, 1960-67

	Correlation
Work Force in Agriculture—Conservative Vote, 1961	.38
Work Force in Agriculture—Conservative Vote, 1960	.37
Autonomous Lower Middle Class—Nation Vote, 1967	.65[a]
Autonomous Lower Middle Class—Conservative Vote, 1963	.54[b]
Autonomous Lower Middle Class—Conservative Vote, 1961	.47[c]
Autonomous Lower Middle Class—Conservative Vote, 1960	.59[b]

[a]Significant at .001 level
[b]Significant at .01 level
[c]Significant at .05 level

Table 2

INTERCORRELATIONS OF ALLENDE VOTE, 1958-70

	Correlation
Allende 1964-Allende 1970	.85[a]
Allende 1958-Allende 1970	.79[a]
Allende 1958-Allende 1964	.81[a]

[a]Significant at .001 level

The trend of areal stability in voting patterns with regard to recent presidential elections is also worthy of note. The following table presents the intercorrelations (using communal data) for the Allende vote in the presidential elections of 1958, 1964 and 1970.

Approximately 72 percent of the variation in the 1970 Allende vote is accounted for by variation in the 1964 Allende vote, 62 percent of the variation in the 1970 Allende vote is accounted for by variation in the 1958 Allende vote and 64 percent of the variation in the 1964 Allende vote is accounted for by variation in the 1958 Allende vote.[10]

What is the nature of electoral constraints stemming from these data on electoral stability? On the leftist side, the Communist party remained relatively strong in those areas where it was strong in the 1960s and remained relatively weak in those areas where it was weak. The correlational results, in themselves, say nothing about the absolute size of the Communist vote, but a detailed inspection of individual communes indicates that the party had its strength confined to a relatively reduced bastion or small geographical part of the country. Certain communes in the country regularly returned substantial Communist pluralities without seriously disturbing the essential outlines of the political system. There were, for example, 16 communes in which the mean Communist vote exceeded 30 percent during five elections held between 1960 and 1967. In one of these, the commune of Catalina, the mean percentage was an impressive 55.7. Catalina is a clear example of a commune with a stably high Communist plurality. Located in the province of Antofagasta, it returned a Communist plurality of 48.3 percent in 1961; 56.8 in 1963; 57.6 in 1964; and 60.1 in 1967. Another such example is the commune of Mincha in the province of Coquimbo, which had a Communist vote of 31.5 percent in 1961; 35.9 in 1963; 36.8 in 1965; and 36.5 in 1967.

Using a somewhat less restrictive definition of Communist communes, 26 of Chile's 286 communes can be identified as "principal areas of Communist electoral strength."[11] Of these 26, 21 are located either in the four northernmost provinces (Tarapaca, Antofagasta, Atacama, Coquimbo) or in the industrial coal-mining regions of the provinces of Concepción and Arauco. Principal areas of Communist electoral strength are to be found in only 10 of the country's 25 provinces. Briefly, there are several additional characteristics of these 26 communes. The mean percentage of urban population is 60.1 (by contrast, the mean urban percentage of the principal areas of Radical electoral strength is only 28.4). The mean percentage of the active work force in agriculture is only 29.1 (by contrast, the mean for the communes of the entire country is 52.5, and for principal areas of Radical electoral strength 64.6). In 12 of the 26 communes, mining is the leading occupation in terms of percentage of the active work force employed. Finally, the percentage of these 26 communes possessing labor unions in 1964 was 53.8 (by contrast, the percentage of principal areas of Radical electoral strength possessing labor unions was only 16.7).[12]

The stability in Communist communal vote percentages was a mixed blessing for the Communists: it provided them with a "rock-bottom" electoral strength upon which they could customarily count, but it prevented the extension of their influence. The obverse of the stably high Communist communes was a great number of stably low Communist communes in which Communist electoral inroads, during the decade of the 1960s, were very scant. The most common feature of such communes is their rurality. Using communal data, we find the following correlations between "percentage rural" and "percentage Communist vote": -.36 in 1967; -.20 in 1965; -.25 in 1963; -.38 in 1961; and -.33 in 1960.[13] A clear example of an overwhelmingly rural, stably low Communist commune is Paredones in the province of Colchagua. In Paredones, which was 93.9 percent rural according to the 1960 census, the Communist party received 2.9 percent of the vote in 1960; did not run candidates in 1961; received 2.8 percent in 1963; did not run candidates in 1965; and received 1.7 percent in 1967. Communist weakness in rural communes is also illustrated by the characteristics of those communes where the party is apparently so weak that it does not even bother to run candidates. In the municipal elections of 1967, for example, the Communists did not run candidates in 50 communes with a mean rural percentage of 71.8. In the preceding municipal elections of 1963, they did not run candidates in 66 communes with a mean rural percentage of 77.3.[14]

At the national level the Communist vote in 1971 changed the least in comparison with 1969. The Communist vote in the 1971 municipal elections was 17.0 percent; in the 1969 congressional elections, it was 15.9 percent. The lack of change is also illustrated in our mean communal change figures. From 1961 to 1969, the mean communal change in the Communist vote was only +3.5 percent. From 1963 to 1969, it was +3.4; from 1965 to 1969, +1.2 and from 1967 to 1969, +2.0 (i.e., after eight years of perhaps unparalleled vicissitudes in Chilean politics, the Communist vote in the "average" commune was only 3.5 percent higher than it was in 1961). The remarkably high stability of the Communist vote, which detailed inspection of individual communes reveals to translate into geographical confinement, augered well for the electoral extension of this prime component of UP.

On the side of UP, the case of the Radicals must also be considered. The Radicals have also had "their" communes in Chilean electoral history. In five nonpresidential elections held during the 1960s, the Radical party obtained a mean vote greater than 40 percent in 13 communes. Its stable strength in some communes is quite remarkable. In the commune of Santa Juana in the province of Concepción, the Radicals polled 52.1 percent of the vote in 1967; 70.4 percent in 1965; 66.2 percent in 1963; 57.7 percent in 1961; and 62.0 percent in 1960. Radical electoral strength is also notoriously high in some northern mining communes such as Negreiros in the province of Tarapaca. The mean vote for the Radicals in Negreiros was 68.9 percent for the five nonpresidential elections held between 1960 and 1967.

The bulk of principal areas of Radical electoral strength is south of Santiago, particularly in the rural and agricultural areas of such provinces as Nuble, Concepción, Osorno and Chiloe. Only 9 of the 36 communes designated as principal areas of Radical electoral strength are in the north of the country, the majority of these in the province of Tarapaca.

These facts are of some importance in discussions of the Radical party, for the social base of the party is generally alleged to differ between northern and central-south regions. Gil, for example, refers to "northerners from the mining districts" and "southern landowners."[15] More generally, the party appears to have attracted electoral support from working-class elements in the north and from the provincial middle class in the central-south region. The heterogeneity of the social bases of the Radical party, in part a result of the regionalization of Chilean politics, is frequently related to other characteristics of the party—most notably its historical record of ideological schizophrenia. What is interesting here is not so much the lack of a clearly definable Radical ideology as the fact that the principal communal contributors to a history of Radical electoral stability are in the center and center-south of Chile, regions where the party has generally had more of a right-wing coloration than it has had in the north or in the populous capital city.

The importance of such areas in the social base of the Radical party has influenced the magnitude and direction of findings regarding the party's electoral behavior. In modern elections, the party's vote has shown an increasing tendency to positively correlate with an indicator of "percentage rural." At the communal level, this correlation was .22 in 1965 and .29 in 1967. In the 1967 municipal elections, the party had the second highest vote in the most rural and agricultural of Chilean communes, trailing only the Christian Democrats, but clearly outdistancing the right-wing National party. And, in an analysis of the correlates of the Radical vote with subdivisions of the population active in agriculture, the following dramatic contrast was revealed:[16]

Table 3

CORRELATES OF THE RADICAL VOTE WITH TWO
SUBDIVISIONS OF THE POPULATION ACTIVE IN
AGRICULTURE (PROVINCES)

Sub-division	1967	1965	1964	1963	1961	1960	1958	1957
Rural middle and upper class	.32	.11	$.53^b$	$.51^b$	.31	.33	$.55^b$	$.43^c$
Inquilinos, Medieros	−.13	$−.41^c$	$−.44^c$	$−.44^c$	$−.64^a$	−.36	$−.44^c$	−.27

[a]Significant at .001 level
[b]Significant at .01 level
[c]Significant at .05 level

The ideological instability of the Radical party was particularly obvious in the 1960s, when the party shifted from membership in Alessandri's Democratic Front to an allegedly Social Democratic party which, by 1970, wound up in the Allende camp. This was essentially an elite phenomenon and as such raised some interesting questions about elite-mass relationships in multiparty systems. During the 1960s, the Radical party manifested considerable ideological instability at the elite level while maintaining considerable stability in its mass social base. It is quite possible that this peculiar function of the Radical party contributed to the stability of the Chilean party system by introducing an element of flexibility which did not depend upon sudden movements of voters from one party to another. But, in late 1969, the ideological schisms at the elite level in the party precipitated an open split with the formation of the Radical Democracy Party (Partido Democracia Radical), composed largely of the rightist elements in the party and supporters of Alessandri in the 1970 election. In the 1971 elections, the Radical party obtained only 8.0 percent of the vote, while the Radical Democracy party obtained only 3.8 percent.

In the light of the 1969 party split and the 1970 election results, a debate ensued concerning the contribution of the Radicals to the votes for Allende or Alessandri. This debate was especially vigorous on the Left, with the Socialists claiming very little Radical support for the Allende victory. Preliminary data for the 1970 election have a bearing on the issue. The data are of relevance, not only with regard to the specific triumph of Allende, but also in terms of larger concerns with the stability of the Radical vote and the areas largely responsible for it.

First identified were those communes where the Radical party had appeared electorally strongest throughout the 1960s. There were, as previously noted, 36 principal areas of Radical electoral strength. Then, trends were surveyed in the Allende vote from 1964 to 1970 in these 36 Radical communes. In 23 of the 36 communes, the Allende vote showed a decline from 1964 to 1970. In one commune (La Serena), it stayed exactly the same. There were 12 increases over 1964, of which five occurred in the north. From Santiago south, there were only seven Allende increases out of 27 Radical communes and only two of these were substantial. The mean change in the Allende vote, 1964 to 1970, was -.26 percent in the Radical communes. In the Radical communes south of Santiago, the mean change was - 4.5 percent.

Additional data of relevance stem from a correlational analysis of party votes in the 1969 congressional elections with the vote for Allende in the 1970 presidential election. The communal correlation between the 1970 Allende vote and the 1969 vote for the Communist party is +.73. The correlation between the 1970 Allende vote and the 1969 vote for the Socialist party is +.24. But the correlation between the 1970 Allende vote and the 1969 vote for the Radical party is a faintly negative one, -.02. Thus, in terms of a communal-level correlational analysis, there is virtually no relationship between Radical voting in 1969 and Allende voting in 1970. And what relationship exists is a slightly negative one (i.e., the higher the vote for the Radicals in 1969, the lower the vote for Allende in 1970).

It is likely that if the votes for the two Radical parties were combined by communes and then correlational analyses were made, the total Radical vote would continue to manifest high interelection stability. But the Radicals were decreasingly able to lend an aura of bourgeois respectability to the coalition which Allende headed. If the "regular" party could still count on a social base which was relatively strong where it had always been so, the absolute level of voting for the Radicals nevertheless dramatically declined, substantial numbers of old Radicals went over to anti-UP political forces and the schism with its right wing eliminated the flexibility role of the official Radical party.

On the opposition side, the electoral stability coefficients also had some constraining implications for the future of UP. Although the absolute vote percentages for the parties of the Right declined from 33.0 percent in 1957 to 21.1 percent in 1971, it is still a valid inference that substantial numbers of people in important social aggregates (who voted for the parties of the Right consistently throughout the 1960s) would continue to vote for the National party. (Indirect evidence on this score may be gleaned from the provincial ecological correlates between some social aggregates and rightist voting in modern national elections. The correlations between "upper administrative class" and voting for the Conservative party were .27 in 1957, .23 in 1960, .30 in 1961, .56 in 1963, and .48 in 1965. In 1967, the correlation between "upper administrative class" and voting for the National party was .50. The correlations between "urban middle class" and voting for the Conservatives were .23 in 1957, .56 in 1960, .52 in 1961, .61 in 1963, but only .13 in 1965. In 1967, however, the correlation between "urban middle class" and voting for the National party was .62.)

In 1965, the Conservative and Liberal parties together polled only 12.5 percent of the national vote, leading some observers to speculate about their ultimate demise as important forces in the

Chilean political system. In the 1971 municipal elections, however, the parties of the Right (National and Radical Democracy) rebounded to the extent of receiving 21.1 percent of the vote. In the election interval of 1967-69, the National party was one of only two parties (the other being the Communists) whose mean communal change figure showed an increase. In the "average" Chilean commune between these two elections, the National party gained 3.4 percent. All of the vicissitudes of Chilean politics in the 1960s did not sway large numbers of people in important social aggregates from their habit of rightist voting. An electoral breakthrough that would decimate the Right did not occur.

While definitive judgements are difficult to make on such matters, the material under discussion boils down to the assertion that there is some evidence for a modern history of electoral stability on the part of at least four of the six major Chilean parties in the 1960s.

THE POLITICAL STANCE OF THE PETITE BOURGEOISIE

Of relevance as an electoral constraint for UP is the voting behavior of the petite bourgeoisie. It is difficult to pinpoint those Chileans who fall into this social category. Among the rural population, they might be identified as small- and medium-scale farmers. Unlike *inquilinos* or *medieros,* they are landowners, but of relatively small parcels. A rough operational definition of such farmers, frequently employed in Chile in connection with discussions of agrarian reform, identifies as small- and medium-scale farmers all those owning fewer than 80 hectares of land. In general, such small- and medium-scale farmers were considered exempt from expropriations under the agrarian reform program.

Among the urban population, the petite bourgeoisie is still harder to locate precisely. They may be identified as members of small-scale industry and artisanry, as well as members of the burgeoning tertiary sector (small-scale service occupations). According to estimates of the Chilean Development Corporation (CORFO), there exist in Chile more than 80,000 small-scale industries and more than 50,000 artisans' workshops.[17]

The prevailing attitude of UP toward these petite bourgeois sectors of Chilean society was one of "not touching them." Concerning the small-scale urban industrial sector, the Basic Program of UP was quite explicit. In discussing "The Construction of the New Economy," the program referred to areas of social, private and mixed property. Referring to the area of private property, the program noted: "These businesses will be the numerical majority. The State will procure the necessary technical and financial assistance for the businesses of this sector, so that they may fulfill the important function which they perform in the national economy, keeping in mind the number of persons who work in them and the volume of production which they generate."[18] Far from being eliminated as important features of the economy or having their interests subordinated to those of the state in a systematic manner, small-scale industry and artisanry were promised a flourishing future under the Allende government. This position was reiterated by Allende throughout his regime.

A similar stance was adopted with regard to small- and medium-scale farmers. While the basic program promised the liquidation of the latifundia, it also was quite specific about the smaller farmers: "Only the small- and medium-scale farmers will have the right not to be expropriated."[19] In the first months of the Allende administration, conflicts in the agrarian sector were the most serious political issues faced by the government. The rights of small- and medium-scale farmers were brought into question as land invasions, instigated by the extreme leftist Revolutionary Peasant Movement (Movimiento Campesino Revolucionario), led to takeovers of numerous small properties falling well below the 80-hectare figure. Finally, on February 15, 1971, the government issued a new official declaration of agrarian policy. The declaration read in part: ". . .the Government does not intend to expropriate in any way the small- and medium-scale farmers, understanding by that those who possess fewer than 80 hectares of irrigated land or its equivalent throughout the country."[20]

In the light of this unwillingness to "touch" the interests of the petite bourgeoisie, whether in urban or rural areas, it is interesting to examine the direction of political preferences among these sectors in modern Chilean electoral history. Some aggregate census and electoral data may throw some light on the question. Provincial electoral data and an occupational classification scheme borrowed from Di Tella will be used in a correlational analysis designed to examine the relationship between party voting and various indicators of the petite bourgeoisie.[21]

Tables 4 and 5 contain the correlations between the percentage vote obtained by various major Chilean political parties and two occupational subdivisions of the lower middle class, the "administrative lower middle class" and "the autonomous lower middle class."

None of the major parties comprising UP (Communist, Socialist and Radical) exhibited positive relationships with two indicators of the occupational lower middle class. In recent elections, an indicator of the "administrative lower middle class" is strongly and positively correlated with voting for the PDC and strongly and negatively correlated with voting for the Radicals and Socialists (the relationship between "administrative lower middle class" and Communist vote is virtually nonexistent). In the case of the "autonomous lower middle class," which might be thought the better of the two indicators in terms of petite bourgeoisie, the strongest positive correlates are generally with the parties of the traditional Right. Correlations between an indicator of the "autonomous lower middle class" and votes for the Radical, Socialist and Communist parties are always strongly negative.

The relationship between party voting and the proportion of petit bourgeois provincial population is further illustrated by a comparison of the voting behavior of the "autonomous working class" and that of the "dependent working class." By definition, the category of "autonomous working class" more closely approximates the petit bourgeois aggregate.

Tables 6 and 7 present the findings of an analysis correlating major party votes with these diverse segments of the worker population.

Members of the "autonomous working class," i.e., self-employed workers (for example, plumbers, carpenters, painters, etc.), constitute a large occupational category in the Chilean context. As can be seen from Table 6, an indicator of this

Table 4

CORRELATES OF PARTY VOTES WITH INDICATOR OF
ADMINISTRATIVE LOWER MIDDLE CLASS (PROVINCES)

	1957	1958	1960	1961	1963	1964	1965	1967
PDC	-.03	.40[c]	.15	.01	.42[c]	.59[b]	.60[b]	.68[a]
Radicals	-.31	-.54[b]	-.33	-.31	-.42[c]	-.63[a]	-.46[c]	-.41[c]
Socialists	-.20	-.28	-.36	-.35	-.23	-.41[c]	-.37	-.33
Communist	—	—	-.07	-.28	-.08	—	-.10	.07

[a]Significant at .001 level
[b]Significant at .01 level
[c]Significant at .05 level

Table 5

CORRELATES OF PARTY VOTES WITH INDICATOR OF
AUTONOMOUS LOWER MIDDLE CLASS (PROVINCES)

	1967	1965	1964	1963	1961	1960	1958	1957
PDC	.17	.17	.54[b]	-.04	.28	-.10	-.05	-.43
Radicals	-.05	-.41[c]	-.26	-.34	-.48[c]	-.33	-.26	-.35
Socialists	-.33	-.20	-.49[c]	-.38	-.29	-.30	-.66[a]	-.69
Communists	-.44[c]	-.16	—	-.45[c]	-.54[c]	-.52[b]	—	—
Nationals	.65[a]	—	—	—	—	—	—	—
Conservatives	—	.13	—	.54[b]	.47[c]	.59[b]	—	.39
Liberals	—	.26	—	.50[c]	.27	.60[b]	.69[a]	.30

[a]Significant at .001 level
[b]Significant at .01 level
[c]Significant at .05 level

Table 6

CORRELATES OF PARTY VOTES WITH INDICATOR OF
AUTONOMOUS WORKING CLASS (PROVINCES)

	1967	1965	1964	1963	1961	1960	1958	1957
Socialists	-.36	-.17	-.70[a]	-.24	-.19	-.22	-.79[a]	-.63[b]
Communists	-.80[a]	-.49	—	-.76[a]	-.84[a]	-.80[a]	—	—
Nationals	.71[a]	—	—	—	—	—	—	—
Conservatives	—	.53[c]	—	.63[b]	.46[c]	.36	—	.23
Liberals	—	.37	—	.53[b]	.34	.54[b]	.71[a]	.15

[a]Significant at .001 level
[b]Significant at .01 level
[c]Significant at .05 level

Table 7

CORRELATES OF PARTY VOTES WITH INDICATOR OF DEPENDENT WORKING CLASS (PROVINCES)

	1967	1965	1964	1963	1961	1960	1958	1957
Socialists	.42[c]	.28	.72[a]	.33	.29	.34	.79[a]	.66[a]
Communists	.63[a]	.41	—	.65[a]	.78[a]	.72[a]	—	—
Nationals	-.73[a]	—	—	—	—	—	—	—
Conservatives	—	-.34	—	.70[a]	-.56[b]	-.55[b]	—	-.26
Liberals	—	-.27	—	-.43[c]	-.22	-.55[b]	-.77[b]	-.11

[a] Significant at .001 level
[b] Significant at .01 level
[c] Significant at .05 level

"autonomous working class" correlates highly negatively with the vote for the Communist party and negatively (less strongly so) with the vote for the Socialist party. On the other hand, the indicator correlates highly positively with the votes for the traditional parties of the Chilean Right (Conservatives, Liberals) and with the vote of their latter-day descendant, the National party (which supported Jorge Alessandri in the 1970 presidential election). A measure of the "dependent working class," workers employed in industrial or commercial establishments, reveals a pattern almost exactly the reverse. Now the strikingly high positive correlations are with the parties of the Left, particularly the Communists, and the strongly negative correlations are with the parties of the Right, particularly the National party in 1967.

Whether the middle class or the working class, the results are substantially the same: that part of each class which most closely approximates a social aggregate that can be called the "petite bourgeoisie," the autonomous lower middle class and the autonomous working class, has not been historically associated with voting for the parties that comprised UP. Quite to the contrary: to the extent that ecological analysis can throw any light on the voting patterns of this social aggregate in urban areas, petit bourgeois voting appears historically associated with voting for the parties of the Right or for the newer PDC. The Radical party was the only member of the UP coalition for which it might be argued that the petite bourgeoisie contributed some support. But the pattern of findings with regard to the Radicals, while occasionally revealing some grounds for arguing the case, more often led in the opposite direction.

When the rural sector is considered, it is more difficult to formulate social categories that correspond perfectly to the petite bourgeoisie. This is because Di Tella's category of "autonomous rural middle class," which on the surface appears to be exactly what is needed, includes several other agricultural categories as well as the aforementioned small landowners.[22] Similarly, the category of "rural managers" includes both middle- and upper-class managers. Although the category of *inquilinos* is more clearly defined, they are distinguished from the rural petite bourgeoisie. There is no simple way of correlating an indicator of rural petite bourgeoisie with voting for the major Chilean parties.

Some shreds of data are, however, revealing. Of the major parties which comprised UP, only the Radical vote correlated positively with the indicator of "rural middle- and upper-class managers." These managers were agricultural employers, of whom many would, no doubt, be classified as "small farmers." The correlates of this indicator with voting for the parties of UP can be seen in Table 8.

These findings with regard to the Radical vote cannot be definitively analyzed in light of the 1969 split of the Radical party which saw its landowning right-wing depart in favor of the Radical Democracy party. One hypothesis is that the historically positive correlation between the Radical vote and this indicator was occasioned by the voting behavior of medium-scale (and in some cases, large-scale) farmers who departed the ranks of the Radical party in favor of the right-wing alternative. The pattern with regard to the Radical party is substantially the same if the indicator of the "autonomous rural middle class" is considered contaminated, however, in the manner already described. The Radical vote correlates consistently and positively with an indicator of the "autonomous rural middle class." Again it could be hypothesized that this relationship was largely attributable to the voting behavior of people who have subsequently deserted the party in great numbers.

The vote for the Socialist party generally correlates moderately negatively with an indicator of "autonomous rural middle class." There is also a moderately positive relationship between Communist voting and this indicator. This is an example of the pitfalls of aggregate analysis. It is entirely possible that there exists a number of small- or medium-scale landowners who regularly voted for the Communist party despite the obvious overall weakness of the party in rural areas. But in addition to being implausible for the Chilean case, this argument is dangerously close to the ecological fallacy that social scientists attempt to avoid. A more plausible argument might be that increases in the number of landowners increase the level of resentment of nonowners and drive them into a Communist vote.

The correlational analysis does not confirm the expectation that the propertyless were voting for the parties of the Left. Although the *inquilino* population is explicitly excluded from the

Table 8

CORRELATES OF VOTES FOR THE PARTIES OF UP WITH AN
INDICATOR OF RURAL MIDDLE-AND UPPER-CLASS MANAGERS
(SOME OF WHOM ARE SMALL FARMERS) (PROVINCES)

	1967	1965	1964	1963	1961	1960	1958	1957
Radicals	.50[b]	.26	.53[a]	.28	.27	.27	.46[b]	.06
Socialists	-.11	-.08	-.34	.07	.06	.14	-.25	.00
Communists	-.35	-.14	—	-.34	-.39	-.36	—	—

[a]Significant at .01 level
[b]Significant at .05 level

category of petite bourgeoisie, it is nevertheless interesting to inspect the correlates of party voting with an indicator of the *inquilino* and *mediero* subdivision of the population active in farming. The correlates are included in Table 9.

Table 9's results are important in view of the amount of attention given to the rural peasantry as a force in Chilean politics. The only two political forces to manifest positive correlations with this indicator of *inquilino* concentration are the Christian Democrats and the right-wing parties. In light of the finding for the PDC from 1960 onward, it is not surprising that the party felt the wrath of the Right. The PDC was the only effective counterweight to right-wing control of the peasantry. The negative correlations between the parties of UP and this indicator are surprising. In view of the depressing results for the parties of UP, their concern (particularly the Communists and Socialists) with buttressing their strength among the peasantry was to be expected.

Petit bourgeois voting behavior was another electoral constraint confronting the Allende experiment. The problem there was similar to that discussed by Huberman and Sweezy in *Socialism in Cuba*. In giving extensive treatment to the private sector in Cuban agriculture, Huberman and Sweezy point to "the high cost a socialist society has to pay to maintain the loyalty of a petty bourgeoisie it cannot afford to antagonize and is not yet strong enough to absorb into the socialist system." In their view, "what is undoubtedly serious is the social and moral cost of having a segment of the population amounting to 10 percent or more of the total as permanent 'carriers' of a petty bourgeois mentality and outlook."[23]

In Chile, the size of the petite bourgeoisie is considerably larger than 10 percent, making its weight in the society all that more important. In view of the apparent persistence of nonleftist voting on the part of these sectors, it is unlikely that governmental assistance would have diverted them away from conservative orientations toward reformist, much less revolutionary orientations. Since the petite bourgeoisie had not supported the forces of the Left in any case, it might be argued that UP could afford to "touch" them without much electoral detriment to itself. But this is apparently not the way the matter was perceived by UP. In

Table 9

CORRELATES OF PARTY VOTES WITH THE PERCENTAGE OF THE
AGRICULTURAL POPULATION CLASSIFIED AS *INQUILINOS* OR *MEDIEROS* (PROVINCES)

	1967	1965	1964	1963	1961	1960	1958	1957
PDC	.33	.52[b]	.14	.30	.58[b]	.40[c]	-.11	-.33
Radicals	-.13	-.41[c]	-.44[c]	-.44[c]	-.64[a]	-.36	-.44[c]	-.27
Socialists	-.34	-.42[c]	.03	-.27	-.16	-.26	-.30	-.54[b]
Communists	-.12	-.46	—	-.12	-.11	-.23	—	—
Nationals	.31	—	—	—	—	—	—	—
Conservatives	—	-.45	—	.32	.31	.28	—	.35
Liberals	—	-.15	—	.24	.11	.32	.45[c]	.38

[a] Significant at .001 level
[b] Significant at .01 level
[c] Significant at .05 level

modern Chilean political history, the petite bourgeoisie has been endowed with a myth glorifying it as the principal repository of Chilean democracy. To attack it is to attack the essence of Chilean democracy itself. Thus, the petite bourgeoisie was allowed to persist and even to flourish. The likelihood that they could have been won over to the Left by tempting governmental policies was never strong, however. Neither was a frontal assault on their interests, such as might be entailed by a commitment to expropriate farms of fewer than 80 hectares or to expropriate retail traders, commercial establishments, small-scale industries, artisans' workshops and so on. What was always more likely was that this large and important element in Chilean society would remain intact and persist in its political orientations.

ALTERNATIVES

The electoral constraints that confronted the Allende government were formidable. Past patterns of electoral and parliamentary politics in Chile cautioned against expecting any significant changes in their operation and outcomes. However, it would be an overstatement of the argument to say that Allende and his coalition were placed in a corner from which there was no room to escape. Certainly Allende and the Chilean Left would not have subscribed to the view that their future efforts to build a peaceful road to socialism were inevitably preordained to failure given the above discussed electoral constraints. What, then, are some possible alternative developments that might have resulted from a modification of the situations described?

The Possibility of an Electoral Breakthrough

An electoral breakthrough would mean the occurrence of such a critical election as we presumed not to have occurred in the recent Chilean past. It would have involved an enduring realignment of political loyalties among the existing electorate at the mass level. Such a realignment would presumably have converted important social aggregates—perhaps most notably the peasants, the marginal urban population and segments of the petite bourgeoisie—into lasting habits of identification with the Marxist parties. It would have translated them into Marxist majorities in future congressional elections and thus put an end to congressional stalemate and obstructionism. This possibility might have been Allende's dream, but the prospects for its realization do not seem to have been great. The obstacles to it were many, including the profound anticommunism of important sectors of the Chilean electorate, the historical organizational weakness of the Socialist party, the resurgence of the Right as a potent electoral force and the likelihood that the Christian Democrats would have had relatively firm support among about one-fifth to one-fourth of the electorate—as well as the persistence of those irrational, symbolic attachments to political parties (such as the Chilean Radical party) or political systems (such as the Chilean multiparty system) which are of importance in other national contexts (e.g., American, French) and which doubtlessly operate in Chile as well.

Future Efforts at Political Mobilization

To argue that a radical transformation of the Chilean electoral landscape was unlikely is not necessarily to argue that there were no devices which the forces of UP could have conceivably used to bolster their electoral support. In particular, the regime could have devoted substantial resources to the mobilization of previously nonparticipant political forces or political forces whose past participation had been unsystematic, non-ideological and allegedly marked by false consciousness. The stalemate or accommodationist model of politics operative in Chile since 1925 has probably depended for its continued existence on relatively low rates of political participation and mobilization. This does not refer simply to the most often cited variable in this regard, i.e., electoral participation, although, in comparison with many other Latin American countries, this has been fairly low in Chile. It refers also to the absence of sustained organizational participation (low proportion of industrial work force unionized, the relative absence of popular community organizations until the Frei administration, etc.) as well as to the almost total absence of politicization of the peasant population.

The possibilities for UP were many. The percentage of the active work force unionized was calculated at 24 for 1970.[24] Probably not more than 10 percent of the peasant population was unionized. The voting franchise was extended to illiterates and to

18 year olds, an extension which should have added several hundred thousand new voters and raised the number in the effective electorate by perhaps 10 or 15 percent. Beyond this, there was the huge population of urban marginals—shantytown dwellers, immigrants from rural areas and so on. In Chile and throughout Latin America, this sector of the swelling urban population has generally been devoid of systematic political organization and has tended toward different variants of the phenomenon known as Latin American populism. They, like the peasants in rural areas, have generally been untouched by political parties of the Marxist Left.

The Marxists with UP were aware of all these facts. Whether they would have developed systematic strategies for dealing with them is another question. The Communist and Socialist parties, particularly the former, have been historically weak or nonexistent in rural areas. The parties have a long history of often bitter struggles over the loyalties of the organized proletariat and such discrepancies might well have impeded attempts to organize and politicize nonparticipants in urban areas. Furthermore, there was the problem that the Communists were generally considered by far the strongest organizational component of UP. In many areas of the country, the Socialists and Radicals were organizations in name only. Hence, mobilizational efforts in which the Communists might have gained the upper hand were likely to receive guarded support from the Communists' major partners in the coalition.

Finally, there was the important question of the quality of the envisioned mobilizational efforts. Few UP strategists or ideologists gave sufficient attention to the substantive content of future politicization efforts. There was much talk of cultural action, consciousness-raising and the replacement of bourgeois values, but precisely what all this signified was difficult to discern. Yet, it was a crucial point. For, if people were to be asked to cast off old ways in favor of new, to adopt participant roles in place of parochial ones, or to attach meaning to ongoing political organizations where before they appeared meaningless, then directions and rationalizations should have been regularly and coherently supplied. In the absence of such qualitative mobilization of the periphery, the result was likely to be an increase in quantitative indicators of mobilization with no payoff in terms of progress toward a socialist regime. Without attention to substantive content, such mobilizational efforts may have backfired in terms of regime support. Eduardo Frei and the Christian Democrats engaged in mobilizational efforts with a vaguely defined communitarian rationale whose operational significance was seldom apparent and whose end results for PDC electoral support were highly questionable.

In short, UP needed to formulate strategies for mobilizing and organizing those many social forces not tied to the existing structure of institutions and needed to organize them in a manner consonant with its vision of the Chilean future. This is an effort that would have gone beyond electoral politics but whose electoral payoffs may well have proved substantial. Even if it did not produce a quasi-permanent electoral majority in the future (for other political forces, most notably the Christian Democrats, were also at work among these unmobilized strata), it could have produced enough of a Socialist-inspired mass to guarantee that retreats from major policy initiatives engineered by Allende would have been difficult to undertake in any future post-Socialist government. The first year of UP was not characterized by these sustained mobilizational efforts. In part, this was the result of a preeminent concern for economic performance in the first year, but it was also the result of the lack of a clearly defined strategy for the organization of power relations in the new government.

Where, then, does the current situation leave the Chilean political system for the years immediately ahead? General Pinochet and his colleagues are apparently attempting to effect the definitive termination of some long-standing Chilean political and economic characteristics. In the political sphere, the institutionalized electoral and parliamentary system—which was at once the hallmark of Chilean democracy and a brake on profound new directions in the national experience—is to be replaced by a "corporatist," "authoritarian" structure. In the economy, the perennial economic stagnation is to be replaced by "the Chilean miracle." Chile is to become a little Brazil. Only time will tell whether the constraints surrounding these efforts will ultimately prove as debilitating as those which closed the curtain on the socialist experiment.

NOTES

1. V. O. Key, Jr., "A Theory of Critical Elections," *Journal of Politics,* 17 (February 1955): 3-18; and V. O. Key, Jr., "Secular Realignment and the Party System," *Journal of Politics,* 21 (May 1959): 198-210.

2. Federico Gil and Charles J. Parrish, *The Chilean Presidential Election of September 4, 1964,* (Washington, D.C.: Institute for the Comparative Study of Political Systems, 1965), p. 46.

3. The restrictive definition was as follows: a "critical election commune" is one in which (a) the 1965 vote for the PDC was at least 20 percent more than the 1963 vote and (b) the 1967 vote was greater than the 1965 vote, or the loss between 1965 and 1967 was less than 25 percent of the 1963 to gain. At the time we established this definition we had data from only the 1963, 1965 and 1967 elections—admittedly too short a time span to talk about secular realignment. A quick inspection of 1969 electoral data indicates that many of the 48 communes would no longer be considered "critical election communes" if we continued to apply the 25 percent criterion. This does not blunt the thrust of the argument here, i.e., that very few of the communes where secular realignment has presumably occurred on behalf of the Christian Democrats can be considered urban communes.

4. The assertion cannot be made without some qualifications. There are, as we have noted in the text, some communes where secular realignment has occurred. In communes where the PDC vote returned in 1969 to near its 1963 and pre-1963 level, it is possible that important changes occurred in the social composition of the PDC vote even though the absolute vote in 1969 equalled that of 1963 and thus seems to argue superficially for a stability-of-vote interpretation. In the absence of survey data, hypotheses concerning changes in the social composition of the PDC vote are notoriously difficult to deal with. Fragmentary ecological evidence can be offered: in processing provincial census and electoral data, we were struck by some changes in the processing provincial census and electoral data and by some changes in the PDC correlates between 1963 and the subsequent nonpresidential elections. The correlate (at the provincial level) between the PDC vote and an indicator of the "rural working class," for example, was only .16 in 1963. In 1965, it was .64 and in 1967, .47. With the category of "rural administrators," the 1963 PDC correlate was .02; 1965, .55; 1967, .41. An indicator of the "urban middle class" correlated at .13 in 1967 (following a correlation with the Frei presidential vote of .67). In the absence of survey data, we prefer to hedge our conclusions

concerning changes in the social composition of the PDC electorate. But the aggregate data do suggest some alterations in that composition, even while they indicate a return to the pre-1973 norm in terms of communal percentages obtained by the PDC. How much reshuffling of the electorate has occurred is difficult to estimate.

5. In this and subsequent sections of the paper we present the findings of various correlational analyses. The correlations are performed on aggregate census and electoral data and hence are ecological correlations. The total number of communes employed in our analyses is 286 and the total number of provinces is 25. The bulk of our communal and provincial census data is from Armand Mattelart, *Atlas Social de las comunas de Chile* (Santiago de Chile: Editorial del Pacífico, 1965); Mattelart, "Integración nacional y marginalidad" (Santiago de Chile: Editorial del Pacifico, 1965). Mattelart generated the bulk of his data by performing various manipulations on raw 1960 national census data. The electoral data stem from our own collection of Chilean election data for the period 1957-71 at both communal and provincial levels. Throughout the paper we attempt to differentiate between those analyses which employ communal data and those which use provincial data. This is not the place to engage in the by now familiar debates on the advantages and disadvantages of such correlations. We caution the reader that we cannot legitimately infer the characteristics of individuals from the characteristics of the ecological units within which they reside. Yet many of our results using aggregate data contain very strong statistical relationships and we have accordingly chosen to present them here. Although we readily admit the problems of ecological analysis, there remains considerable utility in employing it in the study of Chilean elections. The demonstration of areal voting patterns has been skillfully used by American political scientists to illumine both the determinants and consequences of electoral behavior. Concerning all these topics the literature is too numerous to mention here. Standard references on this methodological problem include: Hubert M. Blalock, *Causal Inference in Non Experimental Research* (Chapel Hill: University of North Carolina Press, 1965); W. S. Robinson, "Ecological Correlations and the Behavior of Individuals," *American Sociological Review,* 15 (June 1950): 351-7; W. Phillips Shively, " 'Ecological' Inference: The Use of Aggregate Data to Study Individuals," *American Political Science Review,* 63 (December 1969): 1183-96. We would prefer to employ survey data for our generalizations about the social bases of Chilean political parties, but such data of a reliable nature are nonexistent in Chile.

A comment is also needed on the occupational categories used. These are borrowed from Torcuato S. Di Tella, "Economía y estructura ocupacional en un pais subdesarrollado," *Desarrollo Económico,* 1 (October-December 1961): 123-53, who based his occupational scheme on a table in the Chilean census which cross-tabulated Habitual Occupation with Occupational Situation. The categories of Occupational Situation were those of employers, self-employed workers, office workers, farmers, artisans, miners, professionals, technicians. By mixing the two variables, Di Tella obtained some occupational categories which we have employed here and elsewhere in the paper. For example: if we take the first two categories of Habitual Occupation ("professionals, technicians and affined" and "managers, administrators and directive officials"), we label as "medium and large urban entrepreneurs" those who have the Occupational Situation of "employer," and we label as administrative those who have the Occupational Situation of "employee." We thus can have "farmers" who are employers, "farmers" who are self-employed, "farmer" employees and "farmer" workers.

6. Eldon Kenworthy, "Coalitions in the Political Development of Latin America," *The Study of Coalition Behavior,* eds. Sven Groennings et al. (New York: Holt, Rinehart and Winston, 1970), p. 112.

7. Ibid.

8. Using communal data, we correlated the 1965 Communist vote with correlations for the time span covered. Then we computed the mean of all these coefficients. A similar procedure was used with the votes for other major parties.

9. Our treatment of the Radical vote gives an example of the procedure generally employed. We computed a simple regression equation between the 1967 Radical vote and each previous Radical vote back to 1957, including the vote for Bossay in 1958 and Durán in 1964. This produced seven separate equations. We did the same for the 1965 Radical vote and each of the elections preceding it, the 1963 Radical vote and each of the elections preceding it, etc. The result was a total of 28 separate simple regression equations upon which we calculated the mean deviation of the slope from 1.0. A similar procedure was used with each of the other major parties.

10. An analysis of the intercorrelations among the votes of the various other presidential candidates in 1958, 1964 and 1970 would entail too extended a discussion. Suffice it to note that the 1964 vote for Eduardo Frei more resembled the previous vote for parties of the Chilean Right than it resembled the previous vote for the Christian Democrats. The relationships between the 1970 vote for Alessandri, the 1970 vote for Tomic and previous patterns of Chilean presidential voting are too numerous and complex to be analyzed here and can appropriately be made the subject of another investigation.

11. The less restrictive definition is that the Communist party received at least 20 percent of the communal vote in at least four out of five nonpresidential elections held between 1960 and 1967.

12. "Principal areas of Radical electoral strength" refers to communes in which the Radical party received at least 30 percent of the vote in four out of five nonpresidential elections held between 1960 and 1967.

13. The correlations between the two variables using provincial data are understandably higher. They are: -.68 in 1967; -.40 in 1965; -.54 in 1963; -.50 in 1961; and -.60 in 1960. The communal correlations cited in the text are computed using only those communes for which electoral data exist. Since there are no such data for communes where the Communists did not run candidates, such communes have been excluded from the correlations between "percentage rural" and "percentage Communist vote."

14. In presenting the data on these communes and in making our general comments on Communist electoral weakness in rural-agricultural communes, we should add two important social groups manifesting left voting behavior. This has recently been argued by James Petras and Maurice Zeitlin, "Agrarian Radicalism in Chile," *British Journal of Sociology,* 19 (September 1968): 254-70. In analyzing the 1964 vote for Allende, they concluded that "the agricultural municipalities with proportionately greater numbers of agricultural wage laborers were also those in which Allende got a "high" vote. . ." and that "the wage laborers—the propertyless agricultural preletariat—form the major FRAP social base in the countryside." Our analysis in the present section does not extend to the voting behavior of specific groups within rural areas but is content to demonstrate the overall weakness of Communist electoral support in rural areas in the aggregate. Second, by emphasizing the stably low Communist communes, we do not mean to imply that there are no rural-agricultural communes where the Communists (or other forces of the Chilean Left) showed secular gains throughout the 1960s. There are a number of rural communes where the Communists have recently made substantial electoral inroads and an analysis of quantitative and qualitative data regarding such communes would make a highly interesting study.

15. Federico Gil, *The Political System of Chile* (Boston: Houghton Miffin, 1966), p. 260.

16. One of these subdivisions is that of "inquilino" (tenant). We may employ the Petras and Zeitlin, "Agrarian Radicalism," p. 256, definition of the inquilino: "The large fundo's major work force is made up of 'inquilinos', peasants who work the landlord's fields and contribute other types of labor in return for certain minimal perquisites or 'regalias' such as a 'house' for themselves and their families, ration of land, usually from fourth to half an acre, and the right to graze their animals on the patron's land." A full description of the category known as *medieros* (broadly "copartners") would take us far afield. For an excellent discussion the reader is referred to "Chile: tenencia, de la tierra y desarrollo socio-económico del sector agricola" (Santiago de Chile: CIDA, Comité Interamericano de Desarrollo Agricola, 1966), p. 49ff.

17. 'Plan Chonchol: proposiciones para una acción política en el periodo 1967-70 de una via no-capitalista de desarrollo," PEC (Política, Economía, Cultura) no. 239 (July 28, 1967).

18. *Programa Básico de Gobierno de la Unidad Popular* (Santiago de Chile: Impresora Horizonte, 1970), pp. 20-21.

19. *Ibid., p. 45.*

20. *El Mecurio,* Edición internacional, Santiago de Chile, February 15-21, 1971, p. 1.

21. For a more complete discussion of the correlation analysis and the occupational scheme, see note 4.

22. More precisely, it includes subdivisions of the agricultural work force known as *medieros* and *arrendatarios* (lessees). See CIDA (1966:49 ff.).

23. Leo Huberman and Paul Sweezy, *Socialism in Cuba* (New York: Monthly Review Press, 1969), pp. 119-20.

24. Clotario Blest, "La clase trabajadora chilena en cifras," *Punto Final* April 13, 1971.

3
Public Opinion and the Movement of Chilean Government to the Left, 1952-72

James W. Prothro and Patricio E. Chaparro

The thrust of Chilean political development in the last half century has been toward the Left in political orientations and policies. This shift has been associated with, and largely caused by, the mobilization of previously marginal sectors—the middle class, the lower class and peasants.[1] These modernizing forces and the leftist movement stand in sharp contrast to the almost exclusive dominance of Chilean politics by traditional rightist sectors before the 1920s.[2] Federico Gil cites the presidential election of 1920 as a crucial election in the sense that Arturo Alessandri's victory meant the collapse of oligarchical domination. The election of 1952 is pictured as another critical one in that a majority of rural workers and tenant farmers defied the rightist landlords to vote for Carlos Ibáñez.[3] This election is seen further as the first sign of a change of values on the part of a majority of the electorate.[4] In more recent periods the working class has been viewed as a cohesive force that can be politically and socially mobilized by the Left.[5]

From the perspective of the literature, the election of Salvador Allende, a Marxist candidate, as president in 1970 thus appears as some sort of culmination of the processes of mobilization and

Reprinted from *The Journal of Politics* 36 (February 1974) with permission.

This was made possible by a collaborative research training project in Chile supported by the Foreign Area Fellowship Program (FAFP) in the summer of 1972. As graduate students participating in the project, Richard Moore of the University of Texas and Brian Smith of Yale University did much of the work in data gathering, coding and tabulation; José Luis Rodríguez of Yale joined them in criticizing and shaping our ideas. We are also indebted to Luis Quirós of the Centro Latinoamericano de Demografía, Jorge Tapia of the Universidad Católica, Chile, and Federico Gil and David Kovenock of the University of North Carolina. All these individuals share with the FAFP any credit, but no blame, for what follows.

Left movement in Chilean politics. This chapter will not challenge this general interpretation but seek to refine it by examining the specific assumption that the Chilean government and party system have moved to the Left as a response to, or in association with, a shift in mass opinions to a more ideological content and a leftist orientation. We will accept what has been written about the movement to the Left at the system level—our concern is with the public opinion that is assumed to underlie this movement.

Support for the view that Chilean public opinion has moved significantly and decisively to the Left is impressive, particularly at the system level. After all, Chileans enjoyed the unique distinction of being the only nation to elect a Marxist government in a freely held, country-wide election.[6] When one contemplates the support that a Marxist coalition, based on Socialist and Communist parties, would muster in an election for president in the United States, he might realize how far to the Left of their North American counterparts the Chilean voters must have been. As great as this contrast is, however, it does not necessarily mean that Chileans were committed to Marxist ideology. They endorsed a Marxist coalition at the polls, but a wealth of research in other contexts has demonstrated the dangers of inferring, from aggregate electoral outcomes, the true state of mind of the voters.[7] The election of Allende tells us, in itself, that Chileans were not so ideologically committed (in an anti-Marxist direction) as to reject a candidate campaigning on a Marxist platform. But many factors, other than Allende's Marxism, might account for his support. From the election alone one might conceivably argue that Chileans are less ideological than North Americans, for whom ideology is sufficiently salient to assure the rejection of a Marxist candidate. Or, in positive terms, one could conclude from the election that many Chileans became champions of Marxism in their beliefs, no less than with their votes. The fact that neither interpretation is inconsistent with the election outcome underscores the necessity of going beyond electoral data to draw inferences about public opinion. Happily, more direct data can be applied to assess the apparent movement of Chilean public opinion to the Left.

The theoretical perspective which brings us to a new look at Chilean socialism is shaped by research in other contexts, which has demonstrated that imputations to popular beliefs from system characteristics and outcomes are often spectacularly in error. The theory of democracy long held, for example, that public acceptance of majority decisions and recognition of the legitimacy of minority dissent were based, in general consensus, on the fundamental principles of democracy. Although such consensus appeared logically necessary, in view of the characteristics of a democratic polity, empirical examination of the proposition in the United States in 1960 found the alleged consensus to be highly restricted.[8] Similarly, explanations of election outcomes in terms of minute shifts in the ideological positions of voters proved, in confrontation with direct data on popular attitudes, to be highly misleading.[9] In other systems too, notably in France, logical deductions from system characteristics—in this case multiparty competition—to public attitudes proved, on empirical examination, to be in error.[10] The perils of inferring from systemic to individual characteristics are, thus, sufficiently evident to call for the examination of more data before similarly derived explanations are accepted for Chile.

In addition to these theoretical and methodological warnings from general literature, some empirical work on Chile itself suggests that several accepted interpretations may be too facile. One of the major assertions in recent literature, regarding the Chilean working class, is that the workers are a cohesive force which can be politically and socially mobilized by the Left.[11] Applying both survey and ecological data to this
José Luis Rodriguez and Brian Smith find it to be oversimplified to the point of invalidity: if one works out percentage relationships on the dependent variable—Communist and Socialist support—he finds that industrial workers, though not the working class as a whole, form the electoral core of the Left parties; but doing similar calculations based on the independent variable—working-class status—reveals a different picture. Within the Chilean working class, "substantial numbers choose the Right and many make no choice at all. In addition, differential behaviour and attitudinal patterns appear between industrial and non-industrial (service) workers and between men and women in working class families. Thus, things are not as clear-cut as we are often led to believe by the existing literature."[12]

For both empirical and theoretical reasons, then, we need to question the belief that Chilean public opinion has recently shifted markedly to the Left. In this chapter, we propose to examine that belief in the light of three hypotheses which offer a different interpretation. Due to the discovery of a new source of data on Chilean public opinion, not previously known to academicians, our hypotheses can be examined against direct attitudinal data.[13] Although we thus avoid the uncertainties in the inferential leap from system outcomes to individual attitudes, we must accept the inherent limitations of secondary data analysis. Our data were collected by someone else without our purposes in mind—in either questionnaire construction or coding. Fortunately, the purpose of the survey organization—to ascertain political preferences and the reasons for those preferences in Chile—fits our own concern closely. But our theoretical interest in ideology did not guide the original survey work. Code categories were, accordingly, not constructed with the specific purpose of extracting a maximum of information applicable to that interest. Moreover, the extant data include tabular reports, not the original interview protocols or data records which would permit us to recode or rerun the data. Although these are serious limitations, the data available do offer direct evidence on relevant public attitudes. And our inability to ask different questions or to arrange the data differently is, after all, not so far from the problem political analysts have long confronted in analyzing diaries, letters and political documents. Just as scholars are unable to get past political figures to discuss anything not included in historical archives, so are we unable to ask different questions of Chileans about their attitudes. But what they have said, if carefully handled, may be a firmer base for conclusions than aggregate electoral outcomes. Moreover, our survey data will supplement, rather than replace, aggregate electoral data.

Hypothesis 1: *The marked shift of the Chilean government to the Left from 1952 to 1972 occurred without a corresponding increase in the ideological content or Left orientation of public opinion.*

Our concern is with the ideological content or orientation of opinions, not with their structure. We accordingly classify opinions as ideological or nonideological according to their substance, not their correlation with other opinions. For our purposes, any opinion that relates to class rewards or deprivations, any that refers to a Left-Center-Right continuum, and, of course, any that specifically mentions ideology as such, will be taken as ideological. Values common to most ideologies and to most people with no ideology—for example, better housing, higher wages and more jobs—are not regarded as ideological in nature. Individuals may thus engage in ideological reasoning with or without a full-blown ideology in the sense of a highly "constrained" attitudinal structure.[14] We thus focus on the ideological flavor or direction of Chilean attitudes, examining opinions for the presence or absence of such an orientation without going into the more intricate questions of whether the orientation is rooted in a "true," fully developed ideology.

Public perceptions of class bias in the outputs of the Allende government are dramatically revealed in a September 1972 survey of adult opinions in greater Santiago by the respected Chilean news magazine, *Ercilla*.[15] In response to a question as to which class has benefited most from the then present administration a majority, 53 percent, cited the lower (literally, "most modest") class, while 23 percent said that no one benefited; only 9 and 12 percent perceived the middle or upper class, respectively, as having benefited most (see Table 1). Class contrasts in perception were so sharp as to suggest a deep political polarization in Chile: 53 percent of the upper class, for example, as opposed to only 12 percent of the lower class said that no one benefited. Moreover, the notion that the benefits of government can somehow fall, like the rain, on all citizens alike was almost unanimously rejected, with only one percent claiming that everyone benefited. Clearly this government was seen to aim its benefits primarily at the poor, with 61 percent of the lower class avowing that they themselves benefited most. The percentage in other classes who agreed that benefits had gone to the lower class is smaller (47 percent of the middle class and 33 percent of the upper class agreed), but the difference is accounted for by the fact that those in higher classes were more likely to see no one as benefiting.

Table 1

PERCEPTIONS AS TO WHO HAS BENEFITED MOST FROM
ALLENDE GOVERNMENT, BY INCOME LEVEL

Beneficiaries	Weighted Total	Upper	Income Groups Middle	Lower
Lower Class	53%	33%	47%	61%
Middle Class	9	8	9	9
Upper Class	12	9	9	14
No one	23	53	32	12
Everyone	3	—	1	4
Government itself	1	1	2	1
Don't Know, no answer	1	1	3	—
Total [a]	102%	105%	103%	101%
(N)	(300)	(100)	(100)	(100)

a. Some respondents mentioned more than one group.

Source: Ercilla, September 13–19, 1972, p. 11.

At first glance, these findings appear to support the view that the Chilean public was seeing politics in such stark class terms that a revolutionary shift must have produced the Allende victory. But what was really new was not so much the prevalence of class bias as the control of the government by forces more definitely linked to the lower classes. Two of the contenders who dominated the election for president in 1970, Jorge Alessandri and Allende, were also among the five contenders in the field in the 1958 election, when Chilean politics did not appear to the outside world to be nearly as polarized as it did in the early 1970s. Even ignoring the votes of the other contenders, the perceived polarization in the sources of support for Alessandri and Allende in 1958 was starkly revealed by a survey conducted during the earlier campaign (see Table 2). Among those responding to questions about sources of support, 93 percent reported that a majority of rich people would vote for Alessandri, whereas only one percent felt that the wealthy would vote for Allende. A majority of the poor were seen as supporting Allende by 68 percent of those responding, compared with 14 percent who thought the poor would vote for Alessandri. The general public's views of the preferences of industrialists and workers are in almost as sharp a contrast: 83 percent thought industrialists would vote for Alessandri, 4 percent thought Allende; 15 percent expected most workers to vote for Alessandri, 73 percent for Allende.

Table 2

ESTIMATES AS TO VOTE PREFERENCE OF SELECTED
GROUPS IN 1958 PRESIDENTIAL ELECTION

Candidate	Rich People	Poor People	Industrialists	Workers
Alessandri	93%	14%	83%	15%
Allende	1	68	4	73
Bossay	2	4	4	3
Frei	4	8	9	8
Zamorano	0	6	0	1
Total	100%	100%	100%	100%
(N)	(637)	(673)	(681)	(696)

Source: International Data Library and Reference Service, Survey Research Center, University of California, Berkeley, 1958 Presidential Election Survey in Santiago, Chile.

Compared with the mild class differences characteristic of the United States, contemporary perceptions in Chile appear to be those of a country in drastic change. Compared with Chilean perceptions in 1958, however, they appear as a continuity of traditional differences. Moreover, the perception of class differences does not necessarily mean that these perceptions lead to ideological behavior. In 1958, for example, to the question, "Do you think that some people in Chile have better opportunities for advancement than others?" 89 percent said "Yes," only 6 percent said "No," and 5 percent failed to answer. Moreover, the reasons cited for unequal opportunity were predominantly matters of class advantage. Nevertheless, when the same citizens were asked earlier in the interview to name "the most important problem that Chile faces today," their answers mentioned the results of inequality, rather than structural or systemic features to which the inequality might have been attributed. The answers ranged from general economic problems, such as inflation and crises, through housing shortages, high prices and unemployment, all the way down to juvenile delinquency and begging.

At roughly the same time that Chileans were denying the existence of equal opportunities for advancement, an almost equally overwhelming majority of North Americans were denying that "the average man doesn't have much chance to really get ahead" and maintaining that "anyone who works hard can go as far as he wants." [16] Moreover, most North Americans were also citing personal qualities, rather than class advantage, as the explanation of varying success.[17] Such cross-national divergences may suggest that North Americans, in fact, enjoyed greater equality of opportunity than Chileans, that the former are less likely than the latter to perceive actual variations in opportunity, or both. Whatever the explanation, the divergencies may explain the difficulty of North American interpreters in reconciling Chilean perceptions of marked class differences in voting and in life chances with a Chilean conception of national problems that was so largely free of ideology. Having gone, in some respects, so far toward an ideological—at least in the sense of an explicitly class-conscious—view of politics, they are somehow expected to go much further. But do they? Except for the omission of begging as a problem for the United States, the North Americans, who think they enjoy equal opportunities, and the Chileans, who know they do not enjoy such opportunities, describe their national problems in a remarkably similar manner.

The reasons given for liking and disliking political parties and candidates are perhaps our best source for assessing the importance of ideology in the Chilean voter's decision-making. The earliest Chilean survey (1958) to which access is available unfortunately failed to include reasons for liking and disliking parties and candidates. It did, however, include questions which could be searched for ideological implications. With Ibáñez nearing the end of his term in 1958, Chileans were asked their opinions of his administration; this question might have been expected to evoke some ideological responses. Despite his career as a general and as an erstwhile president through military coup, Ibáñez was elected in 1952 with support from the Left in a campaign that included a pledge to repeal legislation outlawing Communist party activity. By 1958, however, as Table 3 indicates, most Chileans were disappointed in the Ibáñez administration—58 percent of the evaluations were clearly unfavorable, six percent clearly favorable. Only two percent of the opinions focused unequivocally on ideology in the complaint that Ibáñez had forgotten the poor in favor of the rich, although ideological orientations might underlie most of the nonpersonality comments. Clearly, however, ideological considerations were not explicit in Chilean evaluations of the 1952-58 regime. These findings, by the very paucity of ideological content, offer a clue

Table 3

OPINIONS ABOUT IBÁÑEZ ADMINISTRATION, 1958

Unfavorable		58%
Promises not kept, deceived the people, disastrous	52	
No personality, weak leader	4	
Favored rich, forgot poor	2	
Mixed		36
Some good, e.g., repeal of law outlawing Communists	26	
Had no support, e.g., in Congress	10	
Favorable		6
Very good, honest, rid country of misery	6	
Total		100%
(N)*		(758)

*N here refers to number of responses, not respondents, because some (38) respondents gave more than one answer.

Source: International Data Library and Reference Service, Survey Research Center, University of California, Berkeley, 1958 Presidential Election Survey in Santiago, Chile.

to Chilean public opinion: despite their relatively great tendency
to recognize class biases in politics, Chileans tend to evaluate
political performance pragmatically; specific achievements take
precedence over their location in an ideological frame of
reference, even with class-related responses counted as ideological.

Table 4

PERCEPTIONS OF 1958 PRESIDENTIAL
CANDIDATES' PLATFORMS

	Ideological Responses		Respondents Unfamiliar with Platform	
	%	(N)	%	(N)
Alessandri	13	(3511)	8	(807)
Allende	45	(437)	61	(807)
Frei	14	(359)	69	(807)
Bossay	0	(180)	81	(807)
Zamorano	53	(74)	91	(807)

Source: International Data Library and Reference Service, Survey Research Center, University of California, Berkeley,
1958 Presidential Election Survey in Santiago, Chile.
The N under the first column heading refers to the
number of responses offered about each candidate's
platform; under the second column heading, N refers
to the number of respondents.

In addition to evaluating the Ibáñez regime, the 1958
respondents were asked "which are the important points of each
platform" of the five candidates for president in that year's
campaign. Like the previous question, this one did not necessarily
call for responses with an ideological flavor. As Table 4 indicates,
however, the platform points perceived by voters included some
with ideological content. The degree to which each candidate was
associated with some sort of ideological stance varied markedly.

The platform of the leading candidate and ultimate winner, Alessandri of the Conservative and Liberal parties, was seen as largely devoid of ideology, with only 13 percent of the responses classifiable as ideological. (The responses classed as ideological included reference to "free enterprise" and to worker and employee benefits including "greater distribution.") Allende, who ran second as the candidate of the FRAP (Socialist and Communist parties), was seen as having a much heavier (45 percent) ideological emphasis in his platform. (The responses so classed included "agrarian reform distribution of the land"; "better salaries for workers" with "better distribution of the income"; "government by the common people, with the common people"; and "free enterprise of basic products.") The third major candidate, Eduardo Frei of the newly organized Christian Democratic party, was seen as advancing a platform hardly more ideological (14 percent) than that of Alessandri. (The responses so classed also mentioned better wages and "better distribution of the national income"; "improvement of public housing"; and "use of new social doctrine, new party, new business orienta-tion.") Luis Bossay, the candidate of the Radical (Centrist) party, was seen in entirely nonideological terms. Antonio Zamorano, on the other hand, as a defrocked Catholic priest representing the independent Left, was seen as even more ideological than Allende. (His 53 percent ideological references were assertions that "he will help the poor.") Ideological clarity was clearly not necessary to victory in 1958, but Chilean voters appeared capable of perceiving ideological messages when they were offered. More consequential for the outcome, however, is the fact that only for Alessandri did most voters show any familiarity with the platforms. Of the other contenders, Allende, the candidate of the FRAP, came closest to getting his platform across to a majority of the voters, even though 61 percent failed to mention any point in his platform.[18]

Explanations of Alessandri's victory and Allende's defeat, immediately after the 1958 elections, are easily classifiable as ideological or nonideological. Confined to people who had voted in the election, the postelection interviews present a contrast similar to the preelection interviews with adults in general. Alessandri's personality and personal qualifications made up 32 percent of the reasons offered, bribery and propaganda, 27 percent (see Table 5). Explanations recognizing the importance of the Left-Right continuum account for 30 percent of the reasons. Allende's loss is explained more in ideological terms, which account for 62 percent of all reasons advanced. Perhaps because of the relative clarity of Allende's preelection ideological appeals, personal factors constitute only 13 percent of the reasons given for his defeat. Impressive in these public explanations is the recognition of the importance of tactical factors like the number of candidates and the role of factional unity or division. As we shall see when we turn to Hypothesis 2, these comments manifest analytical insights that have been insufficiently emphasized in some of the published works on Chilean politics.

Two-thirds of the way through the Alessandri administration, in 1962, Santiago adults were asked not a factual question about platforms (as in 1958), but an evaluative question about the best and worst features of Chilean political parties. As Table 6 indicates, FRAP, the group including the Socialist and Communist parties, evoked the most polarized reactions; only 28 percent of the respondents offered any opinion about a best feature of the FRAP, whereas 45 percent mentioned a worst feature. The FRAP was the only party for which more respondents offered unfavorable than favorable opinions. The rapid ascent of the Christian Democratic party, which first entered into national competition in the 1958 election, is seen in the fact that it emerged as the party with the greatest excess of favorable over unfavorable opinions.

In addition to the favorable-to-unfavorable ratio for each party presented in the party columns, one can see by reading across the rows of Table 6 the comparative favorable and unfavorable pictures of all parties. Because respondents were asked for both positive *and* negative features of each party, rather than for positive *or* negative features, the image of a given party could, in principle, include 100 percent favorable and 100 percent unfavorable perceptions. In fact, the FRAP again emerges as distinctive, receiving the fewest (28 percent) favorable comments and the most (45 percent) unfavorable comments. As the most conspicuous target of negative opinions, the FRAP appeared, in the late

Table 5

REASONS GIVEN FOR ALESSANDRI VICTORY, ALLENDE LOSS IN 1958

Alessandri	%
Personality of candidate (confidence in his person, character, quality, honesty, prestige)	22
Discontent with leftist governments, failure of earlier governments [a]	19
Bribery, duped people	18
Right was united, Left divided [a]	11
Qualifications of candidate (capable, experienced)	10
Propaganda	9
Others	11
Total	100
(N=responses, not respondents)	(390)
a. Ideological response	

Allende	%
Tends to support communism, repudiation of extremist parties didn't help him [a]	19
Division of the Left, because of Radicals (as party of the Left) [a]	18
The Priest of Catapilco [Zamorano] [a]	13
Alessandri could pay, bribery	13
Negative personal references (has no prestige, they didn't believe him, country doesn't owe him anything)	13
Discontent with government of the Left, people wanted to try the Right again [a]	4
Only common people supported him, only attracted modest people [a]	4
Because the government (ex-Ibañistas) helped him [a]	4
Poor propaganda	1
Others	11
Total	100
(N=responses, not respondents)	(364)
a. Ideological response	

Source: International Data Library and Reference Service, Survey Research Center, University of California, Berkeley, 1958 Presidential Election Survey in Santiago, Chile.

Table 6

OPINIONS OF CHILEAN POLITICAL PARTIES, 1962

What do you think is best about the:

	Liberals and Conservatives?	Radicals?	Christian Democrats?	FRAP?
Favorable Responses	40%	42%	39%	28%
Nothing is good	9	8	6	20
No opinion, don't know	51	50	55	52
Total (N=1,000)	100%	100%	100%	100%

What do you think is worst about the:

	Liberals and Conservatives?	Radicals?	Christian Democrats?	FRAP?
Unfavorable Responses	33%	38%	27%	45%
Nothing is bad	13	9	13	6
No opinion, don't know	54	53	60	49
Total (N=1,000)	100%	100%	100%	100%

Source: Salas-Reyes, Ltd. See note 13 for details.

1950s and early 1960s, a weak contender for the presidency. But, as we shall see in examining Hypothesis 2, this apparent weakness depends on the structure of competition in each election. In a two-party race, the clarity and negativism of opinions about the FRAP would appear a crippling handicap because of the necessity of winning an absolute majority of the votes. In a multiparty contest with diverse appeals keeping any party from mustering a majority, however, clarity of position may be more important than the amount of disapprobation involved; a party with a clear position could be expected better to retain the support of its adherents than could a party with a more ambiguous position. And the position of the FRAP does appear clearer than that of other parties.

When we shift to the detailed party images in Table 7, the ideological content in expressions about the best and worst features of parties appear quite high, ranging from a low of 32 percent in the negative references to the Radical party to a high of 89 percent in the negative references to the Liberal and Conservative parties. In characterizing the Chilean political system as a whole, the frequency of ideological comments is significant. For a comparison of parties within Chile, the direction of ideological bias is important. The Liberals and Conservatives, the parties of Alessandri, are seen in mixed terms. Of all favorable comments, 65 percent were ideological; 34 percent of the favorable comments appeared to have a rightist orientation, 24 percent a leftist orientation and 7 percent a centrist orientation. Our classifications are: rightist—*parties of order*, serious, correct, not revolutionary, *Catholicism*; centrist—*ideological freedom,* tolerant; leftist—*help the common people, progressive, future-oriented ideology*. The Liberals and Conservatives, thus, cover a wide range of the ideological spectrum in their positive images. On the negative side, however, 89 percent of the comments are ideological and all of these criticize the Liberals and Conservatives for their rightism. The diverse appeals of the Liberals and Conservatives in positive images are replaced on the negative side by an image unmistakably rightist. For the FRAP, on the other hand, all ideological comments—whether positive or negative—describe it as Left, with the possible exception of the charge of "*despotism*, very rigid discipline." (We have designated this comment with "?" because, although it seems clearly ideological, it could be made about a party of the Right no less than one of the Left.) The Radical party, frequently criticized in the literature for ideological vacillation, is similarly viewed by the public insofar as it is viewed as ideological at all; favorable images are centrist and rightist, whereas unfavorable images include some to the Right, some to the Left and others to the specific effect that the party occupies inconsistent ideological positions. The Christian Democrat is the only party to emerge with both positive and negative images all the way from right to left. As such, the Christian Democrats appear to have had the broad appeal more typical of parties in two-party systems. With such appeals, one would expect this party to fare better in a two-way race than in one with a multiparty character. (As we see in examining Hypothesis 2, this expectation is borne out by the facts.)

By 1964, when Frei and Allende were engaged in a two-way race for the presidency, the disadvantage of unfamiliarity, under which Frei and the Christian Democrats had labored in 1958, had disappeared. Adults in greater Santiago were asked, during the height of the campaign (June 1964), to name "the most important thing said" by the candidates. Whereas 69 percent of those interviewed in 1958 had been unfamiliar with Frei's platform, the unfamiliarity had dropped to 54 percent in 1964. About the same proportion (61 percent) of the respondents were unfamiliar with Allende's platform in both years. Moreover, the much heavier ideological flavor in comments about Allende, as compared with Frei in 1958, was lessened in 1964 by increased ideological content in comments about Frei. Because of unfamiliarity with both candidates' platforms, the overall proportion of respondents with ideological perceptions was not high. Only 15 percent mentioned ideological things said by Allende ("nationalization, agrarian reform"), compared with 11 percent for Frei ("ideology, nationalization, agrarian reform, revolution in liberty"). Otherwise, the things perceived in both campaigns were not ideological. For Allende, they were "mother-child care," "progress in general," "well-being," "salaries," "housing"; for Frei, they were "housing," "well-being," "child care," "salaries," "progress in general." The campaigns as perceived were, thus, surprisingly similar. Although the overall level of their ideological content was not very high, it becomes comparable to that of 1958 when respondents with no opinions are eliminated. Among those who were informed, 38 percent of the Allende comments and 25 percent of the Frei comments were ideological. Neither familiarity with Allende's platform nor ideological flavor in

Table 7

PUBLIC IMAGES OF BEST AND WORST FEATURES OF POLITICAL PARTIES, 1962

A. Liberals and Conservatives

	Favorable	%		Unfavorable	%
R̲	Parties of order, serious, correct, not revolutionary	27	R̲	Capitalists, don't help the common people	33
	Raise up the country, better standard of living, check inflation	14	R̲	Don't renew themselves	24
L̲	Help the common people	14	R̲	Claim class superiority	17
	Govern better, give confidence	10	R̲	Their monopolies	3
L̲	Progressive, future-oriented ideology	10	R̲	Exploit the common people	10
C̲	Ideological freedom, tolerant	7		Their demagoguery	2
R̲	Catholicism	7		Others	11
	Their condition as incumbents	3		Total	100
	Others	8		(N)	(331)
	Total	100			
	(N)	(398)			

Table 7 Continued

B. Radicals

	Favorable	%		Unfavorable	%
C̲	Legislation: works of improvement, benefits for the common people	27		Bureaucracy: monopoly of public functions	26
	Ideology: realistic, forward-thinking, positive	19 (L̲-C̲-R̲)		Lack of defined political position: inconstancy	22
C̲	Party of the center: support the middle class	16		Demagoguery: unreliability, irresponsibility	13
R̲	Discipline: party of order	8	L̲	Undisciplined: factitious, wrangling	12
	Industrialization	7	R̲	Illicit transactions: bad governors	9
	Capacity: youth, professionals	6		"Fellow travellers"; antireligious	5
	Education policy	4		Rightism: support of emergency presidential powers	5
	Pro-administration orientation	4		Others	8
	Others	9			
	Total (N)	100 (417)		Total (N)	100 (380)

Table 7 Continued

C. Christian Democrats

	Favorable	%		Unfavorable	%
L	Forward-thinking: ideological renovation	27	L	Marxist tendency: leftism	22
L	Interested in the common people: social and economic work	25	R	Religiosity: influence of the church	17
		L-C-R		Indefinition: political vacillation	15
R	Catholicism: Christian ideology	19		Don't complete their program: not constructive	12
	Leadership: organization	12		Demagogy: falsity	10
C	Its democracy: sane, idealistic people	7		Wrangling	6
C	Condition as party of the Center: middle class	5		Disorganized	5
	Others	5	R	Little support to the common people	4
				Others	9
	Total	100		Total	100
	(N)	(392)		(N)	(268)

Table 7 Continued

D. FRAP

	Favorable	%		Unfavorable	%
L	People's party: help the common people	51	L	Communism: alliance with Communism	36
L	Ideology: forward-thinking:	20	L	Revolutions: disorders and strikes	20
	Unity: cohesion among its components	9		Demagogy: unreliable	14
	Only hope for betterment	7		Destructive opposition	9
	Its enthusiasm	4		Lack of preparation, ignorant	7
L	Marxism	4	?	Despotism: very rigid discipline	5
	Others	5		Allende as candidate: very ambitious	2
				Others	7
	Total	100		Total	100
	(N)	(278)		(N)	(449)

Source: Salas-Reyes, Ltd. See note 13 for details.
The symbols R, C, and L refer to Left, Center, and Right respectively.

perceptions of it was greater in 1964 than in 1958, whereas both familiarity and the perception of ideological content had increased for Frei.

The motives for voting for Allende and Frei manifest a slightly higher level of ideological content than did the naming of the most important thing they said. The percentages of people offering ideological reasons for supporting and opposing the candidates were:

	Allende	Frei
For	19%	24%
Against	40%	21%

These are percentages of all adult responses. Ideological biases were thus volunteered by a fifth to a fourth of the total population in support of both candidates and against Frei; the proportion opposing Allende for ideological reasons was twice as great as that opposing Frei for similar reasons. Percentages based only on those who offered reasons to be for or against each candidate were:

	Allende	Frei
For	37%	37%
Against	67%	52%

Ideological reasoning was quite common among those able to offer some grounds for their preference; it was more common on the negative than on the positive side, with Frei getting an advantage in the comparison. The ideological motives in reasons to support Allende included ideology as such and his representation of the common people; for Frei, the direct reference to his ideology was supplemented, for a few voters, by his Catholicism and his Right support. Negatively, Frei's Right support was the most common ideological point, whereas, for Allende, ideology as such remained prominent, with a few voters also specifying that his position was antidemocratic. The intense nature of the opposition between these two candidates is better revealed by looking at their supporters, rather than at all respondents. Here the "no response" rate drops sharply: among "Freistas," 59 percent gave clearly ideological reasons for opposing Allende; among "Allendistas," 50 percent gave clearly ideological grounds for opposing Frei. Chilean partisans, thus, had clear images of their choices, and those images remained heavily ideological, by United States standards.

In 1970, Chilean presidential campaigning was essentially a three-man race, with the familiar figures of Allende and Alessandri joined, this time, by Radomiro Tomic as the new candidate of the Christian Democrats. A pre-election survey (July-August 1970) in greater Santiago produced results remarkably similar to those of 1958. The ideological content of the reasons advanced for their preference by the proponents of each candidate was: Alessandri, 12 percent; Allende, 57 percent; Tomic, 7 percent. Alessandri's supporters emphasized primarily his personal qualities and experience. The few who did mention ideological reasons emphasized a rightist orientation, except for one lonely supporter who asserted that Alessandri "is with the common man." Allende's supporters were predominantly ideological in their reasoning and the ideological slant was exclusively to the Left. Allende supporters did not specifically emphasize socialism as such, for the general bias ("candidate of the common people," "is of the Left") and the objectives ("to change the system") of Allende far outnumbered references to socialism per se. Tomic was most liked simply as the standard bearer of the Frei government; the few ideological reasons were scattered in several directions.

From a negative point of view, 57 percent said they would not vote for Allende in any case, 44 percent said the same about Tomic and 40 percent about Alessandri. Although Allende won more support than any other candidate, the relative clarity of his ideological position made him, at the same time, the last choice of a majority. In a two-way race, Allende—the victor in the actual three-way race—would clearly have been the loser. The anti-Allende reasoning was overwhelmingly ideological, with 60 percent of those who rejected him citing his "Leftism, Marxism, Socialism" and such related concerns as "violence, revolution," "Cuba, Fidel," and "less liberty." (Two respondents deviated by calling him an "exploiter of the common man.") The anti-Alessandri sentiments were much more ideological than the reasons for supporting him; 45 percent of the negative reasons emphasized distaste for his rightism: "Capitalist, of the rich, of the Right"; "retrogressive, reactionary"; "enemy of the common man." Anti-Tomic feeling was even less ideological than pro-Tomic reasoning; a scattering of his detractors (five percent) viewed him as rightist and a few as leftist, while most simply denounced him for representing the Frei government and party.

From the perspective of the United States, a cross-section of Chilean opinion, at any time since the 1950s, would look heavily ideological, though by no means overwhelmingly so. When the objects of public opinion—either political parties or candidates—offered clear ideological clues, they were picked up by sizable portions of the citizenry. The ideological characteristics imputed to political actors by the general public in Chile corresponded well to descriptions advanced by learned commentators. The view of Chilean society as ridden with class advantages and the relatively high level of ideology in the electorate go back, however, at least to the 1950s, when Chilean public opinion was first systematically sampled. In 1958, 62 percent of the reasons given for Allende's loss were ideological. Already high, this level of ideological content in political opinions was not increased by party conflicts between 1958 and 1970; in the latter year, 60 percent of the reasons given for being against Allende were ideological. In 1962, 75 percent of the favorable attitudes about the Left coalition, the FRAP, endorsed its Left ideology; in 1970, 57 percent of the reasons for supporting the FRAP candidate were ideological. The data accordingly support Hypothesis 1: the marked shift of Chilean government to the Left from 1952 to 1972 occurred without a corresponding increase in the ideological content or Left orientation of public opinion.

Hypothesis 2: *The shift of the Chilean government to the Left is a result not of an equal shift in public opinion but of the individual campaign alternatives afforded by the political system.*

Actual votes in elections might be thought to represent the best measure of growing leftism in Chile. In examining Hypothesis 1, however, we ignored the distribution of candidate preferences to concentrate, instead, on the level and direction of ideological thinking. That strategy was dictated by recognition of the fact that, although votes have consequences with clear ideological import in Chile, one cannot be certain that they are expressions of ideology in the minds of the voters. Parties of the Left in Chile could have won an increasing share of votes as a result of nonideological factors. Alternatively, a decline in Left votes could have been concomitant with an increase in Left ideology if the original Left votes were cast for mostly nonideological reasons and the remaining Left votes were based on ideology. We found the level of ideological awareness high enough—throughout the period for which we have data—to suggest that election results in Chile can be taken as a valid, though rough, measure of ideological predispositions. In considering Hypothesis 2, we accordingly shift to election outcomes.

In 1952, Carlos Ibáñez was elected president of Chile as a nonpartisan candidate, an ex-general who stood "above parties." In 1958, Jorge Alessandri won as a candidate of the Right. In 1964, Eduardo Frei was chosen as a representative of the Center. In 1970, Salvador Allende triumphed as a candidate of the Left.

The outcome of recent presidential elections in Chile has, therefore, presented the picture of a neat and steady movement to the Left. So far as control of the executive is concerned, this interpretation is correct. Because the primary business of elections is with the question of who takes office, commentators tend to interpret the meaning of elections from that point of view. In terms of policy outcomes, of course, their focus is quite justified. From the point of view of drawing inferences about public opinion and about future election outcomes, however, such a focus may be quite misleading. When we look at popular votes, rather than at who took office, no great change can be discerned. Examination of recent Chilean elections suggests that their varying outcomes have resulted more from the number of parties competing in each election than from a change in public preferences.

The fact that Allende won in 1970 and not in 1958 was an accident as far as public opinion is concerned. As Table 8 shows, Allende won 28.9 percent of the votes in the earlier contest. Unfortunately for Allende, Antonio Zamorano, a defrocked Catholic priest known as "*el cura de Catapilco*" (the priest of Catapilco), entered the contest as a candidate of the independent

Table 8

DISTRIBUTION OF POPULAR VOTES IN CHILEAN PRESIDENTIAL ELECTIONS, 1952–1970

1952	%	1958	%
Carlos Ibáñez (Independent)	46.8	Jorge Alessandri (Right: Conservative, Liberal)	31.6
Arturo Matte (Right: Conservative, Liberal)	27.8	Salvador Allende (Left: Socialist, Communist)	28.9
Pedro E. Alfonso (Center Radical)	19.9	Eduardo Frei (Center: Christian Democrat)	20.7
Salvador Allende (Left: Socialist)	5.5 / 100.0	Luis Bossay (Center: Radical)	15.6
		Antonio Zamorano (Independent Left)	3.3 / 100.1

1964	%	1970	%
Eduardo Frei (Center-Right: Christian Democrat, Conservative, Liberal)	56.09	Salvador Allende (Left: Socialist, Communist)	36.6
Salvador Allende (Left: Socialist, Communist)	38.93	Jorge Alessandri (Right: Independent, National)	35.2
Julio Durán (Center-Right: Radical)	4.99 / 100.01	Radomiro Tomic (Center: Christian Democrat)	28.1 / 99.9

Source: Dirección del Registro Electoral, Chile.

Left and received 3.3 percent of the votes. In the absence of Zamorano, Allende would almost certainly have received those votes, giving him a total of 32.2 percent and the presidency of Chile. Conversely, an additional Left candidate in 1970 could have kept Allende from the presidency by winning only 1.5 percent of the votes at his expense.

We do not mean to suggest here that the number of candidates and parties contesting an election is an accident or a matter of no concern to political scientists. We do submit that the number of such candidates is largely irrelevant for explaining the distribution of popular support for broad political tendencies in Chile, that is, that the combined Allende-Zamorano votes in 1958 are as accurate a measure of Left preferences as are the Allende votes in 1970. The 1952 election reveals little about Right-Center-Left preferences, on the other hand, because Ibáñez's appeal was nonpartisan and he won the support of groups all the way from Right to Left. The Communist party, it should be noted, was outlawed at that time; some of Ibáñez's Left support undoubtedly came from his promise to repeal the law banning the Communist party from the ballot, a promise he subsequently fulfilled. The inability of the Communist party to campaign as such and the appeal of Ibáñez to its supporters undoubtedly reduced Allende's vote in 1952. The election of 1952, thus, provides no measure of Left support.

The election of 1964 was unique in recent Chilean political history in that it became a two-man race between Frei and Allende. The contest began as a three-way race, with a Right coalition known as the *"Frente Democrático"* (Democratic Front) expected to make a strong showing behind Julio Durán of the Radical party. Had the contest developed as expected, with no other Left candidate to dilute his strength, Allende might well have won the office which he had been denied by Zamorano's candidacy in 1958. An otherwise unimportant by-election during the early stages of the campaign in Curicó, a traditionally conservative province, convinced leaders of the Right that just such an unhappy fate was in store for them. To the surprise of all political observers in Chile, the *Frente Democrático* lost the Curicó election, and the Left candidate was the victor. Leaders of the Right coalition accordingly decided to unite behind the candidacy of Frei in order to block Allende. The Radical party candidate remained on the ballot but, without support from the Right coalition, he received a mere five percent of the votes. By winning the by-election, the Left lost the presidency for another six years.

The lesson appears clear: the Left vote in Chilean presidential elections hovered around 36 percent after the 1950s; this vote was not greatly increased or decreased by the number of parties or candidates contesting the election. Hence, in the event of a single major candidate from the Left and two or more major candidates from the Center and Right, the Left had a good chance of winning. In the event of a single major candidate from the Center and Right, the Left had almost no chance of winning. No change in Chilean preferences or perceptions of political forces is necessary to account for the varying outcomes since 1952. The near-miss of 1958 did not make a sufficient impression on forces of the Center and Right and they almost presented Allende with an ideal type of contest in 1964, but the Curicó by-election carried the same message they would have gotten from reading Anthony Downs and they shifted to occupy all of the "ideological space" covering the Center and Right with a single candidate.[19] But the lesson was lost by 1970 and, with two candidates to his right and no Zamorano type to his Left, Allende finally won the presidency.

Our argument that Allende's election did not result from any dramatic shift of Chilean opinion to the Left is supported by votes in Chilean congressional elections. Insofar as there has been a significant shift, it has been *toward* but not *to* the Left. That is, it has been to the Center at the expense of the Right and of independent and minor, unclassifiable political groups. Table 9 presents the distribution of popular votes in congressional elections from 1941 to 1969. Except for the period during which the Communist party was banned (1949-1961), the Left vote varied from about 23 to 29 percent, with no significant increase. The Center parties moved from a position of rough parity with the Left to greater strength in the last three elections. At the same time, rightists and unclassifiable candidates lost strength. Marked individual variations in particular years are explicable by short-term influences, some of which are noted under Hypothesis

Table 9

VOTE FOR MAJOR POLITICAL PARTIES IN
CONGRESSIONAL ELECTIONS IN CHILE, 1941–1969 (IN PERCENT)

	1941	1945	1949[a]	1953[a]	1957[a]	1961	1965[b]	1969
LEFT (Socialist, Communist)[a]	28.5	23.1	9.3	14.1	10.7	22.9	23.3	29.4
CENTER (Radical, Christian Democrat)	25.1	22.6	25.6	16.2	30.8	38.4	57.3	44.7
RIGHT (Liberal, Conservative; National)[b]	31.1	41.5	40.7	21.1	29.1	31.4	12.8	20.8
OTHER	15.3	12.8	24.4	48.6	29.4	7.3	6.6	5.1
Total	100.0	100.0	100.0	100.0	100.0	100.0	100.0	100.0

a. During the period 1948–1957, the Communist party was banned by the Law for the Permanent Defense of Democracy; the Left votes are represented by the Socialist party only for this period.

b. After the 1965 parliamentary election the Liberals and Conservatives joined their forces and became the National party.

Source: Dirección del Registro Electoral, Chile.   Percentages exclude null and blank votes.

3, but the principal secular trend is clear: the Center, but not the Left, increased significantly in appeal in congressional elections in Chile after 1941.

The absence of dramatic change in the Left vote suggests that Allende's 1970 triumph was not a "critical election."[20] Moreover, a *Ercilla* survey in Santiago reports continuing stability. When Santiago adults were asked how they would vote if the presidential election of 1970 were held "today" (September 1972), the proportion who said they would vote for Allende was 36 percent, 1.2 percentage points above his Santiago vote two years before (see Table 10). Alessandri and Tomic received smaller percentages than in the actual 1970 Santiago vote (losing 7.4 and 7.8 percentage points, respectively), decreases partly

Table 10

A. 1972 PREFERENCE IF THE PRESIDENTIAL ELECTION OF 1970 WERE "TODAY" (SEPTEMBER 1972) WITH THE SAME CANDIDATES

	Weighted Total %	Upper Income %	Middle Income %	Lower Income %
Salvador Allende	36	9	28	46
Jorge Alessandri	31	62	37	22
Radomiro Tomic	19	16	22	18
None	14	13	13	14
Total	100	100	100	100
(N)	(300)	(100)	(100)	(100)

B. 1972 PREFERENCE IF THE CANDIDATES WERE ALLENDE AND FREI

	Weighted Total %	Upper Income %	Middle Income %	Lower Income %
Salvadore Allende	39	11	31	48
Eduardo Frei	51	77	58	42
None	10	12	11	10
Total	100	100	100	100
(N)	(300)	(100)	(100)	(100)

Source: Ercilla, September 13–19, 1972, p. 11.

attributable to Allende's increase but mostly accounted for by 14 percent who said, in 1972, they would vote for none of the three.[21] A rerun of the 1964 election between Frei and Allende produced a 3.3 percent gain for Allende and a 9.9 percent drop for Frei.[22]

An extraordinary stability in support for the candidate of the Left rather than a mass movement to the Left thus characterizes modern Chilean elections, and the evidence is that this stable support remained firm in 1972. Moreover, the working class "solidarity" in support for the Left, that some observers have postulated, is no more accurate than the image of a sharp turn to the Left in ideology or votes.[23] Almost half the lower-income voters reported support for Allende in 1972, whether he was listed with two opponents or only one. But even in a two-way choice between Allende and Frei, the "neither" responses were enough to deny Allende an absolute majority. From the point of view of Left support, immobilism rather than radical change thus emerges as the predominant feature of Chilean political opinions.

HYPOTHESIS 3: *The control of the Chilean government by the Left is reversible.*

The election of Allende as president of Chile in 1970 gave rise to concerns dramatically illustrating what political scientists call the "problem of intensity" in democratic politics.[24] Speculation was rife in the press inside and outside Chile whether the opposing forces—which, taken together, had won a majority of the popular votes and which held a majority of seats in the Chilean Congress—would permit Allende to assume the presidency. Although he was first choice for president by a plurality of Chilean voters, we know (from survey results cited earlier) that he was the last choice of a majority. Was the opposition of the majority sufficiently intense to lead to frustration of the recorded preference for Allende over each of this two opponents by a plurality of the voters? The Chilean Constitution vests in the Congress the right of electing the president from the two leading candidates in popular votes; only by democratic tradition is the Congress expected to select the leading choice of the voters.

Had Allende's opposition taken an apocalyptic view of his ascent to the presidency, they had the votes and, technically, the constitutional authority to deny him the office. When Allende reaffirmed his commitment to constitutional guarantees, assuring freedom of the press and of political opposition, however, the opposing Christian Democrats moved unanimously to his support and he was overwhelmingly elected president by the Congress of Chile. This action appears to demonstrate that respect for traditional democratic norms and procedures can coexist with a greater degree of ideological and class conflict than many North Americans are wont to believe. Months after Allende's inauguration, for example, President Nixon of the United States canceled a courtesy call of the aircraft carrier U.S.S. *Enterprise* at the Chilean port of Valparaiso. The explanation was that the United States administration did not want to help Allende "while he consolidates political power," with the implication that some coup by the opposition was expected and, presumably, to be approved by the United States.[25]

Chileans appear no less committed to acceptance of the results of their electoral system than are their neighbors to the north (and more committed than those neighbors would have liked in 1970). In addition to its manifest function of selecting official decision-makers, an election performs the latent function of celebrating and reinforcing the concept of self-rule. Speaking of this function in the United States, one American government text asserts, "The result is to legitimize governmental power, to convince everyone of the right of the elected officials to make general policy. The losers of American elections are expected to show their good sportsmanship by rallying around the winner."[26] When differences among parties are intense, when the stakes are high and when opposition is ideologically based, elections might be expected to fail in the function of creating a "honeymoon" period for the winners. But Chile appears no different from the United States in the tendency to rally around the winner.

Shortly before the election of 1958, for example, respondents in Santiago manifested the mixed feelings about Alessandri that one would expect from his 31.6 percent of the national vote in the subsequent election. Of those who are registered and intended to vote, 28 percent had already decided to vote for Alessandri.

Asked directly whether they liked or disliked Alessandri, 53 percent of all respondents chose the "like" answer, 30 percent "dislike," and 17 percent failed to respond. When prompted to answer "What do you think of the candidates as persons?" 40 percent of all responses about Alessandri could be coded as favorable, with emphasis on positive personal characteristics, specific abilities and his "independence." Positive attributes were outweighed by unfavorable ones, with 51 percent of the responses stressing negative personal characteristics ("maniac," "antisocial," "egotist," "authoritarian," "old bachelor") or disapproved orientations ("reactionary," "capitalist," "rich," "doesn't understand the poor," "demagogue").

The observer might have expected a candidate elected by a small plurality, and viewed with such mixed feelings during his campaign, to face intense opposition as he awaited formal election by the Congress. Voters were accordingly asked, "Now that the presidential elections are over, Congress has to choose between the two candidates who received the majority of the votes. If you were a Congressman, for which one of the candidates would you vote?" The answers were for

the one who received the most votes	35%
Alessandri	47%
Allende	15%
"in blank"	1%
no answer	2%
Total	100%

$N = 339$

Despite the harsh remarks about Alessandri and votes for someone else by a majority of respondents, only 15 percent of the respondents said they would vote against his election if they were congressmen. The voters, no less than their congressmen, were thus ready to accept the popular outcome. The tendency of voters to rally around the winner goes further than a willingness to accept the legitimacy of the election results. When asked how they expected the Alessandri administration would be, now that he was elected, only six percent went so far as to predict that it would be actually bad:

very good	22%
good	53%
fair	15%
bad	6%
no answer	4%
Total	100%

$N = 339$

From a pre-election situation in which a small portion conceded that they "liked" Alessandri and a larger sector emphasized negative personal attributes, his election by a plurality of 32 percent had transformed Alessandri into a president whose administration was expected to be good or very good by 75 percent of the voters. This transformation is a dramatic demonstration of the "bandwagon" effect that is stressed as a stabilizing function of elections. Presidents are more positive figures than candidates.

A similar phenomenon appears to have occurred after the election of Frei in 1964. We have no direct data on expectations as to the new administration, but inferences can be drawn from other survey findings that suggest another process of rallying around the winner. Before 1964, the Christian Democratic party had never received more than 21 percent of the votes as a separate party, but, as the candidate of the combined Center and Right, Frei received 56 percent of the 1964 presidential vote. In February 1965, 58 percent of the respondents in greater Santiago said they would prefer to give their votes to the Christian Democratic party, an impressive increase over its previous peak of 21 percent of the votes. If preferences for all political forces of Center and Right are summed, they come to 77 percent, a 16-percentage-point increase over the 61 percent polled by Frei and the minor rightist candidate in the preceding election. This increment appears attributable to the legitimizing effect of the election. Because it is more difficult to express a change of preference to the winner's party than to express confidence in the winning candidate's administration, this shift is as meaningful as the great confidence in Alessandri produced by his election.

Despite worldwide emphasis on the uniqueness of the Allende victory in 1970, and the expectations of constitutional or unconstitutional efforts to deny him office, the populace of Chile behaved in its traditional fashion. Allende's 37 percent of the popular vote was magnified to a much higher postelection level of support for his party when he became president. In January 1971, 65 percent of Santiago respondents expressed support for Allende's Popular Unity coalition. In a survey the following month on specific party preference, the Popular Unity parties (Socialist, Communist, Radical and MAPU—Movimiento de Acción Popular Unitaria), were chosen by 48.5 percent of all respondents and by 60 percent of those respondents who expressed a party preference. Although opposition to Chilean presidents traditionally intensified before the termination of their terms, they were traditionally given a honeymoon period of broad popular support. Despite contrary expectations and hopes from some in the United States, Allende was clearly no exception.

The surge of support for the political groups winning the presidency in Chile is manifested in elections no less than in survey results. Chile's four-year cycle of congressional elections and six-year cycle of presidential elections scheduled a congressional election a few months after alternate presidential elections. Presidents elected in these years were fortunate because the surge of support for the winner gave his supporters an opportunity to win far more than their usual share of congressional seats. In 1952, for example, Ibáñez was chosen an independent candidate who was "above" political parties. In the congressional election held the following spring, the proportion of votes won by the principal parties of Right-Center-Left dropped from over three-fourths (75.6 percent) to scarcely one-half (51.4 percent). Candidates not associated with these parties had previously won less than one-fourth of the votes; following Ibáñez's lead however, candidates running as independents or with groups supporting his position above party politics captured almost half the congressional votes (48.6 percent) in 1953.[27] In 1965, following Frei's assumption of the presidency, the center parties (Christian Democrats and Radicals) won a full majority (47.3 percent) of the congressional vote, compared with a previous high of 38.4 percent.[28] Allende was not fortunate enough to have a congressional election on the heels of his inauguration, but local elections for *regidores* (councilmen) did ensue, and the parties of his Unidad Popular won a resounding 49.7 percent of the national vote, compared with his presidential vote of 36.6 percent.[29] For Allende, no less than his predecessors, then, the magic of the presidency produced a surge of national support as expressed in both surveys and at the polls.

After an initial wave of enthusiasm for a new president, Chileans typically reverted to their more enduring political loyalties and predilections. The Santiago survey by *Ercilla* in September 1972 indicated that the Allende government had not escaped the posthoneymoon development of criticism. Indeed, this appraisal of national affairs presented a picture of such extreme polarization as to suggest, at first glance, a highly unstable political situation approaching violent upheaval.

When asked whether it is easy or difficult to buy the essentials for living, Chileans responded with almost unbelievably contrasting perceptions (see Table 11-A). Overall, they were in almost complete dissension, with roughly half finding it easy and half finding it hard to buy essentials. Class differences (as represented by variations in income) revealed a truly startling degree of polarization; virtually all (99 percent) of those in the upper group thought it was hard to buy daily necessities, while a large majority (75 percent) of those with the lowest incomes thought it was easy. Polarization of this magnitude is the more remarkable in view of the substance of the opinions reported. By definition, those with the highest incomes could more easily buy daily necessities than could those with the lowest incomes, yet perceptions differed in the opposite direction. But this statement is true *by definition* only if ease of purchase is defined monetarily, and it is necessarily true *empirically* only if "ease" is viewed in comparison with other purchasers rather than in comparison with one's own ease or one's relative ease at earlier points in time. Higher-income Chileans probably interpreted ease of purchasing essentials as referring to the ability to send servants to a market or store with confidence that they can find what is needed without having to search at more than one place, without having to wait in a queue to make the purchase and without being limited in the amount available for purchase. In 1972, objects ranging from beef to toilet paper could not be purchased on any given day in Chile with assurance that none of these inconveniences would be encountered. Moreover, one could be certain than an upper-income Chilean regarded both toilet paper and beef as "essentials." With these meanings in mind, we can understand why necessities were almost unanimously viewed as hard to purchase by the higher-income group. And if they compared the situation with their own in the pre-Allende period, it probably also appeared more trying.

Table 11
A. PERCEIVED EASE OF PURCHASING HOUSEHOLD STAPLES, 1972

	Weighted Total %	Upper Income %	Middle Income %	Lower Income %
Easy	47	1	17	75
Difficult	48	99	77	19
Neither easy nor difficult	5	1	6	6
Total	100	100	100	100
(N)	(300)	(100)	(100)	(100)

B. PERCEIVED RESPONSIBILITY FOR DEFICIENCY IN HOUSEHOLD STAPLES, 1972

	Weighted Total %	Upper Income %	Middle Income %	Lower Income %
The Government	50	85	60	37
The Opposition	29	9	29	32
Merchants	21	15	19	23
Manufacturers	26	11	24	29
Others	1	–	3	–
Don't Know, no answer	–	2	–	–
Total	100	100	100	100
(N)	(300)	(100)	(100)	(100)

Source: Ercilla, September 13–19, 1972, p. 11.

The Allende government's early policies gave additional purchasing power to those with low incomes, and it established fixed prices and quality standards for some essentials, for example, bread. Despite general inflation and both chronic and sporadic shortages, then, lower-income people correctly perceived the situation as one in which essentials were relatively easy to purchase. Moreover, toilet paper and beef are much less likely to be viewed as essentials by lower-status Chileans. At about the time of this survey, a Chilean man of middle-class dress and demeanor complained bitterly while standing in a queue moving slowly to a meat counter that he never thought he would have to stand in line an hour and a half to buy meat; a woman of lower-class appearance responded, "I never thought I would *get* to stand in line to buy meat!30 Identical situations may thus be experienced as a deprivation by some and as rewarding by others.

The explosive possibilities that seem to inhere in such class polarization were underscored by the perceptions of violence reported in Table 12. An overwhelming majority of Santiago adults believed that Chile was living in a climate of violence in 1972. Despite class differences in these perceptions, a large majority at every income level was in agreement of the existence of a climate of violence. Before concluding that a Chilean revolution was immediately in the offing, however, we must examine related opinions. Such an examination underscores the fact that class differences, rather than class solidarity, underlied Chilean political opinions. Even where class solidarity existed in differences on a question—ease of access to essentials, in this case—it should not be translated into equal class polarization on the most closely related political question—in this case, who is responsible for the lack of supplies. Assuming a lack of essential supplies (and thus begging its own question), the *Ercilla* survey asked Santiago adults who was responsible for the deficiency (see Table 11-B). With each respondent allowed to name more than one group as responsible, the government was named by half the people and others—such as the (political) opposition, merchants and manufacturers—by three-fourths of the people. Class differences on those to blame were not solid. Although the high-income group focused primary blame on the government, the middle-income group more often blamed others (75 percent for all others combined compared with 60 percent for the government), as did the low-income group (84 percent to 37 percent). The other groups listed as blameworthy can all be counted as opposed to the government in this context; while the government received much of the blame, others received an equal share. Moreover, neither the lower nor the middle class attributed blame to a single source among the groups opposed to the government. Most important for its dampening effects on class conflict was the lack of solidarity of the lower class in defending the Allende government. Indeed, 37 percent in the lower class attributed any shortages to the government itself.

Table 12

A. BELIEF THAT CHILE IS LIVING IN A CLIMATE OF VIOLENCE, 1972

	Weighted Total %	Upper Income %	Middle Income %	Lower Income %
Yes	83	98	92	75
No	17	2	8	25
Total	100	100	100	100
(N)	(300)	(100)	(100)	(100)

B. PERCEPTIONS OF SOURCE OF VIOLENCE, 1972

	Weighted Total %	Upper Income %	Middle Income %	Lower Income %
The Government	23	36	27	18
The Opposition	27	7	20	35
Both Sectors	33	54	44	22
Others (Extremists)	–	1	1	–
No Climate of Violence	17	2	8	25
Total	100	100	100	100
(N)	(300)	(100)	(100)	(100)

Source: Ercilla, September 13–19, 1972. p. 11.

Diffusion rather than polarization also occurs when we examine the attribution of blame for Chile's climate of violence (see Table 12-B). For Santiago adults as a whole, 33 percent blamed both the government and the opposition, 27 percent the opposition alone, 23 percent the government alone and 17 percent denied the existence of a climate of violence. Only for the upper-income group did a single "villain" stand out. The lower-income group singled out the opposition most often, but its opinions were spread, with the second most frequent response being a denial of the existence of a climate of violence. The middle-income group was most inclined to blame both government and opposition. Class differences were again clear, but again they failed to reveal classes aligned in solid opposition.

Slippage in the translation of differing perceptions into progovernment and antigovernment attitudes is most clearly revealed in the general evaluation of the Allende government's performance. We began the examination of Hypothesis 1 with the finding that 61 percent of the lower-income group regarded themselves as the principal beneficiaries of the government's policies, with 33 percent of the upper-income group agreeing and 53 percent maintaining that no one benefited (see Table 1). When it came to judging the government's performance, however, these polar differences were muted (see Table 13). A majority in both the upper and middle groups assessed the government

Table 13

EVALUATION OF ALLENDE GOVERNMENT'S
PERFORMANCE, 1972

	Weighted Total %	Upper Income %	Middle Income %	Lower Income %
Good	21	6	16	27
Fair	36	22	32	41
Bad	43	72	52	32
Total	100	100	100	100
(N)	(300)	(100)	(100)	(100)

Source: Ercilla, September 13–19, 1972, p. 11.

performance as bad, but this judgment was balanced for the middle-income group by 32 percent who said "fair" and 16 percent who said "good." The lower class was, again, least certain; the modal judgment (41 percent) was "fair," followed by 32 percent who said "bad" and 27 percent "good."

If lower-class Chileans were as solidly united behind the Allende government as their upper-class countrymen were against it, a modification or violent breakdown of the system would appear unavoidable. As of 1972, however, the alignment of Chilean voters did not appear drastically different from what it was in 1958. As we saw in analyzing Hypothesis 2, a repetition of the elections of 1970 or of 1964 in 1972 would have produced virtually identical results. Even as they reported themselves as the principal beneficiaries of the Allende government, only 48 percent of the lower class said they would vote for Allende against Frei. Although upper-class opposition to Allende was solid, their numbers were small (seven percent by the income criterion used in these tables).

The nonrevolutionary stance of the lower class was demonstrated in response to Allende's proposal to amend the Chilean Constitution in order to replace the bicameral Congress with a unicameral legislature. This was promoted as a measure to enhance popular control of the government and to expedite responses to changes in public preferences by eliminating the Chilean Senate, only a portion of the seats of which were up for election in any given year. A July-August 1971 survey in Santiago found 50 percent in opposition and 38 percent in support of the proposed change (see Table 14). Only among the lower class was there a plurality in support of the change, but the lower class was almost evenly divided on the question. Moreover, when opponents of the proposal were asked to give their reasons, lower-class opponents mentioned "tradition, democracy" more than did those from the middle or upper classes (see Table 15). Although the lower class was the chief source of support for constitutional reform, lower-class opposition to such reform was sufficiently common to make it also the source of greatest resistance based directly on appeals to Chilean constitutional tradition.

Table 14

PUBLIC REACTIONS TO ALLENDE PROPOSAL FOR UNICAMERAL LEGISLATURE, 1971

	All Respondents %	Upper Class %	Middle Class %	Lower Class %
Keep bicameral congress	50	72	55	41
Adopt unicameral congress	38	24	34	44
No opinion	12	4	11	15
Total	100	100	100	100
(N)	(1000)	(116)	(380)	(504)

Source: Salas-Reyes, Ltd. See note 13 for details.

Table 15

REASONS FOR SUPPORTING CONTINUATION OF BICAMERAL LEGISLATURE, 1971

	Upper Class %	Middle Class %	Lower Class %
*For tradition, democracy	50	33	63
Two chambers study proposals better	25	29	14
*Two chambers mean more liberty	11	15	7
Better control of the executive	6	10	5
Two chambers have fewer arguments	1	3	—
No opinion	7	10	11
Total	100	100	100
(N)	(83)	(209)	(206)

*Ideological reasons.

Source: Salas-Reyes, Ltd. See note 13 for details.

The Allende government's efforts to achieve socialism were constrained by a pluralist system. Most of the newspapers in the *kioskos* (newsstands) of Santiago were antigovernment in orientation. Congress was controlled by opposition parties. For that matter, Allende's control of the executive branch itself was based on a fragile coalition of parties and factions, each of which appeared to be maneuvering for its individual advantage in the short run or in future elections. Indeed, one of the complaints about the government, from some leftists who voted for Allende, was that individual office-holders appeared to be seeking maximum rewards from their period in office, as if they took it for granted that a differing government coalition would take office after the presidential election of 1976.[31]

The ideological foundations of the Allende government in popular support appeared neither more nor less solid than those of its predecessors. A plurality of Chilean voters elected a candidate who had long championed socialist solutions to basic problems, and his election gave him and his coalition a typical surge of increased popular support. Although the Allende supporters clearly endorsed socialism, their commitment appeared to be more pragmatic than ideological. In February 1971, during the period of greatest popular support for the new government, when Santiago residents were asked what they like best in its actions, only 16 percent replied in clearly ideological terms: "nationalizations and expropriations," "help to the common man, to the poor, to the workers," "government take-over of the bank." Other comments may have been based on equal knowledge of the ideological rationale behind the government's actions, but they stressed specific ends rather than socialist means: "help to children—half liter of (free) milk," "readjustments of wages and salaries, family support," "stopping inflation—freezing of prices," "mass transit fare, single price for bread."

Chileans were concerned with pressing personal needs. Long aware of extreme class disparities in chances of meeting these needs on an individual basis, many were happy to try socialist solutions. But the focus was on the needs, not the means to their solution. In Cuba, Fidel Castro could occasionally call on his countrymen to sacrifice for socialism, even if it meant masses of urbanites trying their hands at cutting sugar cane. In Chile, it would be laughable to expect a Cuban-style response to a call to sacrifice for socialism; socialism was a means that many Chileans wanted to use to meet their long-standing needs, but it was not an end in itself.

As of 1972, the ability of the Chilean working class to see themselves as the beneficiaries of an Allende government and their failure to unite solidly behind Allende was enough to drive various theorists to despair. From a Marxist view, the second characteristic must be accounted for as "false consciousness." From the point of view of a Downsian "economic theory of democracy," the failure was harder to accommodate because the necessary information for a rational calculus appeared already in hand. Perhaps psychological theories of dissonance reduction would have best integrated these findings. Socialized to a commitment to a variety of values—including the verities of tradition and the Constitution—the working class attempted to promote its interest within the framework of these other values.

The primary thrust of our findings is that the basic immobilism of the Chilean system was rooted in a distribution of opinion that had not changed drastically since the Ibáñez regime of 1952-58. Varying election outcomes since then were explicable more by the specific alternatives and the structure of competition in each election than by a basic change in public opinion. An expanding electorate strengthened the Center and Left, but it had not radically altered the level of ideology or the ideological content of Chilean opinion.

In September 1973, a military coup overthrew the Allende government without waiting for the election of 1976. Our view is that despite this violent disruption of the Chilean political system, the current military junta has won a battle rather than a war. Our data indicate that the election of Allende was overinterpreted as a manifestation of a shift of Chilean opinion to the Left; the military coup should not be similarly misinterpreted as indicating either a massive shift to the Right or an abandonment of democracy by most Chileans. System level changes can occur without close correspondence to public opinion, but too many Chileans are committed to democracy for a military junta to survive unless it imposes active repression.

NOTES

1. Federico G. Gil, *The Political System of Chile* (Boston: Houghton Mifflin Co., 1966); James Petras, *Politics and Social Forces in Chilean Development* (Berkeley and Los Angeles: University of California Press, 1969); Aníbal Pinto Y otros, *Chile Hoy* (Santiago de Chile: Editorial Siglo XX, 1970); Ben G. Burnett, *Political Groups in Chile: The Dialogue between Order and Change* (Austin: The University of Texas Press, 1970); Luis Quirós Varela, "La evolución política de Chile, 1951-1971," *Mensaje*, September-October 1971, pp. 413-21; Richard Fagen and Wayne Cornelius, eds., *Political Power in Latin America: Seven Confrontations* (Englewood Cliffs, N.J.: Prentice-Hall, Inc., 1970), pp. 3-44; Charles J. Parrish, Arpad J. von Lazar, and Jorge I. Tapia Videla, "Electoral Procedures and Political Parties in Chile," *Studies in Comparative International Development* 6 (1970-71): 255-267; Ricardo Cot, *El colapso democrático, visión crítica en Chile,* (Santiago de Chile: Edicones Portada, 1972), pp. 37-61; José Garrido Rojas, "La creciente participación social," in Cot. *Colapso democrático,* pp. 193-212;   Atilio Borón, Movilización política en Chile, 1920-1970," *Estudios FLACP* N° 7, *Santiago de Chile,* November 1970; Herman Godoy O., ed., *Estructura social de Chile* (Santiago de Chile: Editorial Universitaria, 1971), pp. 183-593; Jorge Tapia Videla and Luis Quirós Varela,"El Gobierno de la Unidad Popular;el difícil camino de transición hacia el socialismo," in James Petras and Marcelo Cavarozzi, eds., *América Latina: Economía y política* (Buenos Aires: Editorial Periferia, 1972).

2. Political activity during that time was considered the "sport of the Chilean oligarchy." See Godoy, *Estructura*, p. 188; also see Guillermo Feliú Cruz, "Un esquema de la evolución social de Chile en el siglo XX," in Godoy, *Estructura*, pp. 215-222; Claudio Véliz,. "La mesa de tres patas," in Godoy, *Estructura*, pp. 232-40; Germán Urzúa U., *Los partidos políticos chilenos* (Santiago de Chile: Editorial Jurídica de Chile, 1968), p. 50.

3. Gil, *Political System*,   pp. 51, 557; Borón,"Movilización", pp. 342-46.

4. Quirós, "Evolución." pp. 414-15.

5. Maurice Zeitlin and James Petras, "The Working-Class Vote in Chile: Christian Democracy versus Marxism," *British Journal of Sociology* 21 (March 1970): 16-29.

6. The republic of San Marino appears to be the only competitor for this distinction. See David Lindsey, "Communications," *American Political Science Review* 62 (December 1968): 272-73.

7. See Philip E. Converse, "The Nature of Belief Systems in Mass Publics," in David E. Apter, ed., *Ideology and Discontent* (New York: Free Press of Glencoe, Inc., 1964), pp. 206-61.

8. James W. Prothro and Charles M. Grigg, "Fundamental Principles of Democracy: Bases of Agreement and Disagreement," *Journal of Politics* 22 (May 1960): 276-94. Subsequent work which further substantiated these findings includes Herbert McClosky, "Consensus and Ideology in American Politics," *American Political Science Review:* 58 (June 1964): 361-82; V.O. Key, Jr., *Public Opinion and American Democracy* (New York: Alfred A. Knopf, 1961), pp. 27-53.

9. Compare, for example, Samuel Lubell, *Revolt of the Moderates* (New York: Harper & Row, 1956) and Converse, "Belief Systems," for different views of the 1952 presidential election in the United States.

10. Converse and Georges Dupeux, "Politicization of the Electorate in France and the United States," in Angus Campbell et al., *Elections and the Political Order* (New York: John Wiley & Sons, Inc., 1966), pp. 269-91.

11. Zeitlin and Petras, "Working-Class Vote."

12. "Political Attitudes and Behavior of the Chilean Working Class, 1958-1968," unpublished paper, Yale University, 1972.

13. We refer to Salas-Reyes, Ltd., a survey organization that has carried out surveys in Chile since 1958. Their data were secured by the Instituto de Ciencia Política, Universidad Católica, with funds from the FAFP grant; we are indebted to Prof. Luis Quirós for discovering them and arranging for their purchase. The surveys we cite used area probability samples of voting-age adults. For purposes of longitudinal comparison, only surveys from Greater Santiago are employed in this article. Although surveys from other Chilean locales are available, only Greater Santiago has been consistently surveyed for the period in which we are interested. The occasional surveys of other areas suggest that nationwide data would not alter the trend findings of this article.

14. For our purposes, for example, a response that cited a Marxist commitment in justification of a candidate preference would be classified as ideological, whether or not it predicted other attitudes of the respondent. This usage is justified by our concern for ideological content and direction of opinions. (It is necessitated by our inability to manipulate individual responses.) In contrast, the Converse analysis cited in footnote 8 would not classify such a response as ideological unless it were systematically related to other responses of the same individual, and it would classify responses not manifestly ideological in content as ideological if

they were systematically related to other responses. Converse's usage was justified by his concern for ideology as the structure rather than the content of opinions.

15. September 13-19, 1972, pp. 10-11.

16. See Key, *Public Opinion*, p. 130.

17. See Lloyd A. Free and Hadley Cantril, *The Political Beliefs of Americans* (New Brunswick, N.J.: Rutgers University Press, 1967), pp. 114-15.

18. A caveat that applies to most of this paper deserves emphasis here. The margin of error in our coding of responses is unavoidably higher than would be possible if we had access to original interview schedules. Take, for example, the code category "better salaries for workers, employees, wage earners, better distribution of the national income." The redistributional feature of the last item mentioned clearly requires that it be classed as ideological; but some unknown proportion of the answers falling in this category may have mentioned "better salaries for workers" with no explicit reference to redistribution. These responses are less clearly ideological but they cannot be separated from those that are. Because all responses in the category must be treated as ideological or as nonideological, our decision is governed by the principle of minimizing error. The references to "better salaries for workers," if they could be taken by themselves, *might* be interpreted as referring to workers' income in relation to the income of others, probably employers, and hence be classified as ideological. Because the references to overall distribution of income are clearly ideological, we risk some error by coding the entire category as ideological rather than insuring some error by coding it as nonideological. The content of other categories classified as nonideological is also an aid in making the decision. In this case, for example, other categories mention "improve the standard of living" and "create jobs, end unemployment"; the availability of these categories for references to general improvements in the economic lot of people (in nonclass terms) reinforces the conclusion that "better salaries for workers" belongs in the ideological category. Another example of the importance of a second code category on a given subject in deciding whether or not a particular category is ideological is the ideological classification of the Frei platform point on "public housing." This classification might have been judged as nonideological but for the fact that another Frei point mentioned "housing construction, housing problem" with no reference to a "public" solution to the problem. With this general category available for the coding of any housing references that did not refer to public versus private enterprise approaches, we felt more certain that the "public housing" category was indeed ideological in content and confined to housing references stipulating the public nature of the proposed solution.

Our procedure undoubtedly includes errors of both inclusion and exclusion. Some responses tallied as ideological were no doubt made with no ideological referent intended by the respondent. Conversely, some of the references to general goals, such as "more education," were probably offered with an unstated ideological goal in mind. Nevertheless, our coding procedure appears best calculated to reduce both types of error to a minimum.

19. See *An Economic Theory of Democracy* (New York: Harper & Row, 1957).

20. On the concept of "critical elections" see Key, "A Theory of Critical Elections," *Journal of Politics:* 17 (February 1955): 3-18.

21. Should the 14 percent who say they would not vote for any of the three candidates actually fail to vote in a real election, then Allende's percentage of the vote would increase to 45 percent. As we saw in examining Hypothesis 1, however, Allende was the last choice of a majority of voters even when he won election with his plurality of the votes in 1970. Accordingly, Allende's support is less easily affected by the number or nature of his opponents than is that of other candidates—those who fail to support him not only prefer someone else but are definite about not wanting Allende. Should respondents who say they would not vote for any of these candidates named in an interview actually vote under the necessities of an election choice, they would be least likely to choose Allende.

22. Durán, who remained on the ballot as the Right candidate in 1964, received 3.4 percent of the vote in Santiago, Allende 35.7 percent and Frei 60.9 percent.

23. See Zeitlin and Petras, "Working-Class Vote."

24. On the problem of intensity, see Robert A. Dahl, *A Preface to Democratic Theory* (Chicago: University of Chicago Press, 1956).

25. *New York Times*, March 7, 1971, p. 3.

26. Marian D. Irish and James W. Prothro, *The Politics of American Democracy,* 5th ed. (Englewood Cliffs, N.J.: Prentice-Hall, Inc., 1971), p. 337.

27. *Direción del Registro Electoral, Chile*. For detailed figures, see Table 9.

28. Ibid.

29. *El Mercurio*, International Edition, April 5-11, 1971, p. 8.

30. Conversation overheard by one of the members of the FAFP research group.

31. This observation is based on personal interviews.

4

Three Views of Allende's Chile

Paul E. Sigmund

Like Caesar's Gaul, Allende's Chile was divided into three parts. On the right was the National party, formed in 1966 out of a fusion of the traditional Liberal and Conservative parties following their disastrous electoral defeat in the 1965 congressional elections. Together with the Radical Democrats, who left the parent Radical party in 1969, it secured the support of 20 percent to 25 percent of the Chilean electorate in 1969, 1971 and 1973. The center was dominated by the Christian Democratic party (Partido Demócrata Cristiano—PDC), joined in 1972 by another radical splinter group, the Left Radicals. The PDC's electoral fortune eroded from the 42 percent it received in 1965 to a low of 26 percent in the 1971 municipal elections, then it staged a comeback, receiving nearly 30 percent of the vote in the 1973 congressional elections. On the left was Salvador Allende's Popular Unity (*Unidad Popular—UP*) coalition, increasingly dominated by the Socialist and Communist parties, which rose from 36 percent in the 1970 presidential elections to about 50 percent of the vote in 1971, dropping back to around 44 percent in 1973.

There were many other political groups inside and outside of the Chilean political system. Certainly no description of Chilean politics between 1970 and 1973 could ignore the movement of the revolutionary Left—MIR on the extreme Left or the Fatherland and Freedom group (Patria y Libertad) on the extreme Right. Moreover, the pressures engendered by the changes after Allende's accession to power produced a process of political polarization into pro- and anti-government groupings which was clearly evident in the 1973 congressional elections. Yet dichotomous divisions, whether the labels were "progressive" and "facist," or "totalitarian" and "democratic," concealed an enduring political reality in Chile, a three-way ideological division related to but by no means coterminous with class lines as to the desirable pace and nature of social, economic and political change. The divisions decisively influenced the way in which the complex Chilean scene was viewed and evaluated, so that the same phenomena were interpreted in sharply different ways. The foreign observer who wishes to understand Chilean politics during Allende's regime must be aware of these three views before he can come to an informed assessment of pre-coup Chile. The "evidence" in this chapter will be presented by hypothetical proponents of each of the three positions as each attempts to assess economic, social and international policies of the Allende government during the nearly three years of his regime which began on September 4, 1970.

FROM THE VIEWPOINT
OF A POPULAR UNITY ADHERENT

The basic program of Popular Unity was approved by the Communist, Socialist, Radical and Social Democratic parties, as well as by the Movement for Unitary Popular Action (MAPU) and Independent Popular Action (API) on December 17, 1969. The program attributed the profound crisis in Chile to the capitalist system which was "dependent on imperialism and dominated by sectors of the bourgeoisie which are structurally linked to foreign capital."[1] The remedies UP prescribed included the "construction of a new economy" by nationalization of the basic riches of the country in the power of foreign capital and domestic monopoly; acceleration of the process of agrarian reform; constitutional reform to create a single legislative chamber which in turn would appoint the members of the Supreme Court; and extension of medical care, housing and education to the masses. The mass media were asked to assist in the formation of a "new culture and a new man." International relations were to be carried out on the basis of self-determination and diplomatic relations with all countries of the world and would be characterized by "a strong Latin American and anti-imperialist sense." The policy of the Popular Unity government would be directed at carrying out "the transition to socialism" through the united action of "the immense majority" of Chileans.

This is the program which brought Salvador Allende to victory on September 4, 1970. Allende received 36.2 percent of the votes and if that figure is combined with the 27.8 percent of the ballots that went to the Christian Democratic candidate, Radomiro Tomic, whose program also called for the replacement of capitalism and the termination of international dependence, it is clear that the immense majority of Chileans rejected capitalism in Chile. As in the 1964 election, the reactionaries organized a "campaign of terror" with horror stories about the effects of a victory of Popular Unity. However, this time the Chilean people were not deceived and they elected Allende as their president. Tomic recognized Allende's victory immediately after the election when he went to *Compañero*, Allende's residence, to congratulate him, and announced to journalists, "I have come to greet the president-elect of Chile, my grand old friend, Salvador Allende."[2]

Yet, within a few days, the capitalists and the rightists attempted to frustrate the popular mandate. According to the Chilean constitution, if no presidential candidate receives an absolute majority of the votes, the Congress is to meet in 50 days to choose one of the two candidates with the largest pluralities. A strong constitutional tradition prescribes that the leading candidate should be elected by the Congress, but shortly after the election, Jorge Allessandri, the rightist candidate who received 34.9 percent of the vote, offered to resign if he were elected and thus pave the way for a new election in which the Right could repeat its 1964 maneuver and throw its support to Eduardo Frei (who would then be eligible to run again).

The International Telephone and Telegraph Company (ITT) papers published in April 1972 contained documented proof that the United States government, the foreign monopolists and Eduardo Frei plotted together to prevent the victory of Allende. The September 17, 1970 memorandum speaks of U.S. Ambassador Korry receiving a "green light" from the U.S. Department of State "to do all possible, short of a Dominican Republic-type action, to keep Allende from taking power"; it quotes Frei as stating "that the country cannot be allowed to go Communist and that Allende must be prevented from taking office," and says that Frei saw and approved the Alessandri statement before it was released to the public.[3]

The Frei government also cooperated with foreign interests in attempting to create an economic panic. Andres Zaldivar, Frei's finance minister, made a provocative speech on September 23, 1970, in which he spoke of mass withdrawals from the banking system and mounting production crises. The collusion of the Frei government with foreign interests is proven in the September 29, 1970 ITT memorandum which asserts that "an economic collapse is being encouraged by some sectors in the business and political community and by President Frei himself."

When Allende agreed to the Christian Democratic proposal to add a Statute of Democratic Guarantees to the Chilean constitution, thus assuring his election in the Congress on October 27, 1970, the Right resorted to more desperate maneuvers. Later judicial investigations indicated that members of the Frei government knew that a military coup was being prepared and did nothing to prevent it and that the conspirators met with National party and Radical Democrat senators in September and October 1970. Their plotting resulted in the attempted kidnapping and consequent assassination of the army chief of staff, General René Schneider, two days before the congressional election. A wave of revulsion was felt throughout Chile at the murder of the army leader, who was known to be dedicated to the defense of Chilean constitutionalism, and, on October 25, 1970, an overwhelming majority of the Congress adhered to constitutional precedent by electing Allende president by a vote of 153 to 35.

At the inauguration ceremonies on November 3 of the same year, Allende was sworn in at a ceremony attended by members of the diplomatic community and by representatives of the Korean People's Republic, the People's Republic of Vietnam, the

German Democratic Republic, the People's Republic of China and Cuba. In a speech delivered two days after his inauguration, Allende quoted Friedrich Engels on the possibility of "peaceful evolution from the old society to the new in countries where the representatives of the people have all power." He concluded, "This is our Chile. Here, at last, the anticipation of Engels is fulfilled." Allende's strong commitment to democracy was reaffirmed in his first State of the Nation address the following May when he spoke of Chile as a "second model of the transition to a socialist society ... anticipated by the classics of Marxism."[4]

Despite the efforts of foreign intrigue and domestic reaction, *Compañero* Allende had come to power with full respect for the democratic process. He pledged to carry out the transition to socialism through the institutions of bourgeois democracy despite a hostile majority in Congress and a judiciary composed of adherents of the old class-oriented legal system. The Congress blocked Allende's attempt to democratize the judicial system by the establishment of neighborhood courts composed of a government appointee and two representatives of community organizations. It also opposed the Popular Unity proposal for a unicameral legislature, but if the *vía chilena* had not been so brutally interrupted, the expansion of mass support for the Popular Unity government would have permitted the use of plebiscite provisions of the Constitution to impose the popular will on the bourgeoisie.

In the area of economic policy the opposition was not able to impede the revolutionary process in the same way. For the first time Chile's natural resources, including nitrate, coal, iron and above all copper, were developed for the benefit of the Chilean people. In the case of copper, a constitutional amendment was unanimously adopted by Congress in July 1971 which provided for independent appraisal of the value of the American-owned mines (independent Soviet and French teams determined that the mines had been seriously mismanaged and despoiled by the American companies prior to nationalization). The amendment allowed deductions for profits in excess of 12 percent computed for the period since the *Nuevo Trato* ("New Deal") agreements with the companies in 1955. The Anaconda and the Kennecott companies had such exorbitant profits in that time that after deduction for excess profits no compensation was due.

In fulfillment of its commitment to the Chilean people, the Popular Unity government also began to acquire control of private banking through the purchase of stocks from private investors. By 1973, the people's government had majority control of nearly all private banks. In industry through negotiated purchase, intervention or requisition, massive changes in ownership took place, making the area of social property the dominant sector of the economy, including over 250 industrial enterprises and banks and most of the foreign trade. All of this was done with strict respect for Chilean law and within the existing institutional framework.

Basic changes were also carried out in Chilean agriculture. The agrarian reform law, adopted in 1967 under the auspices of the Christian Democratic administration, was used by the Popular Unity government to take over two and a half times as many *fundos* (estates) in two years as the Christian Democrats took over in six years. The reformed sector was farmed through cooperative *asentamientos* or in state-run Centers for Agrarian Reform, and the Chilean peasants and Indians, for the first time, were paid a living wage.

The Allende government checked the development of capitalist attitudes and practices among the beneficiaries of the agrarian reform, who, under the Frei regime, were on the way to becoming a new privileged elite in the countryside. The Cautin district, the "breadbasket" of Chile and an area scarcely affected by the Frei administration, became the center of operations of the Ministry of Agriculture in early 1971. Virtually all land that occupied more than the 80 basic hectare (195-acre) legal limit became part of the reformed sector.

The social advances of Popular Unity were as striking as its progress in extending national control over the economy. The first budget of the Popular Unity government raised the exemption on income and property taxes for the benefit of small property owners and the poorest wage earners. It also secured the adoption of pension increases and wage readjustments which gave the largest raises to those in the lowest income groups. At the same time, price controls were enforced more stringently so that the inflation rate for the first three months of 1971 was 3.4 percent compared to 16 percent in the preceding year. As a result of the increased purchasing power of the masses produced by these measures, the economy staged a spectacular recovery. In 1971, industrial production was up 12 percent, the gross national product increased by over 8 percent and unemployment dropped from 8 percent to a record low of 3.8 percent. The former class distinctions between employees and workers, which even led to separate social-security systems, were eliminated. In 1971, 80,000 houses were built; university enrollments rose by 30 percent; and 48 million liters of milk were distributed in the form of a free pint daily to every school child.[5]

In the municipal elections of April 1971, the Popular Unity government scored an impressive victory. Omitting blank and invalid votes, the parties supporting the Allende government received 50.8 percent of the votes and Allende's own Socialist party increased its percentage from 12 percent in the 1969 congressional elections to 22 percent in the municipal elections.

The political advances made by Popular Unity were accelerated in July 1971 when the Christian Democratic party split for the second time in two years. The PDC's declaration earlier in that year that it favored "communitarian socialism" had been revealed as fraudulent when the Christian Democrats accepted the support of the right-wing parties for their candidate in a Valparaiso by-election. After the party plenary council rejected a resolution prohibiting such understandings with rightist groups, Bosco Parra, the leader of the *tercerista* faction of the party, along with leaders of the party youth organization and six PDC deputies left the party to form the Christian Left, a new political movement which declared its support for the Allende government.

After mid-1971 there was a clear pattern of collaboration between the *momios* ("mummies") of the right and the PDC to use the opposition's control of Congress to impede implementation of the Popular Unity program. In October 1971, two Christian Democratic senators introduced a constitutional amendment severely limiting the government's recourse to intervention and purchase in bringing enterprises into the social area. The Christian Democrats and the right-wing parties also began to cooperate in the impeachment of ministers for various trumped-up charges. This attempt to transform the Chilean presidential system into a parliamentary one was not successful, however, since each time a minister was impeached, Allende simply transferred him to another ministerial post. There was also collaboration between the PDC and the so-called March of the Empty Pots, a demonstration carried out by matrons from the *Barrio Alto* (a middle- and upper-class section of Santiago) who had never known what it was like to be without food and who were seen banging new pots purchased just for the occasion.

Shortages of certain types of food and consumer goods can be explained by the increased demand resulting from the redistribution of income carried out by the Popular Unity government. According to the planning office (ODEPLAN), the share of the national income received by wage and salary earners rose from 51 percent to 59 percent in 1971 and much of this was spent in increased consumption by the 220,000 families that had never been able to eat meat, sleep in sheets or enjoy other benefits of modern life.[6]

The shortage of beef was a result of sabotage by wealthy *latifundistas* (large landowners) who preferred to sell their meat on the black market or to smuggle it to Argentina rather than to sell it to the government distribution agency. Shortages of replacement parts were the consequence of what Allende called the "invisible blockade" which denied Chile credits from U.S. agencies, private banks or sources of international assistance subject to United States influence. In the three years of Allende's tenure, the only new foreign aid authorized by the United States went to the Chilean military. The economic problems in Chile under Allende must be blamed chiefly on the maneuvers of the imperialists and their domestic allies.

The redistribution of income and the refusal of Congress to vote sufficient taxes to cover wage readjustments led to an increase in the inflation rate in the second half of 1972. However, this was compensated for by a 100 percent readjustment for inflation in October 1972 and a special bonus for the national holidays (*Fiestas Patrias*). Further wage readjustments, to cover the inflation in the last three months of 1972 and the first part of 1973, were delayed by congressional unwillingness to accept the government's proposal to limit readjustments to incomes below three times the minimum wage. Demonstrating their class bias, the Congress refused to vote additional taxes on the wealthy to finance the readjustment and finally forced the government to raise the upper limit to five times the minimum wage.

The opposition created even greater pressures on the economy when it organized the Employers' Strike (*Paro Patronal*) of October 1972. More accurately described as a lockout than a strike, it was an attempt to topple the government by shutting down industry, small business and the normal operation of the professions. The strike demonstrated the solidarity of the working classes when even Christian Democratic-controlled labor unions refused to support it. The strike's principal result was a considerable increase in the number of firms taken over by the government.

The strike was settled when Allende reorganized his cabinet to include representatives of the three armed services with the understanding that they would only serve until the March 1973 congressional elections. Those elections, held in an atmosphere of complete freedom, destroyed the hopes of the opposition for the two-thirds majority it needed to impeach the president. Instead, for the first time in recent Chilean history, an incumbent administration increased its electoral support in a mid-term election as the Unidad Popular candidates received nearly 44 percent of the vote, compared to the 36 percent which Allende had received in 1970.[7] It was evident from the vote that despite material difficulties which are inevitable in the transition to socialism, the masses still supported the Popular Unity government. (As one Chilean worker put it, "It may be a government *de mierda*, but it is *our* government *de mierda*.") The economic power of the industrialists, the landowners and foreign companies was severely curtailed. The worker and the peasant became involved in new relationships which compelled them to take responsibility for their own futures supplanting their former dependence upon employers and big landowners. Although there were occasional instances of violence or injustice, the social price of the immense transformation which Chile was undergoing was far less than that of any of the great revolutions of the twentieth century. As Allende approached the midpoint of his presidential program, Allende would have to seek the cooperation of sectors outside of the Popular Unity coalition. At the peak of his popularity in the municipal elections of April 1971, after an artificial economic boom created by the reckless spending of the government, his candidates still did not have the support of a majority of the voters.[9] In nearly every one of the by-elections held subsequently, in elections in universities, student organizations, trade unions, copper mines and, above all, in the 1973 Congressional elections (in which, for all the government's claims to the contrary, the Allende forces were defeated) it became apparent that the government had little hope of securing majority support by relying exclusively on the parties and groups of Popular Unity, dominated as it was by the two Marxist parties, the Socialists and the Communists. (To demonstrate the increase in influence of the Marxists it is only necessary to look at the decline of the Radical party since its alliance with the Marxist Left. As early as July 1971, a group of Left Radicals including Alberto Baltra, the Radicals' presidential candidate in the 1969-70 Popular Unity negotiations, left the party over the issue of Marxist domination and in 1972 joined the opposition. In 1973, the once-great centrist Radical party received only 3.5 percent of the vote.)

Yet, instead of seeking cooperation from the Christian Democrats, Allende encouraged his supporters and the government-controlled press to attack the PDC—in particular former President Frei—in a campaign which confirmed all our earlier fears. On the basis of unsubstantiated rumors contained in the ITT papers, rumors which, as Frei said, could have been picked up on any street corner in Santiago in September and October of 1970,[10] Frei was accused of conspiracy to overthrow the constitutional system and of involvement in the assassination of General Schneider, accusations which are refuted by other parts of the ITT papers themselves. The important social advances made by the Frei administration—the adoption of the 1967 agrarian reform law which the Allende government later used, the distribution of land to 30,000 families as beneficiaries of the agrarian reform, legislation making the minimum wage and union organization a reality in the countryside, the extension of trade union membership from 10 percent to 18 percent of the working term, it seemed that the social, economic and political advances made by his regime were not reversible and that Chile would demonstrate that a politically mature nation could advance in full democracy toward national liberation and socialism. It took a military coup, the murder of Allende and months of bloody repression to reimpose the will of the bourgeoisie on an awakened people.

THE CHRISTIAN DEMOCRATIC VIEWPOINT

The Christian Democratic party committed itself to "democratic, popular, pluralist and communitarian socialism." As was already evident in the 1970 campaign its objectives and those of Popular Unity were similar.[8] Both groups agreed on the need to replace capitalism, on the necessity for a thorough and rapid agrarian reform and on the need to enable the marginal elements in the countryside and the *poblaciones* (shantytowns) to participate fully in modern society. Where they disagreed was on methods. For the PDC these goals could only be achieved in an atmosphere of freedom and democracy with full respect for the rights of others. Instead, during the Allende regime and as a direct result of Popular Unity policies, Chile was racked by violence, torn by partisan and class strife, paralyzed by demonstrations and strikes and in a state of near civil war which was only avoided by the military intervention of September 11, 1973.

Allende received only 36 percent of the vote on September 4, 1970, and he could not have won his majority vote in the Congress that October without the support of the PDC. That support was given only after he had agreed to the addition of the Statute of Democratic Guarantees to the Constitution as an assurance that his government would not use its powers to destroy the foundations of Chilean democracy: its free press, radio and television; its political parties, churches and trade unions; its pluralist education; and its politically neutral armed forces and judiciary.

Instead of respecting the rules of constitutional democracy and attempting to secure the support of a majority of the Chilean people through persuasion, the Allende government deliberately encouraged violence, sectarianism and class hatred. It seemed obvious to the PDC that, to secure majority support for his population, the redistribution of income so that the salaried and wage-earning sector increased its participation in the national income from 48 percent in the last year of the Alessandri regime to 53 percent in 1969, the expansion of education and housing—all these were simply dismissed as "the new face of reaction."

These attacks would have been less disturbing if they had not been accompanied by a systematic attempt to control the mass media and education. The Communist party alone bought 11 radio stations between 1970 and 1973. A deliberate campaign of discrimination was carried out against the Catholic university's television station and in favor of the Marxist-controlled University of Chile station and the government television network. Zig-Zag Publishers were bankrupted by a government decree granting massive wage increases in a labor dispute thus enabling the government to acquire Zig-Zag's presses for its own *Editorial Quimantú*. Government attempts to take over the only privately owned paper company were successfully resisted as a direct threat to freedom of the press, but the campaign against the *Papelera* continued until Allende's overthrow. Most serious were the attempts to politicize and dominate the entire educational system of Chile through the National Unified School (ENU) decree issued in March 1973, the implementation of which was only postponed because of the protests of the Church, the armed forces, educators and students.

The government encouraged an atmosphere of lawlessness and violence from the moment that it took office. It made no effort to restrain the armed groups of the Left and then, in June 1971, when members of one of the Left's extremist groups assassinated Edmundo Perez Zujovic, Frei's minister of interior, the regime blamed the U.S. Central Intelligence Agency! It attributed the food shortages to sabotage and imperialist maneuvers, when it was clear that the principal cause of the decline in food production was violence and uncertainty in the countryside.

Besides sectarianism and violence, the Allende government was also guilty of bureaucratism and inefficiency in its economic policy. It was easy enough for the Allende administration to create an artificial prosperity during its first year when it enjoyed the cushion of $350 million in international reserves left to it by the Frei administration and when existing stocks and unused capacity permitted some initial expansion of production. However, the economy could not go on operating at a deficit for a prolonged period. By the middle of 1972, the reserves were gone, existing stocks had been depleted and inflation began a runaway upward spiral which reached 323 percent for the 12 months prior to July 31, 1973. The root cause of the economic crisis in Chile just before the coup was the disastrous economic policy of the Allende government. Using measures of at best doubtful legality, it took over 250 business enterprises, appointed inexperienced and sectarian intervenors to run them and then blamed the resulting declines in production on the imperialists. With the PDC's support the Allende government completed the process of recovering national control of the copper industry initiated by Frei; it then so alienated the copper workers that the industry was racked by prolonged strikes of increasing intensity.

The Christian Democratic party favored a restructuring of the Chilean economy but insisted that it be done legally. The constitutional amendment on the areas of the economy, which the PDC proposed and the Congress adopted, delineated the areas of state control and provided for worker-controlled enterprises that would involve the workers directly in decision-making. This would have been far more workable than the complex and overlapping bureaucratic structures elaborated by the Popular Unity government in order to maintain its hegemony and centralized control. What occurred in the industrial sector was not nationalization or socialization but "statification" (*estatización*)—the establishment of a system of state control which principally benefitted the government appointees and the parties of Popular Unity. Technical knowledge or the ability to gain the support of the workers were not qualifications for running a factory. Party affiliation practically determined who would be appointed according to the *cuoteo* (quota) system, which assigned jobs to the party faithful.

The extent to which the Allende government betrayed its promises can be judged by rereading the famous "Forty Measures" promised by Popular Unity in 1970. The first five measures were: (1) suppression of high salaries for presidential appointees, (2) no more government advisors (*asesores*), (3) an end to persecution for political and religious ideas, (4) no more luxury trips abroad for government functionaires and (5) no more government automobiles for personal use. If we add to this list measure number 30, which promised an end to inflation, and measure number 37 which called for the dissolution of the mobile group riot squad (it was simply renamed Special Services), we can see why the opposition deputies laughed bitterly when the list was read in Congress in December 1972.[11]

The government defenders often spoke of the redistribution of income to the urban and rural masses. Yet a secret report of the MAPU in March 1973 admitted that wages and salaries did not increase as rapidly as food prices.[12] If increases for lower income groups are wiped out by inflation and the economy is destroyed in the process, where is the social progress? The two groups on whose behalf Allende claimed to be governing, the workers and the peasants, were increasingly dissatisfied. The copper strikes showed this in the industrial area and, in the rural sector, it was demonstrated by the refusal of the Agrarian Reform agency (CORA) to permit the peasantry to decide whether to divide the agrarian reform settlements (*asentamientos*) into private plots after three years, as was provided in the 1967 law.

The imperialists alone cannot be blamed for Chile's problems. The Christian Democratic party has always favored a policy of national and continental independence as demonstrated by the important steps the Frei government took in this area: establishment of the Andean Subregional Group with a common investment code, the Latin American Foreign Minister's meeting in 1969 which produced the Consensus of Viña del Mar summarizing Latin American complaints against United States economic policies, the creation of CIPEC (The Intergovernmental Committee of Copper Producing Countries) for the coordination of copper policy and the expansion of Chile's relations with Europe, the Soviet Union and, in 1970, with Cuba. But a policy of supposed independence should not create new types of dependence: the accelerated indebtedness and the economic weakness of the Allende government made it the most dependent in Chile's history. Only the involvement of all Chileans in a national effort to create a democratic, productive and just society can repair the damage done by the disastrous policies of the last three years.

THE OPINION OF A RIGHTIST

Jorge Alessandri, in his 1970 presidential campaign, diagnosed Chile's fundamental ailments: excessive politicization and ignorance of even minimal knowledge of sound economics. The debility grew to mortal proportion after the election of Salvador Allende. To avoid the destruction of Chile as a land of *convivencia* in which Chileans of a variety of political orientations could live together, Don Jorge made his offer to resign if elected by the Congress in October 1970 so as to permit an election in which one candidate could receive the support of a majority of Chileans. That majority was opposed to Marxism but, because of a regrettable division in the anti-Marxist forces between two candidates in 1970, it was not able to express that opposition then. Later, that plurality did receive concrete expression in the formation of the Democratic Confederation (CODE) alliance in 1972 and the victory of the opposition candidates by a 56 percent majority in the March 1973 elections.

Even during the Alessandri administration between 1958 and 1964, political pressures prevented the execution of a sound economic policy. In his first three years, Alessandri embarked on a stabilization program which had virtually brought Chile's chronic inflation to a standstill in 1960. But then electoral pressures and restructuring expenditures after the 1960 earthquake set the inflationary spiral off again.

The 34.9 percent of the vote that Alessandri received in 1970 was an indication that Chileans remembered his administration as one of honesty, stability and economic efficiency. Alessandri's administration also carried out important social programs, especially in the areas of housing and education, and adopted Chile's first agrarian reform law. But, as that law demonstrated, social reform was carried out in a nondogmatic fashion. It gave priority to the use of abandoned or inefficiently exploited land instead of attempting to overturn the entire social and economic structure of the countryside as the Frei and Allende administrations did.

The basic problem of Chilean agriculture, after all, is lack of productivity. Since 1940, Chile has been a net importer of foodstuffs and this is directly attributable to the lack of an adequate system of price incentives for the farmer. The low prices for farm products were, in turn, the result of price controls that were adopted out of excessive concern for the urban sector on the part of successive Chilean governments since the Popular Front in 1938. If the agrarian sectors had received half the protection and assistance that the industrial sector received in that period, we would not be in our present predicament.

When Allende was elected, of course, the situation went from bad to catastrophic. In 1973, according to the National Agricultural Society, Chile will be compelled to spend $500 million for food imports, four times the annual amount spent for food imports in the last part of the Frei administration in which there was a severe drought.[13] This disastrous situation was the result of the chaos that reigned in the countryside from a conscious government policy of encouraging violence and indiscriminate seizures and occupations.

The Allende government attacked the *latifundistas* instead of making a clear-headed analysis of the economic errors of its agricultural policy. The regime established stockpiles and monopolies of essential foodstuffs, which were bought from the farmer at absurdly low prices, and then wondered why so much of that food found its way into the black market. The so-called Centers of Agrarian Reform were nothing more than Soviet-style state farms but they were even less efficient than their prototypes. The experience of the Soviet Union and of Communist Eastern Europe demonstrates that collectivized agriculture will not work, which is why Yugoslavia, Hungary and Poland now rely principally on the private sector in agriculture.

This comparison can be further extended. It is ironic that, at the very time that the Soviet Union and China were buying wheat from the West to make up for their own production deficiencies, the Allende government was following the same agricultural course that had led to their difficulties. And at the same time that the Soviet Union made an agreement with Pepsi Cola International (the vice-president of which is the former owner of El Mercurio) for the distribution of Pepsi Cola there, the Allende government took over the soft-drink industry in Chile. While the Soviet Union and China sought Western technology and know-how, Chile cut herself off from the latest technological advances and tried to go it alone. When every other country including those that call themselves socialist attempted to secure additional foreign investment, Chile denounced foreign investors and forced them to discontinue operations in Chile.

In industry as in agriculture, figures during the Allende regime show a precipitous decline. In the last four months of 1972, industrial production dropped by 8 percent to 12 percent from the previous year and a negative 5 percent to 10 percent growth rate was expected in 1973. Copper production declined precipitously. Inefficiency and disorganization meant that in the world's largest open copper mine (at Chuquicamata), 9,500 miners produced 245,000 tons of copper in 1972, while in 1970, 6,500 miners produced 285,000 tons.[14] Fifty-two percent of the national budget in 1972 went to cover budget deficits and even larger amounts went to support the so-called Area of Social Property (APS). The National Strike of October 1972, initiated as a protest by small independent truckers against the government's attempt to establish a state trucking agency, demonstrated the opposition of all sectors to the destruction of independent business, commerce and the professions in Chile.

The Allende government called us facists (*momios*) and coup-mongers (*golpistas*). One of the characteristics of fascism is the glorification of violence, yet who was more eloquent in encouraging and practicing violence than the MIR, which included many members of the president's own party? There are many kinds of coups, and one of them is the steady expansion of state power over all aspects of life so that any political opposition or independent sectors are denied the resources with which to survive. This was how the Allende government operated. It expanded its control of the economy by the use of devices which were clearly illegal and unconstitutional and used "the decree of insistence" to overrule the objections of the controller general. It violated the clear intention of the framers of the 1970 constitutional amendments by claiming that the Congress can only overrule the president's vetoes by a two-thirds majority. It bought out industries and banks by the use of Development Corporation

(CORFO) credits, a procedure not authorized by the legislation establishing that body. And it tried to change the price and supply committees into centers for political control through what was in effect a system of rationing.

The ultimate goal of the Allende government was control of Chile by a Marxist totalitarian state. Lenin once said that the first step in the attainment of such a goal is to debase the currency; the Allende government increased the amount of currency in circulation by over 1,000.[15] Efforts to take over Alessandri's paper company and to orient the educational system toward Marxism were directed toward the same objective. As the economy declined and inflation spiraled upward, only the timely intervention of the armed forces prevented the Allende government from transforming this beautiful country, with its vast mineral resources and its talented and able people, into another Bolivia or another Cuba.

EPILOGUE

Students of Weimar Germany and of the Third and Fourth Republics of France have written about the problem of the "negative majority," which is a continual possibility in a multiparty system. In Chile, proportional representation, ideological parties, staggered elections and a basically stable three-way division of political opinion made it almost inevitable that no government could govern for long without the support of a majority of the population.[16] What enabled the Chilean system to survive up to now has been the inherent strength of the Chilean presidency and the strong commitment of the overwhelming majority of Chileans to the rules of the game of constitutional democracy. In 1973, however, the constitutionalism of the armed forces was eroded and eventually overcome by the combination of (1) hyper-inflation fueled by uncontrolled currency emissions to cover the enormous deficits of the government and the nationalized or intervened industries, and (2) an ideologically motivated class polarization which had turned Chile into an armed camp and, ironically, had greater success in uniting the middle class and professional trade associations against the government than in expanding its support among low-income groups.

The tragic death of Chilean constitutionalism raises some disturbing questions about the experience of the last three presidencies, based respectively on the Right, Center and Left: (1) Must economic development be carried out at the expense of social justice (Alessandri)? (2) Does the attempt to achieve a balance between these goals within the framework of constitutional democracy make it impossible to achieve either (Frei)? (3) Must a regime which attempts to carry out a broadly redistributive program do so at the price of runaway inflation and economic growth collapse (Allende)? (4) Now that all three policies have been tried and none has been able to secure majority support, is there any future for democracy in Chile?

NOTES

1. *Programa Básico de Gobierno de la Unidad Popular* (Santiago, 1970), p. 4. Substantial excerpts from the program are translated in Richard E. Feinberg, *The Triumph of Allende* (Mentor: New York, 1972), pp. 260-72.

2. *Ercilla*, no. 1838 (September 9-15, 1970): p. 12.

3. "Secret Memos from ITT," *Latin America and Empire Report* 6 (April 1972).

4. *El Mercurio*, November 6, 1970, p. 23; *La Via Chilena*, State of the Nation Address (Santiago May 21, 1971) translated as "The Chilean Way to Socialism" in Paul E. Sigmund, *The Ideologies of the Developing Nations* 2nd. ed. (Praeger Publishers: New York, 1972), pp. 447-53.

5. *La Lucha par la Democracia Económica y las Libertades Sociales*, Second State of the Nation Message, May 2, 1972, pp. 113-21.

6. *El Mercurio*, International Edition, February 5-11, 1973 p. 1 (President Allende's speech in the National Stadium).

7. President Pedro Aguirre Cerda, elected in 1938, increased his electoral support in the March 1941 Congressional elections.

8. On the 1970 programs, see Fréderic Debuyst and Joan Garcés, "La opción chilena de 1970. Análisis de los tres programas electorales," *Revista Latinoamericana de Ciencia Política*, vol. 2, no. 2 (August 1972): 279-369.

9. Including blank and invalid ballots (voting is compulsory in Chile) candidates supporting Allende received 49.86 percent of the vote.

10. *Política y Espíritu*, 27 no. 331 (April 1972): 87. (Radio address by Eduardo Frei, April 10, 1972.)

11. *El Mercurio*, International Edition, December 25-31, 1972, p. 8.

12. *El Mercurio*, March 1, 1973, p. 24.

13. *El Mercurio*, International Edition, February 12-18, 1973, p. 5.

14. *El Mercurio*, International Edition, February 12-18, 1973, p. 8; (March 28, 1973). Later estimates have raised that amount to $575 million.

15. *El Mercurio*, International Edition, April 16-22, 1973, p. 2.

16. On the permanence of the divisions in Chilean public opinion during a period in which the system as a whole has moved to the Left, see James W. Prothro's and Patricio Chaparro's "Chilean Public Opinion, 1952-72," in this volume.

5

The Chilean Labor Movement:

The Institutionalization of Conflict

Julio Samuel Valenzuela

The Chilean labor movement has a long tradition of struggle in favor of the socioeconomic demands of organized workers. The movement's history has been closely intertwined with various political groups, in particular the Communist and Socialist parties. Since these parties were the principal force behind the presidential candidacy of Salvador Allende in 1970, his success at the polls was interpreted as a victory for the workers. Labor leaders were assigned to important positions in the new government and replaced private business representatives in the administrative boards of some of the semiautonomous state agencies. A number of unions promoted the expropriation of their respective enterprises, thereby helping to accelerate the process of economic socialization. In times of crisis for the Popular Unity (Unidad Popular—UP) coalition, numerous unions served as a basis to mobilize workers in support of the government. Workers in the newly enlarged social sector of the economy, composed of industries under state control, were given a voice in management.

The position of industrial workers during the Allende government was not, however, without its ambiguities. The institutional mechanisms for worker participation in management were never fully established in the majority of the industries

The author wishes to thank Jacques Zylberberg and Arturo Valenzuela for their comments.

within the social sector. In many cases the opposition to these mechanisms of worker participation was led by the unions, since their leaders feared a displacement of their traditional functions or feared that workers associated to a different political party would be elected to the administrative council.[1] Even in those cases in which the workers did select their representatives to the enterprise's administrative council, the usual union structures remained intact and their leaders continued to pursue "vindicationist" goals.[2] As in the private sector of the economy, workers retained the right to petition for wage increases and to declare strikes. Unions zealously guarded their members' benefits and prerogatives, declaring work stoppages whenever they felt these were threatened.

The Communist and Socialist parties had in the past supported and even encouraged the unions' socioeconomic demands. In so doing, they had become an essential component in the relative success of the workers' vindicationist pursuits. Therefore, unionists had every reason to expect that a government of the Left would decree higher wages and social security benefits. These expectations were fulfilled during the Popular Unity's first year in office; it applied a short-term policy to reactivate the economy by increasing demand, and to strengthen the coalition's relatively tenuous political support among the lower strata.[3] However, partly as a consequence of this increased demand, numerous economic dislocations (including a very high rate of inflation) occurred during 1972 and 1973. Consequently, the administration began to give more restrictive wage increases, although they still equalled the rise of the official price index. The opposition parties quickly seized the opportunity to obtain political advantages from the tensions which developed between some unions and the government as the former pursued economic demands in excess of official guidelines.

The most noteworthy example of union-government tensions occurred during the April 19-July 2, 1973, strike at El Teniente copper mine. Wage readjustment law no. 17,713 had increased all September 30, 1972, salaries by an amount commensurate with the steep rise in prices. Since El Teniente miners had a unique arrangement by which their salaries had already been raised to partially compensate for inflation, the government decided that to grant the copper workers a "readjustment over the readjustment" would be unfair. Therefore, it deducted the previously anticipated amount from the increase provided by law. The unions, pointing to a literal reading of the law's transitory article 1, clause P, declared that the administration's action was illegal and demanded full payment. When the special conciliation board for the copper industry sided with the government, the miners voted to strike.[4] The opposition parties and press supported the miners by organizing solidarity campaigns in all major cities. Former El Teniente union officials in government service faced the difficult tasks of negotiating with the strikers and maintaining order in the city of Rancagua, the scene of frequent demonstrations. The issue was finally settled, largely in favor of the administration's position, in the wake of the abortive June 29, 1973, military coup. During the 76-day strike, Chile lost critically needed foreign-exchange income.

The purpose of this chapter is to provide the necessary background for an understanding of the role of Chilean labor during the Allende government. Accordingly, it sketches relevant aspects of the labor movement's history; examines union structures, goals and labor-management relations; and discusses the ties that existed between unions and political parties in Chile's highly competitive political arena.

A final introductory comment on the membership of Chilean unions is necessary. By 1972, approximately 30 percent of the active labor force was unionized[5] in basically four types of organizations: the industrial, craft and peasant unions, and the associations of public employees. Industrial and craft unions were legalized in 1924, while peasant unions have legally existed since 1967.[6] Public employee associations, in so far as they function as unions, remain outside the legal framework. In 1972 roughly 65 percent of all unionists were affiliated to the Central Unica de Trabajadores (Central Workers' Federation—CUT).[7]

This chapter focuses on industrial unions, since they were the most representative urban blue-collar organization. Affiliation in this union was legally required of all *obreros* (in general, blue-collar workers) in an enterprise once a majority of 55 percent had agreed to its formation.[8] A 1967 survey revealed a high degree of rank-and-file participation in union meetings: 55

percent of the workers interviewed always attended; 11 percent attended frequently; 17 percent attended sometimes; 2 percent never attended.[9] Each year the union membership elected five union officers to the directorate by secret ballot. The directorate in turn chose the union president, secretary and treasurer from among their number. Union leaders usually continued their regular work in the enterprise and were rarely paid for time dedicated to union activity. A profit-sharing scheme provided industrial unions with their major source of income; dues were also deducted from workers' salaries. Roughly 70 percent of the labor force in industries with more than 25 workers (the legal minimum for forming an industrial union) were unionized.[10]

THE "SOCIAL QUESTION" AND THE 1924 ENACTMENT OF LABOR LEGISLATION

> Is it possible to speak of "apolitical trade-unionism"—or of direct action in search of purely economic gains—when even the smallest worker vindication clashes with the whole society, confronting the combined forces of employer and state?
> —Leitmotif of the periodical *Justicia*, official organ of the Chilean Communist party and Labor Federation in the 1920s.

As in other latitudes, the "social question" came to occupy a prominent place in the concerns of the dominant sectors of the nation around the turn of the century. Labor conflicts which prompted this new concern had become more frequent. Between 1849 and 1884, historians of the workers' movement have documented only nine major strikes. By contrast, from 1885 to 1910 there were 290 and from 1911 to 1925 their number increased to 747.[11] The abandonment of the worksite was, of course, only a last resort. If brief work stoppages and other incidents are included, the number of labor conflicts increases considerably. For instance, in the nine-year period between 1891 and 1900, there were 18 major strikes[12] but approximately 300 labor disputes and street incidents involving workers pressing their demands.[13] Many of these strikes and protests were violently repressed by the police and armed forces.[14] The most serious incident took place in December 1907 in the northern port of Iquique where, according to some estimates, over 2,000 striking miners and their families were shot to death by the army.[15]

Occasionally, these strikes had a serious economic impact which highlighted their importance. The Chilean economy was heavily dependent on the export sector which furnished foreign exchange for the acquisition of vital consumer items and capital goods. The main exports were mineral products, principally saltpeter. For instance, in 1904 (a typical year), 88 percent of all export earnings were derived from mineral sales and 74 percent of the total came from nitrate exports alone.[16] Moreover, a high percentage of the revenues of the state were generated by taxation of the export trade.[17] Forty-seven percent of all strikes between 1885 and 1910 occurred in the nitrate-rich northern-most area of the country.[18] They involved saltpeter, railroad, dock and maritime workers who were clearly, as Adolfo Gurrieri and Francisco Zapata have pointed out, "in the axis of the national economic system." [19]

Between 1911 and 1925, the spark of worker discontent spread from the isolated north to the center of the nation. The number of strikes in the nitrate region shrunk to 30.9 percent of the total, while the Santiago-Valparaíso area accounted for 40.4 percent.[20] This process was aided by the migration of miners and labor leaders, the latter forced to relocate frequently because of black-listing by local employers.

The living conditions of urban workers were especially difficult due to the wide fluctuations in employment opportunities. For example, Gurrieri and Zapata indicate that the number of manufacturing establishments decreased during the 1910-15 depression from 5,722 to 2,406, with a corresponding reduction in the number of employed personnel from 74,618 to 45,551.[21] Migration from rural areas compounded the over-supply of labor, contributing to an actual reduction in wages.[22] It was not surprising that the militancy of the mining areas was quickly emulated across the country; the adept organizational efforts of the early labor leaders found a sympathetic reception among urban workers. Thus, by 1920, the Federación Obrera de Chile (Chilean Worker's Federation—FOCh), founded in 1909, represented "80 percent of all the organized workers in Chile" with estimates of membership figures of over 100,000.[23]

The eruption of the worker's movement was a serious defiance of the prevailing social order. Laborers were not expected to formulate demands and much less to pursue them through concerted action; their organizations and activities were neither legal nor considered legitimate. The dominant sectors viewed with particular alarm that leaders of the new labor movement espoused socialist and anarchist ideals. Commenting on a railroad strike in 1907, the National Agricultural Society noted with distress that it was "brought on by subversives and professional agitators who 'today slip into the unions to anarchize and exploit them.' " The Society blamed management for not taking the "elementary precaution of eliminating from its shops those pernicious elements who upset worker tranquility and are the permanent cause of disorder and anarchy." [24] The conservative newspaper, *El Diario Ilustrado*, was wary of a 1919 legislative proposal to create plant unions. James Morris recounts the paper's argument: "Who could prevent plant unions from setting up federations and who could predict what the future 'spirit' of these organizations would be? Would this spirit be prudent and conservative or one of blind resistance and revolution?" [25]

The alarm expressed by dominant groups was not completely unwarranted. The labor movement consisted of more than a multiplicity of unionlike organizations. It was closely tied to the mushrooming working-class political parties intent on a radical transformation of society. The most important of these, the Socialist Workers party (Partido Obrero Socialista—POS), was founded in 1912 by the principal leader of FOCh, Luis Emilio Recabarren, a typographical worker. In 1921, despite the corruption of electoral procedures, POS succeeded in electing Recabarren and one of his associates to Congress.[26] A year later, POS changed its name to the Communist party (Partido Communista) when it joined—along with FOCh—the Third International. The labor movement also presented a challenge with its numerous periodicals. They analyzed the political situation, furnished information about labor activities in various parts of the country and disseminated socialist ideals.

Endless discussions in Congress, the press, universities and professional and employer associations were devoted to analysis of the "social question" and the means to resolve the problems it raised.[27] There was widespread agreement on the necessity of eliminating the "agitators" from union ranks. However, there were disagreements on the means to accomplish this end. Reformers stressed the need to legislate some benefits for the working class, since the "agitators" took advantage of precarious living conditions. They argued that this should be done to promote social justice, to put Chilean legislation in line with the recommendations of international conferences on labor and within the spirit of the *Rerum Novarum* encyclical. Reformers also stressed that blue-collar organizations should be permitted to exist for legally specified ends. As liberal President Arturo Alessandri noted, it was counterproductive to continue to repress them: "It converts public associations, which live under the light of day and are subject directly or indirectly to the vigilance of the State, into secret associations living in shadows and mystery at the margins of common laws; sooner or later, they turn into permanent conspirators against social and public order."[28] Conservatives retorted that these laws would not terminate strikes, demonstrations and disruptions and that they were unsuitable under Chilean conditions.

Conservative opposition to legislative measures designed to improve the living conditions of the working class subsided when agriculture and commerce were exempted from regulation. Welfare provisions were then approved in Congress without much difficulty. Agreement was more elusive on the key question of union structures. Once a majority of the legislators accepted the necessity of granting unions legal recognition, there were disagreements on the specific forms the workers' organizations should take. Although there was consensus on the propriety of placing them under strict state supervision and of restricting their bargaining power, liberals favored craft while conservatives preferred plant unionism. Both types of union structures were finally included in the labor legislation package approved under military pressure in September 1924. The laws which were then enacted became the basis for Chile's industrial relations system.

THE LEGAL APPARATUS, UNION STRUCTURES AND LABOR MANAGEMENT RELATIONS.

It is my pleasure to inform you that this labor inspection office has authorized the Wagner Stein union of Tomé to withdraw from its savings account number 133373 the sum of 738.38 Escudos.

—Letter from a local labor inspection office to a branch of the State Bank, January 24, 1967.

Definitions of Union Goals

In peremptory terms, article 367 of the labor code indicates that "unions formed in accordance to the provisions of this title will be institutions of mutual collaboration between the factors which contribute to production and, therefore, the organizations whose procedures impede discipline and order in work will be considered contrary to the spirit and norms of the law." [29] It is obvious that any union action leading to a socialist transformation—thereby removing "one of the factors contributing to production"—is contrary to the intent of the code.

Referring to the permissible goals of plant unions, article 387 indicates:

The aims of industrial unions are:
(1) To draw up collective work contracts with the enterprise and to press for the fulfillment of rights contained in those contracts in favor of the workers . . . ;
(2) To represent the workers in the exercise of the rights which emanate from individual labor contracts, when the interested parties so demand it;
(3) To represent the workers in collective labor conflicts, especially, in case of conciliation and arbitration;
(4) To organize mutual aid programs complementing social security laws; to create stores for consumption by members, to construct clinics, mausoleums, and halls for shows . . . ;
(5) To install industrial or professional schools and popular libraries;
(6) To organize cooperatives. Production cooperatives will only be permitted when the aim is to produce articles which are different from those made by the respective enterprise; and
(7) In general, to tend to the cultural, solidarity, cooperation

and social security ends which the members agree to and which are determined in the statutes.

The union is thus designed to redress the rightful grievances of its members and to petition management (clauses 1, 2 and 3). It is also characterized as an organization with social welfare and security aims (clauses 4, 5, 6 and 7), albeit in a direction not injurious to the interests of the enterprise (clause 6).

As a result of the legislature's efforts to restrict the bargaining power of unions, article 388 prohibits the use of funds for "any activity which directly or indirectly damages the interests of the respective enterprise," and article 632 proscribes labor federations from declaring strikes.

Did union leaders pursue goals that contrasted sharply with those permitted by the labor code? A survey of nearly all union presidents of the principal industries conducted in 1962 requested them to single out their first, second and third choices of *long-range* goals from a list of previously prepared options. The results are presented in Table 1.[30]

The objectives of union presidents were reasonably congruent with those of the labor code.[31] The goal which most violated the spirit of the law, namely, that of elevating the political consciousness of the workers, received a negligible number of preferences. The first and overriding concern of the labor leaders, that of obtaining economic betterment, is permitted by clause 3 of article 367 cited above. The preoccupation with elevating the moral and educational level of the workers was also a recurrent theme in the legislation. The goal of producing more worker unity and greater unionist consciousness was somewhat at odds with the intent of the labor code. The legislators, as noted earlier, attempted to create weak union structures. Nonetheless, in general, the desire for greater union strength was aimed at fulfilling goals which were perfectly legal.

Unions also operated, in conformity with the code's dispositions, as social security and welfare agencies for their members. They administered subsidies in case of sickness, disability, old age, forcible unemployment or death; they had special arrangements for medical and dental care at reduced rates. Larger unions sponsored mother's clubs, furnishing sewing machines and

TABLE 1

Long-Range Objectives of Union Presidents

Percentage Preferences in Order of Priority (%)

Objectives	First	Second	Third	Total
Economic Betterment	62	9	5	76
Better working conditions	1	6	11	18
Higher moral and educational level for workers	8	23	15	46
Unity of the union movement	10	19	14	43
Greater unionist consciousness	6	15	15	36
More weight for the union in the industry	5	12	9	26
Political consciousness in the workers	1	4	5	10
Social activities	1	1	7	9
Union influence in the community	6	11	19	36

100 (230) 100 (230) 100 (228)

preparing educational activities; formed cooperatives to purchase appliances; established sports clubs, barber shops and so on. However, given the small size of most Chilean unions,[32] a large majority did not have the resources to function effectively in that respect.

Finally, with very few exceptions in which there was mutual agreement between labor and management, industrial labor federations did not engage in collective bargaining. This task was restricted to the multiplicity of plant unions which proliferated throughout the country.

State Controls Over Union Activities

To insure close observance of legal provisions and limitations, special state labor inspection offices were created to exert strict control over unions. The following analysis is based on a detailed study of the actual operation of one labor-inspection office with 43 unions under its jurisdiction, among which are three large unions connected with important textile firms.

In the first place, the state exercised the strictest control over union finances. Unions had to deposit their funds in the closest branch of the state bank and were not entitled to have much cash on hand (article 395). They had to request authorization for withdrawals from the labor inspectorate in order to meet virtually all expenses. This measure was partly intended to prevent violations of the prohibition contained in article 388, cited above. Thus, unions had no recourse to their own funds for strike purposes.[33] The request for fund-withdrawal authorization had to be accompanied by a detailed explanation regarding its intended use, documentation on the state of accounts and receipts for previous expenses. Prior to granting permission for funds, the labor inspectorate had to approve the yearly budget and all fund requests had to conform closely to it. When the budget was larger than a certain sum specified under Labor Ministry guidelines, it was sent for approval to the General Labor Inspection Office in Santiago. Moreover, article 383 indicated that unions had to furnish any other information requested of them by the labor inspectorate.

Second, each union section had to adopt by-laws which were to be submitted to the labor inspection office for ratification. Even small unions were forced to comply with this legal requirement. For example, a September 9, 1965 letter from the labor inspectorate reminded the officers of a 57-member union that they should promptly send the internal statutes for (a) viatica for union leaders, (b) medical services, (c) sports, (d) various activities and (e) sickness subsidies. Since this was the second time these documents had been requested, the letter concluded by warning union leaders that "if on this occasion there is no compliance with these instructions the relevant sanctions will be levied against those who are responsible."[34]

These internal union statutes corresponded quite closely with general legal dispositions. For instance, the Internal Statute of Aid and Social Security of one of the large textile unions indicated in its third article: "no aid can be given to those members who lose their jobs for not meeting the terms of their contracts, for bad conduct or because of an illegal strike, and in general, for the causes indicated in the . . . Labor Code." Thus, if a worker was fired for insulting a superior (law 16,455, article 2, clause 2) he or she could not receive unemployment compensation drawn from union funds.

Labor inspection officials also controlled union elections. The union first sent the list of candidates designated by the assembly of members to the labor inspectorate, where the position of each candidate on the ballot was drawn by lot.[35] During the election itself, the inspectors screened the voters and counted the votes in the presence of the interested parties. To be valid, all ballots cast had to bear the labor inspector's signature.[36]

Labor Management Relations

Labor legislation established an elaborate set of procedures to be followed during labor conflicts. The process to declare a legal strike was a case in point. Workers were allowed to petition management for a new collective contract when the old one expired (usually after a year), or to raise new points not covered in the contract in force. The petition had to be presented in writing to the employer within 24 hours of its approval by majority vote in a union assembly in which at least two-thirds of the membership was present (article 592 and *Dictamen*[37] number 4 of article 590). The employer could then no longer fire workers without labor court permission (article 596). After 48 hours, if no agreement had been signed between the parties, the dispute had to be presented to a special council, the Junta de Conciliación, for the compulsory process of conciliation (articles 609 and 597). These boards existed in every department of the Republic; special ones were also created for certain industries. They were composed of seven individuals: three employers, two workers, one white collar employee and the highest-ranking labor inspector in the department who acted as president. Junta members were drawn each year by lot from lists furnished by unions and employer associations. The *gobernador*,[38] in whose offices the selections were made, had considerable power to appoint substitute and regular members if the various lists were not made available.[39] Since the juntas were often paralyzed because of three-to-three ties, a 1967 law gave the labor inspector the right to vote.[40] Thus, the inspector's role was a crucial one.[41]

The importance of the juntas lay principally in the fact that they examined and judged the legality of petitions presented by the workers.[42] The strategy of the employers usually was to deny that union grievances and demands conformed to the strictures of the law. Thus, a worker representative had to be well versed in the intricacies of labor legislation in order to successfully defend the union's case. If the junta decided that a petition lacked merit, the union was barred from declaring a legal strike.[43]

The Junta de Conciliación had 15 days in which to reach an agreement satisfactory to both parties (article 609). If such an accord was not reached, the dispute could be submitted—if both parties were willing—to binding arbitration by a tribunal of one to three members designated by mutual consent (articles, 617, 619, 620 and 625). This procedure, however, was rarely used. Unions had 20, or if the junta so decided, up to 50 days to declare a legal strike (*Reglamento* 839, and law 16464 of 1966). The strike had to be voted favorably by a majority of the workers in a secret vote in which at least two-thirds of the membership participated. An officer from the junta was required to oversee the election. If any of these procedures were not strictly followed, the strike could be declared illegal. Thus, before the labor inspector was allowed to vote on the junta many unions had to delay the declaration of a strike because board members could not agree on sending a representative to observe the union election.[44] If a strike was legally proclaimed, the union assembly had to nominate a committee of five workers to inform it of the development of the negotiations, to represent it before management and to call its meetings to declare an end to the conflict (article 627).[45]

Though a large number of labor conflicts took the form of "legal strikes," there were between two and four times as many "illegal strikes" than legal ones in any given year.[46] The high incidence of illegal strikes might suggest that the industrial relations system was only loosely institutionalized and that labor legislation played only a small part in these conflicts. In fact, most illegal strikes followed elaborate and well-established routines in which the legal apparatus played a prominent role.

Furthermore, very few illegal strikes pursued goals that were not permitted by the provisions of the labor law.[47]

The term "illegal" strike is actually quite misleading because unions did have, in most instances, a strong legal case on their side. As Jorge Barría indicates, labor legislation presumed that the union was responsible for overseeing management compliance with legal dispositions and agreements.[48] However, if the company did violate any laws or agreements, the only legal recourse the union had was to file a complaint with the labor inspector. He in turn could only publicize the violation (article 616), or institute time consuming court action which could eventually result in a small fine (articles 554 and 555).[49] The union could not initiate the process to declare a legal strike, since the Junta de Conciliación would not classify a violation of labor laws or contracts as a rightful cause for it.[50] Labor legislation consequently provided no effective and legal recourse for a union to insure management's compliance. The union's only alternative was to declare a strike, which would automatically be classified as illegal because it did not conform exactly to the procedures delineated in the labor code. Many strikes of this nature occurred in response to management violations.[51] The probability of union success in these cases was considerably enhanced by the solidity of the legal arguments it could present in defense of its actions.

In other instances, illegal strikes resulted from worker displeasure with management innovations in work routines, scheduling, dismissal of employees and so on. In preparation for these conflicts, both union and management carefully considered the legal arguments in defense of their respective positions. This point is illustrated by the following letters, exchanged between the parties in a large textile industry in anticipation of a confrontation. Due to peculiarities in the scheduling of shifts, some employees of the firm would work 46 hours a week instead of the legal 48. Management decided to force them to work the extra two hours. The union assembly voted against accepting the change. In an August 5, 1968 letter, the union leadership communicated the workers' decision to management:

According to the debate, this determination was taken due to the fact that the present 46 hour week has been in force ever since the shift system was introduced in the enterprise. Moreover, the Dictámenes of the Dirección General del Trabajo and the verbal and written statements of the Ministers of Labor and Social Welfare themselves—determine that all perquisites and benefits in favor of the workers which have been established in writing, verbally, through arbitration or simply by mutual consent and which have been in force for years, will become a part of the set of perquisites and benefits which are established with the enterprise, since they are to be considered an acquired right of the workers.

The company answered in a letter dated three days later:

We think you should take into account the following considerations . . .

1. You have been informed of the situation in which the enterprise finds itself. It requires, if there is interest in its subsistence, the adoption of all measures which will lead to greater productivity and efficiency.

To struggle for the subsistence of the enterprise is to struggle for the maintenance of a source of employment. To oppose legal, logical and rational measures is to undermine that source of employment.

2. The work schedule which you refuse to accept is the most rational; the proof is that most industries in Chile that work with shifts have established it to the full conformity of their workers.

3. The refusal to work the 48-hour week without logical grounds nor legal backing of any type is a determination which harms the enterprise and the workers. The enterprise because it eliminates the possibility of greater production, and the workers because it deprives them of a 4.35% raise in their salaries. . . .

It is not easy to understand a position of this nature. The workers always like to earn more, but in this case they do not wish to when they could. What is worse, they refuse to work the required number of hours. . . .

4. We must warn the workers affected by this measure that their non-compliance will result in our taking the necessary legal measures.

The workers took a position which they believed carried legal weight. The enterprise not only pointed out that its proposed changes were legal, but also indicated that they followed a well-established Chilean norm.

Since local labor inspectors invariably received their instructions from the appropriate authorities in the capital, the nature of government policy was important in determining the outcome of strikes in which it was not clear which side had a more lawful case. The matter became one of interpretation. The labor inspector handling the dispute over work schedules found fault on both sides. In his detailed report to the General Office of Labor, he wrote:

> The undersigned wishes to indicate that all the affected workers are hired on an hourly basis, and that, therefore, by working 46 hours they only receive payment for their production during this period; if they work two more hours, they would produce more and therefore augment their salaries in the same proportion. If the employees had worked 46 hours and received payment for 48 hours, there would undoubtedly be a case of acquired rights, but this is not so. In any event it is proper to also consider the fact that the principal responsibility in this matter rests with the enterprise, since it should not have permitted and maintained for several years an irregular work system.

Officials in the Labor Office instructed the inspector to side with management in this particular case.[52]

Since negotiations to resolve these conflicts were dominated by the parties' defense of the greater legality and propriety of their respective positions, the unions had an inherent disadvantage: the illegal nature of the strike itself. It undermined the workers' attempt to put the full weight of the shared normative system in their favor. It also constituted grounds for a court authorization to fire the union leadership (*Jurisprudencia* number 1 attached to article 627). This was an effective tool which management could use in its favor, as the textile firm did in the case in point. However, if the workers had a strong legal position, the judge could deny the firm's request.

The declaration of a strike and its duration depended partly on management's calculations of the losses it would suffer relative to the cost of settling the issues in the workers' favor. During illegal strikes, it was particularly important for a union to insure that the enterprise suffered the greatest possible economic loss, since labor code provisions prohibiting management from continuing operations were applicable only to legal strikes, and the union leadership was vulnerable to dismissal. For these reasons, a union would occasionally decide to take over the installations of the enterprise. It could then immobilize the marketable stock and disrupt the work of executives and of other employees affiliated to unions which were not on strike. It could also insure that the industry did not hire strikebreakers, and that union members would not be tempted to disobey the decision to strike. During a takeover, workers normally took pains not to damage equipment, since this would constitute a serious offense which could undermine the legal basis of their bargaining position. In some cases, the police or the army were ordered to dislodge the workers. Despite the widespread routinization of labor-management relations, the recent history of the labor movement had included incidents of violence, imprisonment and even death.

To sum up, the following characteristics constituted the principal features of the Chilean industrial relations system:

1. The importance of labor legislation—it not only delineated the internal organization of labor unions but had also become a shared normative standard to which both workers and management appealed during all labor conflicts.

2. The preponderance of the state—the courts, the Congress and, most importantly, the executive branch of government were crucial actors within the system. This is hardly surprising, given the importance of labor legislation. The courts and the executive applied and interpreted it; the Congress had a role in reforming it. Moreover, through the network of labor inspectorates the executive exercised a series of strict (but well-defined) controls over the unions, oversaw management's compliance with labor laws and mediated in all labor conflicts. It could also order the use of legitimate force. Given the importance of the executive's role, a change of administration could produce noticeable changes in the industrial-relations system. However, all administrations were bound to act within its general legal framework, which bore

the imprint of the correlation of political forces at the time of its enactment.

3. The multiplicity of closely controlled labor unions engaged in separate collective bargaining. The most important form of blue-collar organization was the plant union, and labor federations were prohibited from representing their members at the bargaining table. Therefore, Chilean unionism consisted mainly of many small associations with, given their size and lack of control over their own resources, little power of their own.

The following section analyzes the historical process that led to the implementation of the 1924 labor laws, and therefore, to the constitution of this industrial relations system.

THE HISTORICAL PROCESS OF WORKER INTEGRATION TO THE LEGAL APPARATUS

It is the proletariat . . . by virtue of its organizational activities which makes the bourgeoisie enact laws to satisfy many social needs. The bourgeoisie has never made these reforms on its own. Why should it then be said that social reforms are nothing? That they are mere scraps of food *[piltrafas]* thrown at the workers? They are created by virtue of the revolutionary activities of the working class.
—From an article by a leader of the FOCh, *Justicia*, November 27, 1924, refering to the 1924 reforms

The ultimate goal of most labor leaders in the first two decades of this century was the total restructuring of society. And yet, the great majority of strikes that occurred during that period were aimed exclusively at obtaining better salaries and working conditions.[53] The concern was with particular, albeit highly beneficial, reforms. Furthermore, despite the fact that the most prominent labor leaders rejected the possibility of attaining full social justice through the legislative process,[54] in its day to day activities the FOCh pressured Congress to pass laws that would benefit the working class. Numerous articles published in *Justicia*, the official organ of both the Communist party and FOCh, stressed the importance of the congressional arena. For instance, referring to the imminent enactment of a law which would proscribe night work in bakeries, Carlos Lafferte, a prominent FOCh leader, wrote that "our organization obtains a victory after ten years of struggle." [55]   FOCh's demand for the law had brought criticism from an anarchist publication which claimed that the law would be worthless and that changes could be attained only "through revolution." In a commentary published along with Lafferte's article, a bakery worker affiliated to FOCh responded by saying that: "This is an urgent matter. We want it soon. And we try to obtain it through the only viable means we presently have: through law and authoritarian coercion." FOCh's early organizational success was undoubtedly due to its ability to focus on the workers' most pressing demands.

Since it regulated working conditions, established the 48-hour week, provided social security benefits and minimum wages, obliged employers to prepare work contracts and so on, the 1924 legislation contained many provisions which were beneficial to the workers.[56] Luis Víctor Cruz, who assumed a major role in FOCh after Recabarren's death in December 1924, attributed them to the pressure of the organized working class:

> Social reforms are nothing but the fruit of the revolutionary activities of the proletariat. The bourgeoisie never make a single social law which would ameliorate even partially the situation of the working class, if it had not felt the pressure of proletarian strength . . . .[57]

Although FOCh's initial reaction to the creation of labor courts and authorities (and by inference, to the control of union activities) was negative,[58] Cruz later argued that the workers should make use of the union structures envisioned by the reforms. On March 30, 1925, *Justicia* reported a speech given by Cruz in which he "analyzed the recently enacted laws, especially those dealing with industrial unions . . . [and] called on the workers to take the greatest possible advantage of the new laws, since the proletariat does not have the necessary strength to impose its absolute and total emancipation from the bourgeoisie." He argued that both the profit-sharing scheme and the legalization of unions and their activities promised greater security to the workers' organizations. The former provided a stable source of funding and the latter would go a long way to help end repression. Cruz further realized that since membership in the plant union was made compulsory, many more workers could be brought into the labor movement. The FOCh congress which convened in December 1925 endorsed most of Cruz's views.[59]

In the short run, Cruz proved to be much too optimistic. Under President Carlos Ibáñez's (1927-31), semidictatorial rule, legal unions were created for the sole purpose of providing political support to his government. The FOCh was disbanded. Its leaders were jailed or exiled, its presses and headquarters confiscated or destroyed. At the same time, Ibáñez created an officially controlled labor federation in an effort to gain complete control of the labor movement. It is thus not surprising that, after Ibáñez was forced out of office, the crippled FOCh called for the immediate abolition of the "Fascist" labor code. Referring to the legal unions, *Justicia* editorialized wryly:

> It would be erroneous to believe that violence has been the only means by which Ibáñez and the bourgeoisie fought the working class and its vanguard; there were other methods of more dismal consequences for the workers . . . . We refer to labor legislation, to the laws and the vast network of legal, fascist and police unions conceived by Alessandri and implemented by Ibáñez . . . .

> But let us not be deceived. Unfortunately the fascist unions . . . still have strength, and what is even graver, the ideological venom inculcated by the bourgeoisie of "peace between the classes" and the "equitable justice" provoked by the conciliation tribunals still remains in the minds of the workers.[60]

With the demise of the Ibáñez regime, his labor organization collapsed and the labor movement was left with no numerically important central organization. The FOCh was able to muster representation from only 25 *consejos* (councils) for a meeting in August 1931, a far cry from the convention of 1925 which had representatives from 127 *consejos*.[61] The anarchists, who had also suffered persecution, attempted to revive their movement under a new name. The legal unions, in turn, proceeded to organize two new federations aimed at pursuing the restricted objectives allowed under the labor code. The organized workers were thus deeply divided.

The proclamation in 1932 of a "Socialist republic" by a group of military officers and prominent civilians opened a new chapter in the history of the labor movement. The new government raised the hopes of a people suffering the consequences of the devastating economic depression. It was supported by all kinds of unions, professional and white-collar worker associations, student organizations and political parties with middle- and working-class constituencies. Pro-government committees were spontaneously organized across the country. The following telegram sent from a small town to the capital captures the flavor of the times:

> Governing Junta, Santiago. The Revolutionary Committee of Penco was formed agreeing to adhere to the present Governing Junta and to fight with it until death for the advancement of socialist ideals. Revolutionary Committee.[62]

Even though the Socialist Republic was short-lived (June 4-16, 1932), it was soon to be considered a period of "transcendental historical importance for the working class." [63] The overthrow of the government by a right-wing coup turned the leaders of the frustrated experiment into instant heroes for a large sector of the populace.[64] It is thus not surprising that when these leaders founded the Socialist party of Chile, the party soon acquired strong support in the working class. Its militants easily took over leadership positions in a majority of the country's legal unions, since workers within them realized the importance of having outside political and organizational support. The Communist and anarchist movements could not provide the same support because of their general unwillingness to accept labor-code procedures. To further strengthen their position in the labor movement the Socialists created a new labor federation in 1934, which called for the "collective or common ownership of the instruments of production and exchange." [65] Much to the distress of government authorities and employers, leftist leaders began to make serious inroads into legal unionism.

FOCh accepted the Socialist call for unity[66] of the labor movement in 1935, after the Communist International encouraged the formation of coalitions of progressive parties and groups to combat fascism. The ensuing creation of the Confederación de Trabajadores de Chile (Chilean Workers Confederation—CTCh) in 1936 brought together most blue- and white-collar federations. CTCh soon became the organized worker's arm of the Popular Front coalition formed by the Radical, Democratic, Socialist and Communist parties. This coalition succeeded in electing a Radical senator to the presidency of Chile in 1938.

The labor movement identified closely with the new Popular Front government. It was given representation on key political committees as well as government agencies.[67] This close cooperation led to a widespread implementation of the 1924 labor legislation.[68] The administration encouraged the creation of new unions in conformity with legal provisions, and many "free" unions sought state recognition. The negative aspects of extensive state control over the unions were offset by government interpretations of the labor code favoring the workers.[69] Abiding by the legal precepts had definite advantages, as Cruz had foreseen. His interpretations of social reforms were revived.[70] This was not surprising, since in the wake of the depression, many of the benefits enacted to separate workers from "agitators" had not been implemented. The platform of the Popular Front coalition called for their immediate implementation, lending credence to Cruz's notion that "social reforms are ours, they belong to us, they are products of our revolutionary sacrifices." [71]

The full incorporation of unionism into the legal apparatus occurred, therefore, during an administration in which the Communist and Socialist parties participated. The integration of leftist labor leaders to this apparatus resulted in its legitimation. Labor legislation was no longer to be perceived as an instrument of fascism, a tool of the bourgeoisie, but rather as a series of complicated procedures containing some beneficial and some negative aspects for the workers. The task of the labor movement was to perfect it by means of congressional action.

POLITICAL STRUCTURES AND UNIONISM

> Congress is a battle trench; that is where laws benefiting the
> workers are made.
> —Luis Figueroa, Congressman and President of the Central
> Labor Federation, quoted in *El Sur*, July 10, 1970.

It is not surprising that the labor movement of the first two
decades of the 20th century gave rise to working-class parties
dedicated to radical transformation of society. Organized
workers' militant actions in the pursuit of economic and social
improvement represented a type of conflict which was not
permissible under existing normative frameworks, and which
shattered the expectations of compliance and subservience
associated with the workers' role. Thus, despite the fact that
union demands were, as indicated above, of a purely vindicationist nature, they represented in themselves a defiance of the
social order. As *Justicia*'s leitmotif indicated, worker vindications
clashed "with the whole society," a perception that was
reinforced by the constant repression of the labor movement by
state authorities. Since the sociopolitical system had no channels
for the presentation and implementation of worker demands,
many labor leaders were led to embrace maximalist ideologies.
The obtainment of concrete benefits appeared possible only after
the realization of drastic macro-societal change. As was asserted
in 1904, "socialism is the only ... system capable of giving ...
workers the welfare and security which they lack today." [72]
The integration of industrial unionism to the legal apparatus
undermined the earlier bridge between a vindicationist and a
revolutionary consciousness among the workers. The 1924 labor
legislation incorporated the specific socioeconomic demands of
workers to the range of the normatively permissible and created
procedures for channeling them. It also set up the elaborate
control system which contributed to the maintenance of
unionism in the pursuit of lawful goals. With this alteration of the
normative apparatus, the satisfaction of the workers' vindicationist aspirations did not have to be postponed until a total
restructuring of society. The 1904 assertion could, therefore, be
substituted for the leitmotif of a 1967 union publication stating

that "the labor union is the tool which forges worker welfare." [73] The raising of the membership's "political consciousness" could hence become a low-priority goal of union leaders. The fulfillment of union objectives did not necessarily lead to a confrontation with the overall system, but became another one of its uneasy conflict-ridden parts. Given their vindicationist objectives, the workers could herald, following Cruz, the establishment of legal unionism and its related procedures as their victory.

Despite appearances to the contrary stemming from a tendency to shroud trade-unionist conflicts in Marxist terminology, the existence of a revolutionary consciousness was, by the end of the 1960s, a minority phenomenon among Chilean workers. The Central Unica de Trabajores'[74] principle that "the capitalist regime should be replaced by an economic and social system which abolishes private property" was, for example, rejected by 66.7 percent of a 1968 sample of 448 industrial workers.[75] The same survey asked workers to choose the slogan with which they agreed the most from a list of options. The resulted are contained in Table 2.[76]

TABLE 2

Slogans Selected by a Sample of Industrial Workers (1968)

There is no other country like Chile	4.1%
Chile needs a strong leader	21.7%
Chile needs changes and progressive reforms	60.4%
Chile needs a genuine revolution, violent if necessary	13.3%
No answer	0.5%
N:442	100.0%

A majority of the workers chose the reformist option. The rightwing slogan ("the country needs a strong leader") received nearly twice as many preferences as the revolutionary alternative.

While the incorporation of the workers into legal unionism reaffirmed the particularistic nature of their activities and consciousness, it did not end the close connection between unions and political parties. These links were maintained partly because unions and the industrial-relations system were strongly affected by government and congressional decisions. The manner in which the authorities handled illegal strikes had decisive influence on their outcome.[77] Executive representatives at the local level determined to a considerable extent, as noted earlier, the composition of the *Juntas de Conciliación* which assessed the legality of union petitions. The executive also authorized the use of force against workers' demonstrations or occupations of enterprises. The administration's anti-inflationary policies had an important effect on the content and the success or failure of worker demands. Congress in turn discussed and approved wage readjustments, social security benefits, classifications of occupations in *empleado* or *obrero* (roughly, white or blue collar) categories, reforms of the labor code and other matters of direct concern to unions.

To have some control over the government and congressional measures affecting the workers' well-being, it was imperative for unions to seek the support of political parties. The latter could intercede before the executive branch and instruct their legislators to vote in favor of union interests on issues facing congressional action. In return, parties expected to receive electoral and other forms of support from the workers.

Union-party links were further reinforced by the structural characteristics of Chilean unions. As Alan Angell indicates, party support helped to compensate for the bargaining weakness of unionism imposed by labor-code provisions.[78] The financial restrictions made it imperative, for example, for unions to seek outside material aid, particularly food, during lengthy strikes.[79] The favorably inclined articles of a party's newspapers, the declarations of its congressmen and the door-to-door canvassing of its youthful militants were often essential to the success of a union's campaign for public support. Since financial restrictions limited the unions' capacity to hire legal counsel, they were dependent on parties and CUT for this essential service. On occasion, individual congressmen served in this capacity.

The partisanship of the union leadership was another important source of party-union ties. Ironically, this partisanship was partly the result of the importance of labor legislation for the regulation of labor-management relations and union activities.[80] The most effective union officers, hence, those with the greatest probability of re-election, were the ones who could readily obtain the legal advice provided by parties; independent union leaders were often forced to seek such legal support, thus establishing ties with one or another political group. Finally, since little reward accrued to union leaders by virtue of their position, many individuals sought union office out of party loyalty.[81] They responded to the efforts of Chilean parties to gain leadership control of the greatest possible number of associations.

The preceding observations provide some insights into the reasons for the maintenance of a close connection between political parties and blue-collar unionism in the post-Popular Front period. They do not clarify, however, why these ties were continued principally with Communists and Socialists. This is not to be expected necessarily given the vindicationist nature of most unions' goals. A brief reference to some features of the political system is necessary to clarify this question.

Chilean politics could be usefully conceptualized as being composed of an ideological and a clientelistic level.[82] The first was associated with national debates of a programmatic nature. The second pertained to the particularistic patterns by which socioeconomic benefits flowed to organized groups and to individuals. The nation's parties were associated closely with both tiers. On one hand, they were a fundamental source of ideological and programmatic debates reflecting view points which covered the full range of the political spectrum. On the other, they consituted a crucial linkage structure between the multiplicity of groups and individuals and the center of power.

It would have been impossible for a single party to establish clientelistic relationships with all groups. The weakness of the Chilean economy precluded giving even minimal satisfaction to all; moreover, some groups had objectively contradictory interests. Consequently, each party was associated roughly with different sections of the organized population. Proportional representation insured the electoral viability of a party's strategy of securing close links with a relatively narrow base.

It follows that the establishment of clientelistic linkages presupposed processes of mutual selection. By means of these processes the parties forged ties with certain groups occupying visibly different positions in the class structure. The Left's relationship to blue-collar unions, the Right's connections with employer associations, and the middle-of-the-road Radical party's traditional ties with teacher's organizations are notable examples. However, the overall clustering of clientelistic linkages along class lines was by no means clear cut. The intensity of electoral competition led the parties to attempt an expansion of their bases of support by establishing new clientelistic ties. This was done, first, by articulating new demands and interests. Party militants, for example, would mobilize a previously disorganized segment of the population in order to obtain a specific goal. A case in point: the homeless urban poor who were led by different parties to establish squatter settlements. Second, clientelistic ties were expanded by capturing the representation of the vindicationist demands of existing groups. This was done, for instance, by legislating certain benefits in a particularistic manner (typically in social security areas) or by presenting partisan slates of candidates in the internal elections of a wide variety of associations. As a result, similar organizations were often divided in their partisan attachments. These differential attachments offered convenient channels for a party in power to grant benefits which could not be given to all groups due to budgetary limitations. By the same token, since an electorally victorious party or coalition could not satisfy all the aspirations it aroused, opposition political groups were able to take advantage of the ensuing discontent to broaden their support. They hastened to organize demonstrations and petitions for groups whose socioeconomic demands had not been fulfilled.

Nonetheless, despite sporadic efforts by other parties, the majority of the nation's blue-collar unions remained attached to the Left since the Popular Front period. One reason for this lay in the fact that the Communist and Socialist parties were, by self-definition, of the working class. They therefore made a determined effort throughout the years to create workers' unions and to strengthen them organizationally. Their intervention in the original articulation of workers' demands and in the early formation of the labor movement created loyalties and a tradition of certain durability. Moreover, the Communist and, to a lesser extent, the Socialist parties recruited many of their members from union ranks.

Although undoubtedly important, the preceding explanation does not suffice. If the workers' material aspirations had been supported with greater effectiveness by non-leftist parties, the Communist and Socialist ties with the unions would have suffered regardless of the loyalties stemming from past experiences. This however, was not the case. The position of industrial workers in the social relations of production, and the underdeveloped conditions of the economy, made it virtually necessary for unions to receive support in their socioeconomic demands from a contestatory force. A party in favor of the private enterprise system could not grant all union demands and at the same time create adequate conditions for private capital accumulation. Moreover, a party in power had to insure the adequate operation of public enterprises, and had to draft anti-inflationary measures which were normally demand-restrictive. By contrast, the parties of the Left were able to give almost unconditional support to the workers' vindicationist aspirations. They had both a disregard for the rationality of private accumulation and were in the opposition for most of their existence. It is therefore not surprising that leftist labor leaders were more effective in obtaining better terms for the workers. They were able to press harder at the bargaining table, and received more efficient support from party sources. Since the weakness of the economy made low salaries for blue-collar workers the rule, a small difference in wage or benefit increases was of considerable importance for the basic necessities of life. Thus, it would have been difficult to convince the workers of the necessity for moderation in wage demands in order to maintain new investment levels or to hold the line on inflation. This was particularly the case since the nation's regressive income distribution—a virtual requirement to support the market for locally produced durable consumer goods—offered a visible and desirable model of a higher level of consumption. Hence, a party rejecting both the socioeconomic structures and in political opposition could capture union support with greater ease.

Despite the fact that the leftist parties' ideology (characterized, to repeat, by a rejection of the prevailing socioeconomic system) aided them in the maintenance of union connections, the latter served from a union's point of view simply as a means of obtaining specific benefits. In other words, the ties were primarily a peculiar type of clientelistic linkage not unlike those established elsewhere by other parties. It would therefore be an unwarranted confusion of both levels of politics to assume that the ties necessarily meant a worker commitment to support a program of macro-sociological transformations.[83] In fact, the existence of disparate expectations was a frequent cause of union-party tensions. The latter expected union officials to play a "political" role,[84] while the membership was principally interested in socioeconomic benefits (90 percent of union presidents interviewed in 1962 indicated that the unionists' first choice of long-range goal [see table 1] would be economic betterment). As Angell indicates, union leaders usually ended up subordinating party programs to the union's specific interests. The multiplicity and autonomy of union organizations made it difficult for parties to control each one closely; moreover, considering the existence of party competition within them, a partisan leader could not neglect vindicationist duties.[85]

The inauguration of the Popular Unity government produced little change in the relations between unions and the parties of the Left within the private sector of the economy. No new organizational structures were created at plant level which could substitute union functions, and the Left's support for the workers' material expectations continued as usual. In some cases the administration took advantage of these expectations in order to transfer certain industries to state control. This was done either by making their conditions of operation difficult, thereby inducing the industry's sale to the state or by promoting an illegal strike. Since the latter paralyzed the enterprise, the government could decree its temporary take over by declaring that the production of an essential consumer item had been interrupted.

The fact that the Left was no longer in opposition constituted, however, a potential source of friction with the vindicationist style of unionism. The Communist and Socialist parties had to insure the proper functioning of the social sector and were responsible for overall economic management. A series of official government newspaper editorials stressing the duties of the workers must be seen in this context. One such commentary asserted:

> Reference is often made to the "battle for production" . . . but the people do not fully comprehend the urgency and validity of this call. Thus we see that many workers persist in old "vindicationist" (*economicista*) conceptions. . . . To win the battle for production implies a change of mentality and, we would dare say, . . . of morality. To insure it, it is necessary to see work duties over rights. . . .[86]

The opposition attempted to increase its working-class base by taking advantage of this potential source of friction. It thus supported vindicationist demands in the social sector which the administration was unwilling to accept. The most significant example of the application of this strategy was the support it gave to El Teniente copper mine strike. Opposition legislators also proposed a bill in March 1973 which would increase wages every four months to compensate for the rise in the cost of living. Government spokesmen rejected it arguing that the inflationary spiral would be aggravated further if it were approved.[87] The roles had reversed: the Left was in these cases resisting vindicationist demands while the Right and Center gave them wholehearted support.

Nonetheless, the potential union-government friction remained for the most part latent. On the one hand, the workers did receive, as they expected, greater socioeconomic benefits and employment security. On the other hand, from past experiences they had developed relatively strong attachments to the Left and a distrust of the Right. It is thus not surprising that organized workers supported the Allende government when political pressures from the Right threatened it. While many workers did so out of a commitment to fundamental change, for most it was a question of defending an administration from which they expected to receive the greatest benefits.

NOTES

1. Fernando Castillo, Rafael Echeverría, and Jorge Larraín, "Las Masas, el Estado y el Problema del Poder en Chile," *Cuadernos de la Realidad Nacional*, no. 16 (September 1971):14-15.

2. The term *reivindicación*, translated here as "vindication" to conserve its special connotations, is used to refer to the economic and social demands of workers. It means literally "rightful redress of grievances" and its origins can be traced to procedures under Roman law.

3. For an analysis of this short-term economic strategy and its intended effect see Julio López, "La Estrategia Económica del Gobierno de la Unidad Popular," *Cuadernos de la Realidad Nactional*, no. 9 (September 1971):69-86.
The parties of the Left did not have majority support among all sectors of the lower strata. Traditionally their strongest support came from mining and industrial workers. For instance, a survey conducted just before the 1958 presidential elections, in which Allende almost received a plurality, revealed that 49.1 percent of the industrial workers in the sample indicated Allende as their preference while only 24.3 percent of nonindustrial workers did. International Data Library and Reference Service, Survey Research Center, University of California, Berkeley, 1958 Presidential Election Survey in Santiago, Chile. However, industrial workers comprised only about 20 percent of the active population.

4. For a summary explanation of the issue involved in the strike see *Chile Hoy*, vol 1, no. 52 (June 8-14, 1973):14.

5. Castillo, Etcheverría and Larraín, "Las Masas," p. 7.

6. For a discussion of these unions and the peasant movement in general see Brian Loveman's contribution to this volume.

7. Castillo, Etcheverría and Larraín, "Las Masas," p. 8.

8. For a detailed review of the complicated procedures involved in the creation of an industrial union see Revista Técnica del Trabajo y Previsión Social, *Tratado Práctico sobre Organización Sindical y Conflictos del Trabajo* (Santiago: Arancibia Hnos., 1970), chapter 2.

9. Víctor Nazar, "El Autoritarismo en la Clase Obrera Chilena y el Proceso de Cambios en las Relaciones Sociales de Producción,'' *Cuadernos de la Realidad Nacional*, no. 13 (July of 1972):227. The survey was based on a sample of 920 workers of industries of different sizes.

10. Alan Angell, *Politics and the Labour Movement in Chile* (London: Oxford University Press, 1972), p. 46.

11. See Manuel Barrera, "Perspectiva Histórica de la Huelga Obrera en Chile," *Cuadernos de la Realidad Nacional*, no. 9, (September 1971):125-

34. Barrera points out that the number of strikes in the early period may be underestimated. The increase is, nonetheless, highly significant.

12. Ibid., p. 125.

13. Hernán Ramírez Necochea, *Historia del Movimiento Obrero en Chile* (Santiago: Talleres Gráficos Santaro, 1956), p. 314.

14. See Julio César Jobet, "Las Primeras Luchas Obreras en Chile y la Comuna de Iquique," in *Estructuras Sindicales* ed. Torcuato di Tella (Buenos Aires: Ediciones Nueva Visión, 1969), pp. 62-67.

15. Ibid., p. 67. Other authors, following newspaper accounts at the time, put the casualty figure at 500. See Aristodemo Escobar Zenteno, *Compendio de la Legislación Social y Desarrollo del Movimiento Obrero en Chile* (Santiago: Talleres San Vicente, 1940), p. 212.

16. See República de Chile, *Estadística Comercial Correspondiente al año 1904* (Valparaíso: Sociedad "Imprenta y Litografía Universo," 1905), pp. 225, 226 and 228.

17. In 1897, for example, roughly 74 percent of fiscal income was generated by custom receipts and 42 percent of the total was furnished by saltpeter sales abroad. See República de Chile, *Sinopsis Estadística en 1897* (Santiago: Imprenta Mejía, 1898), pp. 203 and 212.

18. See Barrera, "Perspectiva Histórica," pp. 125 and 128.

19. Adolfo Gurrieri and Francisco Zapata, *Sectores Obreros y Desarrollo en Chile (Algunas Hipótesis de Trabajo)*, (Concepción: Instituto de Sociología de la Universidad de Concepción, mimeo. no. 192, 1967), p. 11. Gurrieri and Zapata conclude that this fact played a decisive role in the early formation of the workers' movement in Chile. In Argentina and Brazil, by contrast, worker organizations did not acquire similar importance until the growth of manufacturing in the 1930s.

20. Barrera, "Perspectiva Histórica", p. 133.

21. Gurrieri and Zapata, *Sectores Obreros*, p. 13. See also Adolfo Dorfman, *La Industrialización en América Latina y las Políticas de Fomento* (México City: Fondo de Cultura Económica, 1967), p. 42.

22. Rural-urban migrations reached dramatic proportions in this period. See Fredrick Pike, "Aspects of Class Relations in Chile, 1850-1960," in *Latin America: Reform or Revolution* eds. James Petras and Maurice Zeitlin (New York: Fawcett Publications, 1968), p. 207.

23. James O. Morris, *Elites, Intelectuals and Consensus* (Ithaca, N.Y.: Cornell University, 1966), p. 111.

24. Ibid., p. 188. Morris cites the *Boletín de la Sociedad Nacional de Agricultura*, vol. 38 (June 15, 1907).

25. Ibid., p. 195. The legislative proposal, presented by the Conservative party, prohibited the formation of federations. The newspaper's editorial appeared on May 29, 1919.

26. Recabarren had been elected to Congress previously in 1906, but was at that time still in the Partido Democrático. He was not allowed, however, to assume his office by Congress. As one congressman put it, "it is not possible to tolerate the representation of ideas of social dissolution." Julio César Jobet, *Ensayo Crítico del Desarrollo Económico Social de Chile* (Santiago: Editorial Universitaria, 1955), p. 142.

27. For a detailed analysis of these discussions see Morris, *Elites*, chs. 7 and 8.

28. Cited in Escobar Zenteno, *Compendio*, pp. 222-23. This passage forms part of Alessandri's message to Congress introducing a bill on union organization.

29. All citations from the labor code are drawn from Alfredo Gaete Berríos, *Código del Trabajo (Anotado, Concordado y con Jurisprudencia Judicial y Administrativa)*, (Santiago: Ediciones Encina, 1969). All legal references indicated in the text hereinafter are drawn from this source, unless otherwise indicated.

30. Manuel Barrera, *El Sindicato Industrial: Anhelos y Métodos de Lucha* (Santiago: INSORA, 1969), p. 64.

31. This information must of course be taken with reservations. Since they record attitudes expressed at one point in time, surveys cannot be expected to predict individual and much less group behavior in specific conjunctures.

32. Angell, *Politics*, p. 46, estimates Chilean unions had an average of 127 members in 1967. A large union in the Chilean context is one with more than 800 affiliated workers.

33. See Arnoldo Camú Veloso, *Estudio Crítico de la Huelga en Chile* (Santiago: Editorial Jurídica, 1964), p. 25.

34. These sanctions are based on *Jurisprudencia* no. 2 of article 383 of the Labor Code. A *Jurisprudencia* is a court interpretation of a law which establishes precedents.

35. Workers were entitled to indicate five preferences, which counted double if the voter has been employed in the enterprise for over three years (article 390). If the ballot was deposited blank, its votes were given to the first five names on the list. If a voter indicated a number of preferences which did not permit an even distribution of the five or ten votes, the candidates whose names were highest on the list were favored. It would thus appear that the drawing of lots for positions on the list could decide a close election in favor of candidates placed toward the top.

It has been pointed out that the election system favored well-organized minorities, since they could load all their votes on one or two candidates (Morris, *Elites*, p. 10; Angell, *Politics*, p. 60). In fact, labor inspectors indicated that it was very rare to find votes marked with more than two preferences; such widespread loading of votes limited the effectiveness of a possible minority-group strategy to elect its candidates.

36. It must be noted that the labor inspectorate also exercised a series of lax controls over the enterprise. This amounted to not much more than an inspection visit every six months. While fines could be levied for infractions of certain legal dispositions, the enterprise's lawyers could usually thwart costly demands for changes by appealing to local labor courts. However, some improvements obviously resulted from these periodic "fiscalization" visits.

37. A *Dictamen* was an interpretation of the Labor Code by the Dirección General del Trabajo (the General Office of Labor, which controlled the national network of labor inspectorates). Like a *Jurisprudencia*, it established a precedent.

38. The *gobernador* was the representative of the executive at the departmental level.

39. Camú, *Estudio Crítico*, p. 17, indicates that the *gobernadores* often exceeded their attributions and appointed junta members at their discretion even though lists were available. This practice tended to convert the juntas into an instrument in the hands of the executive.

40. See Gaete's annotation to article 601 of his *Código del Trabajo*.

41. The importance of the labor inspector in the junta was further reinforced by the fact that he had greater knowledge of all the facets of each labor conflict. Moreover, the labor inspector could decide issues before the junta alone if, at third citation, no one showed up. This was not uncommon, given the low attendance record at junta meetings.

42. The junta's power in this respect derived to a great extent from the *Reglamento Sobre Conflictos Colectivos no. 839* of November 1944. See Revista Tecnica del Trabajo y Prevision Social, *Tratados Practicos*, pp. 218, 220-21. A *Reglamento* is an executive-branch ruling on the details necessary to implement laws. In subtle ways, they sometimes improperly go beyond the framework of the law they regulate, which Camú argues occurred in this case (*Estudio Critico,* pp. 72-74).

43. See Camú's analysis of this situation, *Estudio Crítico*, pp. 16, 18, 72-74.

44. See Revista Técnica del Trabajo y de Previsión Social, *Tratado Práctico*, pp. 225-26.

45. The labor union directorate can be, as in fact occurs most of the time, designated to this committee. See Barrera, "Perspectiva Histórica," p. 150.

46. See Angell, *Politics*, p. 76. Angell's figures refer to all strikes, not only to those sectors which had the legal right to strike.

47. See Barrera, "Perspectiva Histórica," p. 148-49. Barrera analyses strikes during the 1960s.

48. Jorge Barría, *Las Relaciones Colectivas del Trabajo en Chile* (Santiago: INSORA, 1967), p. 37.

49. See Camú, *Estudio Crítico*, p. 70. Article 639 of the labor code established a maximum fine of one-half of the minimum monthly wage for violations of its provisions, unless otherwise indicated. Other labor-law violations carried more onerous fines, but they were well within the capacity of almost any enterprise to pay.

50. See articles 44 and 45 of *reglamento* 839 and the interpretation of the General Office of Labor contained in Revista Técnica del Trabajo y Previsión Social, *Tratado Práctico*, p. 259.

51. Barría, *Las Relaciones*, p. 38. Management was thus keenly aware that any violation of labor laws or agreements or any innovations related to them could cause a worker walk-out. A fundamental part of the union leadership strategy in dealing with management was precisely the threat of such a strike.

52. The author was not allowed access to files containing communications from the General Office of Labor. The inference is based on interviews with participants.

53. See Barrera, "Perspectiva Histórica," p. 130. A FOCh and Communist party leader wrote reflecting on this situation: "Our activities until this day in our struggle against capitalism have only been limited to the narrow framework of immediate, trade-unionist betterment; an improvement of salaries, a few minutes of reduction in working hours and other reforms of this nature." *Justicia*, November 26, 1924.

54. Luis Emilio Recabarren's February 1921 congressional campaign speech was indicative of this attitude within the labor movement. He said, in part: "We, the workers, know that the social problem cannot be resolved by laws, for the bourgeoisie will never permit laws benefiting the people and if any were passed, they would not respect them. . . . Any apparently beneficial law that a Socialist deputy might obtain would be of no use to the people. . . . They contribute instead to strengthen the capitalist system and they postpone and retard genuine popular emancipation because they arouse hopes in the people which can never be translated into social welfare." Cited in Morris, *Elites*, p. 205.

55. *Justicia*, August 22, 1924.

56. For a dramatic analysis of the benefits a FOCh leader saw in just one aspect, the obligation of a written contract, see ibid., October 12, 1924.

57. Ibid., November 27, 1924.

58. See the article entitled "Laws and more Laws" in ibid., October 12, 1924.

59. See ibid., December 30, 1925. The workers from Tocopilla, who had met repression after attempting to act within the legal framework, dissented from the majority.

60. See ibid., August 15, 1931.

61. See ibid., February 12, 1932, and December 30, 1925.

62. *El Sur*, June 9, 1932.

63. Alejandro Chelén Rojas, *El Partido de la Victoria* (Chañaral: Imprenta Avance, 1939), p. 3.

64. An article appearing in *La Razón*, June 18, 1932, on Marmaduke Grove, one of the leaders of the "Socialist Republic," is indicative of this.

65. Cited in Morris, *Elites*, p. 260.

66. See Jorge Barría, *Breve Historia del Sindicalismo Chileno* (Santiago: INSORA, 1967), p. 34.

67. See Barrera, "Perspectiva Histórica," p. 137.

68. See figures on legal trade-union formation during the Popular Front period in James O. Morris and Roberto Oyanader, *Afiliación y Finanzas Sindicales en Chile, 1932-1959* (Santiago: INSORA, 1962), pp. 18-29.

69. See Barrera, "Perspectiva Histórica," p. 137. Unions, in turn, sharply restricted strike activity as a measure of collaboration with the government.

70. For an example of this, see *Justicia*, January 1-7, 1936.

71. Ibid., December 6, 1924.

72. The 1904 statement was cited by Recabarren in a speech to Congress. See Luis Emilio Recabarren, *Obras Escogidas* (Santiago: Editorial Recabarren, 1965), vol. 1, p. 41.

73. The union publication is the *Folleto del Sindicato Industrial Paños Oveja Tomé*, (Concepción: Imprenta El Sur, 1967).

74. CUT was formed in February 1953. It replaced CTCh which was torn apart by conflicts between Socialists and Communists and by its excessively close identification with the Popular Front governments.

75. Christian Lalive and Jacques Zylberberg, "Dichotomie Sociale et Pluralisme Culturel: La Dispersion de la Classe Ouvrière Chilienne," paper presented to the Ninth World Congress of Political Science, Montreal, August 1973, p. 17.

76. Ibid., p. 13. If this question had been asked in June 1973, it would probably have reflected the polarization which took place after 1970. It is also likely that the increase in leftist preferences would have been larger than the increase in conservative options.

77. A dramatic example of this was the use of illegal strikes to justify government take-overs of industries during the Allende administration. An analysis of the legal basis of these take-overs can be found in Eduardo Novoa, "Vías Legales para Avanzar hacia el Socialismo," *Mensaje*, no. 208 (April 1971). The government relied on decrees dating back to the "Socialist Republic."

78. Angell, *Politics*, p. 59.

79. See Barrera, "Perspectiva Histórica," p. 150.

80. J.S. Valenzuela, *La Integración del Sindicalismo a través del Aparato Legal: Un Estudio Socio-Histórico del Movimiento Obrero Chileno* (Concepción: Instituto de Sociología de la Universidad de Concepción, Memoria de Prueba, 1970), pp. 168-69. By the same token, the legalistic union environment helped to insure the election of those individuals who were most socialized in the spirit of labor legislation provisions.

81. Angell, *Politics*, pp. 62, 128. It must be remembered that union leaders normally did not stop working at the enterprise after their election, and usually did not receive remuneration for time lost on union business. Furthermore, since most unions were small, a position of leadership was not normally identified with much power.

82. See Arturo Valenzuela's contribution to this volume.

83. Similarly, it would be misleading, as Jacques Zylberberg says, to take support for the Communist and Socialist parties as an indicator for leftist radicalism at the individual level. Moreover, the employer-antagonistic consciousness of many workers should not be confused with such a political attitude. It is rather the product of frequent frustrations at the vindicationist level (personal communication).

84. See Angell, *Politics*, p. 126.

85. Ibid., p. 128 et passim.

86. *La Nación*, March 16, 1973.

87. Ibid.

6

Nationalization, Socioeconomic Change and Popular Participation

James F. Petras

In Chile, where workers are found in a variety of industries, on different economic levels and in varied geographical regions, they are bound to have widely differing political experiences.[1] It was logical, therefore, that there would be differences in outlook and attitude toward participation in the nationalizations of the Allende period. The manner in which nationalization occurred—the degree to which there was prior politicization and mobilization—also affected workers' attitudes toward forms of participation.[2] The working class was not a homogeneous entity with the same level of class consciousness throughout; even within the same industries there were often significant variations between workers—in many cases among workers working at the same machine with similar backgrounds and experiences. Because of this complexity, workers' attitudes toward participation in industry were not easy to determine. One could also not assume that workers were only oriented toward participation through higher salaries, or that they were by nature prone toward participation in the decision-making structure of the firm.[3]

In addition to industrial and mining workers, four other groups linked to the productive process had potentially important roles to play in defining participatory aspects within the structural transformation that took place in Chile: the agricul-

---

This chapter previously appeared in *Studies in Comparative International Development* 8 (Spring 1973).

tural and nonindustrial urban workers and the mining and industrial technicians and supervisors. The sweeping changes that occurred in Chile embraced almost all important sectors of the economy (although the degree of change within each sector varied considerably) and all levels of enterprise.[4] Socialist policymakers had to face fundamental issues—such as who was going to run the newly nationalized enterprises and what role the industrial workers, miners, agricultural workers, technicians and supervisors would play within the new system. Before those points are discussed, the workers' attitudes toward their role in the process will be examined. A series of open-ended, unstructured interviews were conducted to obtain an overview of the attitudes of several different working-class, peasant, technical and supervisory groups.[5] All the enterprises visited were either nationalized or requisitioned property, no longer in the hands of their previous private owners. Interviews were taken at two copper-mining enterprises (Chuquicamata and El Teniente), the Hirmas Textile, Inc., factory (or ex-Hirmas as the workers referred to it), farms in southern Chile (provinces of Nuble and Cautín), and a land-squatter settlement on the outskirts of Santiago (Nueva Habana).

COPPER MINERS

In discussing the nationalization of the copper mines, one of the directors of the new state copper-mining directorate said that consciousness was the biggest problem. This may appear incongruous, since a plurality of the copper miners—even in Chuquicamata—voted for Allende in 1970. The proportion of left-wing voters increased in the municipal elections of April 1971, six months after Allende took office. The majority of industrial mining workers voted for the Socialist ticket in the union elections and 70 percent of the industrial union leaders in Chuquicamata were either Socialists or Communists.[6]

There were a number of political problems: half of those employed in Chuquicamata were classified as employees, not manual workers. The employees' union was led by nonleftists (Christian Democrats, independents and so on), whose only concern was to increase salaries and improve the financial accounts of the union treasury and the income and expense accounts of union officials.[7] Leftist unions (with the possible exception of Communist unions) were only nominally under party discipline. For the most part, Socialist trade unionists formulated policies independently of the party; in fact, the union controlled party policy regarding the mining sector. The division between workers and employees was not the only one. Supervisors and technicians belonged to an association that worked closely with United States managerial personnel and whose leadership was allied with the Right. The introduction of modern technology reduced the number of manual workers, increased the number of other employees and thus reduced the political influence of the Left.

A number of factors contributed to the formation of a "sectoral economic consciousness,"[8] as opposed to genuine working-class consciousness. The copper miners, especially those employed in Chuquicamata, were geographically isolated from the rest of the working class. Workers came to "Chuqui" for one reason: to make money. After a few years, many of them would leave, so there was little community feeling among the working class. Outside of the common pursuit of higher salaries, there was little that held the workers together; outside of work, there was little of the social solidarity that flourished in other working-class areas of Chile. Geographically separated, socially isolated, uprooted from their normal class environment, in transition toward new occupational opportunities, the copper workers in Chuquicamata were salary-conscious, but not class-conscious. The nationalization of copper was celebrated throughout Chile as a historic national occasion—in Chuquicamata, workers went about their routine business.

Participation in the copper mines was very low, except in some sections of the mines. The worker representatives on the directorate of the firm reflected the leadership of the trade unions who worked closely with the government. Despite their support of the government, trade union leaders faced continuous pressure from the rank and file to increase wages beyond the guidelines established by the government. Occasionally, trade union leaders functioned as if they were still combating foreign capitalists, failing to discipline absentee workers and not taking adequate measures to systematically reeducate rank and file workers and prepare them for responsible positions. In discussing the problem of the copper workers' attitudes in Chuquicamata after the nationalization of the mines, the president of the Industrial Union noted:

> There was fear that they would lose their social gains. There is no change in their political level. They vote for Left trade unionists because they are more effective negotiators of new contracts. Alessandri was popular but he does not have one trade union leader. The workers may turn to conservative unions if the workers' leaders identify too strongly with the government thus not leading the struggle for improved benefits. The government can help Left trade unionists by granting a 60 percent increase.

The workers' demands were the same as before and the response of the trade union leaders was no different—albeit they made attempts to square the government's overall development plans with the workers' immediate demands. The results in terms of participation were symptomatic. The same trade union leader noted:

> In the struggle for [economic] demands 95 percent of the workers are active but in informative meetings they are very few. The working class was accustomed to the old system, they have not entered into participation in the leadership of the administration—the workers see it as a change of owners. Presently, temporarily, the trade union leaders represent the workers in the administration.

Though salaries were high in comparison with the average wage of Chilean industrial workers, the cost of living in the isolated desert area was also high—the location offered few extra-monetary compensations. The government began some programs of social improvements—installation of private sewage systems, and so on—but this type of program had only a limited impact. In the meantime, the business unionism fostered by companies and union officials still held sway among the workers occasionally encouraged by conservative middle-level government function-

176   JAMES F. PETRAS

aries and plant supervisors held over from the previous government (Frei's).

MANAGEMENT IN THE NEW CONTEXT: CONSERVATIVE ATTITUDES AND TECHNOCRATIC IDEOLOGY

Some of the top personnel of the mines were competent and had a favorable attitude toward the socialization program of the government. The new superintendent of mines at Chuquicamata spent five years working in the United States, had ten years experience as a mining engineer and saw the new responsibilities as a challenge to Chilean professionals. Regarding the new situation he stated:

> There is much more responsibility. We have to make our own decisions—not the people in New York. Before we did most of the routine work; now we must find ways to better exploit the mines—according to our national interest. To avoid exhausting the mine we no longer want maximum exploitation for short-term gains. The fundamental positions were in the hands of the United States—planning and operations; as a result there were not sufficient Chileans trained for executive positions. Many went to the United States and learned, and a new mine, Exotica, was a learning experience, providing executive training. The sacking of the mine by the U.S. companies left waste deposits accumulating—this imposes new investments on the government. The multinational corporation owns many mines around the world: it exploits at the least cost and takes the cream. It does not have a long-range perspective because of its many holdings—this is what conflicts with the national interest of Chile.[9]

While a number of supervisors made the transition from private to nationalized industry, a substantial number showed signs of hostility and outright opposition, cloaking their political opposition in technocratic jargon. One supervisor at Chuquicamata stated: "I don't have any position on nationalization. My only interest is that this enterprise produces." Another Chuquicamata supervisor noted: "If politics are not mixed with technical questions, the technicians will stay. Politics must take second place to technical problems."

Three weeks after these interviews, the supervisors walked off the job to protest government hiring of executive personnel. The top leadership maintained that "we are not in bad condition nor are we in very good condition." Yet problems arose—serious conflicts between the government and the supervisors. The latter attempted to take control of the hiring of management—a prerogative they had never assumed under U.S. ownership. On the one hand, the supervisors claimed that they were only concerned with production and technical questions and had no objections to the government's policy; on the other, they attempted to convert nationalization of mines into a vehicle for their own domination. Using technological ideology (opposing the introduction of politics), many supervisors attempted to control the appointment of managers and executives to the mines, thus controlling mining policy—a highly political issue.

ATTITUDES OF COPPER WORKERS

One of the paradoxes during the first months of nationalization was the decline in the number of strikes and the low level of absenteeism among the relatively less politicized and radicalized copper workers in Chuquicamata—compared to the coppermining workers in El Teniente or El Salvador. The lower level of absenteeism in Chuquicamata was not so much a positive response to the revolutionary goals of the government as it was a commitment to staying on the job to make more money. In the short run, workers with a trade union consciousness were more disciplined and more prone to continue working as well as before than were the more radicalized workers. The latter probably perceived the victory of the Left as a means of easing off on the job. To the more radical workers, socialism was associated with redistribution, not production. To the more conservative workers, "the job had to be done" regardless of who was in power. Political efforts by parties on the Left to raise the consciousness of mining workers were very sporadic and unsystematic. Worker representatives were elected by trade union officials and the new management personnel functioned much the same as before. Salaries, status and the prerogatives of management were little changed. Nevertheless, trade unionists were aware of the larger political issues involved in the nationalization of mines: "This is a long-term process. Workers have to learn that the national interest comes before private interest. All profits are not to be distributed to the workers, but to be used for development of the whole country."[10]

The militancy of workers was most clearly seen in the issue of paying compensation to former U.S. owners. Most workers felt that the government should pay little or nothing. The treasurer of the Chuquicamata Industrial Union stated: "I believe that the company should not be paid, they should pay us for all the riches that they took out; they left us misery and sabotaged the mines. They were the thieves, not the Chileans."[11]

While mining workers appeared to be primarily interested in increasing their personal income, they also expressed considerable nationalist sentiment on the issue of compensation. This might have been caused by the belief that if the Chilean government paid high compensation it would come out of their pockets. The combination of economic self-interest and nationalism blended and made the compensation issue a significant factor in Chilean politics and in U.S.–Chilean relations.

While more mine workers in El Teniente favored national-ization of mines (as opposed to Chuquicamata), their perception of what nationalization meant was different from that of leftist leaders. For the workers, it was seen as a means of substantially improving their economic levels—not as a stimulus to national development—though the national-development theme was being promoted by trade union leaders. As one copper worker in El Teniente stated: "I am in favor of nationalization of the mines—it will bring more work for everybody—as long as we keep our social benefits and they arrange our collective bargaining contracts." Another worker emphasized: "We are the ones who produce for the country, therefore, we should receive better salaries at the end of the year."

On the question of who should make policy within the plant, workers tended to split between a majority favoring bipartite committees (worker-technicians or worker-professional super-visor) and a smaller group favoring only workers' committees. In contrast, supervisors tended to favor a structure in which management would be rooted in the upper reaches of the supervisory hierarchy and workers' councils would form a consultative body dealing with limited areas in labor relations. Altogether, mining workers were much closer to a democratic-socialist participatory position than were the supervisors. In El Teniente, there was a closer identification between workers and government than in Chuquicamata; El Teniente workers expressed more hostility toward their supervisors. One worker stated that "up to now this government has done more in six months than the previous government in six years—even though they [referring to the supervisors] don't believe it."

There was considerable naïveté among the new Socialist managers: they assumed that the mere fact of nationalization—the formal change of ownership from private to public—was sufficient to motivate the workers to produce more. One manager thought that as a result of nationalization "the miners will be obligated to be more responsible." Many Socialist executives avoided the question of who would control the nationalized industries.[12]

In regard to the charge that they were privileged workers, the miners usually reacted with indignation: "We don't believe it. Here in the mines you have to mortify yourself a great deal. Those people in Santiago simply don't know the conditions of the mines. They don't know the kind of work involved in the mines. They think it is the same [kind of work] as they do."

The same mining workers in El Teniente who supported Allende, who thought that his was the best government Chile ever had, were the same workers who saw the process of change in narrow economic terms and were among the 30–50 percent of workers absent each Monday. Radical political beliefs were not linked to a disciplined commitment to socialist production.

The copper miners, accustomed to struggling for welfare and redistributive programs, had difficulties in viewing themselves as leaders of the whole society. While trade union leaders had, to some degree, modified their behavior, this may have led them to misinterpret the attitudes of rank-and-file workers. One example was the case of a former mine leader (later a government official in Rancagua) who asserted that "with a few exceptions most workers perceive nationalization as welfare for the country. The workers will see that there is a limit to demands. There will be increased demands for national development and less demands for individual satisfaction." It is interesting to note that, subsequent to his opening declaration, the rest of his response was in the future tense.

While trade union leaders tended to regard nationalization as a means of capitalizing the economy and developing new industries, workers tended to view it in terms of better living standards and other immediate benefits.

INDUSTRIAL WORKERS, PARTICIPATION AND THE TEXTILE INDUSTRY

In May 1971, textile workers employed in the giant, modern plants owned by industrial families Yarur and Sumar went on strike, occupied the plants and called on the government to nationalize them. The government requisitioned the plants and the firms passed over unofficially to the state sector of the economy.[13]

The major textile firms in Chile were largely in the hands of immigrant Middle Easterners—successful businessmen whose labor policies reflected a carefully organized paternalistic system: low wages and company-organized social facilities, opposition to unionization and a network of constituent groups (section chiefs, foremen and others) which filtered information and served to check militant workers.

The industrial workers' union in Hirmas originated with textile firms, becoming organized in 1945. Prolonged (60-day) strikes did not occur until 1961 and 1965 and were largely over wage issues. The employees' union was founded in 1964 and became engaged in strikes in 1969 and 1970. Until 1961, the company was largely in control of the union—manipulating it to serve its own ends. Subsequently, the Left, mainly the Communist party, became active. Eventually, Communist unionists were elected to the leadership of the union. Through pressure, organization and struggle, the workers improved their treatment on the job—though salaries remained quite low. The union began to replace the company in the organization of the firm's social and cultural activities. The trade union's role in the enterprise was largely confined to raising purely economic issues. On occasion, usually during elections, spokesmen for the left-wing parties were presented to workers' assemblies. At Hirmas Textile, Inc., union leaders estimated that 70 percent of the industrial workers and 60 percent of the employees voted for Allende in 1970. Nevertheless, few of the workers were members of any political party. The Allende government had strong support from trade union leaders and the sympathy of the great majority of workers—yet the level of consciousness within the plant did not go very far beyond "economics." They were mostly concerned with trade union issues.

Unlike the nationalization of copper, which was almost wholly a product of executive and congressional action, workers and employees took an active part in the takeover of the textile industry. From the time Allende was elected until the firm was requisitioned, the owners lowered production (as did almost all private industrialists). The trade unionists correctly viewed this as part of a campaign to sabotage production and to create shortages and public unrest leading to the overthrow of the government. Trade union officials met with the minister of economy (Pedro Vuskovic) to discuss the problem. Subsequently, the trade union called a mass meeting of textile workers in which the overwhelming majority decided to strike and proceeded to occupy the plant. After three days, the government requisitioned the plant and appointed an intervenor to manage the firm along with the leaders of the trade unions.

While trade union leaders acted out of socialist convictions and understood that the strike and occupation were first steps toward nationalization of the industry, many of the workers who supported the strike did so in response to the low salaries and intensely exploitative conditions of their work. Behind a general support of the trade union leaders' political demands were the workers' economic and social grievances against the employer.

After nationalization, forces in the government interested in worker control of industry initiated a series of broad educational programs to prepare workers for participation in the management of the firm. Unlike the supervisors in the copper industry, the government intervenor in charge of Hirmas Textile was a professional with strong democratic-socialist ideas. While textile workers shared the same "economic" orientation as the copper workers—the trade union leaders were not too different from the union leaders in the copper mines—the way in which the requisition took place, the direct and active mobilization of the workers themselves and the active political intervention of a technically competent Socialist intervenor created a situation where the workers could deepen their political understanding of the whole process.

THE SOCIALIST EXECUTIVE IN HIRMAS TEXTILE, INC.

The importance of a class-conscious democratic Socialist in the top executive position of a newly nationalized plant cannot be underestimated, especially in light of the need to transform workers from capitalist to socialist consciousness. At the time of the takeover, the government intervenor acted decisively, disposing of all vestiges of the authority of the previous owners; some workers, partly fearful of the return of the old owners, had been reserved and refused to openly commit themselves. However, once the intervenor insisted that the owner would not return, there was a general expression of support for the new administration. The Socialist executive faced two principal problems: maintaining the efficient operation of the plant and creating a new structure of authority in which workers and employees participated directly in all major policy decisions. He began by working closely with trade union leaders who were in day-to-day contact with the workers; second, he took measures to reassure the older professionals and employees. At the same time, he had to make them understand that they were under his and the trade union leaders' orders. He also took other closely related measures. The content of company publications was changed: articles on worker involvement began to appear; courses in worker management were established. More importantly, the executive encouraged the development of an executive council which would include five representatives directly elected by the workers, five representatives selected by the government and a general administrator appointed by the government. As a first step, in every section of the plant, workers formed production committees to advise on policy and to exercise control over the productive process.

Organizational measures taken in the nationalized firm reflected the socialist ideology of the intervenor. In his words: "The goal is for workers to participate in the discussion of national politics—not only the production goals of the government. The workers should participate on all levels of planning—both on the level of the firm and on the national level."

Regarding the attitudes of the workers, the intervenor had an accurate perception of how much support existed as well as of the problems related to political consciousness:

> There are two tendencies among the workers: some identify with the new structure and produce more; others take advantage of the new structure and work less. To maintain work discipline we need workers' committees to pressure the workers—not administrative measures. The basic reason that workers support change is because there are better working conditions—there is more tranquility. For others there is a wait-and-see attitude: to see if we can run the plant efficiently and can maintain authority. Even if workers do not have the capacity to decide today, they will learn through practice.

TRADE UNION LEADERS IN HIRMAS

Most leaders of the industrial union were Communists who had spent many years improving working and salary conditions in the factory and urging workers to vote for left-wing candidates during elections. They felt somewhat uncomfortable being interviewed in the plush meeting room of the former board of directors. The trade unionists were men and women who were close to the level and style of life of the skilled worker. In discussing the role of the trade union in the post-takeover period, one Communist trade union leader noted:

> It [the trade union] has to change without losing its autonomy.[14] We must defend the interests of the working class. With the bosses the struggle was frontal; now we have to participate directly in the firm. Now we have to know all aspects of the firm—we must consider our collective bargaining demands in relationship with the overall performance of the firm. We have to make the workers conscious and prepare them for the elections to the council. I think the trade

unionist should stay in the union to make the rank and file aware.

While the Communist trade unionist favored the elimination of capitalism, he also favored a gradual transformation:

This is a government in transition: at this stage the government defines the areas to be expropriated, forms mixed enterprises and eliminates it [capitalism] little by little. Politically it may not be suitable to expropriate some enterprises at this stage—in the long run they might be expropriated as we head toward socialism.

In contrast to the Socialist intervenor who favored acceleration of the process, the Communist trade union leader said that "the rate of expropriation [during the first eight months] is dizzy, the working class was not prepared for the rapid rate of change. The government is complying with its program. We are pleasantly surprised by the rate of change." It appears that the political leadership outside the factory took the initiative supported by the leadership of the trade unions and backed by rank-and-file workers with economic and social grievances.

TEXTILE WORKERS' ATTITUDES TOWARD PARTICIPATION

There are at least four different types of workers to consider in discussing their attitudes: the section chiefs (foremen), the union delegates (equivalent to shop stewards), the various skilled workers and the unskilled or semiskilled workers (who were mostly women).

The foremen were deeply divided between those who favored the changes and those who were uncertain or somewhat opposed. For example, one foreman, who had been with the firm for 22 years, stated:

I am not sure that the social benefits gained in the past will stay because it [the change] is all new, it is not secure. I cannot say whether it will turn out well or not. With the boss it was hard to get a raise but through the trade union one could get raises. We do not know if this practice will continue.

Questioned about the issue of worker participation, this same individual responded that "the principal issue is the factor of money. With pay the workers will be successful: if there is no money there will be more work; if the present boss doesn't pay more we should return to the old one."

In contrast, another foreman analyzed the situation from a totally different perspective:

> This change was long awaited. We have to thank President Allende. We are content and have to produce more. The workers and employees are capable of running the enterprise. We are not manual workers or white collar workers but workers. I participate in all the meetings and assemblies.

If lower management was divided, the skilled workers tended to be overwhelmingly favorable to the changes—though they differ somewhat in terms of their understanding of specific issues. Many of the skilled and unskilled workers felt that the lack of constant pressure—what some referred to as "persecution"—on the job was the most important change. Others felt that there was less conflict and more peaceful labor relations—social relations were more humane.

Among most skilled workers interviewed, there was a clear understanding that wage increases were dependent on production increases. Unlike their unskilled counterparts, skilled workers felt confident that workers and employees were as capable of managing the enterprise as the previous owners. One class-conscious mechanic stated:

> This is what we had always hoped for. We are going to work under a new system—socialism—for all Chileans. It is a principle to nationalize all vital industries. Of course with facilities, spare parts, the workers can run the industry. Working 22 years for private owners—why can't we work for ourselves? Here [among the mechanics] all the workers think the same as me. Here and there some workers, those who are not very smart, can't understand. If there is an increase in production then there will be an increase in salary. We have to show the intervenor. Some of the fellows want more money now—but we have to prove our capacity to produce first.

Most skilled workers actively participated in meetings and discussions. They felt the importance of the change and the opportunity that this change represented from their own point of view much more so than the unskilled workers did. The skilled workers were also more likely than the unskilled to take a "longer view" and to see the whole process.

There were articulate, class-conscious workers among the semiskilled or unskilled, but they were a small minority. A young semiskilled worker, who was a section delegate to the union and active in the nomination of the new directorate, summed up the meaning of nationalization in the following terms:

> I feel integrated in the firm, before I felt alienated. The biggest change is that the very workers are organizing committees, the people are actually participating in the firm. As it is new, the workers are learning and the university people with theoretical training will contribute. There are differences occasionally, workers who want more salary (differences in work result in different demands), problems inherited from the past; we should equalize salaries. Workers' salaries should be adjusted to take account of inflation and then the rest should be in the form of social improvements [not individual increases], something visible like child-care centers for four- and five-year-olds in addition to the infant centers that already existed, a football field, more housing—50 percent of us live in temporary shacks. It is important that the changes come from this government and not through strikes. I have to participate as a worker in this change. I want change for my children even if I don't see it.

Most unskilled workers were not very clear about the changes and had less to say, though they were generally sympathetic. One worker stated, "it is a little better—more work. The talks are very good—they explained things I didn't understand. There is more comradeship. I am in favor of increased salaries as well as increases in production." A woman who had been a semiskilled machine operator for five years commented: "We are better off but I don't go to meetings or to talks. Now we are more peaceful. It is better to have workers as leaders than a boss. Before we worked because we had to, now one knows one has to." Another female machine helper blandly noted: "Same conditions as before. I haven't participated in meetings. There are some people better trained in the industry. Up to now the government has been very good. Our job is to produce good fabrics."

The main base of support for the notion of worker participation lies with trade union activists and skilled workers; lower management and unskilled workers were less involved and tended to view the process of change in somewhat more capitalist terms. The acceptability of the larger issue of worker participation depended upon the ability of the more politically conscious workers to draw their less involved fellow workers into activity. The alternative to worker participation was the gradual bureaucratization of the new structure—and the subsequent focus exclusively on salary demands.

AGRARIAN WORKERS: FROM SUBJECTS TO PROTAGONISTS

The process of land expropriation was vastly accelerated with the election of Salvador Allende. Organized peasant land seizures and government-initiated expropriations made deep inroads in the old latifundia structure, especially in areas little affected by the previous Frei government. As the large farms were being expropriated a process of massive peasant unionization was taking place. Concurrently, left-wing organizers—Socialists, MIR and MAPU[15]—began creating peasant assemblies which elected peasant representatives who helped formulate postagrarian reform policy.

Due to intense party competition in rural areas along with organizational and political breakthroughs during the period 1965-71, four types of peasant organizations emerged: (1) Socialist-, Communist- and MAPU-led peasant unions, closely linked to the official left-wing parties and including a variety of social forces from moderate, "legalist" and Communist to militant Socialists who worked closely with MCR;[16] (2) Christian Democratic peasant unions which contained a variety of moderate and left-wing Catholic peasant unions; (3) the MCR, a largely MIR-led peasant movement which took the lead in the organization of peasant land occupations outside official legal channels; and (4) the traditional peasantry, loyal to the large landowners' associations and a vanishing phenomenon. The degree of politicization and radicalism in rural areas rose considerably during the Allende administration, as did the complexity of political affiliation.

In southern Chile—an area of extreme poverty and tyrannical landlord rule—the organization of the peasantry was delayed. Peasants were violently prevented from unionizing; repression was much more intense than in the rest of the country. With the election of Allende, the late-developing peasant consciousness of the south responded to the most advanced revolutionary ideas, methods of struggle and organization. Rural collectivism, nonlegal land occupations, under the leadership of the most resolute and determined revolutionary organizations, characterized the southern peasant movement. The sudden and radical change expressed the latent political demands which previous governments had inhibited. Allende's election was the green light for a rapid and thorough transformation. Consciously or not—depending on the level of awareness of each peasant—throughout the south scores of farms were occupied as peasants learned that the armed forces would not be used to repress them. Many peasants interviewed claimed that they were "only helping President Allende carry out the agrarian reform and increase production for the country." There may be two elements involved in this response: the peasants may have genuinely thought that they were helping Allende and/or they may have felt that this was a historic opportunity to bring about changes that Allende might later be unable or unwilling to carry out. There is some rational basis for peasant doubts about government action. In the past, Chilean leftists have promised far more than they have ever actually carried out.

A local peasant leader of a seized farm described the process of political action in the following terms:

> Trade union activity began in 1965 but there was no unity among the workers, since most were afraid that the owner would cause trouble and they would lose their jobs. With the Allende victory the owner disappeared[17] and the son managed the farm. After September 4, 1970, they started to sell the

[farm] machinery and the animals: of 400 cows only 140 remain.[18] In October we formed a union—108 of the 120 workers participated in the assembly. On November 13 the farm was taken by 78 peasants, the employees [management] did not participate—they were allies of the owner. On November 25 CORA (the government's Agrarian Reform Corporation) arrived with an intervenor—we lost only one-half day of work. During the intervention the Socialist Party gave us legal aid. There is little "politics"—work and technical assistance is basic. There are no Christian Democrats ... before there were some *alessandristas*. The majority are with the Socialist party though few attend meetings. Allende is very good: on all aspects he is with us. The program is being fulfilled. Before I was with the Right: always eat with the Right but vote with the Left.

On the issues directly affecting the peasantry, local peasant leaders moved closer to the Left—shedding their inhibitions and openly collaborating with the government. Concerning other areas of the government's program, there was some radical spillover but the local unionists were not very sure of their own opinions: "I understand little about copper. It is a big step. The riches will not go abroad but will stay in Chile. To have the State own the banks is not a bad idea. The funds of the rich will be controlled."

In discussing their relationship with peasants on and off the farm, the unionists had a realistic appraisal of their possibilities:

Production on this farm will increase—we are expanding the amount of land to be seeded from 50 to 100 hectares. Milk will drop since the cows were sold . . . . The peasants on the adjoining farm are with the boss; he is very paternalistic. We are surrounded by small proprietors—there are no direct discussions. We participate in the municipal peasant council—which seems to unite the peasants. We agree that, in principle, we should work the farm collectively. Work discipline varies: we levy fines but we cannot throw out offenders. Concerning drinking: he who doesn't drink is a Protestant—with this cold we all take a drink.

The more radical peasants—many of them Mapuche Indians from southern Chile—were attracted to MCR. Living in abysmal poverty—even by Chilean peasant standards—many of their children walked barefoot on the frozen mud. In Camilo Torres' settlement in the municipality of Lautaro and in the province of Cautín, a local MCR peasant, leader of an illegal land occupation, clearly defined the revolutionary socialist outlook:

> We favor collectivizing the land. This land seizure was self-organized. We support the government by land seizures. I am with Allende. This was an abandoned farm that we are making productive—which is what the president has asked us to do. We support the nationalization of copper.

Most peasants described the Allende government's performance as favorable in comparison to previous governments—but many still thought the agrarian reform was too slow. Most attributed the decline in production to the sabotage of the former landlords, the slowness of the expropriation procedure and the inefficiency of government agencies in the delivery of supplies. Peasants in areas of intense conflict—where farms were seized or expropriated during the Allende regime favored collective ownership.

The left-wing factions disagreed over the organization of agriculture after the expropriations. The relationship between the Socialists and Communists in rural areas was tense: the more militant Socialist-organized unions grew rapidly and threatened the existing Communist leadership in the unions. In the peasant-council elections the Socialists displaced the Communists as the leading force in the rural sectors. However, the relationship between the Socialist militants and MCR was still very good in agrarian southern Chile.

In summing up his position regarding the government, one rank-and-file peasant from Coihueco (province of Nuble) put it very succinctly: "Our hope is with the government that we have, it is completely with the peasant. It is more or less good—better than before. We are beginning, much has been done, more to be done. The opposition is strong. We need to organize trade unions to put the opposition to rest."

The president of the Socialist Lands Peasant Federation of Nuble claimed that 80 percent of the peasants favored collectivizing the land. The other 20 percent favored individual holdings and were described as still under Christian Democratic influence. According to this militant leader, son of a rural worker, "we should work the land collectively and not divide the land, because then conflicts will continue; conflicts between small proprietors and workers."

The process of radicalization in the rural areas continued: first the Christian Democrats displaced the traditional Right; then the Communists, Socialists and Christian Left (ex-MAPU and ex-Christian Democrats) displaced the Christian Democrats; at the same time, MIR began to put pressure on the official Left and put itself in a position to become a major force if the government should fail to carry through its promise to accelerate agrarian reform. The peasant commitment to the government, while strong, was conditional: performance was emphasized; comparisons were made with the past; and support was hedged with the proviso "Up to now it is fulfilling its program ..." which suggested that support depended upon the government's ability to keep up with radical peasant demands.

LAND SQUATTERS: THE NEW URBAN REVOLUTIONARIES

Comparing the best years of the two predecessor presidents to the performance of the Allende government in the area of public housing, a picture emerges of the specific improvements which led to increased support of the Left among the lower class:

Table 1

COMPARISON OF HOUSING CONSTRUCTION UNDER ALLESANDRI, FREI AND ALLENDE

Time Period	Number of Houses Built
Allende (November 4, 1970-March 26, 1971)[a]	31,018
Frei (1965)[b]	26,196
Alessandri (1961)[b]	28,297

[a]By July 1, 1971 nearly 50,000 houses had been built—by the end of 1971 the government hopes to build 100,000 houses.

[b]We are comparing the best years of the Frei and Allesandri governments to the first five months of Allende's. Part of the data taken from CORVI, Sub-Oficina de Campamentos.

In many areas, unemployment committees in the land-squatter settlements provided the manpower to build the houses. The settlements themselves varied a great deal in terms of their internal structure, degree of organization, politicization and capacity to make basic decisions concerning community development. The settlements around Santiago, under MIR leadership, were generally recognized as the best organized: there was a greater degree of participation, law and order and sense of purpose among residents.

One of the major land-squatter movements began in January 1970 when groups of homeless families (usually given the run-around by Frei's housing officials) undertook a massive occupation of unused land sites. Not infrequently, these squatters were attacked by special units of the riot police established by the Frei government to deal with mass movements. As a result, the squatters set up self-defense units to protect themselves from external government-sponsored violence, as well as to maintain internal order.

After the election of Allende, government policy began to change, as did the attitudes, policies and organization of the settlements. The chief of Campamento Nueva Habana[19] (population 7,000) discussed these changes:

After September 4 there was a fundamental change. Before, the Housing Ministry was enemy No. 1. After September 4, the doors of the Housing Ministry were wide open. The self-defense unit was dissolved, and our popular militias in part also were dissolved because some militiamen became delinquents for lack of sufficient political education. We are reorganizing the militia. After September 4, mobilization and confrontation ended—in part because the squatters began to criticize leaders of the settlement; they said 'Allende is now

President and you have to change your politics.' The land here was given over to the squatters. All the settlements began to divide. Some went to the Socialists, many stayed with MIR. The squatters demanded that the leaders solve their problems. When the National Health Service came to our settlement they had to join the Health Front. The nurses and doctors had to discuss the organization of the policlinic with the squatters— thus avoiding paternalism. A doctor is just another comrade who happens to know more . . . .

The high degree of active participation in the settlement reflected the emphasis given to it in the ideology of MIR and the latter's capacity to create organizational structures and tangible goals which allowed individuals to channel their energies. In discussing Nueva Habana's housing policy, its leader[20] revealed the degree of political and organizational sophistication achieved by the squatters:

CORVI [the State Housing Corporation] came with their little shanty houses. The squatters demanded that they participate and discuss the planning of the houses. Along with the squatters were a group of left-wing architects who advised them in their discussion with CORVI. The squatters made the architects conscious of the need to work together. The squatters rejected private construction firms and provided voluntary labor to build. CORVI set up a construction firm to work with the squatters. With the money saved, the size of the houses was expanded from 36 square meters to 46 square meters and up to 65 square meters. We know how we want to live even if we are not architects. We discussed and approved the plans. Squatters who are paying for their houses want a say in how it is going to be built. The bureaucracy of CORVI resisted but we mobilized and threatened to seize their building. In private enterprise workers don't care about materials because they have no say in the organization of work. The squatters organize tripartite committees: (a) settlement leaders and workers; (b) university technical advisors; (c) CORVI officials. Once Nueva Habana is finished the workers will have the experience to form a construction firm; they will elect their foremen and supervisors and there will be no inequality between workers and management.

In regard to internal political structure, the settlement's fundamental unit was the block: each block and each front elected delegates to the directorate which met on a weekly basis. In 1971, the community completed the construction of a community cafeteria, laundry and supermarket. The leader pointed out that these social services were built to allow women to participate in the tasks of the community.

Nueva Habana was not a typical settlement—it was exceptional. The degree of order, organization and achievement was a function of the political level of the squatters which, in turn, reflected the policies of the political leaders. In comparing MIR to the official Left (Communist and Socialist parties), the leader of Nueva Habana made some interesting distinctions that should aid in understanding the political and social basis of popular participation in basic community decisions:

> The traditional left-wing agencies organize the squatters until the next elections, when they introduce lighting, water, etc. MIR rejects elections in principle—we work continuously with squatters. The leaders of the settlements of U.P. [Unidad Popular—the coalition of left-wing parties in the government] don't live in the settlement, they come in a car twice a week to attend meetings. The absentee leaders are not present to execute the program. MIR leaders are totally integrated in the settlement—involved in all relations within it. We work because we believe in the revolution. There is a strong sense of comradeship.

From Nueva Habana sprang the first socialist experiment and the building of the new socialist man that Che Guevara spoke of: the self-organized community, in which state property was an instrument of the democratically organized community. Socialist political organization and behavior appeared to be higher among the squatters of Nueva Habana than in any other working-class stratum in Chile.

AN OVERVIEW

There was an inverse relationship between degree of participation and decision-making, on the one hand, and level of income and status. Workers with the highest degree of interest in participation, interaction and solidarity were found among the squatters of Nueva Habana; next highest were the peasants of the Socialist and MIR peasant unions in the Nuble and Cautín areas; the textile workers from Hirmas were next highest in their interest in participation; the copper miners in El Teniente were next to last; and the miners in Chuquicamata were in last place.

Table 2

RANK ORDER OF SOCIAL STRATA ACCORDING TO
LEVELS OF PARTICIPATION AND SALARY

| | Rank Order | |
Group	Participation in Leadership	Salary and Status
Squatters (Nueva Habana)	1	5
Peasants (Nuble, Cautín)	2	4
Textile Workers (Hirmas)	3	3
Copper Workers (El Teniente)	4	2
Copper Workers (Chuquicamata)	5	1

The inverse relationship between salary and status and participation does not explain very much—in fact, *it* needs to be explained. Low income and status in themselves do not explain high levels of participation or interest in participation. If the two groups high in participation (squatters and southern peasants) are compared to the two groups ranked low in participation (copper miners of El Teniente and Chuquicamata), we find some interesting differences. Those scoring low in participation had been organized in trade unions for over a half century and had engaged in a great number of strikes and job actions led by leftist trade union leaders. The high scorers had been organized only since 1970 and most of them lacked previous organized political experience. The newest organized groups were MIR and the left wing of the Socialist party. Paradoxically, the groups with the longest experience of class strugggle and the longest tradition of class organization under leftist leadership were the ones least interested in participating in decision-making within the nationalized firms. A closer view, however, reveals several factors which help explain the problem.

The newly organized squatters and peasants were led by revolutionary socialist political cadres whose vision of the process led them to constantly infuse immediate piecemeal changes with a broader perspective embracing the whole system. The older organized groups (the copper miners) were led by Socialist trade union leaders who had achieved leadership positions on the basis of their trade union skills (ability to organize strikes, negotiate substantial wage increases) rather than because of their political militancy. The copper miners supported leftist politicians because of their ability to reinforce the demands of their trade union leaders.

Partly because of past experiences and partly because leftist trade unionists focused primarily on economic issues (mainly salaries), the copper miners developed little in the way of a radical political consciousness which would enable them to see themselves in decision-making positions, rather than as mere wage workers.[21] The newly organized workers on the other hand—beginning with their initial organizational experience—came into contact with the most progressive political groups in Chilean society: MIR and left-wing Socialist political leaders whose demands went beyond state control of the economy to a socialist program based on worker and peasant control as the central issue. The most exploited and lowest paid groups—those literally without houses, work or land—were the major groups not organized by the established left-wing organizations; thus, they were susceptible to the more revolutionary groups like MIR and the left-wing Socialists.

The better-organized and better-paid workers were those who had been socialized over the years to electoral and union politics; they were conditioned to think of politics as casting a ballot once every three or six years for a parliamentary representative. Once elected, there was very little direct contact and discussion between the representative and the worker-voter—except insofar as a wage dispute necessitated parliamentary support. The only meetings to directly affect the copper workers (under the previous private ownership system) were those which discussed salary questions. Hence, the only periods of activity and discussion revolved around the periods of salary negotiations. As a result, in the postreform period, copper miners tended to identify greater participation with a greater share in the profits— not greater responsibility in the decisions of the enterprise.

The land squatters and peasants began their activity with the expropriation of land and thus immediately faced larger questions concerning the management and administration of the whole community. There was little prior schooling in electoral or union policies. The very act of land expropriation was, in many instances, organized from below and carried out by the people themselves—creating a tradition of solidarity around global issues. The copper miners' solidarity was based on limited goals—wage demands for themselves—and they were very reluctant to participate in solidarity action with other oppressed groups—if it meant a day's lost pay. The expropriation of the copper mines themselves was carried out through parliamentary action and executive negotiation. At best, the copper miners voiced support for the action. In some cases, however, they had serious reservations concerning possible effects on their social and economic welfare.

Thus, those sectors of the working class which were organized late and led by extraparliamentary political groups infused by a global vision of the process, showed greater interest in the democratic participatory mode of organizing the nationalized industries than did the established organized union workers led by electorally oriented trade unionists.

The key question facing the Allende government was not, as Eric Hobsbawm[22] suggests, one of increasing the number of leftists among the lower classes (a careful analysis would show that the Left practically exhausted its possible support among the urban and rural workers, although perhaps not among urban-slum women voters). The Left had the support of the great majority of the productive sectors of the society—peasants, miners, industrial workers, land squatters. The real question facing the Left was its ability to transform the trade union consciousness of its supporters into socialist consciousness. If this was indeed the key issue, then the program of the Left should not have concentrated

198   JAMES F. PETRAS

on the populist redistributive measures (Perón style), which
Hobsbawm suggests as a means of increasing popular support.
Instead, the Left should have focused on creating institutions for
worker participation. Only through direct participation in the
management of an enterprise—with all the errors and risks that
may result—could the workers get the experiences that would
deepen their political awareness and make them conscious of the
socialist nature of the transformation.

NOTES

The author conducted a series of interviews with various union officials
at different ranks. In each case, the ranks of the officials with whom the
interviews were conducted are listed in the body of the text.

1. For a detailed dicussion of the voting behavior of different
working-class segments, see James F. Petras and Maurice Zeitlin, *El
radicalismo político de la elase trabajadora chilena* (Buenos Aires: Centro
Editor de América Latina, 1970). For a historical treatment of working-
class parties, see James F. Petras, *Politics and Social Forces in Chilean
Development* (Berkeley; University of California Press, 1969), ch. 5.

2. Maurice Zeitlin, *Revolutionary Politics and the Cuban Working Class*
(Princeton: Princeton University Press, 1967).

3. For a discussion of the issue of worker control, see: A.F. Sturmthal,
Workers' Councils (Cambridge: Harvard University Press, 1964); J.T.
Kolaha, *Workers' Councils: The Yugoslav Experience* (London: Tavistock,
1965); F. Fleisher, *The New Sweden* (New York: MacKay, 1967); E.C.
Brown, *Soviet Trade Unions and Labor Relations* (Cambridge: Harvard
University Press, 1966); Drago Gorupic, "Trends in the Development of
Workers' Self-Management in Yugoslavia," *Eastern European Economico*, 8
(Winter, 1969-70):   107-82; Jaroslav Uanek, "Decentralization under
Workers' Management: A Theoretical Approach," *American Economic
Review* 59 (December 1969) 1006-14; Milton Derber, "Plant Labor
Relations in Israel," *Industrial and Labor Relations Review* 3 (October
1963) 39-59; Anthony Sylvester, "Workers' Councils: Signposts for the
Future," *Problems of Communism:* 13 (January-February 1964) 43-48;
Fred Singleton and Tony Topkam, "Yugoslav Workers Control: The Latest
Phase," *New Left Review* (January-February 1963): 73-84; George
Graham, "Labor Participation in Management: A Study of the National
Coal Board," *Political Quarterly:* 38 (April 1967) 184-99; Dusan Diland-
zic, "Workers' Management in Factories," *Socialist Thought and Practice*
28 (October-December 1967): 30-47; Jean-Jacques Bonnard, "Participation
by Workers' and Employers' Organizations in Economic Planning in France,"
International Labor Review 93 (April 1966): 337-61; Joye Taira,
"Participation by Workers' and Employers' Organizations in Economic
Planning in Japan," *International Labor Review* 94 (December 1966):

511-34; Guy Caire, "Participation by Employers' and Workers' Organizations in Planning," *International Labor Review:* 96 (December 1967): 557-80; Edward Marek, "Workers' Participation in Planning and Management in Poland," *International Labor Review:* 101 (March 1971): 271-90.

4. *NACLA Newsletter*, 5 (September 1971). James F. Petras, "The Transition to Socialism in Chile: Perspectives and Problems," *Monthly Review:* 23 (October 1971): 43-71.

5. Hubert Blalock, *Social Statistics* (New York: McGraw-Hill, 1960).

6. The voting results for both the 1970 and 1971 elections were compiled from raw data at the Registro Electoral (Santiago).

7. This style of unionism was also one of the by-products of U.S. ownership of copper mines.

8. By sectoral economic consciousness we mean concern with and social action directed toward issues solely related to salary and job considerations within a particular firm or sector of industry.

9. The superintendent of mines at Chuquicamata provided data which suggested that despite the changeover (or perhaps because the changeover meant so little in terms of work and production) production had not declined but had increased over the previous year:

| January | June 1970 | 139.632 short tons |
| January | June 1971 | 142.052 short tons |

10. Treasurer of Chuquicamata Employees Union.

11. The reference to thieves was in response to an article published by the New York *Daily News* which was reproduced in Chile and which accused the Chilean government of robbing U.S. investors.

12. This "socialist" position is not very different from the bureaucratic collectivist position adopted by the technocratic supervisors who justified their elitist position by arguing that workers were not prepared to participate, that the majority were peasants who lacked a cultural base even if they were literate.

13. The owners contested the expropriation and a definitive legal decision was never reached.

14. All trade unionists that I interviewed throughout Chile maintained that trade unions should be autonomous and have the right to strike. One socialist union leader stated that the day they lost the right to strike he would stop supporting the government.

15. MIR (Movimiento de Izquierda Revolucionaria–Movement of the Revolutionary Left) was a revolutionary socialist group which critically supported the Allende government but stood outside of the formal government coalition. MAPU (Movimiento de Acción Popular Unitario– Unitary Popular Action Movement) was a former left wing Catholic group which turned increasingly to Marxism-Leninism.

16. MCR (Movimiento Campesino Revolucionario–Revolutionary Peasant Movement) was the peasant affiliate of MIR.

17. It appears that the owner fled to Argentina, implicated in the Schneider assassination plot.

18. After Allende's victory on September 4, 1970, the large landholders began selling and slaughtering animals and dismantling farm machinery.

19. Campamento Nueva Habana had several organizations that dealt with different areas such as health, education, cultural activities, and so on. Community development was expressed through functional differentiation and organizational specialization.

20. The leader of Campamento Nueva Habana was formerly a construction electrician who left his trade to become a full-time settlement organizer for MIR. He lived in the settlement and received less than $1.50 (official rate) per day.

21. Conservative political leaders like Jorge Alessandri received substantial electoral support among these workers in the 1970 elections, especially in Chuquicamata, though there are no *alessandrista* union leaders.

22. Eric Hobsbawm, "Can Allende Make It?" *New York Review of Books,* September 23, 1971, 23-32.

7

Occupation and Lower-Class Political Orientations in Chile

Alejandro Portes

[The waiter's work gives him the mentality not of a workman but of a snob . . . .

George Orwell, 1933.]

Students of the political orientations of the poor have consistently emphasized that an individual's occupational situation is a fundamental influence upon many other aspects of his life. The particular location of an individual in the process of economic production determines his level of social and economic rewards, the relative long-range stability of these compensations and the nature and orientations of the social context within which he interacts during most of his working hours.

Discussion of the politics of poverty has concentrated, by and large, on those conditions that determine the impoverished masses' allegiance to the existing order or which render them at least politically indifferent and apathetic versus those which incite them to revolt. From the viewpoint of political authorities, such groups present a particular problem; a social order which relegates the poor to the least desirable conditions of life must somehow be made legitimate to them. The tension intrinsic to these situations, which has attracted the attention of almost all political theorists, is that between constant economic deprivation and social humiliation on the one hand, and the conditions which lead to transformation of this ever-present radical potential into a political reality on the other. For this reason, the political sociology of poverty has often been synonymous with the sociology of class consciousness and militant populism. The crucial question is: what triggers, at certain historical moments, the potential built up by massive deprivation into effective support for radical movements?

That question cannot be given an exhaustive answer in this chapter. It furnishes, however, an appropriate framework for approaching the more specific problem of this study: in what manner have different factors linked with occupational situation affected political orientations among Chile's urban poor? Though the subject is relevant to the quest for general theoretical answers, emphasis will be placed on the way that the data clarify certain persistent trends in the politics of Chile's lower classes.

There is little doubt that the strength of both the Communist and Socialist parties in Chile and the fate of their 1970s experiment with socialist democracy hinged largely on the support they commanded among the popular masses. The inexorable polarization that characterized Chilean politics in modern times prevented the leftist parties from turning to any other sector for effective support. Neither the middle sectors nor the upper sectors ever responded to Unidad Popular (Popular Unity—UP) appeals for votes; likewise, they would not provide any backing for the government in times of crisis.[1]

The crucial point, however, is that lower-class support for extreme Left parties and for radical politics was anything but secure. While it is true that copper, nitrate and coal miners have provided traditional bulwarks for both the Communist and Socialist parties, leftist militance, among other popular sectors, was problematic. Two such sectors seemed critical during Allende's regime: the rural peasantry and the urban marginal population. The first had recently been freed from the constraints of quasi-feudal arrangements in rural areas, coming to age as an independent political force.[2] The second formed a new and fast-growing sector in the major cities.[3] Both had in common numerical vastness and the fact that neither had consolidated an overriding loyalty to any political orientation. Leftist parties

competed in both urban and rural areas with Christian Democrats, other minor forces and the weight of traditional political
apathy for the support of these groups.[4] In Chile, where upper-,
middle- and even working-class sectors were already politically
organized and supported one or another of the existing parties (in
defense of their interests), the newly mobilized peasantry and
urban marginal population constituted the last available frontier
for massive political proselytism. Their huge numbers guaranteed
them a decisive role in any political contest.

This chapter deals with the second of these sectors—the
marginal urban lower classes. In Santiago, lower-class settlements
occupy the entire western, northern, southern and southeastern
peripheries, comprising about one-half of the physical metro-
politan area.[5] Residents of these settlements—called *pobladores*
or *marginales*—represent up to 30 percent of the greater Santiago
population.[6]

Several other analysts have discussed general political characteristics of the *pobladores* as well as aspects of their communities and past residential histories that have affected their
political orientations.[7] This chapter will tackle the problem from
a different perspective and concentrate on the occupational
situations of these groups. An individual's place of work, like his
place of residence, can affect his political preference through its
recurrent impact on his everyday life. Occupation, or the place an
individual has in the process of economic production, is the most
direct determinant of a condition of marginality in the first place.
This perspective should provide new insights into the emergence
of political orientations among the urban poor and their long-run
effects on the Chilean polity.

THE POLITICAL IMPACT OF OCCUPATION: THREE HYPOTHESES

Political theorizing on effects of occupational situation on
individual orientation has traditionally emphasized three con-
cepts. Status, or the place particular occupations occupy in the
social-stratification hierarchy, is probably the most general
concept and is most consistently discussed in political writings.[8]
Occupational role, or nature of the work performed, has also

been emphasized, insofar as it determines different types of contexts for social interaction and political learning.[9] Occupational insecurity, measured by length or frequency of unemployment, is a third dimension, often linked to emergence of radicalism, either of the Left or Right.[10]

Occupational status is important insofar as it determines differential access to social and economic rewards. The very simple relationship thus postulated predicts that those sectors with greater access to socioeconomic benefits will be most inclined to maintain allegiance to the existing order, while the most deprived groups will tend to deny its legitimacy. While numerous historical exceptions have been documented, the postulated inverse relationship between status and leftism/ liberalism remains a basic principle of political theory. Thus, an initial hypothesis can be stated as follows: *The higher the status of occupations, the lower the tendency to endorse change-oriented movements of a leftist or radical nature.* In a well-known passage, Seymour Martin Lipset[11] speaks, for example, of

> the fairly logical relationship between ideology and social base. The Socialist left derives its strength from manual workers and the poorer rural strata; the conservative right is backed by the well-to-do elements . . . . The democratic center is backed by the middle classes, especially small businessmen, white-collar workers, and the anticlerical sectors of the professional classes.

Occupational role or nature of the work situation is emphasized, in contrast, not for its effect on differential rewards or deprivations but rather for the way in which it conditions opportunities for political socialization. For all sectors, but especially the lower classes, the way in which occupational frustrations are experienced can make all the difference. Menial-service workers, such as maids, janitors and street vendors, tend to be isolated from class peers and placed paradoxically in closer contact with higher-status individuals. The nature of political learning in these situations is not conducive to translation of a reality of poverty and deprivation into militant consciousness. As Daniel Goldrich[12] states:

> Some occupational factors that probably retard politicization include the very high proportion of Latin Americans who are

engaged in service work and petty commercial activities such as street vending. Such people tend to form an atomized labor force, and their lack of regular contact with others like themselves probably does very little to generate an orientation toward government and politics.

Also, the frustrations of lower-class life are suffered by the industrial proletariat as a collective phenomenon. An everyday routine of factory work facilitates recurrent interaction between workers, bringing into sharper focus the structural roots of their situation. Marxist writing has long emphasized the close link between emergence of "consciousness" among the lower classes and those work situations which bring ever-greater numbers of them together, facilitating political socialization. Thus, it is logical that, despite a better objective position in terms of social and economic rewards, industrial workers exhibit higher levels of leftism and political militance than their class peers in the menial-service sectors.[13] The hypothesis held by writers in the Marxist tradition, along with many theorists from other orientations, can be formulated as follows: *Lower-class occupations in work settings conducive to continuous interaction among workers will yield higher levels of leftism and radicalism than those in other areas.*

Occupational insecurity, in the form of recurrent unemployment, has been consistently believed to lead to lower-class leftist radicalism. Two different though not mutually exclusive interpretations usually accompany these arguments. First, emphasis is most often placed on the deprivation-frustration aspect of insecurity. "Little-but-secure" may prove less frustrating to the poor than "more-but-unstable." Psychological tensions associated with the prospect and reality of unemployment may prove so frustrating as to lead individuals into the arms of radical movements. Thus, for Lipset,[14] extremism brought about by occupational insecurity is essentially "an expression of discontent, an indication that needs are not being met."

A second, but less frequent interpretation, is that insecurity promotes radicalism by the unique way in which it helps clarify the structural sources of a lower-class situation. Frequent switches from employment to unemployment are bound to increase preoccupation in the individual with the origins of his situation. Also, liberation from everyday work routine may help concentrate attention on more general social issues. Finally, unemployment tends to occur as a collective phenomenon following in the wake of economic recessions. This weakens the tendency to impute responsibility for personal situations to structurally irrelevant factors such as fate, bad luck or individual shortcomings. As Maurice Zeitlin[15] notes in the case of Cuban workers:

> It is not the contrast between their (unemployed) situation and that of unemployed workers which makes them amenable to the appeals of radical politics, but also the fact that they can so easily recognize the source of their problems to be in the concrete economic order.

The same general hypothesis applies to both interpretations of the impact of unemployment upon political orientations: *The greater the occupational insecurity among the lower classes, the stronger the tendency toward leftist radicalism.*

Underlying the three hypotheses thus proffered are two different theoretical orientations. While not mutually exclusive, they represent different viewpoints toward the problem of lower-class politics. As already noted, the interest of all theoreticians in this area has centered on conditions which transform lower-class deprivation into politically relevant beliefs and actions. One view centers on those situations which exacerbate or deepen frustration among these groups. Anger thus generated will be channeled into increased support and sympathy for militant, extremist movements. This frustration-political aggression viewpoint finds its most systematic expression in the writings of contemporary theorists such as Ted Gurr in 1970 and Eric Hoffer in 1966. Leftist radicalism is defined from this perspective as, first, a highly emotional response and, second, a reactive formation triggered by the intolerable situation in which these groups live.[16]

The second orientation is characterized less by concern with conditions increasing frustration than with the particular cognitive framework in which the lower-class situation is interpreted. Low levels of frustration, defined in terms which tie them to the existing social order, may provoke more radical responses than extreme deprivation interpreted in traditional terms. Interpretation of a lower-class situation in structural terms does not arise spontaneously, but must be learned. For this reason, such a viewpoint emphasizes cognition, not emotion, and envisions lower-class radicalism less as a reaction to suffering than as the logical product of processes of political socialization. From this perspective, which may be labeled the socialization-political consciousness interpretation, the particular context in which individuals interact becomes the key factor for predicting their eventual political orientations.[17]

While emphasis on occupational status is linked to the first of these general orientations, the hypothesis relating occupational role with lower-class political attitudes draws its rationale from the second. Both perspectives converge on the importance of occupational insecurity but, as already seen, for different reasons.

This discussion has not been intended as an exhaustive treatment of current theories of lower-class politics, nor has it aimed at formalizing parameters for a "crucial test" between the two general viewpoints. It has attempted, instead, to advance ideas which may provide a systematic framework for the following analysis. The impact of occupational situations on political orientations among Chile's urban poor will be examined within the guidelines provided by the preceding hypotheses and their underlying rationales.

DATA AND METHOD

Data for this study were collected from a sample of Santiago's lower-class settlement dwellers early in 1969. The same data have been employed previously in analyses of the situation and determinants of political orientations in these groups.[18] However, no exhaustive analysis of the role of occupation in the emergence of political attitudes has been conducted. The data seem appropriate for this purpose since, first, they contain measures of all relevant variables within acceptable levels of reliability and, second, they were collected at a time when the parameters of national problems and popular concerns which eventually led to the Unidad Popular victory in 1970 had already crystallized. Leftist party preferences and general leftist radicalism, both tapped in the questionnaire, had already evolved to a level closely linked and, hence, directly relevant to the Chilean situation in the early seventies. This was, in fact, the last set of data on urban lower-class political attitudes collected in Santiago prior to the election of Salvador Allende and his coalition.

The data, however, are not statistically representative of the entire periphery of lower-class settlements in Santiago. Absence of an adequate sampling framework and difficulties in constructing one, due to the vastness of these areas, prevented drawing a probability sample. As an alternative strategy, a classification of main types of marginal settlements in the city was developed. Four such types emerged: squatter settlements, spontaneous slum settlements, decaying government projects and new public resettlement areas.

Squatter settlements in Santiago were the product of organized land invasions. They required protracted periods of organization and planning by would-be invaders. This experience, plus the confrontations with police forces after the invasion, tended to generate high levels of solidarity among settlers. Spontaneous slum settlements were also the product of popular initiative. Unlike squatter settlements, however, they grew in accretive fashion following individual uncoordinated decisions. This generated an irrational physical layout and created barriers for organized cooperative action by settlers. Decaying government projects were initially established for the purpose of eradicating spontaneous slums. Cheap materials and a housing layout which impeded improvement soon transformed these areas into slums themselves. Their inhabitants exhibited the highest levels of discontent with the government which was blamed for placing them in a worse situation than the one they had before. Finally, new resettlement areas were government projects patterned after the experience of successful squatter invasions. They offered land, basic services and opportunities for development and expansion at cheap prices. These "Operación Sitio" settlements, as they were called, were in high demand among popular groups.

For the present study, a settlement was selected as representative of each type. This design maximized variation between sampled areas in residential and related social and economic characteristics. Areas were selected in the north, west, southwest and southeast sectors of the city, thus increasing geographic representation. Detailed maps of each area were available from the Chilean Corporación de la Vivienda (Housing Corporation—CORVI). These were used to draw 10 percent simple random samples of dwellings in each area. In each dwelling, the family head was interviewed. The total sample size was 382.

To ensure that results would be truly indicative of tendencies among the marginal urban population, we evaluated not only quality of measurement but also external validity or ability to generalize findings beyond the present sample. It was possible to test the last dimension, albeit tentatively, by comparing results based on the present sample with those yielded by other surveys. At the time data collection was completed, two more representative studies of the same population were available. The first, conducted by Promoción Popular (Popular Promotion), the government agency for community development, was based on a nonrepresentative but very large sample of peripheral settlements. Total sample size was 71,570. The second study, conducted by CELAP (the Latin American Population Center), was based on a probability sample of the same areas developed by the Statistical Institute of the University of Chile. Total sample size was 1,231. Relative frequency distributions of variables, for which measures were available in either of these studies and in the present one, were compared. The results yielded close similarities.[19] Not only were specific percentages close in most cases, but the shapes of frequency distribution were, without exception, identical. Variables in this analysis included educational level, length of urban residence, occupational sector and amount of media exposure, among others. The analysis provided evidence that findings based on the present sample can be generalized to include the entire lower-class periphery of Santiago.

Political orientations were measured by two different indicators: leftist party preferences (LPP) and a general leftist radicalism index (LRI). The importance of the difference between these two indicators lies in the need to insure validity of results in the face of changing Chilean politics. In earlier work, scholars studying political beliefs employed measures of leftist radicalism based on preferences for the Chilean Communist or Socialist parties.[20] In Chile, an important sector of the Socialist party has been traditionally acknowledged to be more leftist than the Communists, a fact which facilitated their inclusion in the extreme-Left category.

Yet, even before the 1970 elections, new militant groups, such as the Leftist Revolutionary Movement (Movimiento Izquierda Revolucionaria—MIR), posed an effective challenge to Unidad Popular parties as standard bearers of proletariat and peasant revolution. While they did not deny the role of the other parties in promoting proletarian consciousness, they accused them of having evolved toward an institutionalized Left, incapable of revolutionary action. By 1969, MIR and similar movements were defining the Communist party as no longer a radical organization oriented toward defense of lower-class interests within a bourgeois-democratic framework.[21] Thus, preferences of lower-class respondents for the large Chilean Marxist parties at that time could be challenged by some as invalid indicators of leftist radicalism. For this reason, a measure based on more general orientations relevant to this dimension was also included in the analysis. The first indicator, "Leftist party preferences" was based on an item asking respondents which political party they trusted most. Responses were dichotomized into:

1. non-leftist preferences for the Christian Democratic, Radical or National parties, or no political preferences;
2. leftist preferences for the Communist or Socialist party, or FRAP (the previous Communist-Socialist alliance).

The test-retest reliability coefficient for LPP was .61, which is high for a single attitudinal item.

Leftist radicalism was defined as the endorsement of revolution and violence as legitimate means to overthrow the existing social order and bring about one more just toward the poor. Following this definition, the leftist radicalism index evolved from a selective procedure considering all items that appeared to tap this dimension. The technique of matrix inspection and factor analysis, through which the index was constructed, has been documented in detail elsewhere.[22] Table 1 includes the seven components of LRI and their frequency distribution. Taken as a whole, they furnish evidence of face validity of this measure. Internal consistency reliability of LRI reached .78, which is again high (see Table 1).

Table 1

FREQUENCY DISTRIBUTIONS FOR ITEM COMPONENTS
OF LEFTIST RADICALISM INDEX (LRI) (1969)

Item	Categories	Code	Percentages (N = 382)
1. Do you believe that a popular revolution would be:	Very good for Chile	5	6
	Good for Chile	4	27
	Does not know	3	5
	Bad for Chile	2	49
	Very bad for Chile	1	13
2. A progressive government should break diplomatic relations with the U.S.	Should not be done; not very important	1	77
	Very important that it be done	2	23
3. A progressive government should establish friendly relations with Cuba	Should not be done; not very important	1	60
	Very important that it be done	2	40
4. A progressive government should expropriate the properties of the rich and put them under state control	Should not be done; not very important	1	38
	Very important that it be done	2	62
5. A said: A social change must be revolutionary. It is necessary to sweep away the past. B said: A social change should not	A	3	27
	Neither; don't know	2	3
	B	1	70

Table 1 continued

Item	Categories	Code	Percentages (N = 382)

be revolutionary. It is necessary to maintain many things from the past.
Who was right?

6. <u>A</u> said: the best way for a progressive government to attain power is through democratic elections.	A	1	75
	Neither; don't know	2	2
	B	3	23

<u>B</u> said: The best way for progressive government to attain power is through a popular revolution.
Who was right?

7. <u>A</u> said: Force does not lead anywhere. To achieve true social change it is necessary to seek the cooperation of all.	A	1	66
	Neither; don't know	2	32
	B	3	32

<u>B</u> said: To achieve true social change it is necessary to use force against the powerful.
Who was right?

* In Items 2, 3, and 4 "don't know" responses were included in the category "not very important that it be done." Percentages of

"don't know" answers for these items are 8, 12, and 4 respectively.

Because of the emphasis one of the general theories places on frustration as the crucial mediating factor leading to leftist radicalism, it seemed necessary to use a measure of this psychosocial dimension as a control in the analysis. The subjective frustration index (SFI) was created from the same procedures as those used with LRI. Data on this index have also been presented elsewhere.[23] Table 2 presents five items pertaining to SFI and their frequency distributions. Beyond face validity of these items, there is evidence of construct validity in the correlations of SFI with income. Income can be one of the objective dimensions most closely correlated with lower-class frustration. In effect, the correlation of SFI with personal income is -.50 ($p < .001$), that with total family income, -.45 ($p < .001$). Internal consistency reliability of SFI reaches .73 (see Table 2).

Table 2

FREQUENCY DISTRIBUTIONS FOR ITEM COMPONENTS OF SUBJECTIVE FRUSTRATION INDEX (SFI) (1969)

Item	Categories	Code	Percentages (N = 382)
1. Comparison between Present and Past Occupations	Better now than before; best occupation R has ever had	1	40
	Better now than before; not best occupation R has had	2	5
	Same as before	3	29
	Worse than before; unemployed	4	26
2. Comparison between Present Occupation and Initial Occupational Aspirations	Better than aspired	1	16
	Same as aspired; no initial aspirations	2	34
	Worse than aspired	3	24
	Much worse than aspired; unemployed	4	26

Table 2 Continued

Item	Categories	Code	Percentages (N = 382)
3. Comparison between Present Income and Initial Income Aspirations	Better than aspired	1	14
	Same as aspired; no initial aspirations	2	16
	Worse than aspired	3	23
	Much worse than aspired; does not earn anything	4	47
4. Comparison between Present Situation in General and Initial Life Aspirations	Better than aspired	1	26
	Same as aspired	2	18
	Worse than aspired	3	36
	Much worse than aspired	4	20
5. Evaluation of Present Income in Relation to Family Needs	Earns enough; can save	1	5
	Earns just enough	2	30
	Does not earn enough; has difficulties	3	48
	Does not earn enough; suffers serious deprivations	4	17

*R = respondent

Measures of different dimensions of occupation will be described as they become relevant in the analysis. Occupational status and role, measured by the respondent's statement of his main occupation, have a test-retest reliability of .93. The corresponding coefficient for occupational insecurity, measured by length of unemployment in the past, is .91.

THE IMPACT OF OCCUPATION: RESULTS

The first noteworthy result is that the proportion of those expressing sympathy for the Communists, Socialists or FRAP is only 38.5 percent. This figure is slightly higher than the 36 percent of the vote received by Allende and the Unidad Popular coalition in the national elections in 1970.[24] It shows the absence of unanimous support for the Left in marginal urban areas and their tendency toward political pluralism, rather than toward a crystallized majority orientation. The Christian Democratic party received 31 percent of the total, a figure not far from the combined preferences for the two Left parties and their coalition. Those expressing no political preference amounted to 24 percent, also a sizable proportion. Further support was distributed among the centrist Radical and the rightist National parties.

The existence of considerable variability in political orientations among lower-class urban people has been a consistent finding of research in Chile and other countries.[25] These results have effectively superseded previous stereotypes of lower-class areas as hotbeds of political radicalism. As frequency distributions in Table 1 show, those expressing radical orientations in the sample are, without exception, a minority usually less than one-third of the total.

The examination of the effect of occupation on these varying political orientations begins by correlating occupational status with dependent variables. Status was measured by recording principal occupation and classifying responses into four hierarchical categories:

1. minor services;
2. unskilled blue collar;
3. semiskilled and skilled blue collar;
4. intermediate services and white collar.[26]

It is significant that, despite relative physical homogeneity of sample area, considerable variation was found in occupations. Respondents ranged from shoeshinemen and street vendors to established white-collar workers such as teachers, secretaries, social workers, bookkeepers and small merchants. Thirteen percent of those surveyed had white-collar or established service jobs which, in the Chilean context, rank much higher than blue-collar work. Skilled and semiskilled workers, amounting to 45 percent of the sample, were in a much better position than the quasi-tertiary sector of sporadic menial services. Income, which is closely associated with these occupational categories, had a wide range: from below the official 1969 subsistence level of $40 per month to $250 per month, or more.

While variability within the sample was not as large as in the entire population, it was wide enough to justify testing the first hypothesis. As already discussed, this hypothesis predicted a linear relationship between status of occupation and political orientation: the higher the individual in the occupational ladder, the less his support for leftist radicalism. Zero-order correlation between status and LPP is .002; with LRI, .05.[27] Both are insignificant and in the direction opposite to that predicted. These and other relevant correlation coefficients are presented in Table 3.

Table 3

ZERO-ORDER CORRELATION MATRIX BETWEEN
OCCUPATIONAL DIMENSIONS AND
POLITICAL ORIENTATIONS†

Variables*	X1	X2	X3	X4	X5
X1	–	.15	.16	.002	.05
X2		–	.03	.22	.17
X3			–	.12	.22
X4				–	.36
X5					–

* X1 – Occupational status
  X2 – Occupational role (secondary occupations coded highest)
  X3 – Occupational insecurity
  X4 – Leftist party preferences
  X5 – Leftist Radicalism

† Correlations larger than .15 are significant at the .01 level, those larger than .10 at the .02 level.

Absence of linear relationships between these variables can be clarified by Table 4. As was indicated, the underlying rationale for the hypothesis is that higher levels of deprivation, associated with lower occupations, are bound to promote intense frustration which will lead to radical orientation. Accordingly, the first row of Table 4 presents mean level of frustration (SFI) for each status category while the second and third rows present proportions of leftism (LPP) and leftist radicalism (LRI).[28]

The pattern of frustration means corresponds fairly well to that predicted by the theory. The two lowest occupational categories exhibit the highest frustration, while the two best-established ones are the least frustrated. If the rationale for the hypothesis is correct, political orientations should follow an identical pattern: the higher the frustration, the higher the party leftism and radicalism. This is not what happens, however. The two intermediate categories—unskilled blue collar and semiskilled and skilled blue collar—show uniformly high levels of party leftism and leftist radicalism, despite wide differences in frustration. Minor services, the most humble and most frustrated category, has the *lowest* proportion of leftist radicalism and next-to-last proportion of party leftism. The low levels of minor services in both measures of leftism are quite similar to those exhibited by the highest and least frustrated category—intermediate services and white collar. Finally, the semiskilled and skilled blue-collar category, while being less frustrated than the average, shows the *highest* proportion of leftist radicalism.

There is, therefore, a relationship between occupational status and political orientation, but it in no way corresponds to that predicted by the first hypothesis. Status relates to both subjective frustration and leftist orientations, but in a different fashion. Relationship with the first is almost linear, as predicted by the hypothesis. Relationship with the second, however, is nonlinear. Intermediate blue-collar categories, that is, those employed in factory and construction, exhibit higher levels of party leftism and radicalism than service and white-collar occupations. These results not only conclusively reject the first hypothesis, but also have obvious implications for the second.

The second hypothesis makes occupational role the determinant of differential opportunities for political socialization.

Table 4

OCCUPATIONAL STATUS, FRUSTRATION AND POLITICAL ORIENTATIONS (1969)

Status	Minor Services (N = 77)	Unskilled Blue Collar (N = 80)	Semiskilled and Skilled Blue Collar (N = 174)	Intermediate Services and White Collar (N = 51)	Totals (N = 382)
Mean Frustration* (SFI)	.620	.972	.207	–1.750	.000
Percent Leftist Party Preferences †	29.9	46.3	42.5	25.5	38.5
Percent Leftist Radicalism **	7.8	20.0	24.1	13.7	18.5

* In this and subsequent tables, higher scores represent higher frustration.
† $X^2 = 9.29$ 3 df p < .03 V = .16
** $X^2 = 10.37$ 3 df p < .02 V = .16

Secondary occupations, those in industry and construction, offer more opportunities for class-relevant socialization than the relatively isolated occupations of the tertiary or service sector. Figures in Table 4 lean strongly in that direction.

A more specific indicator of occupational role was developed by splitting main occupation into:

1. tertiary and others (service and agriculture);
2. secondary (factory and construction).

This breakdown is separate from occupational status. Six subjects reported agriculture as their primary occupation and were placed into the first category, which also included: those performing established services, such as barbers and cab drivers; white collar workers, such as teachers and bookkeepers; and the large quasi-tertiary sector of oddjobbers, maids and servants, street vendors, etc.

Correlation of this variable with leftist party preferences in Table 3 is .22 (p < .01), with LRI, .17 (p < .01). Both correlations are significant and in the predicted direction. The relationship which they convey is clarified by tabular results similar to those presented for the first hypothesis. Results are presented in Table 5. Proportions of party leftism and leftist radicalism appear in the second and third rows, respectively. To clarify the extent to which results can be imputed to differential frustration, mean SFI are presented in the first row.

Although the level of frustration is, in fact, lower for industrial workers compared to service workers, the former exhibit almost twice the proportion of party leftism and more than twice the proportion of leftist radicalism found among the latter. There is little doubt as to the conclusion to be drawn from these findings. No support is provided for the theory which stresses the role of frustration. On the other hand, results run clearly in the direction predicted by the socialization hypothesis.

The findings would be more significant if it could be shown that leftist orientation among respondents increased as a function of time of exposure to secondary versus tertiary work experience. If the relationship between occupational role and political orientation is, in fact, due to differential socialization, longer periods of industrial and related work would yield greater party leftism and radicalism than shorter ones.[29]

One item in the questionnaire asked respondents about their principal occupations in the past. Answers were again split into secondary (including mining) versus tertiary and others. An Index of Work Experience was then computed by adding this new variable to present occupation. The index recognized the following values:

0—no secondary work experience;

1—some secondary work experience in the present or past;

2—extended secondary work experience in the present *and* past.[30]

Associations between this index and the dependent variables are presented in Table 6. As can be seen, significant monotonic

Table 5

OCCUPATIONAL ROLE, FRUSTRATION AND POLITICAL ORIENTATIONS (1969)

Role	Tertiary (Services) and Others (N = 222)	Secondary (Factory and Construction) (N = 160)	Totals (N = 382)
Means Frustration (SFI)	.235	-.324	.000
Percent Leftist Party Preferences	29.3	51.3 $x^2 = 18.04$ 1 df	38.5 $p < .001 \, \Phi = .22^*$
Percent Leftist Radicalism	13.1	26.3 $x^2 = 9.83$ 1 df	18.6 $p < .002 \, \Phi = .17^*$

*In 2x2 tables, Φ coefficient of association equals Cramer's V

Table 6

INDEX OF WORK EXPERIENCE AND POLITICAL ORIENTATIONS (1969)

Work Experience	No Secondary Work Experience (N = 132)	Some Secondary Work Experience (N = 176)	Extended Secondary Work Experience (N = 74)	Totals (N = 382)
Percent Leftist Party Preferences	28.8	40.3	51.4 $x^2 = 10.67$ 2 df	38.5 $p < .005$ V = .17
Percent Leftist Radicalism	9.1	19.9	32.4 $x^2 = 17.44$ 2 df	38.5 $p < .001$ V = .21

patterns emerge with both party leftism and leftist radicalism increasing as a direct function of exposure to industrial work experiences. Leftist radicalism is especially affected: those having extended experiences in factories, construction and mining exhibit proportions of radicalism three times as high as those never so exposed.

A third indicator of occupational role in the data permits a final test of the hypothesis. This item, independent of the first two measures, asked respondents the conditions under which they performed their present work. Five closed-response alternatives were provided:

1. no permanent occupation;
2. self-employed without permanent locale;
3. self-employed in permanent locale;
4. salaried as chief or foreman;
5. salaried as worker.

Self-employed respondents were always found in service occupations, ranging from shining shoes and street vending to operating small shops. The few foremen in the sample worked in factories but were, by reason of income and rank, clearly above the average worker. The category "salaried as worker" is thus the only one uniquely identifiable with the industrial proletariat.

In examining effects of this variable, the same procedure followed in Tables 4 and 5 was employed. If whatever relationship that exists between this new variable and political orientation is due to deprivation and frustration, the rank-order of the stated categories of the variable, according to mean frustration, should be identical to that according to proportions of leftist party preferences and leftist radicalism.

Mean SFI levels are presented in the first row of Table 7 and proportions of the two dependent variables appear in the second and third rows. Referring to numerical labels assigned to each category, mean differences in frustration yield the following prediction with regard to proportions of leftism: 1>2>5>3>4. Foremen, the most satisfied groups, should also be the least leftist, while those without permanent employment, the most frustrated category, should be the most inclined toward leftism. In contrast, the socialization hypothesis predicts one major difference: the category of workers (the only one formed by

Table 7

TYPE OF OCCUPATION, FRUSTRATION AND POLITICAL ORIENTATIONS (1969)

Type of Occupation	1 No. Permanent Occupation (N = 56)	2 Self-Employer without Locale (N = 64)	3 Self-Employed in Permanent Locale (N = 27)	4 Salaried as Chief or Foreman (N = 13)	5 Salaried as Worker (N = 222)	6 Totals (N = 382)
Mean Frustration (SFI)	2.601	.213	−.709	−2.969	−.456	.000
Percent Leftist Party Preferences	33.9	26.6	29.6 $x^2 =$ 8.4 4 df	30.8	44.6 $p < .01$ V = .15	38.5
Percent Leftist Radicalism	12.5	14.1	14.8 $x^2 = 11.14$ 4 df	15.4	22.1 $p < .01$ V = .17	18.6

occupations conducive to class-relevant socialization) should exhibit larger proportions of leftism than all others.

Once again, the prediction is supported by results. Associations between the independent variable and leftist party preferences and leftist radicalism are both significant at the .01 level. Significance in both cases is due to only one major difference: workers show higher proportions of leftism than all other categories; differences among the latter are insignificant and follow no consistent pattern.

In sum: the second conclusion to be drawn from the analysis is that lower-class occupational roles are significantly related to political orientations. In Chile, as in other countries, the industrial working class was more prone to the politics of leftism than its status peers in service occupations.[31] Results also show that the association between occupational role and political orientations is not mediated by frustration. Findings lend support, by contrast, to the theory of differential socialization, which finds in occupational roles a crucial channel through which politically relevant lessons are taught and learned.

The study of effects of occupational insecurity, however, yield results which depart somewhat from those already presented. Occupational insecurity was measured by the total amount of time that the person had been unemployed and looking for work in the past five years. Responses were divided into:

1. little or no unemployment (two months or less);

2. extended unemployment (three months or more).

Zero-order correlation of occupational insecurity with LPP is .12 (p <.02) with LRI, .22 (p <.001). While both are significant, the second association is stronger, indicating a greater impact of insecurity on radical orientations than on preferences for institutionalized leftist parties. This is in agreement with past research findings which have consistently linked occupational instability with emergence of generalized radical orientations.[32]

Why does prolonged umemployment affect lower-class political attitudes? The most frequent answer is that this situation aggravates frustration and anger felt by the poor and thus provides a final push leading individuals to political radicalism. Table 8 follows the format of preceding analyses in presenting mean subjective frustration levels for both categories of occupa-

Table 8

OCCUPATIONAL INSECURITY, FRUSTRATION AND POLITICAL ORIENTATIONS (1969)

Insecurity Level	Secure Employment (2 Months or Less Unemployment in Last Five Years) (N = 224)	Insecure Employment (3 Months or More Unemployment in Last Five Years) (N = 158)	Totals (N = 382)
Mean Frustration (SFI)	-.812	1.153	.000
Percent Leftist Party Preferences	33.5	45.6 $x^2 = 5.22$ 1 df	38.5 p < .03 $\Phi = .12$
Percent Leftist Radicalism	12.9	26.6 $x^2 = 10.5$ 1 df	18.6 p < .002 $\Phi = .17$

tional insecurity in the first row and proportions of party leftism and leftist radicalism in the second and third. Results, in this case, do support the pattern predicated by the frustration-political aggression model. There are marked differences in frustration between the occupationally secure and those who have experienced prolonged unemployment. Differences, in this instance, run in the same direction as the dependent variables: the occupationally insecure are both more frustrated and more leftist than those in stable occupations.

Does this mean, then, that insecurity effects on political orientations are entirely mediated by frustration? To answer this question, the relationship between occupational insecurity and the dependent variables within levels of subjective frustration was examined. For this purpose, SFI was cut off at the mean. More control categories, or a different cutting point, would have resulted in cells with too few cases for analysis. If frustration is, in fact, the major mediating factor between occupational instability and party leftism and radicalism, controlling for frustration should render relationships between these variables insignificant.[33]

Results are presented in Table 9. They do not yield a conclusive pattern in either direction. Among the group where frustration is high, relationships between occupational insecurity and indicators of leftism are reduced to insignificance. So far, the above prediction is supported. Within the group where frustration is low, however, the original relationships persist. The original association between insecurity and leftist radicalism is, in fact, significantly strengthened when examined within this group: those suffering from prolonged unemployment in the past exhibited proportions of radicalism four times as large as those securely employed. The tabular coefficient of association for this relationship increased from .17 (for the total sample) to .34.

How can these results be interpreted? In Hyman's terminology, frustration may not be an intervening but rather a "specifying" variable that sets limits within which the association between other variables does occur. If nothing else, findings in the low-frustration group clearly show that interpretation of the link between occupational insecurity and lower-class leftism in terms of subjective frustration is only partially valid. Differences

Table 9

OCCUPATIONAL INSECURITY, STRUCTURAL BLAME AND POLITICAL
ORIENTATIONS CONTROLLING FOR FRUSTRATION* (1969)

Level of Insecurity	Low Frustration (Below SFI Mean)			High Frustration (On or Above SFI Mean)		
	Secure Employment (N = 138)	Insecure Employment (N = 61)	Totals (N = 199)	Secure Employment (N = 86)	Insecure Employment (N = 97)	Totals (N = 183)
Percent Leftist Party Preferences	26.6	37.0	29.6	45.3	50.5	48.1
		$\Phi = .11$			$\Phi = .05$	
Percent Leftist Radicalism	8.7	36.1	17.1	19.8	20.6	20.2
		$\Phi = .34$			$\Phi = .01$	

* Significance levels omitted because varying sub-sample sizes make them non-comparable

detected, especially those in leftist radicalism, suggest that there are factors which play a role in this relationship.

The general nature of these factors is suggested by results found in the last row of Table 9. According to the socialization-consciousness model, effects of occupational insecurity on political orientations are due to increased awareness by unemployed individuals of the structural roots of their situation. If this is true, prolonged unemployment can be expected to lead to processes of cognitive change in which blame for personal situation is shifted from self and fate to the social order. The notion of class-consciousness[34] has, at its core, this perceptual redefinition of causes of poverty. This central dimension has been labeled structural blame.

A crude indicator available in the data is the respondent's belief about whether Chilean governments have concerned themselves with the situation of the poor. Belief that governments have been concerned with the poor implies nonstructural blame, while belief that they have not indicates a measure of structural blame.

Correlation of this variable with occupational insecurity is .17 ($p < .01$). More important, however, is the pattern of structure-blaming responses for categories of occupational situation, using controls for frustration. In the bottom row of Table 9, these proportions perform exactly like those in leftist party preferences and leftist radicalism: the relationship between occupational insecurity and structural blame disappears under conditions of high frustration, but remains quite visible among the low-frustration group. These parallel results in the behavior of indicators of structural blame and leftism suggest that the former is potentially an intervening factor between insecurity and political orientations.

Thus, the final step of the analysis consists of examining the "unexplained" associations between occupational insecurity, party leftism and leftist radicalism in the low-frustration group, within categories of structural blame. These results are presented in Table 10. Coefficients of association—Φ—are employed for comparison since they are unaffected by varying sample sizes.

The original association between leftist party preferences and occupational insecurity in the low-frustration group is .11.

Table 10

OCCUPATIONAL INSECURITY AND POLITICAL ORIENTATIONS
WITHIN CATEGORIES OF STRUCTURAL BLAME FOR LOW FRUSTRATION GROUP* (1969)

Level of Insecurity	No Structural Blame			Structural Blame		
	Secure Employment (N = 73)	Insecure Employment (N = 22)	Totals (N = 95)	Secure Employment (N = 65)	Insecure Employment (N = 39)	Totals (N = 104)
Percent Leftist Party Preferences	16.4	22.7	17.9	36.9	46.2	40.4
		Φ = .04			Φ = .07	
Percent Leftist Radicalism	24.7	34.6	27.0	39.6	68.6	51.5
		Φ = .07			Φ = .26	

Placing controls on structural blame reduces this figure to .04 for those who do not blame the social order and to .07 for those who do. Relative differences between original association and those controlled by structural blame are, in both cases, sizable. Similarly, the original association between insecurity and leftist radicalism (.34) is reduced to .07 for the nonstructure-blaming group and to .26 for those expressing high structural blame.

Thus, while our measure of structural blame does not succeed in entirely accounting for the original relationships, it nevertheless plays a significant mediating role. The fact that structural blame does not further break down the original effects of occupational insecurity can well be attributed to the very crudeness of the available measure. An indicator based on opinion about governmental concern for the poor can only partially capture the full range of content of that dimension.

In sum: the hypothesis that occupational insecurity affects lower-class political orientations is supported by the data. Unlike other dimensions of occupation, insecurity effects seem at least partially due to subjective frustration. Both this variable—suggested by the frustration-political aggression model of radicalism—and structural blame—suggested by the socialization-consciousness model—play significant intervening roles between insecurity and political orientations.

FINDINGS AND THEIR IMPLICATIONS

What is the significance of these findings for the Chilean political situation? Theoretical conclusions to be drawn from the analysis point to the greater importance of political socialization as opposed to sheer emotional frustration in the emergence of lower-class leftist radicalism. These results, first of all, reinforce, from the perspective of occupation, trends already encountered in studies of the residential settings of these groups. A major theoretical convergence is suggested by the fact that, in the study of political consequences of occupation, as in that of political effects of community of residence, the main determining factors are not those of status, quality or level, but rather those of social context and interaction.[35] Both sets of findings lead away from the notion of emotional anger and reaction and toward those of political learning and cognitive change as major causal forces in the emergence of leftist radicalism. From this, two related lessons can be derived.

First, in Chile, as in other developing countries, predictions of intense radicalism among the urban poor have taken as points of departure vivid descriptions of the misery in which the masses of peripheral slum dwellers live.[36] Later evidence indicates, however, that misery alone does not give birth to leftist radicalism in these areas.[37] One of the reasons that mass poverty has not been translated into mass radicalism is that the large and growing sector of menial services, in which vast proportions of marginal slum dwellers find employment, is not conducive to the type of class-relevant contacts and socialization capable of promoting radicalism.

Thus, in Chile, support for Salvador Allende and the Left among urban *pobladores* never reached the overwhelming levels that their class situation would have led us to expect. Despite the much publicized case of *Nueva Habana* and other such radical *campamentos* (squatter settlements), the truth is that leftist radicalism was never the dominant orientation in these areas.

The core of urban support for the Allende government lay precisely where the above findings would have predicted: among the industrial workers. An industrial proletariat affected for decades by recurrent unemployment offered the greatest receptivity to leftist radicalism. In this situation, class-relevant political socialization, combined with occupational insecurity, promoted high levels of structural blame and political militance.

The historical experience of Chile during the decades preceding the advent of the Unidad Popular government was conducive to this situation. The Chilean economy was in a transitional stage where industrial advancement had not crystallized into self-sustained growth and where the relatively favorable positions of the industrially employed were constantly threatened by the "reserve army" of the unemployed.[38] In this situation, the import-substitution industrialization of those decades was accompanied by the rapid growth of a militant proletariat and the progressive strengthening of the Left, previously dominant only in the mining areas.[39]

Thus, the conclusion supported by the above findings is that the industrial proletariat was more militant and more supportive of leftist radical ideologies than the rest of the urban poor not employed in the industrial sector. However, our interpretation also suggests that the situation was not necessarily unchangeable. Leftist parties and, especially, a Marxist-led government could have provided alternative means for socializing other sectors of the urban poor into militant leftist ideologies. It is here that community of residence and voluntary organizations linked to it became especially strategic. Efforts were clearly made in this direction. They lacked, however, sufficient impetus or sufficient time to produce a drastic reversal of traditional political orientations among the marginal poor.

A second lesson derived from the above findings concerns the resilience of lower-class support for the Allende government. In more general terms, this is the issue of how a Socialist regime could manage to maintain its popularity among the proletariat despite its shortcomings and the inevitable tensions of a transitional economy. Support for leftist parties that is essentially a reaction to the frustrations of lower-class life would tend to disappear when the same conditions persisted or even deteriorated under socialism. On the other hand, support for a leftist government which has its basis in political socialization of these groups and the resulting cognitive redefinition of the origins of their situation would follow a different path. A conscious radicalized proletariat might accept further sacrifices if they were perceived as legitimate costs of bringing about a new social order.

Generalized expectations of a major defeat for the Unidad Popular coalition in the 1973 parliamentary elections took, as their point of departure, the assumption of "fickleness" among the popular masses who voted Allende in as a reaction to the inflation and shortages during the Frei period and would, presumably, vote him out as these same frustrating conditions persisted during the Allende regime. These predictions did not consider that a large proportion of the working-class vote which brought that regime into power did not arise from passing enthusiasm, but rather from having been exposed to a leftist interpretation of poverty in structural terms.

The above results show that lower-class individuals who supported leftist parties and leaned most heavily toward leftist radicalism were not found among the most frustrated, but rather among those more exposed to class-relevant political influences. Fruits of political socialization were more lasting than those due to emotional frustration. In a situation of rapid class polarization in Chile and under the dual threats of external pressures and internal reaction, proletarian support for the Allende government solidified.

Despite growing scarcities, inefficiencies and widespread reports of corruption in official circles, industrial workers remained the most loyal partisans of the regime. The crucial issue was not how much sacrifice and deprivation had to be endured, but to what extent the government remained the legitimate standard-bearer of the working class and the ideology of revolutionary change. Such attitude left far behind conventional frustration theories of lower-class radicalism.

The legitimacy of the Unidad Popular regime was at times rendered problematic by its vacillations and its own internal contradictions. A radicalized proletariat seemed to go beyond the official leadership in its efforts to accelerate the process of change. Factories were occupied, popular distribution systems organized and, finally, the industrial belts (*cordones industriales*) formed. It was precisely the fear of having to confront an organized, militant, and armed proletariat which lay at the root of the military coup d'etat.

The decision of the Allende government to disarm the *cordones industriales* a few weeks before the coup and the overwhelming force employed during the latter prevented any effective counteraction by workers. This, however, is no indication that proletarian class-consciousness and leftist radicalism have weakened. Our research results as well as broader historical evidence point in a different direction. Working-class radicalism is likely to persist and become a major force in future political confrontations. While specifics are unknown, the last page of the present Chilean drama is still to be written.

NOTES

1. Mauricio Solaún and Fernando Cepeda, "Alternative Strategies in Allende's Chile: On the Politics of Brinkmanship" (Department of Sociology, University of Illinois, mimeo, 1972).

2. James Petras and Maurice Zeitlin, "Miners and Agrarian Radicalism," in *Latin America: Reform or Revolution*, ed. James Petras and Maurice Zeitlin (Greenwich, Connecticut: Fawcett, 1968), pp. 235-48.

3. Guillermo Rosenbluth, "Problemas Socio-económicos de la Marginalidad y la Integración Urbana" (Santiago: University of Chile and Latin American Demographic Center, 1962); Daniel Goldrich, "Political Organization and the Politicization of the Poblador," *Comparative Political Studies* 3 (July 1970):176-202.

4. Arturo Valenzuela, "Political Constraints to the Establishment of Socialism in Chile," in this volume.

5. Joaquín Errázuriz. "Tipología Habitacional del Gran Santiago" (Santiago: Report of the Ministry of Housing and Urban Development, 1969).

6. Charles Abrams, "Squatter Settlements: The Problem and the Opportunity," Report to the U.S. Agency for International Development (New York: USAID, Department of Housing and Urban Development, 1965).

7. Daniel Goldrich, "Political Organization and the Politicization of the Poblador," *Comparative Political Studies* 3 (July 1970):176-202; Daniel Goldrich, Raymond B. Pratt and C.R. Schuller, "The Political Integration of Lower-Class Urban Settlements in Chile and Peru," *Studies in Comparative International Development* 3 (1967):1-22; Lucy Behrman, "Political Development and Secularization in Two Chilean Communities," *Comparative Politics* 4 (January 1972):269-80; Alejandro Portes, "Political Primitivism, Differential Socialization, and Lower-Class Leftist Radicalism," *American Sociological Review* 36 (October 1971):820-35.

8. Seymour Martin Lipset, *Political Man* (New York: Doubleday Anchor Books, 1963).

9. Daniel Goldrich, "Toward the Comparative Study of Politicization in Latin America," in *Contemporary Cultures and Societies in Latin America*, ed. D. Heath and R. Adams (New York: Random House, 1965), pp. 361-78.

10. Maurice Zeitlin, "Economic Insecurity and the Political Attitudes of Cuban Workers," *American Sociological Review* 31 (February 1966):31-51; Erich Fromm, *Escape from Freedom* (New York: Holt, Rinehart, and Winston, 1941); Hans Toch, *The Social Psychology of Social Movements* (Indianapolis: Bobbs-Merrill, 1965).

11. Lipset, *Political Man*, p. 139.

12. Goldrich, "Toward the Comparative Study," p. 365.

13. John C. Leggett, "Economic Insecurity and Working Class Consciousness," *American Sociological Review* 29 (April 1964):226-34.

14. Lipset, *Political Man*, p. 243.

15. Zeitlin, "Economic Insecurity," p. 49.

16. Ted R. Gurr, *Why Men Rebel* (Princeton: Princeton University Press, 1970); Eric Hoffer, *The True Believer* (New York: Harper and Row, 1966).

17. Vladimir I. Lenin, *What is to be Done* (New York: International Publishers, 1929); Ralf Dahrendorf, *Class and Class Conflict in Industrial Society* (Stanford: Stanford University Press, 1965); Petras and Zeitlin, "Miners and Agrarian Radicalism."

18. Alejandro Portes, "Political Primitivism"; "On the Logic of Post-Factum Explanations: The Hypothesis of Lower-Class Frustration as the Cause of Leftist Radicalism," *Social Forces* 50 (September 1971):26-44.

19. Alejandro Portes, "Status Inconsistency and Lower-Class Leftist Radicalism," *Sociological Quarterly* 13 (Summer 1972):361-82.

20. William Kornhauser, *The Politics of Mass Society* (New York: The Free Press, 1959); Glaucio Soares and Robert L. Hamblin, "Socio-economic Variables and Voting for the Radical Left: Chile, 1952," *American Political Science Review* 61 (December 1967):1055-66.

21. Thomas G. Sanders, "Chile—The Elections and After," American Universities Field Staff Reports, West Coast South American Series 27, 1970.

22. Portes, "Political Primitivism."

23. Ibid.

24. Sanders, "Chile."

25. Goldrich, et al., "Political Integration."

26. In minor services were included maids, shoeshiners, messengers, oddjobbers, washerwomen, etc.; in unskilled blue collar, construction and factory workers without training; in semiskilled and skilled blue collar, carpenters, masons, plumbers, factory machinists, mechanics, electricians, etc.; in intermediate services and white collar, barbers, cab drivers, small merchants with their own shops, secretaries, bookkeepers and teachers.

27. Analysis and justification for use of product-moment correlation with ordinal-level variables are found, among others, in Labovitz, "Some Observations on Measurement and Statistics," *Social Forces* 56 (December 1967):151-60 and Richard Boyle, "Path Analysis and Ordinal Data," *American Journal of Sociology* 75 (January 1970):461-80. Readers skeptical of this orientation may turn directly to tabular results.

28. Proportion of leftist radicalism in this and subsequent analyses are the proportions on or above one standard deviation in the radical direction of LRI. This cutting point maximizes validity of the classification by insuring that those labelled "radical" are really so.

29. Herbert Hyman, *Survey Design and Analysis* (New York: The Free Press, 1967).

30. Respondents reporting the same occupation in the present and past were coded "0" if this was a tertiary occupation, and "2" if it was secondary. The only exceptions were young respondents, employed in factory or construction, who never had worked before. These were coded "1".

31. An alternative and perhaps better way of phrasing this conclusion is that the industrial proletariat in developing nations is more aware of its class interests and more militant in defending movements perceived to represent them than other lower-class sectors. Such movements are usually, but not always, of Marxist inspiration. A particularly instructive case is that of Peronism in Argentina, described at length by Gino Germani, "Inquiry into the Social Effects of Urbanization in a Working-Class Sector of Buenos Aires," in *Urbanization in Latin America*, ed. Philip M. Hauser (New York: International Documents Service, 1961), pp. 206-33, and "Social and Political Consequences of Mobility," in *Social Structure and Mobility in Economic Development*, ed. N.J. Smelser and S.M. Lipset (Chicago: Aldine, 1966), pp. 364-94. Touraine has studied the somewhat similar case of the Sao Paulo industrial proletariat; see Alan Touraine, "Industrialisation et Conscience Ouvrière a Sao Paulo," *Sociologie du Travail* 4 (October 1961):389-407. In Chile, however, as in Uruguay and other countries, industrial workers' political consciousness is channeled through traditional Marxist unions and the Communist party. See Antonio Mercader and Jorge de Vera, *Tupamaros: Estrategia y Accion* (Montevideo: Alfa, 1969).

32. Leggett, "Economic Insecurity"; Walter Korpi, "Working-Class Communism in Western Europe: Rational or Non-Rational," *American Sociological Review* 36 (December 1971):971-84.

33. Hyman, *Survey Design and Analysis*; Herbert A. Simon, *Models of Man* (New York: Wiley, 1957).

34. Bertell Ollman, "Marx's Use of 'Class'," *American Journal of Sociology* 73 (March 1968):573-80.

35. Goldrich, "Political Organization"; Portes, "Political Primitivism."

36. Barbara Ward, "The Uses of Prosperity," *Saturday Review*, August 1964, pp. 191-92; Tad Szulc, *Winds of Revolution: Latin America Today and Tomorrow* (New York: Praeger, 1965); Jose Nun, Juan Carlos Marin and Miguel Murmis, "La Marginalidad en America Latina," Working Paper 2 (Santiago, Chile: Joint Program ILPES/DESAL, 1967).

37. Joan M. Nelson, *Migrants, Urban Poverty and Instability in Developing Nations* (Cambridge, Mass.: Harvard University Center for International Affairs, 1969).

38. Jorge Ahumada, *En Vez de la Miseria* (Santiago, Chile: Editorial del Pacifico, 1967); Anibal Pinto, *Chile: Una Economia Dificil* (México: Fondo de Cultura Económica, 1964); Joseph Grunwald, "The 'Structuralist' School on Price Stability and Development: The Chilean Case," in *Latin American Issues*, ed. Albert O. Hirschman (New York: Twentieth Century Fund, 1961), pp. 95-123.

39. Frederick B. Pike, "Aspects of Class Relations in Chile, 1850-1960," in *Latin America: Reform or Revolution?* ed. Petras and Zeitlin, pp. 202-19; Petras and Zeitlin, "Miners and Agrarian Radicalism."

8

The Transformation
of the Chilean Countryside

Brian Loveman

From 1932 until 1973, Chile was the only country in Latin America to maintain a competitive formal democracy with no unconstitutional changes of regime. To a great extent, the success of the Chilean system rested on the pride most Chileans shared in their political institutions. However, a supportive political culture may not be enough, particularly when large segments of the population experience economic and social conditions that directly contradict a system's formal commitment to equality, social mobility and decent living standards.

In Chile, a highly developed party system and presidential government, along with the absence of serious regional, religious or ethnic cleavages, contributed to the continuity of democracy. The party spectrum was one-dimensional—a Left-Right continuum based on ideological differences concerning the role of the state in society and on the "social question."

A very important source of continuity and stability was the Chilean system's combination of multiparty politics with presidential government. Whatever happened in congressional elections, the president, with his vested constitutional powers, remained "in charge." Nevertheless, a "polarized multiparty system"[1] provided a difficult context for presidential dominance. Typically, Chilean presidents elected by coalitions were unable to maintain total support even of their own parties during their six-year terms.[2]

The political struggle between Congress and the president did not mean immobility, only a serious constraint on the ability of Chilean presidents to impose the electoral platform on which they campaigned. Since, generally, the presidential electoral platforms contained more "Left" or populist planks than the Congress would accept, the growing frustration of leftist members of presidential coalitions meant the eventual decomposition of these arrangements and a gradually increased dependence on the Right for essential legislation. The Chilean Congress thus provided the Right with an opportunity to constrain the activity of the Center-Left presidential coalitions which governed the country between 1938 and 1958. As James Petras has pointed out, "though the traditional oligarchy did not 'rule' Chile between 1938-58, it did limit the scope of action of the Left-Center coalitions that elected the president."[3]

The capability of the Right to constrain the action of the Center-Left presidential coalitions depended upon the dominance of the *hacendados* (landowners) over the rural labor force. Control of the votes of rural labor through bribery and intimidation provided the base for the electoral strength of many Conservatives and Liberals as well as some Radicals and contributed significantly to determine the composition of Congress, where rightist elements (as opposed to the Center) maintained veto capabilities as late as 1965. The "stability" of Chilean democracy during these years depended upon the continued domination of the hacienda system in rural areas and repression of the labor movement there in exchange for approval of government programs of industrialization and modernization in the urban areas. In practice, the rightist parties also exacted benefits from the urban and industrial development programs by participating in government-supported private enterprises and channeling credit into "desirable" areas.

Underlying this tacit "arrangement" were important contradictions. The electoral constituency of Socialists, Communists, Radicals and even Liberals consisted mainly of urban dwellers. A most important element in maintaining this support was the effort to keep basic food prices—controlled by government decree—within reasonable limits. Throughout this period, the issue of inflation—reflected in the price of flour, bread, cooking oil, sugar and other staples—was a dominant theme in every election except the presidential election of 1964, which focused on the "danger of communism."

After the great world depression (1929-30), the Chilean government began to fix *minimum* prices for agricultural commodities to defend producers. When the depression ended, the government began to fix *maximum* prices for a variety of wholesale and retail commodities. This development reflected the conflicting interests of urban politicians and landowners. The growing militancy of the urban and industrial labor movement made it inevitable that increases in agricultural prices would have repercussions in demands for higher wages. In addition,

> a direct confrontation with the workers would have entailed a loss of electoral support by the reformist bourgeois parties. In these conditions the bourgeoisie decided again and again to oppose increases in agricultural prices. . . .The bourgeoisie was disposed to find ways to compensate the landowners. The nature of these measures depended upon political exigencies but there was one means which was almost always constant: repression of the rural union movement.[4]

It must be added that the Marxist parties, with the exception of the Trotskyist wing of the Socialists, periodically colluded in this repression. Coalition governments headed by radicals from 1938 to 1952 repeatedly sacrificed the rural labor movement in order to maintain the internal viability of government coalitions and to save programs in Congress. The repression of rural labor, in addition to the nonenforcement of labor law and housing codes and the noncollection of social security and health insurance payments, represented the most important government "subsidy" to rural employers from 1932-64.[5] This compensated farmers for the relatively low prices of agricultural commodities.[6] Indeed, the real income of rural labor experienced a secular decline from 1940-64.[7] Thus, the fundamental basis for maintaining the existing equilibrium among parties, that is, the legal participation of the "anti-system" parties, consisted in the latter's nonintervention in rural areas and their unwillingness to seriously threaten the *hacendados'* domination of the rural labor force. Maintenance of the hacienda system provided the essential exchange for the "stability" of the party system which, in turn, prevented radical transformations of the Chilean policy and economy.[8]

From 1938 onward, middle-class and especially Marxist parties did begin to challenge the *hacendados'* control of rural labor. But from 1938-58, the major thrust of the Marxist parties in rural areas was not electoral politics. Stimulation of class organizations and labor conflicts, agitation for enforcement of existing labor law and ideological penetration took precedence over the electoral struggle. The existence of foci of resistance provided leftist parties with the potential for creating situations of conflict, embarrassing incumbent governments, agitating for improved conditions for rural labor and directly challenging landed proprietors. While the struggle of the *campesinos* (rural workers and "peasants") against the *hacendados* during the period 1932-64 failed, in itself, to destroy the hacienda system,[9] the combination of increased *campesino* militancy and a dramatic turn in national political events did finally bring the end of the traditional rural property system in Chile. This upset the political equilibrium that had persisted since 1932 and set Chile on the "road to socialism."

ORIGIN AND POLITICAL IMPLICATIONS OF THE HACIENDA SYSTEM: THE COLONY TO 1964

From the time of the Spanish conquest of the territory of Chile, rural proprietorship entailed extensive authority over the rural labor force. The *encomienda* (trust), the first institution established by the conquerors, legalized the exploitation of Indian labor in the mines and agricultural enterprises by "commending" the care and protection of the Indians in a territory designated to favored Spanish settlers. Usually the *encomienda* did not vest property rights in land with the conquerors although sometimes the Indians (together with their land) passed into the "trust" of favored Spaniards.[10] Legal titles to the land generally remained with the Spanish Crown. But because the number of sedentary Indians in Chile was small (perhaps 70,000 natives between Aconcagua and the Maule River), the "commendation" of the native population in a given region typically "degenerated" into *de facto* control of large tracts of rural property.[11]

Unlike the *encomienda,* the *merced* (grant) assigned property rights in rural land to designated conquistadores and later settlers. Introduced into the Spanish American colonies in 1495-97, the *merced* played a less important role in Chile during the sixteenth century than did the *encomienda.*[12] During the remainder of the colonial period, other kinds of rural properties were also introduced.[13]

Despite the variety of property types, studies by Jean Borde and Mario Gongora (the Valley of Puange) and by Rafael Baraona et al., (the Valley of Putaendo) conclude that the great majority of large estates (haciendas or *fundos*) that dominated the Chilean rural sector from the seventeenth century until the mid-twentieth century originated with the *mercedes.* By the beginning of the seventeenth century, large amounts of the best agricultural land had been concentrated in relatively few such rural estates.[14]

The estates served as huge corrals for extensive livestock husbandry geared primarily but not exclusively to the domestic market.[15] Near the end of the seventeenth century, some landowners turned to wheat production partially as a response to the demands of the Peruvian market.[16] Because wheat production required more labor than extensive livestock operations, the estate owners attracted a resident labor force by offering rentals *(préstamos de tierra*—loans of land). Thus, by the second half of the eighteenth century, Cristóbal Kay indicates that "the process of cerealization increased the number of *arrendatario* [rent-paying] tenants to such an extent that they generally outnumbered the labourers of the Hacienda Enterprise."[17]

As population increased within the haciendas, the bargaining position of the workers eroded. Toward the end of the eighteenth century, a substitution of money and in-kind rents for labor rents began; this process which gradually eliminated the peon[18] has been cited as the origin of the Chilean system of *inquilinaje,* an arrangement whereby resident workers exchanged varying amounts of labor for access to productive land, a small cash wage and other perquisites.[19] During the nineteenth century, the *inquilino* (tenant farmer) was also required to provide one (or more) *peon obligado* ("obligatory" worker) to the hacienda for a specified number of days, depending upon the amount of land leased and other fringe benefits enjoyed.[20] Some *inquilinos* paid workers to perform their labor services, others sent members of their families or performed the labor obligations themselves.[21]

Given the large number of tenants, sharecroppers and wage laborers that resided within his private estate and the wealth he accumulated, the *hacendado's* influence in rural areas was dominant. It was further magnified by the fact that nearby "independent" *campesino* proprietors were dependent upon him for part-time work, credit, markets or access to irrigation water and pasture. From their position of strength in rural Chile, the *hacendados* exercised a key role in national politics well into the twentieth century.

The extent of land concentration in 1925 is illustrated in Table 1. At most, 3 percent of all rural properties encompassed 79 percent of the agricultural land; 10 percent of the properties contained over 90 percent of the agricultural land. George McBride, citing the *Anuario Estadistico,* (1925-26), reported that in the Central Valley 375 properties, representing 45 percent of all holdings in the valley, contained 52 percent of the agricultural land in the area.[23]

Table 1

DISTRIBUTION OF AGRICULTURAL PROPERTY IN 1924[22]

Size in Hectares Extension (Hectares)	Number of Properties	As Percent of Total Number of Properties	Area in Hectares	As Percent of Total Area
less than 5	46,136	42.5	73,069	0.28
5-20	27,475	23.3	292,411	1.10
21-50	13,853	12.7	470,414	1.80
51-200	12,503	11.5	1,288,048	5.02
201-1000	7,236	7.3	3,245,124	12.80
1001-5000	2,080	2.0	4,245,124	16.70
5001---	570	0.7	15,813,796	62.30

As late as 1930, McBride estimated that 60 percent to 75 percent of the rural population resided within the haciendas. In some rural districts, no rural inhabitants lived outside these large estates.[24] The "typical hacienda" was a political community in which the landowner claimed authority over most aspects of the *campesino's* life. The *hacendado's* authoritative jurisdiction extended into the private lives of the resident labor force although, in comparison to the feudal lord's scope of authority in restricting marriages or the "right of the first night," the Chilean *hacendado* exercised a more limited rule. Authority was personalistic and arbitrary, despite structural organization that resembled a hierarchical bureaucratic organization. Members of the labor force were expected to deal individually with the landowner or, since the *hacendado* normally resided in urban areas, with his representative. Severe sanctions, including "banishment," met any effort to organize worker associations. The *hacendados* kept each other well informed about "trouble makers" and maintained wages at subsistence levels.[25]

The turn of the twentieth century was accompanied by profound changes which threatened the privileged position of the *hacendados.* Particularly during its first two decades, the demographic balance shifted dramatically toward urban areas. Supported by newly created Marxist parties, a vigorous working-class movement sprang to life in northern nitrate fields and burgeoning cities throughout Chile. It was not long before unions were extended into the countryside and rural labor was able to join the broader struggle against the propertied classes. Despite a period of intense repression during the administration of Carlos Ibañez (1927-31), short-term gains were achieved through labor petitions, work slowdowns and strikes.[26] However, these were only temporary advances that left the structure of rural relations basically unchanged. Whenever a significant challenge was mounted against the landed elite, the *hacendados* were able to crush the labor movement—often with the tacit compliance of the highest political authorities. In 1933, 1939 and 1947 presidential decisions, formulated under pressure from the Right, brought administrative and legislative sanctions against rural labor.[27] Restrictive legislation was adopted in 1947 and 1948 aimed at denying the right to organize labor groups in rural areas.

Landowners accompanied these governmental measures with dismissals, evictions and physical violence.

Ironically, while the *hacendados* successfully defended their dominance in the countryside, the hacienda system proved an increasingly deficient mode of agricultural production and Chile was forced to import ever larger amounts of foodstuff to meet internal demand. The production system was not fully used to respond to the growing crisis: nearly 7 percent of all farm units, those represented by the large estates, contained 78 percent of all land under irrigation—but about 30 percent of it remained natural pasture.[28] This underutilization of good farm land not only affected production, but also contributed to rural unemployment. As a result, rural workers migrated to the cities and intensified the problems associated with the provision of urban services. The inefficiency of the hacienda system led many Chilean intellectuals of diverse persuasions to join Marxists in criticizing that system's performance. Ultimately, such mismanagement contributed to the haciendas' final demise.

Despite the early success of the Left in gaining *campesino* votes, it was not until 1958 (and a new electoral reform law) that *hacendado* control over rural suffrage weakened significantly.[29] The reforms established a single official ballot that carried the names of all candidates and was available only at the polling place. By replacing the old system, which distributed individual ballots for each candidate (both privately and officially), it became impossible for landowners to determine how individual *campesinos* voted; thus coercive reprisals and bribery became next to useless. Admittedly, the sense of "duty" of some *campesinos* might still have led them to vote for a candidate that offered compensation—but now the landowner had no way of knowing if they chose to ignore this "duty." The performance of the *Frente de Acción Popular* (Popular Action Front—FRAP)—a coalition of Communists and Socialists—in rural districts during the 1958 elections left little doubt that landowner control over rural votes had declined.[30]

In the 1961 congressional election—for the first time in the twentieth century—the Right (Conservatives and Liberals) failed to gain one-third of the seats in congress. In contrast, FRAP obtained more votes than any other single-party slate, gaining control over 27.5 percent of the seats in the Chamber of Deputies (40) and electing 13 out of the total 45 senators. The Christian Democrats, in turn, received more votes than the Conservatives for the first time. The outcome of the election left the incumbent conservative government dependent upon the centrist Radical party. In exchange for their congressional support, the Radicals demanded ministerial participation and, according to the news magazine *Ercilla,* hoped to gain popular backing to win the presidency in 1964 "(by). . .sponsoring several reforms, including an agrarian reform bill."[31] The "availability" of the *campesino* vote contributed to a reevalutation of the rural work force by the middle-class parties and a consequent reemergence of the "agrarian question" as a central issue in national politics. The Alessandri administration, in response to these electoral changes,[32] as well as to increased *campesino* militancy[33] and the insistence of the U.S. Alliance for Progress,[34] finally proposed an agrarian reform law. This law, enacted in 1962, contained the legal basis for a radical transformation of rural Chile, but its implementation barely affected the hacienda system during the remainder of Alessandri's term of office.[35]

After the 1961 congressional elections, the rural labor movement was courted and stimulated by the middle-class parties as well as by the Marxists. In particular, the Christian Democrats sought to capture an important rural constituency through contacts in the Catholic labor movement, and by encouraging the creation of the *Movimiento Campesino Independiente* (Independent Peasant Movement—MCI) and the *Movimiento Nacional de Liberación Campesina* (National Movement of Peasant Liberation—MONALICA). The Christian Democrats also emphasized the need to unionize rural labor and to expropriate *latifundia.* According to Federico Gil, since the Christian Democrats were "convinced that the two keys to victory in the 1964 presidential contest were the votes of the women and of rural workers and *inquilinos,* they concentrated their most strenuous campaign efforts on these two groups."[36]

The principal presidential candidates in 1964, Eduardo Frei of the Christian Democrats and Salvador Allende of FRAP, promised the *campesinos* that they would soon be owners of the land they worked. They also promised them the right to organize unions and to strike. Both candidates offered improved technical assistance, better access to credit, improved family-allowance payments and a government more responsive to "the people." To the landowners, the majority of whom backed Frei, the candidates offered a poor choice between the lesser of two evils.

THE REVOLUTION IN LIBERTY: THE CHRISTIAN DEMOCRATIC GOVERNMENT (1964-1970)

Victorious in the presidential election of 1964, the Christian Democrats labeled their program "Revolution in Liberty." Revolutionary change was to be accomplished by establishing numerous intermediate organizations linking *campesinos* and urban workers to national centers of political power and by introducing innovative legislative and administrative measures benefiting the "popular classes." But their political slogan emphasized the fact that fundamental alterations would be carried out within the framework of existing legal norms and procedures.

In fact, the Christian Democratic government frequently neglected or deliberately violated existing law in carrying out its program, particularly in the rural areas. Some violations involved policy decisions by high-ranking government officials—to the consternation of other government and party personnel. These decisions were often the result of pressure by some Christian Democrats, the Marxist parties and the rural labor movement to speed up and intensify the transformation of the rural sector. This pressure took the form of illegal strikes and land seizures or temporary land occupations to dramatize *campesino* demands.

At stake was the capability of rural proprietors to demand that the police power of the state enforce property rights in the face of illegal pressure. The restrictive nature of existing labor legislation and the extensive scope and domain of proprietary authority did not always allow government officials to act within the law in their zeal to carry out basic changes in the countryside. The law required that police had to be used when *campesinos* refused to carry on their struggle within the framework of existing norms. At times, officials would enforce the law strictly. This type of support for proprietors, insofar as it occurred, disillusioned activist *campesino* elements and provided propaganda for the Marxist press—which proclaimed that the Revolution in Liberty meant the same old repression of rural labor. In general, the program was neither a revolution nor was it fully constrained by existing legal norms: the Chilean idiomatic expression, *"ni chicha, ni limonada,"* aptly described the situation.[37]

The dilemma posed by a commitment to both revolution and legality was not the only fundamental problem for the Christian Democratic agrarian program. Fundamental disagreements existed within the party on the nature of land reform and its role in the Revolution in Liberty. For some Christian Democrats, land reform was an essential part of a broader effort to redefine and redistribute property. Rejecting either capitalism or state socialism, they advocated rapid introduction of "communitarian" property to eliminate the class antagonisms implicit in a social system separating labor from capital. Communitarian property could unite capital and labor and give rise to an integrated, harmonious social order—a "Christian" alternative to the evils of capitalism and Marxist socialism. These notions were rejected by others who favored redistribution of land to the benefit of selected *campesinos* while maintaining, or only marginally modifying, existing proprietary arrangements.[38]

Though political difficulties and internal conflicts prevented the Christian Democrats from adopting full-fledged unionization and land-reform laws until 1967, they succeeded in carrying out a program of legal and administrative innovation as well as quasi-legal mobilizational activity in the rural sector during the period 1964-67. The program consisted of (1) legislative acts and administrative reforms to improve the position of rural labor while further delimiting the authority of rural proprietors;[39] (2) intensified enforcement of labor law;[40] (3) stepped-up use of the provisions of the 1962 Alessandri land-reform law along with further modification of existing property rights;[41] (3) establishment of a transitional form of rural property for use with the acreage acquired for land reform;[42] and (5) mobilization of rural labor in legally recognized unions, cooperatives and committees and in illegal associations employing both legal and illegal tactics in confronting the landowners. In practice, these measures were interdependent. Effective enforcement of labor law and increased willingness of landowners to sell their rural estates to the Corporación de Reforma Agraria (Agrarian Reform Corporation—CORA) largely depended on mobilized *campesino* pressure. Rural mobilization was facilitated by government legislation protecting workers from dismissal, increased Labor Department responsiveness to *campesinos'* demands, and the material benefits directly and indirectly provided by the government, especially the *Instituto de Desarrollo Agropecuario* (Institute of Agrarian Development—INDAP), to those *campesinos* who joined government-sponsored organizations. *Campesino* mobilization brought landowner retaliations similar to those of earlier epochs. Dismissal of workers in mass, subdivision of properties in order to avoid the terms of the proposed land reform law and persecution of labor leaders gave urgency and justification to government legislation dealing with these immediate problems. By 1967, prior to either the land-reform law or the rural-unionization law, Christian Democratic programs had greatly altered the political meaning of property in rural Chile.

Perhaps the most important change in the countryside was the massive mobilization of rural labor by government agencies and by Marxist and Catholic labor organizations. This multipronged attack on the hacienda system not only produced the largest number of legal and illegal rural labor conflicts in Chilean history,[43] but also overwhelmed the institutional channels for handling these confrontations. Labor Department personnel processed so many disputes that they were soon unable to properly report them to Santiago headquarters. In the province of Colchagua, one of the areas most affected, the provincial labor inspector wrote, in early April 1966, that "because of the lack of sufficient personnel, it is physically impossible to inform you of each conflict as opportunely as is desirable."[44] The official in charge of the labor conflicts section of the department likewise indicated, "we have established. . .that, in Colchagua, the surprising number of 39 conflicts have already been solved without ever being reported to headquarters."[45]

Legal petitions were employed where possible. However, Law 8.811, by prohibiting rural unions from operating on more than one farm, by barring petitions during harvest and by denying the right to strike, precluded an activist *and* legal rural labor movement. While *campesinos* organized some legal unions, illegal commune-wide and even regional federations also appeared.[46] The federations presented landowners with commune-wide labor petitions and conducted strikes on up to 70 farms at a time even though such tactics were clearly illegal. The workers not only demanded enforcement of labor laws, higher salaries and other benefits, but they also pressed for expropriations. In many instances government personnel (especially those from INDAP and CORA) supported the labor conflicts and even assisted in the preparation of labor petitions. Frequent appearances by INDAP promoters at Labor Department offices in representation of *campesino* groups finally forced the labor office to declare that: "the functionaries. . .of the *Instituto de Desarrollo Agropecuario* do not have the legal right to intervene in the presentation of labor petitions and in the process of negotiating conflicts in the agricultural sector."[47] In response, INDAP personnel received instructions to act only "informally" when stimulating or supporting labor petitions.[48] The massive mobilization of rural labor and the expansion of labor conflict is illustrated in Table 2.

In a rear-guard defense of their proprietary authority, land-owners could only invoke the law and hope that the government—no longer under their control and barely subject to their veto—would enforce it.[49] Consistent with the ambiguity which characterized the Christian Democrats, the Frei government sometimes did, and sometimes did not, enforce the law. At some farms, police squelched illegal strikes and the government ordered the workers to go back to work. In other cases, however, the government used the existence of labor conflicts as a pretext to place a government representative (*interventor*) on the farm and begin organizing the *campesinos* for expropriation of the property. Special treatment provided by the government to the Catholic rural labor organizations (Union de Campesinos Cristianos—UCC, and Asociación Nacional de Organizaciones Campesinas—ANOC) affected the outcome in many cases. The government rarely sent in police against the non-Marxist rural unions in this early period and the Catholic, government-oriented unions

Table 2

LABOR PETITIONS AND STRIKES IN
RURAL CHILE, 1963-66

Year	Labor Petitions	Strikes
1963	33	13
1964	49	45
1965	646[b]	155
1966	752[b]	457[a]

Source: Brian Loveman, *"Antecedentes para el estudio del movimento campesino Chileno: Pliegos de Peticiones, Huelgas y Sindicatos Agricolas,* 1932-1966" (Santiago, ICIRA, 1971.)

a. Almino Affonso et al., *Movimiento Campesino Chileno* 2 vols., (Santiago: ICIRA, 1970) reports 586 strikes for this year by counting each farm involved as one strike. We have reported strikes involving more than one farm as only one strike.

b. The figures on labor petitions were arrived at by combining the petitions reported by Affonso et al. with those we substantiated in the Labor Department archives and that the other authors had not reported. The inability of the Labor Department to process the large amount of information on conflicts during this period means that both the data reported by Affonso and reported here is subject to error in the form of (1) missing data and (2) repetition, when conflicts in the same farm are reported for different dates but, in reality, represent only one labor conflict. This problem is further complicated because it was not uncommon for a strike settlement to be reached at a farm followed shortly thereafter by a second (or more) labor petition(s)—thus a "new" labor conflict.

received clear preference in expropriation of farms and establishment of *asentamientos.*[50]

Until mid-1967, the combined activities of government agencies and rural unions maintained a constant state of conflict in the rural sector. CORA itself sometimes found this pressure a

nuisance when *campesinos* forced confrontations over expropriation in areas where CORA had not yet intended to expropriate farms. This conflict between INDAP and CORA reflected
the ideological and programmatic differences between Jacques
Chonchol, director of INDAP, and CORA's director, Rafael
Moreno. It also represented growing tensions within the Christian
Democratic government over the scope and content of the rural
program. The government periodically reasserted its commitment
to legality and CORA made public statements refusing to expropriate farms taken over illegally by *campesinos*. The landowners
realized, however, that this commitment was not as firm as the
government publicly proclaimed. By mid-1967, the large landowners faced their most serious challenge in Chile's history.

Campesino Unionization and the Agrarian Reform Law of 1967

The passage of the Christian Democratic legislative proposals
dealing with the agrarian sector was delayed for three years
primarily by the opposition of rightist congressmen. During that
period, Frei sought congressional approval of his "copper Chileanization" program, for which, faced with FRAP opposition, he
needed support from the Right in the Senate. Despite their
numerical weakness, compared to the combined forces of the
government and the Left, Conservative forces were able to first
delay and then bargain for a weaker agrarian package by
threatening to vote negatively on the copper bill. Thus, it was not
until mid-1967 that the Christian Democratic rural unionization
and agrarian reform laws were enacted.

The Rural Unionization Law

Law 16.625, replaced the existing legal restrictions on unionization. It guaranteed the right of all rural workers, including
those employed by the government, to join *campesino* unions.
The latter, except in special cases, "must be formed by a
minimum of 100 persons who work either in the same or separate
farms, enterprises or properties"   located in the same commune
(Article 1). Within this territorial limitation, union committees
would form the base organization of the new structure on each
farm. Unions could create provincial federations, and these, in
turn, national confederations. In character with the ideological
and programmatic conflicts within the Christian Democratic

party over the rural program, the law also contained provisions to encourage employers' unions for the purpose of negotiating with rural labor. This indicated that the Christian Democrats still contemplated a role for private commercial farms in the agricultural sector.

As already noted, INDAP, as well as the Catholic and Marxist labor unions, anticipated the provisions of Law 16.625 by creating illegal commune-wide unions and submitting commune-wide labor petitions. When the law was passed, they hastened to comply with it by organizing legal communal unions and presenting a flood of legal labor petitions. By the end of 1967, *campesinos* had organized communal unions with over 50,000 members grouped in 21 provincial federations.[51] By June 1970, 488 rural labor unions with a total membership of 127,688 were grouped in three national confederations.[52]

Soon after passage of Law 16.625, Labor Department functionaries began to make inspection visits at the request (and in the company) of *campesino* leaders. Union leaders assisted in preparation of inspection programs. The department processed literally thousands of *campesino* complaints against individual proprietors. At the same time, the agrarian reform law provided incentives for *campesinos* to press their demands vigorously and to refuse solutions to labor conflicts in the hope of speeding up expropriation. Thus, land reform through *campesino* mobilization was becoming a reality.

The Christian Democratic-Agrarian Reform Law

Complete review of the agrarian reform law would be too complex in this chapter, so we will only provide a brief overview, with emphasis on the redefinition of rural proprietorship that emerged.[53]

The first article of the law contained a series of definitions of terms used in the law. Included among these were legal definitions of "abandoned property" and "poorly exploited property," two categories of land made subject to expropriations:

A property will be considered "poorly exploited" if the proprietor has committed any of the following violations more than twice during the last two years before expropriation:

appropriation of family allowances, dismissal of workers without just cause as specified in Law 16,455, non-payment of salaries or in-kind debts to workers or non-payment of social security taxes. . . .

The burden of demonstrating compliance with these provisions rests with the proprietor (Article 1).

The law embodied the principle that no right to property existed where the proprietor did not comply with existing labor legislation and norms of justice in dealing with rural labor.

Article 2 and its succeeding articles stipulated that "in order that rural property fulfill its social obligation, the following types of properties are hereby declared to be of public utility" and subject to total or partial expropriation:

1. All privately held farms that exceed 80 basic hectares of irrigated land (80 BIH) with the land held by married persons considered as a single unit.

2. Abandoned and poorly exploited land (not to be applied in the case of properties less than 80 BIH for three years).

3. Properties resulting from the subdivision of farms larger than 80 BIH since November 4, 1964, unless physical subdivision has taken place and the land is worked personally by the owner. [Farms could *only* be expropriated under this clause during the first three years following passage of the law.]

4. Corporate and government farms, except those of *campesino* cooperatives and CORA.

5. Rented farms, land given in sharecrop or land otherwise not directly exploited by its owner if the legislation regulating such arrangements is violated.

6. Commonly held properties not meeting the stipulations of the law.

7. Properties in the zone of application of the Law of Southern Property (under specified circumstances) (Article 9).

8. Properties necessary for the agrarian reform program offered by their owners to CORA.

9. *Minifundios*, for the sole purpose of consolidation and reassignment (with preference to ex-proprietors).

10. Properties located in a zone where the State undertakes public works to rehabilitate the land for agricultural production.

11. Properties in an area where the State plans irrigation projects or areas designated "irrigation zones."

It should be noted that the possibility of being expropriated did not apply to agricultural machinery, livestock, tools or other movable items. Also, the expropriation clause lacked the mandatory "shall be expropriated" phrase. The law established categories of "expropriable" land. The decision to carry out expropriation remained discretionary.

Expropriated landowners, with the exception of those expropriated under the "abandoned" or "poorly exploited" clause, retained a right to 80 hectares BIH. This right could be extended under very special circumstances to 320 hectares BIH, but this never occurred in practice. Unless the proprietor rented or otherwise allowed indirect exploitation of the farm, the law allowed him to choose the land to compose the "reserve"—provided that the shape, location and quality of the reserve did not impede rational exploitation of the expropriated land and water supply. Since the law made all waterways the property of the state, this provision was intended to safeguard the reform beneficiaries' access to irrigation canals. The law also declared that the reserve should include the proprietor's house and that the proprietor be given preference in locating farm buildings and installations within it. This provision created great difficulties in the expropriated farms and caused CORA to make large initial investments in farm infrastructure.

The authority to expropriate any particular property resided in CORA's Consejo. The decision to expropriate, thus, was administrative. If proprietors objected to the expropriation, questioned its legality or the clause under which CORA acted, provincial agrarian courts heard appeals.

The law required CORA to pay the owner the tax-assessed value of the property (not the commercial value) plus the value of improvements not included in the last assessment. All improvements made since November 4, 1964, had to be paid for in cash (as per value assessed by CORA). If the proprietor objected to CORA's assessment, appeals could be taken to the appropriate agrarian court. Expropriations under the "abandoned clause" entitled owners to a down payment of one percent and the remainder in Agrarian Reform Bonds type C (amortization in 30 years). The "poorly exploited" farms received a 5-percent down payment and the balance in the same type of bonds. When expropriated because of "excess size," corporate ownership or "voluntary" sale, owners received a 10 percent down payment and a slightly superior grade of bonds with amortization in 25 years (articles 42-55).

From the time that the CORA *consejo* decided to expropriate a farm, CORA had a full year to deposit the down payment with the *Juez de Letras de Mayor Cuantía del Departamento* (Department Court). If CORA failed to fulfill this obligation, the proprietor could petition the court to cancel the expropriation and the transfer of the property title to CORA. For three years, CORA could not again expropriate this property for the same reason. Prior to depositing the down payment and registering the property in its name, CORA could not take material possession of the property. In practice, a shortage of personnel and funds delayed "taking of possession" of many farms for almost a year, although delaying payment of a fixed cost in the Chilean case (inflation of 25 percent a year and up) did not produce a totally negative result for CORA. Landowner appeals of CORA assessments, however, could seriously delay CORA's "taking possession" of the property.

One of the main additions to the agrarian reform bill, which resulted from right-wing congressional pressure, was the creation of special agrarian courts to handle legal conflicts over expropriation and compensation. The law provided for one court in each province and ten courts of appeal—whose verdicts were final. Since legal procedures before these courts made landowner victories possible, CORA tended to favor grounds of expropriation not subject to appeal (e.g., "excess size" and "voluntary" transfers).

To leftist critics of the government, these courts were simply another example of the government's lack of commitment to the real revolution—one which would not allow legality to interfere in a rapid, massive and complete elimination of privately held agricultural properties larger than family farms. To the landowners, the agrarian courts represented an important legal channel for slowing down or stopping government expropriations.

"Upon taking possession of the expropriated property, CORA shall install an *asentamiento campesino*" (Article 66). The law established a three-year minimum for the period of *asentamiento,* extendable to five years in special cases. As a general rule, the law provided that, at the end of this transitional period, the land would be *subdivided and assigned to individual campesinos* (Article 67). However, CORA could assign the land as communitarian properties if individual parcels were not desirable for technical reasons or if the *campesinos* demanded it. For legal purposes, communitarian properties included those "that belong in common to all those who work it, or a cooperative formed by these, constituting a human and economic community. Each member contributes with his personal work to the common labor and participates in the product obtained in relation to the nature and amount of labor he realizes" (Article 1). The law listed several types of such property arrangements as acceptable.

Article 171 of the land reform law specified that, in cases of lockouts or illegal strikes on rural properties, the president of the republic could order the workers back to work by decree. A government official (*interventor*), assisted by police if necessary, could then take over management of the farm until the conflict was settled. Any illegal strike on a rural property was cause for such intervention under the terms of Article 171. As noted below, this overlooked provision became particularly significant after 1970 when the Allende government assigned *interventores* (intervenors) to hundreds of farms in response to worker strikes, not to deal with strikers, but to gradually divest proprietors of their land holdings. This article of the law provided the basis for either government repression of the labor movement or for worker-pressured takeover of private properties.

By July 1970, CORA had organized 910 *asentamientos* on 1,319 expropriated properties.[54] Table 3 details the legal causes of expropriation most frequently invoked:

Table 3

LEGAL CAUSE FOR EXPROPRIATION, 1965-1970

	Number	Percent
Abandoned or Poorly Exploited	604	45.7
Voluntary Transfers	392	29.8
Excess Size	171	13.0
Corporate Farms	41	3.1
Properties of 80 BIH resulting from division of larger properties from Nov. 21, 1965 to July 26, 1967.	88	6.7
Units resulting from the division of properties larger than 80 BIH after Nov. 4, 1964, whose material subdivision did not effectively take place.	23	1.7
	1,319	100.0

Source: CORA, *Reforma Agraria Chilena, 1965-1970* (Santiago, 1970), p. 38.

After the publication of Reglamento 281 of May 15, 1968, which set up a point system for judging the efficiency of exploitation of rural properties, expropriation of "poorly exploited" farms gradually increased. Prior to this time, CORA relied heavily on voluntary transfers and "excess size" expropriations. The application of the "poorly exploited" or "abandoned" clause reduced CORA's initial cash outlay from 10 percent of a farm's assessed value to 5 or 1 percent. Thus, more land could be acquired. From 1965 to mid-1970, the cumulative process of expropriation is indicated in Table 4.

Table 4

EXPROPRIATIONS, from 1965 to July 14, 1970

| | Number of Properties[a] | *Area in Hectares* | | |
		Irrigated	Unirrigated	Total
1965	99	41,260.1	499,923	541,183.1
1966	265	57,877.4	468,326	526,203.4
1967 (law 15.020)	131	20,141.8	115,155.4	136,297.2
1967 (law 16.640)	86	30,443.1	119,285.4	149,728.5
1968	223	44,681.1	612,566.3	657,247.4
1969	314	54,478.8	807,361.8	861,840.6
1970 (to July 14)	201	30,986.6	604,181.5	635,168.1[b]
TOTAL	1,319	279,868.9	3,128,919.4	3,408,788.3

a. Some *asentamientos* were formed by combining two or more properties. Source: CORA, *Reforma Agraria Chilena, 1965-1970*, p. 36.

b. Error in original.

By August 1970, CORA had made 98 definitive land assignments to the benefit of 5,668 families. Another 23,471 *campesino* families still remained in legally constituted *asentamientos.*[55] In all, CORA land-reform projects included approximately 35,000 *campesinos* or 35 percent of the government's original goal of 100,000 new proprietors. Ninety percent of these land assignments were made to communitarian enterprises. In practice, CORA found it technically necessary to stimulate communitarian assignments of land. In this regard, CORA overtly defied the legislative intent of Law 16.640 as defined by its framers. It imposed the communitarian solution as a "technical necessity" in a clear victory for the leftist sectors of the government party. CORA justified this development by stating:

Cooperative tenancy...permits a much greater flexibility and adaptability than a traditional, rigid, individual system in which personal interest takes priority over that of the community.

This system of land tenure greatly facilitiates the creation of regional production cooperatives and commercialization, so useful and necessary in Chile.

Other reasons which support this decision are that the cooperative system allows great economy in the management of machinery, water, pastures and generally, the indirectly productive infrastructure like warehouses, silos, corrals, etc.

...The exploitation of a property in cooperative tenancy signifies that the *campesino* community that owns the property freely decides by the common accord of its members the form in which the land is exploited, deciding that each *campesino* works individual parcels or exploiting sections in common.[56]

A Changing Countryside, 1964–1970

The most dramatic alteration of the rural sector from 1964 to 1970 consisted of the formation of a multiplicity of *campesino*-class organizations. Whether union, cooperative, committee or *asentamiento,* some 50 percent of the rural labor force had been incorporated into some kind of organization related to the work situation. Nonetheless, migrant workers and nonresident day laborers still generally remained outside these organizations and, thus, benefited little from the transformation of the rural sector. Indeed, for many, the reform produced unemployment. Contrary to the Christian Democrat commitment to reduce class distinction in rural areas, the reform further stratified the rural labor force.

The reform also created new types of proprietors and, therefore, new interests, while failing to wholly eliminate any of the ownership structures that existed in 1964. Thus, by the end of Frei's term, the rural sector still contained three to four thousand private farms with over 80 hectares BIH. While 1,300 expropriated properties passed into the hands of "land-reform beneficiaries," the small *campesino* landholders and indigenous communities remained untouched, though a system of cooperatives did link many of the former to a variety of services.

The rural proprietor's right to make decisions about land-use management, and transfer of ownership, was considerably reduced in comparison to the pre-1964 period. Investment decisions, especially the authority to leave the land idle, were subjected to increasingly restrictive government regulation. Piecemeal reform had effectively redefined rural proprietorship.

Whatever seignorial-like jurisdiction over the labor force remained in 1964 disappeared with the unionization of the work force and with a provision of Law 16,640 that guaranteed the right of entry to outsiders wishing to organize workers within *fundo* territory. Recurrent visits by labor inspectors, INDAP promoters and union organizers subjected individual landowners to intensive government regulation of management-labor relations.

The legal obligations of rural proprietors toward rural laborers multiplied greatly. Many decisions previously within the exclusive sphere of the landowners now required participation of unions. Social legislation and unionization placed proprietors on the defensive in negotiating labor contracts. The country-wide programs of labor-law enforcement—by special teams of inspectors—turned theoretical rights into concrete benefits. Many small proprietors, unable to assume the costs of the new labor legislation, refrained from hiring day laborers, even on a temporary basis. Since most *asentamientos* deviated from the ideal model and became, in fact, employers, the legal provisions of the labor laws also applied to them. The communitarian enterprises thus also faced regulation by labor department officials and strikes by hired laborers.

Access to credit remained preferentially available to the *hacendado*. Despite the large infusion of credit to the small landholder and to the *asentamiento* system, private commercial banks preferred to do business with their traditional customers. Similarly, some government agencies, such as CORFO and the *Banco del Estado,* continued their support to private agriculture in accord with the Christian Democratic plan for modernization while developing the new communitarian enterprises.

The Christian Democratic experience modified the distribution of rural ownership in Chile. Almost 20 percent of the country's irrigated land passed from control of private landholders to that of newly instituted communitarian proprietorships. The state also acquired large proprietory responsibilities in the rural sector.

Newly created employers' unions sought to protect land-owners from the threat of expropriation and the pressure of rural unions. Christian Democratic efforts to discriminate between "inefficient" and efficient producers initially served to divide the landowners and weaken their determination to resist. But the growing tide of expropriations, including that of many well-managed farms, produced a notable increase of employer membership in class organizations. Because of the conflict between the rural and urban sectors these organizations began to seek alliances with *asentados, campesino* cooperatives and small holders. The old political stability, based on low agricultural prices and compensated for by repression of rural labor, could no longer prevail. The organization of the rural work force and transformation of *campesino* laborers into *campesino* proprietors provided the possibility for new linkages among a more diverse set of rural owners. The existence of strong class organizations—previously in conflict and suddenly sharing some interests vis-a-vis the national government—thus also became a legacy of the Christian Democratic experience in the rural sector.

After six years of drastic change in rural Chile, the mix of rural proprietorship remained extensive and most Chileans knew that the transformation of the countryside had not been completed. The direction of future alterations hinged on the outcome of the upcoming presidential contest. The high degree of *campesino* involvement in class organizations meant that the incoming regime would have much less flexibility in imposing solutions on the rural labor force than did the Christian Democrats. For those with a vision of a "classless society," the new "classes" created by the Revolution in Liberty would represent a serious obstacle to their visionary dreams.

THE FIRST TWO YEARS "ON THE ROAD TO SOCIALISM": *UNIDAD POPULAR* IN RURAL CHILE

The confirmation of Salvador Allende as president of Chile

triggered a wave of panic in the private sector of the Chilean economy.[57] Pledged to eliminate the hacienda, nationalize foreign mining interests and expropriate the largest industrial and commercial enterprises, Allende symbolized the end of the existing system of property and the political regime which served as its foundation. Rafael Moreno, CORA director during the Christian Democratic years, had declared "the road is open." Allende announced that the road led to the establishment of a socialist society to replace the existing formal democracy and exploitative capitalist economy. During the first two years of the Allende government, political conflict revolved around this preliminary redefinition and redistribution of property in the transition to socialism.

The Allende regime made a prime commitment to the final destruction of the hacienda system.[58] Initially, this meant expropriation of all rural properties larger than 80 hectares BIH. Allende appointed Jacques Chonchol—the former director of INDAP who had been fired when the Frei government moved to the Right in 1968—as minister of agriculture. Chonchol immediately proceeded to carry out his earlier recommendations for a "massive, rapid and drastic" agrarian reform. In Allende's first year of government, CORA expropriated almost as many properties as had the Christian Democrats in six years (approximately 1,300). Chonchol promised to take over all farms in excess of 80 hectares BIH before the end of 1972. The government had essentially fulfilled this promise by mid-1972.

Despite intensification of the land-reform process, unresolved issues plagued the Unidad Popular (Popular Unity—UP) government as they had the Frei administration. Allende, like Frei, proclaimed his intentions to operate within the law and the constitution until the existing "bourgeois institutions" could be legally replaced with a people's assembly and people's courts. Lacking control over the armed forces—which had seemingly decided to forego intervention in politics unless Allende exceeded constitutional norms—Allende's tactics corresponded to a realistic interpretation of the limits of his power within the existing balance of forces at the national level. The UP coalition controlled the presidency and the several thousand administrative appointments which Chilean presidents can make to the policy-making positions of the national bureaucracies. Opposition parties controlled the Congress. The court system and the *controlaria* (controller's office) remained effective constraints on mobilizational politics so long as the government coalition lacked the strength to overtly defy the commitment to legality.

Elements within the government coalition (especially Left-Socialists and the Movement of United Popular Action—MAPU) and the *Movimiento de Izquierda Revolucionaria* (Movement of the Revolutionary Left—MIR) rejected UP's commitment to operation within the framework of legal norms.[59] These leftist critics argued that existing laws and institutions served only to retard the transition to socialism and to protect monopoly capitalists, landowners and the agrarian bourgeoisie. In the rural area, these groups resorted to land occupations, illegal strikes and confrontations between *campesinos* and landowners.[60] In the aftermath of Allende's inauguration (November 1970 through March 1971), the most dramatic confrontations took place in the province of Cautín where MIR's rural faction, the *Movimiento Campesino Revolucionario* (Revolutionary Peasants Movement—MCR), supported numerous efforts by Indians to recover ancestral lands.[61] These movements were also supported by Socialist and MAPU militants and, within the first year, resulted in several deaths.[62] From the start, the government lost the initiative to its leftist critics and was forced to react to militant *campesino* movements. Chonchol temporarily moved the Ministry of Agriculture to Cautín to deal with the first challenge to the government's claim to represent the vanguard of the revolution.[63]

The Problem of "Lawful Revolution"

Allende, like his predecessor, faced the dilemma of maintaining some semblance of order and authority while carrying out a proclaimed revolutionary program. Again, in concrete terms, the issue was the use of police against *campesinos* in order to uphold the existing property rights of landowners. Much less willing to use police against workers than the Christian Democrats had been, Allende and his minister of interior repeatedly and publicly condemned land occupations, urging the *campesinos* to allow the government to proceed with its program of orderly expropriation without the daily pressure of armed confrontations and the negative implications for production of permanent conflict in the countryside.[64] MIR and other militant groups refused to subordinate the mobilization of the *campesinos* and direct revolutionary action to the government program, pointing out contradictions in the government's efforts.[65]

The Popular Unity government found itself in a crucible not too different from that experienced by the Christian Democrats: how to make a commitment to revolution credible while upholding, if only temporarily, existing property rights. The problem for Popular Unity was even greater since, after six years of Christian Democratic administration, some 200,000 *campesinos* had been organized, illegal tactics had become increasingly common and the willingness of *campesinos* openly to resist the government and police had increased. Furthermore, the MIR-, Socialist- and MAPU-directed movements seriously threatened production in the rural sector. Landowners attempted to sell off all movable property, cattle herds and farm machinery, anticipating expropriation or illegal occupation of their farms. Decapitalization of the countryside created serious problems for the government and the *campesinos* who received the farms. Soon *campesinos* occupying farms tried to prevent landowners from removing machinery, animals and other movable stock. In some cases, they were successful.[66] Until the end of 1971, however, auctions of these items, including fine dairy herds, continued. This indicated that the government remained unwilling to fully defy the existing agrarian reform law in order to carry out a confiscatory program in rural areas. The rhetoric of total revolution produced a panic in landowning circles that led to decapitalization, even though the government refused to carry out a clear-cut revolutionary program.

The Allende government did move much further, however, than the Christian Democrats in removing private proprietorship from the protection of the state. Infrequent use of police to uphold private-ownership rights did nothing to convince rural proprietors of the government's willingness to apply legal sanctions against *campesino* movements which dispossessed the landowners. In the first 18 months of the Allende government, *campesinos* temporarily or permanently occupied some 1,700 rural properties.[67] Landowners responded with vigilante groups to "retake" many of these properties, while, at the same time, pleading with the government to enforce the law.[68]

Under the provisions of Article 171 of the agrarian reform law the government used these "labor conflicts" as grounds for covertly transferring rural properties from the control of their owners to government "interventors" (intervenors) and the *campesinos*. Indeed, some government personnel and members of government parties encouraged *campesino* land occupations since work stoppage "for any reason" could legally bring government intervention and, in special circumstances, government administration of the enterprise. This procedure avoided the bureaucratic-judicial routine of expropriation and legally introduced government administrators onto private farms.

A set of instructions regarding intervention, developed at ICIRA, demonstrated the deliberate application of this policy by some government officials.[69] Publication of this document in the conservative *El Mercurio* caused a scandal within the government and recriminations between the minister of agriculture and ICIRA functionaries. These instructions explained the nature of "intervention" and proposed tactics for the use of this procedure in the rural sector to circumvent the more lengthy regular procedures. The only restraint on the intervenor consisted of restrictions on disposal of the property in full or part, including its rental to third parties. In practice, the debts accumulated during the period of intervention, especially when it was used to alleviate unemployment problems, could leave the enterprise so debt-ridden that expropriation required little, if any, payment to the landowner.[70] Thus, interventions provided the Popular Unity government with a legal tool to speed up the program of expropriation. But the use of this tool depended upon mobilization of *campesinos* for direct action. The government still faced the dilemma of controlling militant *campesino* movements which used illegal confrontation tactics without deploying police and, at the same time, maintaining the official posture of respect for law.

The Design of Production Units for "Socialist Agriculture"

Highly critical of the *asentamiento* and the resultant agrarian reform cooperatives, intellectual and party leaders within the government coalition could not, at first, agree upon the structural foundations for a "Socialist agriculture." This constituted a serious problem. The government's massive expropriation of large farms during the first year was unaccompanied by a program for reorganization of the rural sector. Some new *asentamientos* were created, but the government announced, in May 1971, that no others would be formed.[71] Instead, some sort of regional *campesino* enterprise would be created.[72]

The matter was intensely debated within the coalition. Some Socialists favored *haciendas del estado* (state farms).[73] Other Socialists and the Communist party proposed large cooperative farms with *campesinos* assigned private rights to garden plots and their own housing.[74] Members of MAPU supported both *haciendas del estado* and commune-wide enterprises with ownership of the land shared by "all the *campesinos* in the commune."[75] In general, the government parties favored increasing the size of agricultural units, destroying the *campesinos'* localist identification with a particular *fundo* and preventing the kulakization of the countryside which they saw in the *asentamiento*. But these general orientations provided no program for reorganization of the rural sector.

While this internal discussion continued, the Christian Democrats and other opposition groups rallied numerous *campesino* organizations against any effort by the government to impose state farms. *La Prensa* regularly featured articles calling upon the *campesinos* to defend themselves from government efforts to become their new *patrón*.[76]

The lack of definition by Allende's government also contributed to a sense of disorder in the rural sector. Attacks on the *asentamiento* system and the *asentados* as a new privileged class brought the resistance of the *Federación de Asentamientos,* the agrarian reform cooperatives and *campesinos* living in *"pre-asentamientos."* Another source of difficulty for the Popular Unity government derived from the fragmentation of the *campesino* movement into unions, *asentamientos,* cooperatives, committees and groups of *afuerinos* ("outsiders" or day laborers), migrants, traditional small holders and Mapuche Indians of southern Chile. Intellectually committed to a participatory role for *campesinos* in policy-making, the government found that this commitment was inconsistent with a parallel commitment to national planning and the imposition of a new system of property. In short, many *campesinos* simply did not have the same goals for the country-side as the intellectual leaders within the government. This tension became more acute when the government started to introduce two institutional innovations into the rural sector in the form of: (1) consejos communales (commune councils) and (2) the new *centro de reforma agraria* (Agrarian Reform Center) proprietorship which the government finally sought to substitute for the *asentamiento*. These innovations became UP's major rural reforms during the first two years of Allende's government.

Consejos Comunales Campesinos

On January 11, 1971, the government decreed the creation of the *Consejo Nacional Campesino* (National Peasant Council —CNC). Promised as one of the "20 points" in UP's electoral program for the rural area, the government proclaimed that CNC, supplemented by communal and provincial *consejos,* would provide a participatory role for *campesino* organizations in the rural policy-making process. *Campesino* representatives would also replace the landowners within government agencies and semifiscal services like the State Development Corporation, CORA and the central bank.

Through the creation of the CNC, Chonchol sought to gather representatives from diverse *campesino* organizations into a single national framework with the hope of legitimizing government policy through formal *campesino* participation. However, despite his repeated commitment to a participatory role for the *campesinos,* he rejected the wording of the decree establishing the *Consejo Nacional Campesino* suggested by some *campesinos* in favor of a more restrictive interpretation. Instead of declaring that "the *Consejo Nacional Campesino* will be charged with working with the government in all agricultural matters," Chonchol insisted that the decree read: *"Consejo Nacional Campesino* will be charged with transmitting the opinion of the *campesinos* to the government in regard to agricultural matters, especially those related to (a) national plans of rural development, rural production and agrarian reform; (b) policies on prices, credit, commercialization and taxation and others related to development, production and agrarian reform; (c) programs and budgets of public and semipublic agencies in the rural sector; and (d) general policies related to the social and economic conditions of rural labor."[77] The advisory role, instead of a formally determinative one, apparently corresponded to Chonchol's notion that "the state, as representative of the majority of the nation, cannot renounce its right to decide to initiate its plans to fulfill the program of the Popular Government."[78]

Membership in the CNC was limited to two representatives of each *campesino* union, *asentamiento* and cooperative confederation, as well as from a national organization of small holders which was to be formed. The decree excluded two small organizations, *Provincias Agrarias Unidas* (United Agrarian Provinces)—generally assumed to be controlled by landowners or *amarillo*—and the federation *Sargento Candelaria (ex-Movimiento Campesino Independiente)*. It also provided no representation for unorganized *campesinos,* migrant workers or Indians. The *campesino* organizations retained the authority to change their representatives whenever they desired; normal terms of office lasted two years. The decree gave the *campesino* organizations 30 days in which to constitute the *consejo,* after which time the minister of agriculture could convene it with representatives from organizations which had designated participants.

The decree further stipulated that, in each province, two representatives of each legally recognized *campesino* federation would form a *consejo provincial campesino.* The base organization in the *consejo* system, organized at the level of the commune, consisted of representatives of "all the *campesino* organizations existing in the commune and those represented in the *consejo provincial*" (Article 14). The minister of agriculture was to name a representative to each provincial and communal *consejo.* The decree left the precise manner of constitution of the provincial and communal *consejos* to the discretion of the *Consejo Nacional.*

In practice, government organizers attempted to form communal and provincial *consejos* prior to the establishment of any norms by the *Consejo Nacional.* Seeking to preempt opposition groups, government officials from different agrarian bureaucracies founded *consejos* and, at times, deliberately excluded opposition organizations.[79] The influence of Christian Democrats in many areas led government agents to adopt a "modified" form of *consejo communal* which included the possibility of at-large representation for unorganized *campesinos.* Even with all this maneuvering, many *consejos* remained in the hands of the opposition. Conflicting interests within the *consejos* between *asentados,* small holders and workers in small commercial farms and migrants, combined with the addition of party competition, disrupted the government's efforts to create a national instrument to control rural labor. The unions, cooperatives and *asentamientos* generally refused to be subordinated to these new government-fostered institutions.

Of a possible 225 communal *consejos,* 177 had been formed by January 1972. Of these, 22 originated in direct elections of "special assemblies," 45 were "modified" *consejos* and 110 followed the pattern set out in the decree that created the CNC. In some areas, the *consejos* played an important role in selecting farms for expropriation,[80] channeling INDAP credit and pressuring the agrarian bureaucracy. However, preliminary evaluation of the *consejo's* functioning by ICIRA investigators revealed that only 10 percent functioned "well" and another third failed to function at all.[81] According to these investigators, almost 90 percent of the *consejos* that failed to function had been created by decree; those formed in special assemblies by direct election—the formally "illegal" *consejos*—and those dominated by Socialist-directed unions tended to operate "more effectively."[82]

The inability of the Allende government to dominate the *consejos* nationally reinforced the coalition's unwillingness to give them a participatory role in policy-making and in administration of rural programs. By maintaining the advisory role of the *consejos,* the government remained free to work through those which were favorably inclined to it, rejecting the recommendations of *consejos* dominated by independent worker organizations or opposition parties, especially Christian Democrats. In effect, the *consejos campesinos* represented another area of conflict in an already complex organizational environment. Conceived as institutional arrangements potentially responsible for commune-wide rural planning (with some degree of *campe-*

sino participation in policy-making), they became another arena in which the government and opposition forces contested for the control and support of rural labor. Thus, the efforts to bring together the diverse *campesino* interests in a loose national association with local and provincial branches did not provide the Allende government with more leverage or legitimation to aid in constructing a "Socialist agriculture." The precise function of the *consejos* became ambiguous and existing *campesino* unions and *asentamientos* were assured a significant place in the daily life of most of the rural population.

Unions and Asentamientos in the New Order

In the first year of Allende's government, great efforts were made to increase the number of members in unions sympathetic to parties in the Popular Unity coalition. Membership drives focused on taking members from the existing unions and organizing those rural workers left out of the union movement from 1964 to 1970, particularly migrant workers, day laborers and owners of *minifundio* plots. When the left-wing Christian Democrats left the party in late 1971 to form the *Izquierda Cristiana* (Christian Left) a similar split took place in *El Triunfo Campesino*, the union confederation fostered by INDAP (Chonchol) during the Christian Democratic government. Most of the unions which left *El Triunfo Campesino* formed a new organization called *Unidad Obrero Campesino* (United Peasants and Workers), dominated by the MAPU and *Izquierda Cristiana* parties.

The resources of government provided the Allende coalition, as it had provided the Christian Democrats, with a means for attracting *campesinos* to unions it favored. A year after Allende took office, the number of rural workers affiliated with unions had increased to 210,000; of these almost two-thirds now belonged to unions favorably inclined toward government parties, exactly reversing the situation in 1970 when opposition unions claimed almost two-thirds of organized *campesinos*. In response, the Christian Democrats and other opposition groups formed a new organization, the *Central Unica Campesina*, uniting the majority of *El Triunfo Campesino* unions, *Provincias Agrarias Unidas* and the Federación de Asentamientos. Federación Libertad remained "independent." This confederation, grouping the unions created by the UCC and ANOC, rejected cooperation with the political Right and insisted on *campesino* rather than bureaucratic control over rural policy.

Despite their continued significance as organizational structures for *campesinos,* the role of unions in "Socialist agriculture" remained unclear. If all the private farms that employed substantial hired labor were expropriated and replaced by collective enterprises of one form or another, only small farms employing family labor or, at the most, occasional hired labor would remain in the private sector. This implied, over the long run, that only day laborers and migrants would remain in unions while other *campesinos* joined the organizations appropriate to the type of production unit in which they worked. Further, while the Popular Unity government persisted in establishing a single class of rural labor without stratification, there would appear to have been no justification for the continued existence of a large rural labor movement.

Recognizing this logic during the Frei administration, many unions diversified the type of services provided to members. Legal services provided an important attraction to workers; union lawyers on retainer could represent workers, not only in labor negotiations, but also in civil and criminal proceedings.[83] The unions also moved into cooperative purchasing arrangements, providing members with consumer goods, while continuing to act as intermediaries between *campesinos* and government agencies. Nevertheless, there remained some question about the ability of unions to survive on a wide scale if the occupational and social life of rural workers was linked to new kinds of production units in which new types of associations exercised the functions that unions had performed. In the short run, unions survived on the strength of their opposition to government-imposed solutions in the agricultural sector, or as government-subsidized mass organizations demanding more radical land reform. Demands for elimination of landowner "reserves," reduction of "reserve" rights below 80 hectares BIH and alteration of the law to allow expropriation of farms larger than 40, or possibly 20, hectares BIH provided concrete issues for union activity. Still, as the restructuring of the agricultural sector occurred, the relative importance of unions in relation to other *campesino* organizations was called into question.

In the case of the *asentamientos,* the Allende government decided on a policy of "benign neglect." Unwilling to pay the price necessary to disestablish them, the government, nevertheless, remained temporarily noncommittal on their fate. Until the government officially announced its plan for the creation of new production units in agriculture, Christian Democratic leaders insisted that the Popular Unity Coalition intended to create *haciendas del estado* to replace the *asentamiento;* only in September 1971, under intense opposition pressure, did Chonchol categorically declare that *asentamientos* created during the 1964-70 period would be maintained.[84]

For many *campesinos,* the *asentamiento was* the agrarian reform. For the government, on the other hand, the *asentamiento* represented a deficient rural enterprise, an obstacle to social justice, a source of new class cleavages, a basis for a "kulak" class and, perhaps most importantly, an opposition stronghold in the countryside. Though some *asentamientos* contained elements loyal to the UP, the leadership of the federations of *asentamientos* and the national confederation maintained close Christian Democratic alliances.

Centros de Reforma Agrarian (CERA)

The internal debate within the government concerning the nature of rural production units resulted in a provisional solution satisfying to no one. Unable to resolve the ideological and practical differences between the various coalition parties, the government found itself obliged to introduce some alternative to the *asentamiento* which it had so scathingly denounced. What emerged, the *centro de reforma agraria,* represented a highly innovative, complex and untried regional production unit which took on some aspects of a territorial government for purposes of planning and administering programs of regional development. It was conceived by intellectuals; *campesino* participation in development of the CERA concept was notably absent.

Defined as a "transitional form of property," as had been the *asentamiento,* the *centro de reforma agraria* took its name from clauses in the agrarian reform law which gave CORA the exclusive authority to "create, direct and administer. . .*centros de reforma agraria.* . . ." Completely undefined in the law, this wording provided the opportunity for the government to introduce a totally new concept of rural property while claiming to be operating within the legal framework. Again, as in the case of administrative intervention as a means to speed up expropriation, the elastic application of existing law made it unnecessary for the government to seek new legislation—which the opposition-controlled Congress would have rejected—or act illegally in carrying out its program. The initial description of the *centros de reforma agraria,* however, produced immediate charges by the opposition and by many *campesino* organizations that the *centro de reforma agraria* was merely another name for state farm—or, at best, a government-controlled production unit in which the *campesinos* would enjoy little effective decision-making capability.

At the time of Chonchol's August 1971 announcement that the government intended to create the *centros,* ICIRA's Santiago office circulated a booklet to explain them.[85] It indicated that they would be substitutes for the *asentamientos* in order to: promote class solidarity; eliminate the *campesino's mentalidad predial* (localist orientation) instilled by the *latifundio* system; create larger economic units; facilitate commune-wide planning and administration of production; and (5) improve cultivation and management of the farms. Most importantly, the booklet noted that the *asentamiento* would be replaced because it "did not give land to all, but only to a small minority. . . .giving the few many privileges and the majority much misery."[86] According to the publication's description of the way in which the CERA was to operate, the *centros* would deliver 90 percent of all profits to a regional capitalization fund, rely upon government agencies for inputs and marketing of agricultural products, manage the farm in accord with commune-wide, regional and national agrarian plans and adopt a precisely outlined internal structure of organization.

In contrast to the *asentamiento,* membership rights in the CERA would be given to all *campesinos* of either sex older than 16 years of age who worked in an area regardless of whether they actually lived within it. In addition, the legal or common-law spouse of all *campesinos* would enjoy full rights of membership. Incorporation of other members was left to the *consejo comunal campesino,* in cooperation with CORA and the CERA itself, with preference for membership given to seasonal and unemployed workers.

A general assembly, including all the members of CERA, would decide by simple majority vote matters concerning work routines, remuneration systems, plans of production and budgets. Secret ballots were to be used only in the election of officers. All workers would elect a production committee that would be presided over by the president of the assembly and either two or four elected councilors. This committee was to "manage, direct and control the productive activity of the *centro,* taking into account the authority of the assembly. . .propose to the assembly work routines and systems of remuneration, without prejudice to the authority of CORA. . .and inform the assembly, monthly, on the financial situation of the centro."[87] The basic work groups of the CERA were to be the *equipos de producción* (permanent and temporary task-specific work teams). Their purpose was "to plan, improve and execute immediate work tasks, avoid waste, loss of time, absenteeism, negligence,[and so on] . . .to establish a precise mechanism through which to register complaints through the respective responsible member of the committee of production, concerning all deficiencies, omissions and bureaucratisms engaged in by government officials."[88] In addition, a social welfare committee and a control committee to supervise and regulate individual workers and other committees were to be created.

As in the *asentamientos,* workers were to receive salary advances equivalent to the minimum wage, financed by loans from the *banco del estado.* The assembly would have the authority to establish different rates of remuneration or salary advances, limited only by the stipulation that the salary paid "be taken into account in preparing the plan of exploitation of the *centro.*" Social security taxes and family-allowance payments would be deducted by the *Banco del Estado* from the loan to CERA and turned over to CORA for payment as due.[89]

Resistance to the CERA concept became intense almost immediately. Minor criticism of the plan centered on restrictions of individual land allotments and pasture benefits, participation of women and teenagers in the assembly and as officers and the ambiguity of the *campesinos'* individual rights within the CERA. The major source of opposition, however, was the belief that CERA was a barely disguised effort to introduce state and collective farms. This objection was raised despite a government announcement that state farms would be created in special cases, but that they would differ fundamentally from the CERA.

The Christian Democrats and the *Partido Nacional* (National party) reinforced their press campaign against the government's implementation of agrarian reform. Led by Rafael Moreno (director of CORA during the Frei presidency) and Andrés Aylwin (congressman), the Christian Democrats made every effort to support *campesino* demands for private farms and the maintenance of the *asentamiento* system. Subsequently, the *Consejo Nacional Campesino* rejected the CERA as defined by the government, insisting that "property in rural land should be turned over to the *campesinos* in cooperatives with a house and a garden plot of two hectares assigned as private property."

On some expropriated farms, *campesinos* independently established *asentamientos* in open violation of government policy. Several national *campesino* organizations (*El Triunfo Campesino,* the *Federación de Asentamientos, Provincias Agrarias Unidas*) supported this tactic in an effort to resist imposition of the CERA model. In response, the government reassured *campesinos* that workers would be granted private titles to their own homes and garden plots, while the remainder of the enterprise would belong collectively to the membership. With the historical development of the rural union movement in Chile and the emphasis of the *campesinos* on improvement in land allotments and other perquisites, government officials had recognized, if somewhat reluctantly, the principle of private rights in housing and a garden plot. This reluctance was due to the worldwide and Chilean experience that private plots within collective enterprises gave rise to competing demands for labor, which the *campesinos* often resolved in favor of the private plots. This is the case because selling private produce provides direct and immediate income, whereas labor on the collective enterprise assumes distribution of a surplus at the end of the harvest season. Where appropriate incentive systems are lacking, or where poor management, corruption or "bad luck" make the worker's share of the collective surplus less attractive than the immediate benefits derived from private plots, then the private sector within the collective enterprise operates as a drag on the latter. This has been a serious problem with the *asentamièntos*. Kay reported that

> the more socialized forms of organization failed in their original intentions. Peasants have shown a clear preference for limiting the number of members and maximizing their private plots and pasture rights. This has resulted in a considerable expansion of the peasant economy within the estates to the detriment of the common land. In 1971-72, about 15 percent of total cultivated land on the reformed units belonged to *goces* [garden plots]. From 1965 the amount of *goces* has doubled. Collective cultivation has been neglected and peasants have even privately appropriated produce from the collective part and used common machinery and implements for private purposes.[90]

More than a year after it was originally proposed, the CERA concept still remained unapplied on a wide scale. The overwhelming majority of the land expropriated by the Allende government had been organized in "pre-CERA committees" on individual farms. These committees bore marked resemblance to the *asentamientos,* but lacked their legal status. By the end of 1972, according to Kay, 45 percent of all the expropriated farms were organized as *asentamientos,* another 45 percent as "*campesino* committees" and only 10 percent were CERA or *centros de producción* (state farm-production centers).[91] The government failed to make clear the proprietary role and interest of the *campesinos* in CERA and to delimit effectively the imposition of bureaucratic intervention, thus making the CERA a much greater failure than the Popular Unity government claimed the *asentamientos* had been. If a more successful production unit was to be created in the reformed sector of Chilean agriculture it, at the least, had to make it worthwhile for the *campesinos* to invest their time and effort in more than a perfunctory fashion in the collective enterprise. The Allende government did not design a rural production unit that met this criterion.

Thus, despite the government's view of the president of the

National Confederation of *Asentamientos* as a spokesman for the opposition, and especially the Christian Democrats, Juan Chacón's opinions represented those of many *campesinos* and *campesino* organizations:92

> The government speaks of collective farms or state farms without consulting with the *campesinos*. . .We have engaged in a struggle. . .to liberate ourselves from the yoke of the *patrón*. . . .We believe that the land should belong to the *campesinos* and we want a Chilean agrarian reform planned in conjunction with the *campesinos*.93

In extreme cases, the government even failed to honor its pledge to respect the existing *asentamientos* when, for "technical reasons," particular properties were needed to supplement specialized state farms.

One such case, *Asentamiento Arquilhue* in Valdivia, led to a temporary *campesino* occupation of the regional CORA headquarters. The government eventually incorporated the *asentamiento* into the *Complejo forestal y maderero del Estado Panguipulli* (State Forestry and Logging Complex of Panguipulli) after serious confrontations between rival *campesino* groups supported by the Christian Democrats on the one hand, and the government on the other. The government did allow those *campesinos* from the *asentamiento* who wished to remain in the newly created state enterprise to seek openings in other *asentamientos*.94 In a joint declaration by various *campesino* organizations in Valdivia opposing government policy, the workers declared: "The *asentamiento* was integrated into the *complejo* overnight without the knowledge or participation of the *campesinos* who categorically reject the implantation of state-owned property in agriculture."95

The government added fuel to the conflict surrounding rural property when a spokesman announced that the government opposed worker enterprises "because worker enterprises are the last bastion of capitalism since they cause the workers to lose their solidarity and unity and create in them a capitalist mentality oriented toward competition and markets."96 This declaration gave credibility to the Christian Democrats' claims that the CERA represented an ill-disguised transition to collective and state farms.

Emilio Lorenzini, the Christian Democratic deputy who led the famous *campesino* strike in Molina in 1953, responded by noting the intellectual sterility and political implications of the government's rigid conception of property and proprietorship. Recognizing that property and proprietorship take on importance as decision-making capabilities, rather than as absolute or holistic assignments of "ownership," Lorenzini remarked:

> the government has been unable to understand that in a new world in which the rules of the game experience revolutionary change, *it does not matter who is the owner of capital, but rather who has the power to decide, to obtain the fruits of the enterprise, and to orient national production. . . .*
>
> We achieve nothing if we merely change the group which exploits the workers in the capitalist system for. . .an 'interventor' designated by bureaucrats. . . .That is, those who control State property—the bureaucrats—control the management of production, receive the fruits of production and orient production to serve the political party of the government.
>
> The workers continue to sell their personal labor to those who control the capital. . . .Before they were stockholders, now they are bureaucrats [emphasis added].[97]

Lorenzini's comments focused precisely on the ambiguities and contradictions of the Popular Unity government's agrarian program: how can a theoretical commitment to social justice, political democracy and rising production be operationalized in a "Socialist agriculture" which recognizes effective worker participation with proprietary interests while limiting the bureaucratization and overbearing paternalism or authoritarianism of the state?

THE DISTRIBUTION OF PROPERTY IN RURAL LAND

At the end of 1972, the reformed sector—that is, all of the properties expropriated under the Frei and Allende governments—accounted for a little under one-half of the total area in irrigated land and about one-third of the land in basic hectares.[98] *Campesinos* in the reformed sector represented about 18 percent of the rural labor force. The other "new" component in the agrarian structure included the ex-*hacendados* who held "reserves" of up to 80 hectares (BIH). Although precise data are not available, the number of these proprietors probably did not exceed 1,500. Preliminary findings show that extensive illegal subdivision of rural properties took place between 1965 and 1970.[99] At the end of 1972, Solon Barraclough and Almino Affonso reported that rural land was distributed, broadly, as indicated in Table 5.

In addition to eliminating the haciendas and creating the reformed sector, the land-reform process, from 1964 to 1972, increased the number of middle-sized private commercial farms through subdivision and the establishment of the landowner "reserves." Table 6 offers a comparative view of the land-tenure situation, by property size, in 1965 and 1972.

While the agrarian reform destroyed the traditional hacienda system, it did not substantially reduce the physical concentration of land into a relatively small number of properties. In December 1972, 6.1 percent of all rural properties contained 65.7 percent of agricultural land (BIH). At the other end of the spectrum, 90.6 percent of agricultural properties contained only 22.7 percent of the land in farms (BIH). Other than the reformed sector, the most important growth in the proportional share of land in particular property categories took place among farms from 40 to 80 hectares (BIH); their area in hectares (BIH) increased from 12.8 to 27.3 percent. These shifts in the locus of proprietary claims in rural land from *hacendados* to cooperative enterprises and commercial farms entailed a dispersion of decision-making capabilities in the rural sector despite the maintenance of a relatively high degree of physical concentration of land in a small number of properties.

The "Non-Reformed" Sector[100]

It may be the irony of the Chilean land-reform process that a growing emphasis on collective and cooperative enterprises produced ever more efficient private farms in which the rural labor force obtained an increasingly important share of income in the rural enterprise. Wayne Ringlein's sample of private farms showed that, in the 1963-64 to 1968-69 period, farm workers' real wages, including payments in kind, nearly doubled.[101] At

Table 5

APPROXIMATE DISTRIBUTION OF LAND AND LABOR IN AGRICULTURE, 1972
(As Percentage of Total)

	Land in Hectares (BIH)	Permanent and Temporary Workers (Including Unemployed)	Value of Gross Production	Value of Marketed Production	Proportion of Production Marketed
Reformed sector (*Asentamientos,* CERA, *Comites, Centros de Producción,* and so on)	36	18	29	29	(80)
Small properties (*minifundios* and farms of 20 hectares (BIH) or less)	22	60	28	15	(45)

Table 5 Continued

Middle-and large-size farms, including "reserves," farms of 20 to 80 hectares (BIH) and 5 percent of land in properties over 80 hectares (BIH)	42	22	43	56	(95)
	100	100	100	100	(76)

Source: Solon Barraclough and Almino Affonso, *Diagnóstico de la Reforma Agraria*, (ICIRA, December 1972), p. 5.

Table 6

Size of Properties (in hectares BIH)	Number of Units		Percentage of Land Area		Number of Units
	1965 percent	1972 percent	1965 percent	1972 percent	
Less than 5 hectares	81.4	79.3	9.7	9.7	189,500
5-20	11.5	11.3	12.7	13.0	26,900
20-40	3.0	3.3	9.5	11.6	8,900
40-60	1.3	2.5	7.1	14.5	5,200
60-80	0.8	1.6	5.7	12.8	3,800
80-	2.0	0.1	55.3	2.9	200
Reformed Sector	0.0	1.9	0.0	35.5	4,700
	100.0	100.0	100.0	100.0	

Source: ICIRA, *Avance del proceso del reforma agraria*, 1972, cited in *"La Batalla Contra el Latifundio"* in *Chile Hoy (Suplemento Agrario 1, Diciembre, 1972)*, p. 8, and *"El Paro de los Conchenchos"* in *ibid.*, p. 2.

the same time, the strength of rural unions, the threat of expropriation and the obligations imposed by labor laws implied a shift in proprietary authority within the private-farm sector.

In some cases, these changes even induced workers to oppose government expropriation of particular properties. *Campesinos* had little success in preventing expropriation, but such resistance by the workers indicated their perception that (at least in some areas) they were relatively well off when compared with workers in nearby asentamientos—despite government subsidies to the reformed units. Some landowners deliberately opted for extended sharecropping, systems of profit sharing or other devices to compete with the lure of land reform and to attempt to block government expropriation of their farms. The overall effect of these tactics was to improve markedly the conditions of rural workers and to vest them with limited proprietary interests within properties in the private-farm sector.

In other cases, after expropriation occurred, cooperative relationships developed between the landowner ("confined" on his "reserve") and the *asentados*. While conflicts between the *asentados* and the ex-*hacendados* over assessment of a farm's value, location of the "reserve," unpaid salaries or other grievances were common, renting of farm machinery, provision of credit to individual *campesinos* or the *asentamiento* and even managerial assistance often linked the *asentados* with their ex-patron. This provided the *campesinos* with alternatives to bureaucratic purveyors of goods and services and provided the ex-*hacendados* with occasional workers, commercial clients and some political leverage in dealing with the *campesinos*.

The Allende government's effort to limit the number of "reserves" granted, and to decrease their average size, may have prevented further evolution of the new relationship between *campesinos* and ex-*hacendados*. For the Popular Unity coalition, the landowner reserves represented a bastion of capitalism in the rural sector and a potential linkage between the *campesinos* and the "social base of reaction." Sixty percent of the expropriated *hacendados* retained reserves during the years 1964-70. The Allende government managed to reduce this figure to 10 percent between 1970 and 1972. The size of "reserves" was also reduced from 80 to 40 hectares through narrow interpretation of the 1967 Agrarian Reform Law.[102]

As the private commercial sector and the *campesinos* in the reformed sector faced common problems vis-a-vis government policies, weather, crop and animal disease and so on, the likelihood of cooperative relationships tended to increase despite public efforts to keep the ex-*hacendados* in "quarantine." The increased productivity of the private commercial sector and the improved position of rural labor within these enterprises might have offered, with appropriate public incentives to agriculture more generally, an alternative model of agrarian reform to the *campesino* enterprises. In a mixed agricultural sector, this might have provided competitive inducements for continued innovation in production and management to the benefit of rural workers, the cooperatives, individually owned firms and the national economy.

For a Socialist regime, of course, this alternative was neither desirable nor feasible. Elimination of the landlord class represented a political goal for the Popular Unity government. Such political goals were given short-term priority over economic problems, including production in the rural sector. From 1970 to 1972, various officials in the government expressed their willingness to sacrifice short-run production in order to eliminate, once and for all, the hacienda system and the *hacendados* from the countryside.

The Popular Unity coalition insisted that the "rural bourgeoisie" remained an obstacle to the creation of a "Socialist" agriculture. In particular, the regime identified those proprietors with 40 to 80 hectares (BIH) who, together, held 27.3 percent of all agricultural land (BIH) as "a powerful and active bourgeoisie."[103] This "powerful agrarian bourgeoisie," however, had very limited access to governmental decision-makers and no control over the credit policies of a nationalized banking system. The rural proprietors in this category were not—with the exception of the ex-*hacendados* on their reserves—a part of the old landed aristocracy with social ties among Santiago's elite circle. Rather, they were capitalist farmers, highly dependent upon government price policy, availability of agricultural inputs (also, to a great extent, controlled by the government) and marketing channels (increasingly under government control or regulation). These farmers lacked the urban linkages that made the *hacendados* so powerful a force in Chilean politics during almost four centuries. They were an obstacle only for those who viewed any private commercial agriculture as inherently incompatible with "Socialist" agriculture and a socialist society. They did constitute a class of relatively prosperous private entrepreneurs and a potential source of political opposition to utopian Marxist elements bent on creating, literally, a classless society. But in comparison with the *hacendados* of the past, this class of farmers lacked the integrated urban, financial, social and governmental linkages to make it a persistently dominant influence in national politics.

Conclusions

The agrarian reform process from 1964 until 1973 upset the fundamental props of Chilean formal democracy: the hacienda system and the repression of rural labor. The stipulations of new rural labor legislation and the 1967 unionization and agrarian reform laws left rural proprietors with more extensive legal obligations toward rural labor than industrialists had toward the urban worker. The combination of intensified enforcement efforts by the Labor Department—noncompliance with labor regulations as grounds for expropriation and militant action by rural unions—forced a transition from paternalism (benign or otherwise) to a system of formal contractual relations between employer and rural worker.

Precisely because repression of rural labor and the nonenforcement of labor law could no longer be the basis of national political alliances between urban middle-class interests and the old landowner class, the increased legal obligations of rural proprietors toward rural labor resulted in intensified sectoral clashes over the relative price of agriculture and industrial goods. The increasing cost of labor could not be financed by rural proprietors at the same time that governmental pricing policy discriminated against the agricultural sector.

No matter what the character of the national regime, if industrialization policies depend upon protective tariffs and discriminate against agriculture in order to maintain lower-than--market prices for urban consumers, then the agricultural sector cannot be expected to finance legislated welfare gains for rural labor. Yet, the sudden introduction of "efficiency prices" for agricultural commodities, or even prices that somewhat more accurately reflected demand, was considered politically unacceptable in an urban society that took for granted price-fixing and habitually blamed the incumbent government for inflation. The Allende government was in a difficult bind not entirely of its own making—inevitably the costs had to be paid.

At the end of 1972, it was not clear how rural Chile would develop in the near future, nor what proprietary arrangements would be worked out between the *campesinos* and the state. The military coup of September 1973 left unresolved the issues surrounding rural property and rural production units. At the time of the coup the struggle in the countryside centered upon the efforts of the Allende government to reduce still further the role of the private farm sector and to restrict private farms to 40 or even 20 hectares (BIH). If the military government decides to apply the agrarian reform law of 1967 *as written, literally,* emphasis will be placed on assigning land titles to individual *campesinos.* This would still leave a mixed agricultural sector, including a number of agrarian reform cooperatives, unless the military government seeks to destroy the cooperative enterprises created by the Christian Democratic government as part of a massive effort to "de-socialize" the rural sector. In some cases simply allowing the *campesinos* to determine whether they desire to continue as co-proprietors or to subdivide the *campesino* enterprises might allow the military to carry out a policy of counterreform in the countryside.

But whatever occurs in the short run, whatever the nature of the political coalition dominating the agencies of the state, the *campesinos* will have to establish veto positions in order to protect their interests against those of the predominant urban sector. Only by maintaining numerous class organizations, autonomous political capabilities and a determination to protect and extend their gains can the *campesinos* hope to press for continued improvement in their income levels and conditions of living.

NOTES

1. For elaboration of this concept see Giovanni Sartori, "European Political Parties: The Case of Polarized Pluralism," in *Political Parties and Political Development,* ed. J. Palombara and M. Weiner (Princeton, N.J.: Princeton University Press, 1966), pp. 137-76.

2. See Frank M. Lewis, "The Political Effects of a Multi-Party System upon the Presidential Form of Government in Chile" (Ph.D. diss., University of Texas, 1955).

3. James Petras, *Politics and Social Forces in Chilean Development* (Berkeley: University of California Press, 1969), p. 100.

4. Sergio Aranda and Alberto Martinez, "La industria y la agricultura en el desarrollo económico chileno" (Santiago: Universidad de Chile, departmento de Sociología, 1970), pp. 78-79.

5. See Brian Loveman, "Property, Politics and Rural Labor: Agrarian Reform in Chile, 1919-1972" (Ph.D. diss., Indiana University, 1973) chap. 3 ("Labor Legislation and Rural Proprietorship) and chap. 4 ("Rural Unions: The Politico Legal Strugge").

6. See Roberto Echeverría, "The Effect of Agricultural Price Policies on Intersectoral Income Transfers," (Ph.D. diss., Cornell University, 1969), p. 107.

7. José Cademártori, *La Economía Chilena* (Santiago: Editorial Universitaria, 1968), p. 109, and M. Mamalakis and C. W. Reynolds, *Essays on the Chilean Economy* (Homewood, Ill.: Richard D. Irwin, 1965), p. 144.

8. Bernardo Yuras perceptively described this trade-off in a letter to the Socialist party in 1938, requesting greater support for the *Liga Nacional de Campesinos Pobres.* The letter was provided to the author by Yuras.

9. While it is commonly argued that the Chilean *campesino* was a "marginal," nonparticipatory element before 1964, this is an historically inaccurate interpretation of the role of rural labor in Chilean politics. See Brian Loveman, "El mito de la marginalidad: Participación y Repression del Campesinado Chileno" (Santiago, ICIRA, 1971).

10. Echeverría, "The Effect of Agricultural Price Policies", p. 59.

11. Ibid.

12. Jean Borde and Mario Gongora, "Evolución de la propriedad en el

Valle de Puangue" (Santiago: Editorial Universitaria, 1961), p. 30.

13. Among others, these included the *repartimiento, mercedes de estancia, comunidad de pastos* and *composiciones.* On various occasions, the Crown also auctioned off land to raise revenues. The different property types involved varying assignments of authority to individuals to possess, use and alienate real estate. For example, after a period of conflict and litigation, the *estancia* came to include the right to pasture animals and to build corrals that enclosed two *cuadras* of land. The right of *demasía* allowed acquisition of property rights (*propiedad*) in vacant lands adjacent to an existing *merced.* Thus, the Spanish rural property system provided "proprietors" with varying legal discretion to possess, use and alienate their "property."

14. Echeverría, "Effect of Agricultural Price Policies," p. 61.

15. Cristóbal Kay, "Comparative Development of the European Manorial System and the Latin American Hacienda System: An Approach to a Theory of Agrarian Change for Chile" (Ph.D. diss., University of Sussex, 1971, and ICIRA, 1971).

16. Ibid., p. 89.

17. Ibid., pp. 92-93.

18. Ibid., p. 94.

19. Mario Gongora, *Origen de los 'Inquilinos' de Chile Central* (Santiago: Editorial Universitaria, 1960).

20. Kay, "Comparative Development."

21. Ibid., and Gongora, *Origen de los 'Inquilinos',* p. 101.

22. This data includes only "properties" in the narrowest sense. Unregistered properties, informally subdivided properties, tenancies, share-croppers and squatters' land and other unregistered properties are not taken into account. Thus the extent of small holds is considerably underestimated. Likewise, the internal proprietorships within the haciendas *inquilino*-held land and sharecroppers land are not accounted for. On the other hand, the concentration of ownership of land is also understated since many *hacendados* had several large estates.

23. George McBride, *Chile: Land Society* (New York: American Geographical Society, 1936), p. 141.

24. Ibid.

25. See the description of the objectives of La Union Agraria, an association formed to unite landowners, in *Boletin de la Oficina del Trabajo* (Santiago: 1922), pp. 129-30.

26. These events are detailed in Loveman, "Property, Politics and Rural Labor, Agrarian Reform in Chile," chap. 5 ("The Struggle in the Countryside)".

27. Comite Interamericano De Desarrollo Agricola, *Chile, Tenecia De la Tierra y Desarrollo Socio-Economico Del Sector Agricola* (Santiago: 1966), pp. 22-23.

28. Ibid., chap. 11 *el passim.*

29. German Urzua Valenzuela, *Los Partidos Politocos Chilenos* (Santiago: Editorial Jurídica, 1968), pp. 128-29.

30. Federico Gil, *The Chilean Political System* (Boston: Houghton Mifflin, 1966), p. 233, suggests, "what was indeed a surprise, however, was the remarkable strength shown by the leftist candidate in the agricultural areas of the central valley—traditional oligarchical strongholds."

31. *Ercilla,* April 15, 1961, p. 17, cited in Gil, *Chilean Political System,* p. 237.

32. In 1961, for the first time, the rightist parties lost joint control of one-third of the votes in Congress—a critical capability in delaying or obstructing reformist programs.

33. In 1962, *campesinos* carried out 29 separate agricultural strikes.

34. On the role of the Alliance for Progress in inducing the passage of land-reform laws in Latin America see Ernest Feder, *The Rape of the Peasantry* (New York: Doubleday, Anchor, 1971), especially pp. 164-91.

35. The government, from 1962-64, acquired only about 18,000 hectares from private owners and did not exercise its expropriation authority.

36. Gil, *Chilean Political System,* p. 214.

37. Literally, "neither apple juice nor lemonade" (neither fish nor fowl).

38. See the debate between Jacques Chonchol and the editors of *Mensaje* in *Mensaje,* no. 123 (Santiago: October 1963), p. 571.

39. For example, Chilean Labor Department Oficio 74, February 26, 1965, Laws, 16.250, 16.270, 16.362 and 16.455—all of which improved working conditions, wages and job security of rural labor.

40. In early May 1965, the Labor Department and the Social Security Department introduced the first joint team of inspectors (Comisión Especial de Fiscalización Agricola) charged with intensive labor-inspection programs and enforcement in the rural sector. The success of this first effort led to the creation of a widespread enforcement effort in the rural area that radically altered relations between *campesinos* and landowners.

41. For example, Law 16.465 (April 26, 1966) prohibited subdivision of all rural properties larger than 80 hectares without prior authorization from CORA.

42. The *asentamiento*. On this see José Campusano and Miguel González, "El Valle de Choapa y la Reforma Agraria," *Principios* (Santiago, marzo-abril 1965), vol. 26, no. 106, p. 88, and José Campusano, "El papel de las organizaciones campesinas en la lucha por la Reforma Agraria," *Principios* (Santiago, marzo-abril 1966), vol. 27, no. 112, pp. 28-35.

43. This period is treated in detail in Almino Affonso et al., *Movimiento Campesino Chileno*, (Santiago: ICIRA, 1970), vol. 1.

44. Chilean Labor Department Oficio 956, San Fernando, 7 abril 1966 (transcribed in Oficio 3043, 14 abril 1966; *Oficios* 16, 1966, 3001-3214).

45. Ibid.

46. From November 1964 to December 1966, 179 rural unions obtained *personalidad jurídica* (legal recognition).

47. Chilean Labor Department Oficio 8914, 11 Noviembre 1966, *Oficios* 45, 1966, 8801-9100.

48. Affonso, *Movimiento Campesino Chileno*, 2:26.

49. For the reaction by the landowners during the period see Robert Kaufman, *The Politics of Land Reform in Chile 1950-1970* (Cambridge: Harvard University Press, 1972), especially chap. 5.

50. In Aconcagua, this pattern was particularly obvious. Farms organized by UCC were made *asentamientos* while FCI-organized farms, with some exceptions, were left for later action.

51. Chilean Labor Department Oficio 2833, 2 mayo 1968; *Oficios* 11, 1958, 2701-3000.

52. CORA, *Reforma Agraria Chilena 1965-1970* (Santiago: 1970).

53. The following discussion draws from ICIRA, *Exposicion Metódica y Coordinada de la Ley de Reforma Agraria de Chile* (Santiago: Editorial Jurídica, 1968).

54. CORA, *Reforma Agraria*, p. 48.

55. Ibid., p. 45.

56. Ibid., p. 9.

57. Solon Barraclough has pointed out that Oscar Lange generally predicted this sort of reaction to a program of socialization. Lange declared: "A Socialist government really intent upon socialism has to decide to carry out its socialization program at one stroke or to give it up altogether. The very coming into power of such a government must cause a financial panic and economic collapse. Therefore, the Socialist government must either guarantee the immunity of private property and private enterprise in order to enable the capitalist economy to function normally, in doing which it gives up its socialist aims, or it must go through resolutely with its socialization program at maximum speed. Any hesitation, any vacillation and indecision would provoke the inevitable economic catastrophe." O. Lange and F. M. Taylor, *On the Economic Theory of Socialism* (University of Minnesota Press, 1938), cited in S. Barraclough, "Agrarian Reform in Chile" (November 1970), p. 27.

58. The preliminary agrarian program of the *Unidad Popular* government was spelled out in the so-called "20 points" which are reproduced in *Avancemos, revista sindical campesino,* FEES, Santiago, *Ano* 3, nos. 6 and 7, 1971 (Points 1-10 in no. 6 and 11-20 in no. 7).

59. See, for example, "Discurso de Miguel Enríquez, Secretario General del MIR," in *El Mercurio*, November 3, 1971.

60. Newspapers headlined these events daily during the first year of the Allende government. Typical are: "Movimiento Revolucionario de Campesinos Ocupó Seis Fundos," *El Mercurio,* January 25, 1971; "Campesinos Ocuparon Fundo San José de Quecherehua," *El Mercurio,* January 26, 1971; "Expropian Fundos Tomados en Parral," *El Mercurio,* March 28, 1971; "Refuerzos del MCR Están Llegando a Zona Conflictiva," *La Prensa,* April 25, 1971; "Las Tácticas del Movimiento Campesino Revolucionario Retardan Acción del Gobierno," *El Siglo,* May 26, 1971; "131 Fundos

Permanecen Ocupados Ilegalments," *El Mercurio*, November 13, 1971; "Entregan Lista de Fundos Ocupados Ilegalmente Por Extremistas de Izquierda," *La Prensa*, November 17, 1971.

61. MIR intervention in Cautín was also widely covered by the press. See, for example, "Veinticinco Fundos Tomados en Lautaro," *El Mercurio*, December 12, 1970; "Sobre un Volcán de Violencia Vive La Provincia de Cautín," *La Prensa*, December 29, 1970; "Campesinos Dispuestos A Morir Por La Tierra," *Puro Chile*, December 31, 1970; "Armados Para Sedición Latifundistas de Cautin," *El Siglo*, January 19, 1971; "50 Fundos Paralizados En Provincia de Cautín," *El Mercurio*, January 22, 1971.

62. "Murió Agricultor Baleado en Toma de Fundo," *La Prensa*, April 20, 1971; "Un Muerto en Incidente a Tiros en Fundo de Cautín," *El Mercurio*, October 24, 1971; "Un Mapuche Muerto y Tres Heridos En Enfrentamiento de Cautín," *El Siglo*, November 23, 1971.

63. "Gobierno Parte hoy a Solucionar Problemas de Cautín," *El Siglo*, January 4, 1971; "A Cautín se Traslada hoy Ministerio de Agricultura," *La Prensa*, January 5, 1971.

64. "El Gobierno Actuará de Acuerdo a Resoluciones Del Poder Judicial," *El Mercurio*, December 30, 1970; "El Presidente de la República Responde a la SNA," *El Diario Austral* (Temuco), January 20, 1971; "La Alianza Oficialista Condenará Publicamente Las Tomas Ilegales," *La Prensa*, July 30, 1971.

65. See "Discurso del Secretario General Del MIR a Nombre de la Dirección Nacional, en Cautín el Lunes 1 de Noviembre de 1971, en Homenaje a Moisés Huentalaf, héroe de la lucha Campesina," Suplemento de la edición. No. 143 de *Punto Final* (Santiago: November 9, 1971).

66. In carrying out research during 1971 the author visited several farms in which *campesinos* physically prevented the landowners from removing tractors, produce and other movables.

67. Chile, Cuerpo de Carabineros, Dirección General O.S. 3, "Relación de ocupaciones ilegales de fundos ocurridos desde el 1 de Noviembre 1970 al 5 de Abril 1972," *El Mercurio*, June 5, 1972, pp. 9-15 and *El Mercurio*, June 6, 1972, pp. 24-28, cited in Cristóbal Kay, "La Participación Campesina en El Gobierno de la Unidad Popular," typed (sent to author directly by C. Kay).

68. "Movilización de Agricultores Ante Ocupacions Ilegales," *El Mercurio*, February 17, 1971; "Lucha a Muerte Por la Tierra en San Carlos," *La Prensa*, February 26, 1971; "Agricultores Impidieron Toma de

Hijuela," *El Mercurio,* March 23, 1971; "Violenta Recaptura de Fundos Ocupados," *La Segunda,* March 26, 1971; "Momios Forman 'Grupos de Despeje' en Linares," *El Siglo,* July 27, 1971; "Empresarios Agrícolas Solicitan Protección," *La Prensa,* February 21, 1971; "Protección Efectiva Piden los Propietarios Agrícolas," *El Mercurio,* March 16, 1971.

69. "Cartilla Sobre Intervención de Predios Agrícolas   ICIRA, n.d.

70. On this see: "Abusiva Actuación de Interventores Agricolas," *El Mercurio,* editorial, February 15, 1971; "Consecuencias de Intervención Agrícola," *El Mercurio,* editorial, February 16, 1971; "Los Interventores Tienen Orden de Arruinar a los Propietarios," *Las Ultimas Noticias,* February 16, 1971; "Cartilla Sobre Intervención de Predios Agricolas," *El Mercurio,* February 18, 1971; "La Intervención en la Agricultura," *El Mercurio,* editorial, February 19, 1971; "339 Predios Agrícolas Intervenidos en un Año," *El Mercurio,* November 28, 1971.

71. For example, "Constituyen Asentamiento en Cautín," *El Siglo,* February 18, 1971, describes the establishment of Asentamiento Santa Rosa in the first property expropriated by the Popular Unity government in Cautín.

72. As early as November 1970, Chonchol's colleague at ICIRA, Solon Barraclough, described the outlines of such an enterprise. See Barraclough, "Agrarian Reform in Chile" (November 1970).

73. Partido Socialista, "Síntesis de la Politica Agraria del Partido Socialista," mimeo (Santiago: 1971).

74. Jaime Lazo, "Informe Preliminar de la Comisión Politica del Partido Comunista," mimeo (Santiago: 1971).

75. MAPU, El Primer Año del Gobierno Popular, Documentos y Posiciones del MAPU, no. 1, Santiago, n.d., cited in Cristóbal Kay and Peter Winn, "Reforma Agraria y Revolución Rural en el Chile de Allende" (Spanish version of article to appear in English in 1973; sent to author by Cristóbal Kay).

76. "Trabajadores Agricolas No Serán Propietarios de la Tierra," *La Prensa,* February 1, 1971; "Defenderemos con energía el derecho del campesino a la propiedad de la tierra," *La Prensa,* January 19, 1971; "Rafael Moreno, ex Vice de Cora, Haciendas Estatales, Una Burla Para los Campesinos," *La Segunda,* March 5, 1971; "PDC Defenderá Dignidad de los Campesinos Ante La Invasión Estatal," *La Prensa,* March 6, 1971;

"Categórico Rechazo de los Campesinos a Haciendas Estatales," *La Prensa,* July 6, 1971; "Dramática lucha de Campesinos Contra Complejo de tipo estatal," July 27, 1971; Más Campesinos Rechazan Centros de Reforma Agraria," *La Prensa,* September 14, 1971.

77. Chile, Ministerio de Agricultura, Decreto 481, "Que Crea Consejo Nacional Campesino." See also "Reglamento del Consejo Campesino."

78. *El Siglo,* November 27, 1971, p. 10.

79. "Funcionarios Impiden Constitución de Consejos Campesinos," *La Prensa,* February 18, 1971; "INDAP e ICIRA Forma Consejos Campesinos al Margen de la Ley," *La Prensa,* October 24, 1971.

80. For example,"Expropriación de 341 Predios Piden Campesinos en Ñuble," *El Mercurio,* January 27, 1971.

81. Emilio Klein and Sergio Gómez, "Informe sobre el Estado Actual de los Consejos Comunales Campesinos," mimeo (Santiago: ICIRA, April 1971), cited in Kay and Winn, *"Reforma Agraria,"* p. 21.

82. E. Maffei and P. Marchetti, "Algunos alcances teóricos sobre los consejos campesinos y el poder de los trabajodores," borrador, March 1972, cited in Kay, "La Participación," p. 11.

83. In the course of carrying out research in Chile, the author became acquainted with several lawyers on retainer with *campesino* union federations. These lawyers represented union members charged with drunkeness, "disorderly conduct" and theft, as well as handling labor negotiations.

84. "Campesinos Rechazan Mero Cambio de Patrón," *La Prensa,* September 5, 1971.

85. "Los Centros de Reforma Agraria," mimeo (Santiago: ICIRA, August 19, 1971).

86. "Centros de Reforma Agraria," (Santiago: ICIRA, September 9, 1971).

87. Ibid., p. 10.

88. Ibid., p. 11.

89. Ibid., p. 13. These provisions indicated the continuing unwillingness of government bureaucrats to turn over effective management of the

CERA to the *campesinos;* CORA retained its paternalistic role and the banco del estado added another layer of bureaucracy.

90. C. Kay, "The Development of the Chilean *Hacienda* System 1850s-1972" (Paper presented to the Symposium on Landlord and Peasant in Latin America and the Caribbean, University of Cambridge, December 20-21, 1972).

91. Ibid.

92. In carrying out survey research in the countryside late in 1971, the author repeatedly heard views of this sort expressed by *campesinos,* especially those in *asentamientos.*

93. Cited in "A Campesinos no les Gusta el Estado de Patrón," *La Prensa,* January 23, 1971.

94. "Protesta Campesina: Tomadas Tres Oficinas de la CORA," *La Prensa,* October 17, 1971, p. 8.

95. Ibid.

96. "Gobierno Se Opone a las Empresas de Trabajadores," *El Mercurio,* November 18, 1971.

97. "Qué Son Las Empresas de los Trabajadores," Responde El Diputado Demócrata Cristiano Emilio Lorenzini, *La Prensa,* November 26, 1971.

98. Kay, "The Development," p. 29.

99. This study is under the direction of Marion Brown of the University of Wisconsin, Land Tenure Center.

100. Discussion in this section is essentially limited to farms of more than 40 hectares (BIH).

101. Wayne Ringlein, "Economic Effects of Chilean National Expropriation Policy on the Private Commercial Farm Sector, 1964-1969" (University of Maryland, Ph.D. diss. 1971), cited in W. Thiesenhusen, "Agrarian Reform: Chile" in *Land Reform in Latin America, Issues and Cases,* ed. Peter Dorner (Madison: University of Wisconsin Press, 1971), p. 113.

102. Kay, "The Development," p. 28.

103. J. Echenique, "La batalla Contra el Latifundio," *Revista Agraria* I, Santiago (Diciembre 1972), pp. 8-9.

9

The Concentration of National and Foreign Capital in Chile, 1966
Maurice Zeitlin
and Richard E. Ratcliff

No less than in the "advanced" capitalist countries, the decisive unit of production in many misdeveloped ("underdeveloped") countries has become the large corporation. A few large corporations now control the bulk of the assets, sales and profits of individual industries and of the economy as a whole. They are able to effectively control their markets to maximize profits. Contrary to the prevalent (though rapidly changing) situation in the developed countries, however, "monopoly capital" in the misdeveloped countries often means foreign capital. An adequate model of the morphology of backwardness and of the processes of misdevelopment must focus on the extent of economic concentration and of the penetration of foreign capital and their interrelations.[1] An empirical analysis of these relationships, therefore, is both of general theoretical relevance and central to a model of Chile's development.

Further, this analysis has a special and intrinsic interest because Salvador Allende, Chile's president, inaugurated in 1970, pledged to put his country "on the road to socialism"—to take over the large American-owned copper companies and other major foreign and domestic corporations, the banks, insurance companies and large agrarian estates, and to institute democratic planning in the interests of the nation as a whole. In its first two

*Printed here by permission of Maurice Zeitlin. All rights reserved. No part of this chapter may be reproduced in any manner without his written permission, except for brief quotations embodied in articles and reviews.

Acknowledgments: This is part of a larger research project with Lynda Ann Ewen, funded by the Ford Foundation, American Philosophical Society, Louis M. Rabinowitz Foundation, University of Wisconsin Ibero-American Studies Program and the Wisconsin Alumni Research Foundation. Judith Eisenberg provided invaluable research assistance.

years in office, the Unidad Popular (Popular Unity—UP) government, aside from implementing immediate welfare measures and economic palliatives, used the executive authority of the presidency imaginatively and decisively to try to gain control of the country's productive apparatus and to put through basic changes in property relations. It intervened and requisitioned plants involved in prolonged labor conflicts or whose production dropped markedly or which were working well below productive capacity. It used the fiscal resources of the state to purchase controlling interests in the largest private banks and several large national and foreign firms (in addition to formal nationalization of the large copper mines of Anaconda, Kennecott and Cerro). It encouraged the establishment of workers' councils to administer the new "socially owned enterprises." It used preexisting agrarian reform legislation to expropriate large estates and to turn them over to their resident workers to run cooperatively. The government—at the time of the September 11 *putsch*—had not yet obtained parliamentary approval to legalize its ownership of intervened, requisitioned and purchased plants and facilities, or of a list of others which it proposes to take over. Indeed, opposition within parliament from the conservative National and centrist Christian Democratic parties (with the exception of a leftist minority in the latter party) made it unlikely that the government would succeed in establishing the legal basis of what it called "social property": public ownership *and* workers' control of the decisive means of production.

In March 1973, the government sent to parliament a bill on social ownership that listed 90 firms in which it declared the public interest to be central, 41 of which had already been intervened or requisitioned, and all of which the government had slated for expropriation and "incorporation into the area of social property." In connection with another study, we analyzed the status of the 37 largest nonfinancial corporations owned by Chilean private capital, on an original list of the 50 largest national and foreign firms in Chile as of 1964-66. (We began with a list of the presumably largest nonfinancial corporations in Chile, excluding the American-owned mining companies and their wholly owned subsidiaries. Of these, 37 turned out to be a majority owned by Chilean private investors and 11 by foreign investors; two had dissolved by the time our study commenced in 1966.) As of mid-1973, at least 19 of these 37 large nonfinancial corporations apparently had not yet been touched by the Allende government. Even among the 18 affected directly, the significance of the changes was not clear. The largest nationalized firm was Pacific Steel Co. (CAP–Campañía de Acero del Pacífico); it had already been a "mixed enterprise" in which the dominant minority interest was held by the government's development agency (CORFO), long before Allende's election. The same was true of Tamaya Mining Co. (Compañía Minera de Tamaya), which was nationalized through stock purchase. Eleven other firms of the top 37 were either requisitioned or intervened, and it would have taken no more than an executive order (if legality had been the only issue) for them to be returned to private ownership. One, the giant Tierra del Fuego Cattle Company (Ganadera de Tierra del Fuego), had itself not been intervened, though much of its cattle lands had been expropriated by Allende under former President Eduardo Frei's 1967 agrarian reform law. The remaining four of the 18 affected had been requisitioned by the government in direct response to workers' seizures of the corporations' main plants. Therefore, although Allende had made it clear that he was seriously committed to putting through a "peaceful transition to socialism," the question was open as to how seriously the social existence and economic base of the capitalist class of Chile actually had been altered by his government's actions.

That the "business community" itself perceived its existence to be at stake, however, can scarcely be denied. As the Allende government continued to implement the platform on which it had been elected, and gained electoral support in the process (increasing its representation both in municipal governments and in the national parliament—the latter in the April 1973 parliamentary elections), the Right went on the offensive. The dominant leadership of the Christian Democratic party and the National party (a fusion of the former Liberal and Conservative parties representing bankers, large merchants, industrialists and landowners) made common cause. They formed a relatively cohesive "Federation of Democracy" in opposition to the Allende government. Business, trade, employers and professional associations became organizational centers of resistance to Socialist policies. Neighborhood associations and rightist paramilitary bands (particularly "Patria y Libertad") were formed in many areas to counter worker and peasant militance and to carry out antigovernment activities. Prominent business leaders called for the military to intervene to save the nation from "chaos," and many reportedly were directly involved in the planning and organization not only of the massive lockouts of October 1972 and the fall of 1973, but of seditious activities, including the successful military *putsch* of September 11, 1973, which destroyed one of the few remaining parliamentary democracies in the world.

In the face of the promise of a genuinely sovereign national economy under democratic control, via the unprecedented route of presidential leadership, constitutional amendment and parliamentary legislation under a Socialist government, the unity of interests of the owners and managers of the largest national and foreign corporations was revealed with brutal clarity. Within 10 days after the *putsch,* while massive repression of Chile's citizenry was still occurring, the new regime returned some 350 plants that had been taken into the public sector to their former owners and managers, and announced its intentions to open negotiations for new arrangements with nationalized American copper and other foreign companies.[2] The National party's leader, Sergio Jarpa Reyes, "had nothing but good to speak of the government. . .and clearly saw his own party as the nucleus of a 'popular national movement' to put political flesh on the military regime" with the slogan "discipline, order, and work."[3] Jorge Fontaine, president of the "powerful National Confederation of Production and Commerce, an association of Chile's economic elite, including the Chamber of Commerce, the National Mining Society, the National Manufacturers' Association, the Chilean Builders Association and the National Farm Bureau," characterized the *putsch* and its aftermath as a "struggle for freedom." Fontaine, leaders of other "elite pressure groups" and employer and trade associations were "quick to claim they played the 'determining role' in the overthrow of the Allende regime and clearly expect returns."[4] Paradoxically, then, recent events in Chile make it all the more clear how critical the theoretical issues and empirical analysis in this chapter are for an understanding of social reality under capitalism in general and Chile in particular.

THE CONCENTRATION OF CAPITAL

In 1966, a few large corporations controlled most corporate property in Chile.[5] Whether viewed in terms of overall aggregate concentration in the economy, among all nonfinancial corporations, or on an industry-by-industry level, the Chilean economy had been similar to such highly concentrated capitalist economies as France, Italy, Canada, England, the United States, Sweden and Japan.[6]

In 1966, the 182 largest nonfinancial corporations controlled 78 percent of the net capital assets of all 1,712 nonfinancial corporations in Chile. There was also considerable concentration within the group of the 182 largest: over half the combined assets

Table 1

SHARE OF NONFINANCIAL CORPORATION ASSETS HELD BY THE 182 LARGEST NONFINANCIAL CORPORATIONS IN CHILE IN 1966

RANK	ASSETS[a]	PERCENT
Top 5	E° 2437.2	25.9
6-25	2196.3	23.4
26-50	1005.8	10.7
51-75	536.7	5.7
76-100	382.0	4.1
101-125	306.8	3.3
126-150	231.2	2.5
151-175	197.1	2.1
176-182	56.3	0.6
TOTAL:	E°7349.4	78.3

a. Net capital assets in millions of *Escudos*.

Source: Unless stated otherwise, the tables in this chapter are based on calculations from the raw data in "The Top 200 of 1966, Chile." See footnote 3.

of *all* nonfinancial corporations were held by the top 25; and only a handful—the top 5—held over a quarter of the total (see Table 1). This seems to be a minimum estimate of the level of aggregate corporate concentration, since it does not take into account the fact that some of these corporations were actually owned or controlled by others.[7]

FOREIGN vs. NATIONAL CAPITAL

One of the principal aspects of the concentration of capital in Chile was that there were both large foreign and national corporations which accounted for the overall level of concentration. Therefore, it is necessary to analyze the relative position of national and foreign capital among the large corporations. Several questions are critical. How many of the large corporations were foreign owned and what proportion of the assets of the large corporations did they control? How is this related to the size of the corporation? What was the level of overall concentration among corporations owned by national capital? Of these, how many had significant amounts of foreign investment (as represented by ownership of shares) and how is this related to the size of the corporation? Several other questions will have to be answered beforehand.

First, it is quite clear that the largest corporations, measured by the absolute size of their assets, were generally foreign owned. This can be seen in the two parts of Table 2 which focus on the same question in different ways.   There were no national corporations (i.e., corporations majority-owned by Chilean investors) with assets as large as E⁰500 million and only one with asets of over E⁰250 million. (E⁰ equals *Escudos,* the Chilean monetary unit. In 1966, one U.S. dollar could be exchanged for E⁰ 4.37.) Of the corporations with assets of at least E⁰100 million, 13.9 percent of the foreign corporations were in that category, compared to 5 percent of the national corporations. The ratio, in the smallest assets group, of national corporations to foreign corporations is 2 to 1. The second part of Table 2 shows that, with one exception, the proportion of foreign-owned corporations rises directly with the size of the assets.

Similarly, the share of the assets of the 182 largest nonfinancial corporations held by the 43 foreign-owned ones among them

Table 2

CORPORATIONS OWNED BY NATIONAL
AND FOREIGN CAPITAL BY ASSETS,
AMONG THE 182 LARGEST NONFINANCIAL
CORPORATIONS IN CHILE IN 1966

Assets[a]	Foreign		National		Foreign-Owned Corporations in Assets Group	
	N[b]	%	N[c]	%	%	(N)[d]
E° 500 plus	1	2.3	0	0	100.0	(1)
250-499.9	4	9.3	1	0.7	80.0	(5)
100-249.9	1	2.3	6	4.3	14.3	(7)
50-99.9	6	14.0	12	8.6	33.3	(18)
10-49.9	24	55.8	76	54.7	24.0	(100)
5-9.9	7	16.3	44	31.7	13.7	(51)
Less than 5	0	0	0	0	0	0
TOTAL:	43	100%	139	100%	23.6	(182)

a. Net capital assets in millions of *Escudos*.
b. Number of foreign- owned corporations in assets group.
c. Number of national corporations in assets group.
d. Number of foreign - owned and national corporations in assets group.

rises directly with the rank of the corporation. Indeed, the 63 percent share of the assets of the top 25 corporations held by the 11 foreign firms in the group is more than five times that held by the four foreign companies among the bottom 32 largest corporations (see Table 3). Further, of the 1,712 nonfinancial corporations in Chile, these 43 largest foreign-owned corporations *numbered* only 2.5 percent, but controlled 38 percent of their combined assets. In contrast, the 139 large national corporations—numbering more than three times as many as the foreign corporations—merely controlled about the same proportion of all nonfinancial corporation assets: 41 percent.

Table 3

SHARE OF ASSETS OF THE 182 LARGEST
NONFINANCIAL CORPORATIONS HELD BY
FOREIGN-OWNED CORPORATIONS (by Rank)
IN CHILE IN 1966

Foreign Corporations

Rank	Number		Percent Assets of Top 182	
Top 5	4			85.9	
6-25	7	19	62.6	36.8	57.0
26-50	8			31.0	
51-75	4	10		15.7	19.0
76-100	6			23.7	
101-125	4	10		15.9	20.2
126-150	6			26.2	
151-175	3	4		11.6	11.9
176-182	1			12.8	
TOTAL:	43			48.0	

These overall-concentration figures indicate the preponderant economic importance of foreign corporations in the political economy of Chile. However, they tend also to distort the relative position of national capital because of the pattern of direct foreign investment. This pattern of foreign investment, in turn, was essentially the reflection of the presence of the subsidiaries of a few giant American multinational corporations. The 23 American-owned firms, among the top 43 foreign ones, controlled 85 percent of these firms' combined assets. Great Britain accounts for 4.9 percent of the assets, Switzerland for 3.8 percent. The rest is divided among the firms of several countries, none of whose combined assets amounted to more than 3 percent of the top 43's combined assets. This may be compared with the following distribution, by country, of all foreign direct investment in Chile: 87 percent was held by American firms; 10 percent by British firms; the rest was divided among more than seven countries, none of whose firms held as much as one percent.[8]

The subsidiaries of just four American corporations (the Telephone Company of Chile, an ITT subsidiary; The Chilean Electric Company, a subsidiary of American and Foreign Power Company;[9] and the four subsidiaries of Kennecott and Anaconda) accounted for nearly three-quarters of the assets of all 23 of the top American firms in Chile. This means, of course, that American investment in Chile was in the classic pattern of foreign investment in less-developed countries. It was overwhelmingly concentrated in the extraction of raw materials and in utilities: 70 percent of the assets of the top 23 firms was in mining and 19 percent was in utilities, compared to only 6 percent in manufacturing (see Table 4).[10] In contrast, British capital, whose direct investments were once predominant in nitrates, was not even represented among the large corporations in mining in 1966 and was split primarily between commerce and manufacturing. Similarly, the firms of other foreign countries were in manufacturing. On the other hand, despite the fact that only a small proportion of American investment was in manufacturing, the American firms controlled more assets than their British, Swiss or other foreign manufacturing counterparts.[11]

The copper mines, while physically located in Chile, had constituted a foreign enclave, essentially unintegrated into the Chilean economy; their profits (less varying amounts taken by government taxes) from operations in Chile were repatriated to American corporations for a half-century or more.[12] "The operations in Chile were the most profitable investment the companies had available to them," as even crude statistics based on the companies' annual reports indicated. The relative return on assets owned by Anaconda in Chile was nearly twice that on its non-Chilean assets from 1955 to 1960 and more than three times its non-Chilean rate from 1960 to 1965. For Kennecott, its returns on assets owned in Chile were nearly three times its return on assets owned elsewhere throughout both periods.[13] Various estimates of the actual share of the consolidated profits which

Table 4

DIRECT INVESTMENTS IN CHILE OF THE 43 LARGEST FOREIGN-OWNED NONFINANCIAL CORPORATIONS BY PRINCIPAL COUNTRIES[c] AND INDUSTRIAL GROUPS IN CHILE IN 1966

Industry	United States			United Kingdom			Switzerland			All Others			Total		
	Assets[a]	%	N[b]	Assets[a]	%	N[b]	Assets[a]	%	N[b]	Assets[a]	%	N[b]	Assets[a]	%	N[b]
Agriculture, Forestry, Fishing	—	—	0	15.6	9.0	2	—	—	0	13.8	7.0	1	29.4	0.9	3
Mining															
Copper	E°1683.5	56.1	5	—	—	0	—	—	0	43.1	19.6	1	1726.6	49.0	6
Nitrates	346.1	11.5	1	—	—	0	—	—	0	—	—	0	346.1	9.8	1
Iron	75.2	2.5	1	—	—	0	—	—	0	—	—	0	75.2	2.1	1
Manufacturing	184.5	6.1	9	75.7	43.7	3	102.3	76.8	3	162.7	73.4	5	525.2	14.8	20
Utilities															
Telephone	425.2	14.1	1	10.7	6.2	1	—	—	0	—	—	0	435.9	12.4	2
Electricity	147.4	4.9	1	—	—	0	—	—	0	—	—	0	147.4	4.2	1
Railroads	7.2	0.3	1	—	—	0	—	—	0	—	—	0	7.2	0.2	1
Commerce	132.9	4.4	4	71.0	41.0	3	30.8	23.2	1	—	—	0	234.7	6.7	8
Total	3002.0	100.0	23	173.0	100.0	9	133.1	100.0	4	219.6	100.0	7	3527.7	100.0	43

a. Net capital assets in millions of Escudos.

b. Number of firms in industry.

c. Countries whose firms in the top 43 control at least 3 percent of top 43 assets.

these companies received from their Chilean operations differ considerably. The Chilean government has claimed that, between 1955 and 1970, Anaconda received 79 percent of its worldwide profits from its investments in Chile; for Kennecott, the government estimated the figure at 21 percent.[14]

Had the mines been under the control of national capital (private or state), the profits generated would have been reinvested in Chile. Production plants and facilities—to refine, and, most important, to fabricate products from the output of the mines—would have been built in Chile. Heavy equipment for mining operations would have been produced in Chile. Financing would have come from Chilean banks and the large cash reserves of the companies deposited with them. Chilean ships, not foreign ones, would have carried refined copper and manufactured products abroad, there to be sold by Chilean sales organizations. In countless ways, the multiple benefits of the mining industry would have been felt in Chile (rather than in the United States) where it would have been a leading sector and spur to further industrialization. Its vulnerability to fluctuations in the world demand for copper would have been much reduced, perhaps to insignificance, as mining became just one more industry in a more balanced capitalist economy. Clearly, the capitalist class of Chile would have possessed a far broader, more independent and affluent economic base than it otherwise had been able to attain.

This is highly speculative, certainly, but Chile's industrial potential in the late 1960s, as well as its past history, suggest that diversification was a genuine historical alternative for Chile. Its penetration by foreign capital and the subsequent appropriation of its mining resources were not—contrary to the usual interpretations—an inevitable result of the fact that exploitation of Chilean copper ore, after 1900, "demanded a complex technology and management and a capital investment which went far beyond the capacity of the Chilean business community to supply."[15] It happened because of specific "historical choices"—policies adopted by a Chilean government responsive to the views of segments of the dominant class which saw no major contradiction between the national interest and the incursion of foreign capital. These choices permitted the rapid consolidation of foreign control of the mines at a critical moment in Chile's capitalist development: Chile had already reached a level of industrialization that—had different social forces prevailed—would have permitted the profitable exploitation of the mines by national capital and stimulated a more balanced and sustained development. This turning point came with the civil war of 1891, which pitted segments of the dominant class—some allied with British capital—against each other and in which the nationalist government of President Jose Manuel Balmaceda was overthrown.

A DECISIVE HISTORICAL MOMENT

Copper mines owned by Chileans had made Chile the leading copper producer in the world from the 1840s to the 1870s when it produced about 60 percent of world output.[16] When the high-grade ores that made this boom possible were depleted, and competition from newly opened copper mines in the western United States took an increasing share of the market in the 1870s, many Chilean producers were wiped out.[17] Global demand picked up with the growth of the electrical industry after 1880, however, and Chilean producers put increasing pressure on their government for subsidies to modernize the industry.[18] Balmaceda, who assumed office in 1886, was responsive to these pressures and to the interests of industrial capital. He favored strong state intervention to protect and encourage the growth of the domestic industry. His was a nationalist government whose policies, though occasionally inconsistent, were opposed to the British nitrate interests that had gained an ascendant position in those years. He revoked the route monopoly of a British nitrate railway and threatened to nationalize the major British nitrate enterprises and to auction them to Chilean private investors.[19] Legislation which forbade the acquisition or exploitation by foreign capital of concessions in the sheep lands of the south also impinged on British investments. Balmaceda urged the establishment of a state bank to act as depository for government revenues, to assume the sole prerogative of note issue and to provide low-interest loans to stimulate development—policies which threatened private bankers and their privileged creditors, principally large landowners in the central valley, and exporters.

Immense state expenditures were made on "productive works" and to encourage the growth of private manufacturing, especially heavy industry. State contracts were let for the manufacture of railroad engines, freight cars, metal bridges and viaducts; roads, irrigation canals, railway tracks and public service water utilities: other major works, including public schools, were constructed. These public works, especially roads and canals, benefited certain agrarian interests but adversely affected others. They undermined the docility of the peasants, drew off labor and pushed up rural wages.

The government projects were possible because seemingly inexhaustible revenues were available from taxes on nitrate production. Most important, however, was Balmaceda's coming to office on the crest of half a century or more of rapid national capital accumulation and internal capitalist development. Chile had already made substantial progress in the development, not only of light manufacturing, but also of the production of pulp and paper, structural clay and glass, locomotives, turbines, flat cars, copper- and silver-mining machinery, foundries and other heavy industrial equipment.[20]

The policies of the Balmaceda government, because they went counter to the accepted free trade and *laissez faire—laissez investir* ideology and encroached on powerful interests, split the dominant class into hostile, eventually irreconciable, factions. Led by a majority in Congress, financed substantially by British nitrate capitalists and organized by leading Chilean bankers and traders, a rebellion against the government exploded into civil war. The navy supported the rebels; the army remained loyal to the legal executive. The war lasted nine months, cost 10,000 lives and more than 100 million pesos and overthrew Balmaceda and, with him, the government's incipient nationalist policies. The war had a shattering and demoralizing effect on the country's leading capitalists—on victor and vanquished alike—many of whom were, in fact, drawn from the same social class and related through kinship. It cost many who supported Balmaceda (and whom his government represented) their fortunes and drove others into exile or retirement from public life.[21] The confidence and sense of destiny of major industrial capitalists and copper-mine owners, and their ability to act self-consciously as a cohesive group, suffered greatly from their defeat in the civil war. They were not likely, at that point, to take great risks to develop the copper mines. The government not only was not ready to support national industrialists, but was, in fact, freely granting concessions to foreign capitalists. The investible funds available at home might have been forthcoming if the results of the civil war were different. Instead, "those who overthrew [Balmaceda], many of them high-minded and self-sacrificing, were able to do no more than to lead their country into a period of apathetic drifting."[22] Whatever their motives or intentions, the rebels opened the way, historically, for the rapid penetration and alienation of the copper mines by foreign capital at a decisive moment in Chile's development.[23]

GOVERNMENT INTERVENTION AND STATE ENTERPRISE

The contrasting fate of Chile's copper and petroleum reserves is instructive, since those in Chile who favored granting concessions for oil exploration and development to foreign investors were defeated—though narrowly. In fact, in 1927, a law had been passed authorizing such concessions. Standard Oil, Royal Dutch Shell and Panamerican Petroleum filed applications for concessions in Magallanes and Tierra del Fuego amounting to a million and a quarter acres. The law was rescinded, however, and in subsequent legislation, funds were allocated for oil exploration under state auspices and the ownership of all petroleum deposits was vested in the state.[24] In 1931, refining was also restricted almost exclusively to the state. Though there were many attempts throughout the years to reverse this, only the importation, distribution and sale of petroleum products were left to private enterprise. Since 1943, the government development agency (Corporación de Fomento—CORFO) has played the leading role in discovering and developing the petroleum resources of Magallanes—the area over which international oil companies almost obtained a monopoly a decade earlier. State ownership has allowed Chile to meet her petroleum needs from domestic sources and to reinvest a portion of the profits of the National Petroleum Enterprise (ENAP—Empress Nacional de Petroleo) into other development projects. An integrated state-owned petroleum industry, from extraction through refining, became established in Chile, rather than one more foreign-owned resource enclave. It became integrated with the domestic economy and served the needs of national capitalist development. Major Chilean corporations were responsible for distribution and sales in the Chilean market of gasoline, kerosene, bottled gas and other petroleum products. The profits of these companies were subsidized to a great extent by the state-owned enterprises. COPEC (compania de Petróleos de Chile). a firm controlled by national private capital, was guaranteed at least 50 percent of local sales by law; even so, the rest of the market was split by Esso and Shell—although all three firms have several joint ventures in tankers.[25]

Another major state corporation, the National Electricity Enterprise (Empresa Nacional de Electricidad—ENDESA) was established in 1945 and tripled the public service generating capacity of the country within 15 years of its founding.[26] Before ENDESA's establishment, a virtual monopoly on public service electricity was held by American and Foreign Power's subsidiary, Chilectra. Other state enterprises operated in the construction of public educational and hospital establishments, beet sugar refining, the manufacture of pharmaceuticals and other chemical products, wines and the canning and preserving of fish. The importance of the state enterprises in reinforcing national against foreign capital is seen in the pattern of their investments: their assets, like those of American corporations, were most heavily concentrated in the extraction of raw materials (petroleum) and public utilities. Of the combined assets of the top 11 state-owned enterprises (not including the state railways), ENAP and ENDESA alone held 75 percent (see Table 5). ENAP controlled all the assets in petroleum extraction *and refining,* while ENDESA had 79 percent of the assets held by the largest corporations in electric light and power; the rest was split about evenly between four private Chilean firms and the American-owned Chilectra (see Table 6).

The mention of these few major state enterprises merely suggests the extent to which private national capital had been buttressed and reinforced by the state. Since the establishment of CORFO in 1939 by the Popular Front government, the state

Table 5

ASSETS OF THE LARGEST NATIONAL (STATE AND PRIVATE) AND
FOREIGN-OWNED NONFINANCIAL CORPORATIONS, BY INDUSTRIAL GROUPS,
IN CHILE IN 1966

| | National Corporations | | | | | | Foreign-owned Corporations[c] | | |
| | State[a] | | | Private[b] | | | | | |
Industry	Assets[d]	%	N[e]	Assets	%	N	Assets	%	N
Agriculture, Forestry, Fishing	—	—	—	283.1	7.4	11	29.4	0.9	3
Mining									
Coal	—	—	—	88.1	2.3	1	—	—	—
Iron	—	—	—	14.4	0.4	1	75.2	2.1	1
Copper	16.8	0.7	1	89.9	2.4	3	1726.6	49.0	6
Petroleum	747.0	30.3	1	—	—	—	—	—	—
Nitrates	—	—	—	—	—	—	346.1	9.8	1
Manufacturing	174.2	7.0	4	2527.8	66.2	87	525.2	14.8	20

Table 5 Continued

Construction	352.5	14.3	2	26.0	0.7	3	—	—	—
Utilities									
Electricity	1114.1	45.1	1	151.8	4.0	4	147.4	4.2	1
Gas	—	—	—	78.7	2.1	3	—	—	—
Telephone	20.9	0.8	1	—	—	—	435.9	12.4	2
Transportation									
Railroads	State Railways[f]			—	—	—	7.2	0.2	1
Shipping	—	—	—	196.2	5.1	5	—	—	—
Commerce									
Wholesale	—	—	—	191.8	5.0	8	169.3	4.8	5
Retail	—	—	—	60.9	1.6	6	30.7	0.9	1
Real Estate	—	—	—	47.5	1.3	2	—	—	—
Other	—	—	—	65.5	1.7	5	34.7	1.0	2
Services (Hotels)	42.9	1.7	1	—	—	—	—	—	—
Total	2468.4	100	11[f]	3821.7	100	139	3527.7	100	43

Table 5 Continued

a. National corporations, State: More than 50 percent of outstanding shares held by an agency of the Chilean government.

b. National corporations, Private: More than 50 percent of outstanding shares held by Chilean private shareholders.

c. Foreign-owned corporations: More than 50 percent of outstanding shares held by foreign shareholders.

d. Net capital assets in million of *Escudos*.

e. Number of firms in industry.

f. The Chilean State Railway owns and operates the public service railroads and owns 80 percent of the tracks in Chile. However, there is no information on their combined assets.

played a major role in investment.[27] State enterprises had also been complemented by mixed enterprises, with the participation both of CORFO and of large private investors. These were established in areas considered in essential need but which private capital would not enter, either because of the uncertainty of profitable returns or the magnitude of the capital required. Once successful, however, the mixed enterprises had been gradually turned over to private ownership.[28] The policies of the state enterprises, while making significant contributions to economic development, also tended to be guided by the profit considerations of the largest Chilean corporations and the needs of the private sector as a whole.[29] This is not unlike the situation in several other capitalist countries where limited and selective state ownership is "employed cooperatively with private-sector interests"[30] and "there is an established intimacy between the representatives of public authority and the practitioners of private enterprise."[31]

NATIONAL CAPITAL IN NON-MINING INDUSTRIES

Private national capital was relatively preponderant outside of mining. Whereas corporations owned by Chilean private investors controlled only 52 percent of the aggregate net capital assets of the largest 182 national and foreign nonfinancial corporations, their share of the assets outside of mining was nearly one and a half times as large. Of the E°5,009.2 million held by the 169 largest nonmining corporations, 72 percent was controlled by the national corporations, principally in manufacturing.

Sixty-six percent of the assets of the 139 largest national corporations in the private sector was in manufacturing (see Table 5). The relative proportion of national to foreign capital was strongest in manufacturing,[32] where Chilean firms predominated in number and in assets controlled: 87 manufacturing corporations owned by Chileans held 78 percent of the combined assets in that sector; together with the four state firms, national capital held 84 percent of the assets in manufacturing controlled by the largest corporations (see Table 6).

These large manufacturing corporations controlled most of the assets of all of the manufacturing corporations in Chile. Of the

Table 6

PERCENTAGE OF ASSETS OF MAJOR INDUSTRIAL GROUPS
OWNED BY NATIONAL (STATE AND PRIVATE) AND FOREIGN
CAPITAL, AMONG THE LARGEST NONFINANCIAL
CORPORATIONS IN CHILE IN 1966

Percentage of Industry Assets[a] Held by:

| | National Corporations | | | | Foreign | |
Industry	State	N	Private	N	Corporations	N
Agriculture, Forestry, Fishing	0		90.6	11	9.4	3
Mining						
Coal	0		100.0	1	0	0
Iron	0		16.1	1	83.9	1
Copper	0.9	1	4.3	3	94.2	6
Petroleum	100.0	1	0	0	0	0
Nitrates	0	0	0	0	100.0	1
Subtotal	24.6	2	6.2	5	69.2	8
Manufacturing	5.4	4	78.3	87	16.3	20
Construction	93.1	2	6.9	3	0	0
Utilities						
Electricity	78.8	1	10.7	4	10.4	1
Gas	0	0	100.0	3	0	0
Telephone	4.6	1	0	0	95.4	2
Subtotal	58.2	2	11.8	7	30.0	3
Transport						
Railroads[b]	—	0	———		—	1
Shipping	0	0	100.0	5	0	0

Commerce						
Wholesale	0	0	53.1	8	46.9	5
Retail	0	0	66.5	6	33.5	1
Real Estate	0	0	100.0	2	0	0
Other	0	0	65.4	5	34.6	2
Subtotal	0	0	60.9	21	39.1	8
Services						
(Hotels)	100.0	1	0	0	0	0
Total:	25.1	11	38.9	139	35.9	43

a. For actual assets figures and definitions, see Table 5.
b. See note f. in Table 5, on Chilean State Railway

E⁰4,389.2 million estimated aggregate net capital assets in manufacturing, the four state firms controlled 4.0 percent; the 87 owned by Chilean private capital, 57.6 percent; and the 20 foreign manufacturing corporations, 12.0 percent, giving a total of 73.6 percent of all manufacturing assets held by the 111 largest manufacturing corporations. (Unfortunately there is no way of ascertaining the amount of manufacturing assets controlled separately by foreign and national firms below the "top 200," and, thereby, of determining the proportion of each controlled by the largest ones. The data provided by the supervisory agency simply listed aggregates for each industrial group. There was, however, information on overall nonfinancial corporate concentration.)

The question is whether these large manufacturing corporations, as a group, were restricted to a relatively few industries or were broadly represented and important in a wide variety of different industries throughout the economy. There were 39 manufacturing industries represented by the 111 manufacturing corporations. What proportion of the aggregate net capital assets in each of these major industrial groups was controlled by those which appear among the top 111? Asking the question this way is an attempt to show the relationship between "overall concentration" in manufacturing and concentration in individual industries, since there was no necessary connection between overall concentration and market structure. Ordinarily, the "concentration ratios" which show the proportion of an industry controlled by the single largest firm in the industry, or by the three, four or eight largest, do not distinguish whether these were among the largest manufacturing firms in the economy as a whole, or merely within the given industry. In contrast, the following discussion refers specifically (and only) to the share of a given industry controlled by those which appear among the 111 largest in manufacturing as a whole.[33]

Generally, economists measuring corporate concentration consider it irrelevant what proportion by number the few large firms are of the population of all firms in an industry. Rather, it is assumed that "concentration ratios" best "reveal that aspect of the number and size distribution of sellers in any industry which is generally considered most relevant for purposes of economic analysis."[34] The ratios indicate the extent to which the largest corporations may exert monopoly or oligopoly power in an industry. "In economic theory," as Adelman puts it, "the fewer the firms, everything else being equal, the nearer to monopoly."[35]

If the level of concentration in the major industrial groups in manufacturing is examined, two facts stand out clearly: each manufacturing industry was highly concentrated, and national capital was dominant in the great majority of industries. If we disregard, for the moment, whether the corporation was owned by private or state, or national or foreign capital, we find that, in 64 percent of the manufacturing industries,[36] not more than the three top corporations controlled over half the total net capital assets. (The actual number of firms represented among our "top 200" may be fewer than three in a given industry.)

The single largest national corporation, owned by private capital, itself controlled over half the total assets in 31 percent of the manufacturing industries and more than a quarter of the assets in another 33 percent. Among the single-firm virtual monopolies were such well-known corporations owned by national capitalists as United Breweries Company (Cervecerias Unidas) with 96 percent of the net assets in breweries and malt manufacturing; Paper and Cardboard Manufacturing Company (Papeles y Cartones) with 75 percent of industry assets; "El

Melon" Industrial Enterprises, with 62 percent; Pacific Steel Company (CAP), a "mixed" private and minority-state-owned corporation at that time, with 82 percent; and MADECO (Manufacturas de Cobre) with 100 percent of nonferrous metal industrial assets. In only 10 percent of the industries did the single largest Chilean corporation control less than a tenth of the total assets. (This included two industries in which no top Chilean Corporation was represented, although a top foreign firm had a share in each.) The three largest national corporations controlled over half the total net capital assets in 44 percent, and over a quarter of the assets in another 39 percent, of the manufacturing industries. With the state-owned firms included, the level of concentration in manufacturing and the preponderance of national capital were even further accentuated.

The three largest foreign corporations controlled over half the total assets in 8 percent of the manufacturing industries and over a quarter of the assets in another 8 percent. While this is a significant level of concentration of foreign capital in manufacturing, it is clearly secondary—compared to the level of concentration of national capital (see Table 7). Top foreign corporations appear in 13 of the 39 manufacturing industries represented by the large corporations. In seven of these, the foreign corporation was the single largest; in the same seven industries, the combined assets of the large foreign corporations also exceeded those of the large national corporations.

Exploring the economic implications of this tendency toward monopoly in a broad range of manufacturing industries is beyond the scope of this chapter. One thing, however, should be clear: the large manufacturing corporations were generally the dominant ones in a broad range of industries, and their position in the political economy was decisive.

THE CONCENTRATION OF NATIONAL CAPITAL

The largest national manufacturing corporations, together with their counterparts in commerce and other industries, formed the highly concentrated base of national capitalism in Chile. These 139 large corporations controlled the overwhelming bulk of the assets of all nonfinancial corporations owned by Chilean private capital. Of the aggregate net capital assets of E^{0}5,926 million

Table 7

DISTRIBUTION OF MANUFACTURING INDUSTRIES BY CONCENTRATION RATIOS, DISTINGUISHING BETWEEN NATIONAL AND FOREIGN CORPORATIONS, IN CHILE IN 1966

Number and Percentage of Industries with Level of Concentration Among:

Level of Firm Concentration (in percentage)	National Corporations						Foreign Corporations				All-Corporations	
	Single Largest		Three[a] Largest		Three[b] Largest		Single Largest		Three[a] Largest		Three[a] Largest	
	N	%	N	%	N	%	N	%	N	%	N	%
75-100	4	10%	7	18%	7	18%	2	5%	2	5%	14	36%
50-74.9	8	21	10	26	13	33	1	3	1	3	11	28
25-49.9	13	33	15	39	12	31	3	8	4	10	13	33
10-24.9	10	26	4	10	4	10	5	13	4	10	1	3
5-9.9	2	5	1	3	1	3	0	0	2	5	0	0
Under 5	0	0	0	0	0	0	2	5	0	0	0	0
No Large Firm Represented	2	5	2	5	2	5	26	67	26	67	0	0

Table 7 Continued

a. The actual number of firms represented among the "top 200" may be fewer than three in a given industry.

b. This column includes four state-owned enterprises in manufacturing.

controlled by the estimated 1,611 national nonfinancial corporations in Chile, 65 percent was controlled by the top 139. Additionally, the top 10 alone controlled 25 percent of the assets and the top 50 nearly half. The top 100 controlled 59 percent of the aggregate net capital assets of all nationally owned corporations (see Table 8).[37] This is a minimum estimate of the level of aggregate concentration. It does not take into account the fact, as already noted, that some large corporations were actually owned or controlled by others. Intercorporate holdings are not accounted for either. Nor does it include the assets of corporations beneath the "top 200" which these large corporations may have owned or controlled. There is some disagreement among economists concerning the significance of overall corporate concentration. From the standpoint of class analysis, however, to control these large corporations was to control the nation's productive property and is of primary interest. By virtue of their decisive structural location in the economy, the families that owned and controlled the largest corporations constituted the dominant segment of the capitalist class of Chile.

It has been shown, of course, that control of the nation's productive property was shared by foreign capital, which, in some areas of the economy—particularly copper mining and nitrates—had virtually excluded Chilean capital altogether. What has not yet been discussed is the extent to which national capital was not merely hemmed in by foreign capital, but was, in fact, structurally integrated with it. There are, of course, numerous ways, aside from common ownership interests, in which national firms could be closely related to (if not dependent on) foreign corporations. National firms were likely to purchase their heavy equipment and machinery and other basic capital goods from foreign firms; they often had management or technical agreements, or produced

Table 8

SHARE OF NATIONAL (PRIVATE) NONFINANCIAL CORPORATION[a] ASSETS[b] CONTROLLED BY THE 139 LARGEST CORPORATIONS IN CHILE IN 1966

Rank	Percent	Cumulative Percent
Top 5	16.6	16.6
6-10	8.2	24.8
11-20	10.1	34.9
21-30	5.6	40.5
31-40	4.2	44.7
41-50	3.3	48.0
51-75	6.4	54.4
76-100	4.9	59.3
101-125	3.7	63.0
126-139	1.8	64.8

a. National corporations: 50 percent or more of the outstanding shares were held by Chilean private shareholders.
b. Aggregate net capital assets of the 1,611 national nonfinancial corporations was estimated at $E^{o}5926.0$ million. See footnote 3.

goods in Chile under foreign licensing or royalty arrangements. The latter's importance as a source of capital export from Chile to foreign corporations was certain, but these remittances cannot be estimated with any precision. Even "efforts" by the U. S. Department of Commerce "to obtain an idea of the financial importance of such arrangements failed to develop much data, official estimates of remittances being clearly understatements of the true volume."[38]

THE COALESCENCE OF NATIONAL AND FOREIGN CAPITAL

The focus here is on the extent to which foreign capital had minority-ownership interests in national corporations. For analytical purposes, and because the corporation is the minimum legal unit of ownership of productive property, this chapter has dealt with corporations that were majority owned by Chilean investors as "national corporations" and those majority owned by foreign capital as "foreign corporations." In most cases, this raised no problem; in others, however, there was a coalescence of national and foreign capital which made difficult any simple distinction between "national" and "foreign" corporations—even though they may have been majority owned by one or the other. Further, the implications of a minority holding by foreign investors in a Chilean corporation cannot be precisely stated. Their usually superior international market position, patent rights and capital and technical resources (and, perhaps, confidential contractual obligations) may have put them in a position to exert significant influence, if not control, over the national firm's policies, even with a minority holding. A "national" firm may have been restricted to the Chilean market or specified export markets or may have been required to buy its raw materials and equipment either from the foreign firm with the minority holding[39] or from other foreign firms with which that was integrated or had established reciprocity relationships.[40] Careful firm-by-firm investigation would be required to obtain this information. Findings on the distribution and extent of minority holdings by foreign capital in nationally owned corporations are still quite relevant. Such holdings may be considered a minimal indication of the significance of foreign investment within the direct domain of national capitalists. Whether these investments also imply that this segment of the class was integrated into a dependent relationship on foreign capital is a question of great importance. Our findings are merely suggestive in this regard.

Among the 139 largest national corporations, only a few had sizable foreign holdings. Of the worth of all outstanding shares of the 139 national corporations, 5.3 percent was held by foreign investors. Some 83 percent of the national corporations had less than 1 percent of their outstanding shares held by foreign shareholders; another 6 percent had less than 10 percent foreign held; foreign-held; and close to 9 percent had 20 percent or more 3 percent had between 10 and 20 percent or more of their stock held by foreign shareholders. Interestingly, there was no consistent relationship between the decile rank (by assets) of the national corporations and the proportion of stock held by foreign shareholders. Depending on what one might choose to define as a "significant percentage (foreign)," the relationship with size varied accordingly. It should be noted, however, that foreign holdings of 10 percent or more of the national corporation's shares were more frequent among the 50 largest, where there were seven such corporations, then among the next 50, where there were five, and the remaining 39, where only one fell in that category. A foreign holding of 20 percent or more may be defined as a "joint venture" with the national corporation, since a holding of this size already indicates not only that the foreign investors had to concern themselves with the national corporation's fate, but also had a significant potential for control. By this criterion, the frequency of joint ventures is not particularly different among the top 50 (where there were four) than in the second-ranking 50 (where there were five), though, again, there was only one joint venture among the remaining 39 corporations. To this extent, therefore, the larger corporations were more likely than the smaller ones to have joint ventures with foreign capital.

Merely examining the percentage of foreign capital in a national corporation, while important, does not reveal enough about the potential for foreign control. It would be necessary to know also how concentrated the foreign holdings were, among how many foreign corporations (or individual investors) this percentage was divided, and how longstanding these holdings were, as well as whether representatives of the foreign investors sat on the board of the national corporation—not to speak of the other considerations already mentioned. It would also be necessary to know how closely the national corporation was held by domestic investors and where they stood in the national political economy as a whole—what powers they could exert in any serious conflict over control. To such questions the raw data under examination in this chapter can offer no answers.[41]

Distinguishing between manufacturing and other firms shows

that sizable foreign holdings were more frequent in manufacturing. Of foreign holdings of 10 percent or more, some 2 percent of the national nonmanufacturing firms, compared to 17 percent in manufacturing, were in this category. Using the 20-percent criterion, there was not one joint venture outside of manufacturing, compared to the 14 percent among manufacturing corporations. In either case, measured by the frequency of sizable foreign holdings, it was clear that the overwhelming majority of national corporations were owned and controlled by national capital.

Moreover, many of the large corporations in Chile which were majority owned by foreign capital, and by that criterion have been treated as "foreign corporations," did, in fact, have sizable percentages of their stock held by Chilean investors. Of the worth of all outstanding shares of the 43 foreign corporations, 10.9 percent was held by Chilean investors. Again, there is no information on the history of these holdings, whether these were foreign corporations that Chileans bought into or national corporations that were taken over by foreign capital.[42] Further, what the criterion of a "sizable percentage" holding by Chilean investors in a foreign-owned corporation may have been is difficult to determine or to state as a general rule. The most that might reasonably be argued is perhaps that when 20 percent or more, and certainly 40 percent or more, of a corporation's shares were held by Chilean investors, such a degree of coalescence of national and foreign capital indicates a rather clear community of interest between them.

Among other reasons, such an investment may have represented the use of domestic capital to establish a foreign subsidiary in Chile with minimum investment by the foreign corporation itself. Typical of a number of multinational corporations is the practice, as *Fortune* explains, of establishing "a foreign operation with a limited amount of equity and a generous supply of debt." The multinational corporation "thus takes advantage of the fact that foreign lenders will often provide it with far more money, as a percentage of equity, than will U.S. lenders. For many firms this leverage advantage is a particularly attractive feature of the international environment."[43]

A sizable investment by Chilean investors may have also

represented an attempt by the foreign corporation to ensure itself against nationalist "interference" or "discrimination," and to secure influential allies among Chilean investors. Especially under the political conditions in Chile of the past several decades, this cannot be ruled out as a major consideration in the decision-making of the foreign corporation.[44]

Whatever the reasons for the sizable percentage of national shares held in foreign corporations, the plain facts were that a quarter of the 43 large foreign corporations had holdings by Chilean stockholders of over 40 (but less than 50) percent; nearly half of the foreign corporations had at least 20 percent of their shares in Chilean hands. Most of these Chilean holdings were in the smaller foreign firms. Two of those over 40 percent were in the top 20 foreign firms, compared to eight among the bottom 23 firms. Moreover, as soon as manufacturing firms are distinguished from others, it becomes clear that most of the sizable national holdings were in manufacturing; of the Chilean holdings over 20 percent, two-thirds were in manufacturing firms. Viewing the same relationship differently, holdings of 20 percent or more by Chilean investors appeared in 70 percent of the manufacturing firms, compared to a frequency of 30 percent among the foreign firms outside of manufacturing. Whether such a marked coalescence between national and foreign capital in manufacturing was the reflection of increasing national presence in foreign corporations or of the erosion of the position of national capital, is a critical question which, unfortunately, cannot be answered in this chapter.[45]

THE OVERALL SITUATION IN SUMMARY

In the 1960s, the large corporation was the predominant form of productive property in Chile, outside of agriculture. The few largest nonfinancial corporations (43 foreign and 139 national) controlled over three-quarters of the aggregate net capital assets of all nonfinancial corporations in the country in 1966. Foreign capital, mainly American, was concentrated overwhelmingly in mining, and controlled the production of copper and nitrates. National capital, buttressed by state enterprises in petroleum and electricity, was dominant outside of mining, especially in manufacturing. National and foreign capital coalesced among a small number of corporations; in fact, many of the largest foreign manufacturing corporations had sizable minority holdings by Chilean investors. The largest national manufacturing corporations also tended to be the decisive ones in most individual manufacturing industries. They, and their counterparts in other industries, controlled almost two-thirds of the aggregate net capital assets of all nonfinancial corporations owned by national private capital. Whoever controlled these large corporations controlled the political economy of capitalism in Chile.

NOTES

1. See Paul A. Baran, *The Political Economy of Growth* (New York: Monthly Review Press, 1957 and 1962); James O'Connor, *The Origins of Socialism in Cuba* (Ithaca, N.Y.: Cornell University Press, 1970); O'Connor, "On Cuban Political Economy," and Theotonio dos Santos, "Foreign Investment and the Large Enterprise in Latin America: The Brazilian Case," in *Latin America: Reform or Revolution?* eds., James Petras and Maurice Zeitlin (New York: Fawcett, 1968); and Maurice Zeitlin, "Camilo's Colombia," in *Father Camilo Torres: Revolutionary Writings* (New York: Harper and Row, 1972).

2. Analysis of the historical background and events of the Allende government may be found in Maurice Zeitlin, "Chile: The Dilemmas of Democratic Socialism," *Working Papers for a New Society* 1 (Fall, 1973); Kyle Steenland,"Two Years of the Unidad Popular," *Socialist Revolution* 3 (May-June 1973); and Andy Zimbalist and Barbara Stallings, "Showdown in Chile," *Monthly Review* 25 (October 1973). The immediate background to the *putsch* is traced in "Chile: The Story Behind the Coup," *NACLA's Latin America and Empire Report* 7 (October 1973). The events of the *putsch* and its immediate aftermath are reported accurately in *Newsweek,* especially the issues of September 24, October 1, and October 8, 1973; and *Latin America,* September 28, 1973, and following issues. The early reports in the *New York Times* were generally neither adequate nor comprehensive. *Le Monde* had the fullest and most detailed newspaper coverage of events. Also, see Laurence Stern, "Chile: The Lesson," *The Progressive* 37 (November 1973); Marilyn Zeitlin, "Antisemitism in Chile," *The Progressive* 37 (December 1973); and Laurence Birns, "The Death of Chile," *New York Review of Books,* November 1, 1973. A study of the ownership and control of the 37

largest national nonfinancial corporations and six largest commercial banks in Chile in 1964–1966 by the authors and Lynda Ann Ewen will **appear** in *Corporate Capital: the Large Corporation and the Capitalist Class* (New York: Harper and Row, forthcoming).

3. *Latin America,* September 28, 1973, p. 311.

4. *New York Times,* October 28, 1973, sec. 4, p. 7.

5. The analysis of corporate concentration in this chapter is based on official aggregate figures on the net capital assets (*valor patrimonial*) of all of the estimated 1,712 nonfinancial corporations and individual figures on the 182 largest ones in Chile in 1966. These data were recorded in Santiago in 1967-1968 by Dr. Weston Agor, then a doctoral student in the department of political science of the University of Wisconsin, who kindly made them available to the authors. Dr. Agor, of course, bears no responsibility for our analysis and findings. The data were obtained from the Supervisory Agency of Insurance Companies, Corporations, and Stock Exchanges in Santiago, which had compiled a list of the 200 largest firms in 1966, ranked by net-capital assets and classified by the United Nations 3-digit International Standard Industrial Classification of All Economic Activities (UN Statistical Papers, series N, no. 4, add. 1. Indexed edition: "Indexes to the International Standard Industrial Classification of All Economic Activities," 1956; and revisions from series M., no. 43, 1966) The net-capital assets, 3-digit SIS number, names of directors but *not* officers, names (but *not* individual shares held) of the top 10 shareholders, aggregate percentage of outstanding shares held by these top 10 shareholders and the percentage held by state, domestic and foreign shareholders, of each of the 200 firms were provided. In addition, the aggregate net capital assets of 1,729 corporations, classified by UN 3-digit SIS category and by top 200 corporations in that category, were provided.

We found that the 200 largest firms were, in fact, distributed as follows: 11 state-owned firms, five Chilean and one foreign investment company, 139 Chilean-owned, nonfinancial corporations and 43 foreign-owned (50 percent or over of shares held by foreign investors). One firm was not identified.

Total state assets (including equity in non-state-owned corporations) were E°2,524.9 million, of a total of E°12,031.9 million estimated aggregate assets for all 1,729 firms, leaving 1,718 corporations in the private sector with E°9,507.0 million. Six investment companies, plus others below the top 200, held an aggregate of E°116.0 million, leaving an estimated E°9,391.0 million aggregate assets held by 1,712 nonfinancial corporations. It was not possible to make similar calculations for firms below the top 200, as only aggregate data were made available. The supervisory agency listed 58 wholly owned foreign subsidiaries below the top 200. Taken together with the 43 majority or wholly foreign-owned corporations in the top 200, this left a *maximum* of 1,611 Chilean-owned nonfinancial corporations, without taking into account majority-owned (but not wholly owned) foreign firms below the top 200.

The supervisory agency estimated aggregate net capital assets for all domestic corporations as $E^O6,042.0$ million; less the assets of the investment companies, this indicates an estimated $E^O5,926.0$ million aggregate net-capital assets for the estimated 1,611 Chilean-owned nonfinancial corporations. Minor discrepancies and errors discovered in the supervisory agency's data have been corrected wherever possible, including several misclassifications of corporations by their relative shares of foreign and domestic assets. Withal, this constituted the most complete and reliable data base available on the relative-asset shares of the largest corporations in Chile. This source of data will be cited hereafter as "The Top 200 of 1966, Chile."

6. Joe S. Bain, *International Differences in Industrial Structure: Eight Nations in the 1950s* (New Haven and London: Yale University Press, 1966), p. 102.

7. For example, the Chilean-owned firm Petroleum Navigation, Inc., which ranked 63rd among all nonfinancial corporations, was jointly owned by four other firms (an insurance company and three shipping companies). Two of these shipping companies, the South American Steamship Co. and the Chilean Interoceanic Navigation Co., were themselves among the largest nonfinancial corporations, ranking 10th and 65th, respectively. What is more, the other shipping company, which was not in the top 182, Inter-Ocean Gas, was itself owned by Chilean Interoceanic Navigation.) Similarly, two of the five largest firms, Chilean Exploration and Andes Copper Mining, ranking first and third, respectively, as well as the 177th-ranking firm, Potrerillos Railway Co. (although separately incorporated),were wholly-owned subsidiaries of Anaconda in New York.

8. Merwin L. Bohan and Morton Pomeranz, *Investment in Chile* (Washington, D.C.: U.S. Department of Commerce, U.S. G.P.O., 1960), p. 11.

9. AFP was purchased by Electric Bond and Share in 1967, which was, in turn, acquired by Boise-Cascade in 1969.

10. This figure does not include assets which were clearly a direct adjunct of mining activities, but classified elsewhere, e.g., Anaconda's Potrerillos Railway Company. Concerning foreign investment in railroads in Chile, the U.S. Department of Commerce explains: "Foreign capital does not appear to have been interested [in lines]... primarily built to serve the Chilean internal market....[C]onstruction more closely followed the pattern common in Latin America, i.e., foreign financing of railways designed to carry export products to the nearest port....These lines had one characteristic in common, a generally west-east [to the

mines] rather than north-south [to population centers] direction." Bohan and Pomeranz, *Investment in Chile,* pp. 195-396. The Chilean government heavily subsidized national private capital to construct public-service railways running the length of the country.

11. The distribution of the $964 million (estimated) direct investment of all U.S. firms in Chile was substantially similar to findings based only on the top 23 U.S.-owned firms: the U.S. Department of Commerce estimated 58.7 percent of U.S. direct investment was in mining, 6.9 percent in manufacturing, 4.2 percent in commerce, 22.1 percent in utilities and the remaining 8.1 percent in other activities. Calculated from figures reported in Edwin L. Dale, Jr., "U.S. Yawns at Chile's Vote," *New York Times,* October 4, 1970, sec. 3, p. 1.

12. Clark Reynolds has calculated that copper taxes as a "share of 'returned value' " rose steadily between 1925 and 1959, but the government's investments in net capital formation did not keep pace. Markos Mamalakis and Clark Reynolds, *Essays on the Chilean Economy* (Homewood, Ill.: Richard D. Irwin, 1965), p. 326.

13. The relative return on assets was calculated by Theodore H. Moran as follows: Anaconda's Chilean assets brought 13.4 percent in 1955-60 and 9.7 percent in 1960-65, compared to its return on non-Chilean assets in those periods, respectively, of 6.9 percent and 3.0 percent. For Kennecott, the rates of return for these periods, on Chilean assets, were 37.9 percent and 19.0 percent, respectively; on non-Chilean assets, the rates were 13.3 percent and 7.6 percent, respectively. See *The Multinational Corporation and the Politics of Development: 1945-1970* (Ph.D. diss., Government Department, Harvard University, June 1970) p. 112

14. Chilean Copper Corporation (a government agency) paid advertisement, *New York Times,* January 25, 1971, p. 72. "U.S. Copper Firms Looking for a Turnaround", *Newsweek,* March 13, 1972, p. 41, estimates Anaconda "formerly got 75 percent of its profits from Chile," while Kennecott got 15 percent. Reynolds estimated: "Approximately 50 percent of the net income of the Kennecott Copper Company, as reported in its financial statements during the 1950s, was derived from its Chilean operation." *Essays* p. 272. Reynolds made no estimate for Anaconda. John B. Place, Chairman and President of Anaconda, is quoted as estimating that nationalization eliminated "two-thirds of our copper production and three-fourths of our earnings," in the *Washington Post,* November 14, 1971.

15. William P. Glade, *The Latin American Economies* (New York: Van Nostrand, American Books, 1969), p. 327.

16. Mario Vera Valenzuela, *La Politica Económica del Cobre en Chile*

(Santiago: Ediciones de la Universidad de Chile, 1961), p. 30. One of the major Chilean banks of that period, built largely from profits in copper financing and trading, was the Bank of Edwards, with branches in London, Paris, Boston and Vienna. Shipments by the Edwards firms alone went to India, China, France and England. At Birkenhead, England, "Dock Edwards" was exclusively used for Edwards shipments. See Enrique Bunster, "Agustin I," in *Chilenos en California,* 3rd ed. (Santiago: Editorial del Pacífico, 1965), pp. 147 ff.

17. Glade, *The Latin American Economies,* p. 621; Marcello Segall, *El Desarrollo del Capitalismo en Chile* (Santiago: Editorial del Pacífico, 1953), p. 167.

18. Segall, *El Desarrollo del Capitalismo,* pp. 168 ff, 253.

19. The Balmaceda episode has been debated ever since by Chilean and other historians. The most relevant sources are: Hernán Ramírez Necochea, *Balmaceda y la Contrarevolución de 1891* (Santiago: Editorial Universitaria, 1958); Segall, *El Desarrollo del Capitalismo* (this is a poorly organized, but very suggestive, study in which see especially pp. 167-207, *et passim)* Osgood Hardy, "British Nitrates and the Balmaceda Revolution," *Pacific Historical Review* 17 (May 1948): 165-180; Joseph R. Brown, "The Chilean Nitrate Railways Controversy," *Hispanic American Historical Review (HAHR)* 38 (November 1958): 465-81, and "Nitrate Crises, Combinations, and the Chilean Government in the Nitrate Age," *HAHR* 43, (May 1963): 230-46; Harold Blakemore, "The Chilean Revolution of 1891 and its Historiography," *HAHR* 45 (August 1965): 393-421; Frederick B. Pike, *Chile and the United States, 1880-1962* (Notre Dame: University of Notre Dame Press, 1963), pp. 31-46 (and the sources therein); Glade, *The Latin American Economies,* pp. 328-31. Blakemore considers the role of British capitalists in Balmaceda's overthrow "not proven," while British capital and the banks are not even considered as factors in Balmaceda's overthrow by Pike. Still Pike can conclude, "To a large extent [Balmaceda's] quarrel with the opposition rested upon economic rather than political considerations. Once he was removed, his successors agreed among themselves on basic economic and social policies." We agree with Pike that this was "the real crux of the matter."

20. Jack Pfeiffer, "Notes on the Heavy Equipment Industry in Chile, 1880-1910," *HAHR* 32 (February 1952): 139-44; also see J. Fred Rippy and Jack Pfeiffer, "Notes on the Dawn of Manufacturing in Chile," *HAHR* 28 (May 1948): 292-303.

21. With Balmaceda's overthrow, "the triumphant revolutionaries [sic] dedicated themselves to pillage and persecutions, imprisoning, shooting and ferociously persecuting the supporters of the defeated government."

Balmaceda took asylum in the Argentinian Embassy. Refused legal or personal guarantees of his safety by the rebels' provisional government, he remained in the embassy from August 28 to September 19, 1891, the date his legal term of office expired. That morning he shot himself.

What befell Adolfo Eastman Quiroga, son-in-law of the great mine owner José Tomás Urmeneta, and himself a major leader in the mining community as well as a deputy and senator from a mining center, may be illustrative of the fate of many copper-mine owners and industrialists who supported Balmaceda. When Balmaceda's government fell, Eastman's "fortune was taken away and his home destroyed and pillaged." He fled Chile and lived in European exile for the next three years before returning to Chile and becoming active in public life again. See Jordi Fuentes and Lia Cortes, *Diccionario Histórico de Chile* (Santiago: Editorial del Pacífico, 1963); and Luis Galdames, *A History of Chile,* 8th ed. (Chapel Hill, University of North Carolina Press, 1941), pp. 347.

22. Pike, *Chile and the United States, 1880-1962,* p. 46. Pike also comments: "If Balmaceda had succeeded in imposing his economic policies, there is little question that Chile would, in the twentieth century, have been in vastly better condition" (p. 45).

23. The initial capital outlay that established the Braden Copper Company at El Teniente, in 1905, reportedly amounted to $2.5 million. The initial outlay in 1913 at Chuquicamata was a mere $1 million, according to Mario Vera, though an estimated total of $100 million "was poured into the desert [over an eight-year period] before the property was in successful and profitable operation." Bohan and Pomeranz, *Investment in Chile,* p. 90; Vera, *La Politica Económica del Cobre,* pp. 45, 47. That investible funds in these amounts were available from Chilean capitalists seems clear "if for no other reason," as Clark Reynolds points out, "than the existence of extremely high profits from nitrate which were accruing to Chilean entrepreneurs well into the twentieth century." The current value of Chilean investments in Bolivian tin mines, alone, in 1920 was $100 million, aside from the capital in nitrates, beef production, and coal mining. *Essays,* p. 220.

It should be noted here that the ascendance of British capital in nitrates in the 1880s was also the result of Chilean government policy and that the British acquisition of many of the nitrate properties in the aftermath of the War of the Pacific was largely financed by Chilean capital. The Peruvian government had issued certificates in compensation for the properties it expropriated, many belonging to Chileans, just before the outbreak of the war. (The expropriation itself had precipitated the war.) The certificates were selling at a discount when the war ended, since it was not clear whether the Chilean government would nationalize the nitrates or restore them to the holders of the certificates. A group of three British speculators, led by the soon-to-become "Nitrate King" John Thomas

North, having inside information that the government had decided to honor the certificates, bought them up at greatly reduced prices with funds advanced by John Dawson in his capacity as manager of the Chilean Bank of Valparaíso. He advanced North and Robert Harvey (the inspector of nitrates for the Chilean government who provided the information that the government would honor the certificates) the bank's money to buy the certificates, requiring little collateral and allowing them to delay repayment until 1885, with considerably devalued pesos. When, in 1881, the Chilean government honored the certificates, the industry passed into the North group's control. See Hardy, "British Nitrates," 169ff. (Several of the nitrate capitalists were later knighted by the British government, including North's brother and Harvey.) Most of the British corporations (in many of which the North group was dominant) that were to rule the nitrate industry in Chile for more than a quarter of a century were established in these few years. See also J. Fred Rippy, "Economic Enterprises of the 'Nitrate King' and His Associates in Chile," *Pacific Historical Review* 17 (November 1948): 457-65, and "British Investments in the Chilean Nitrate Industry," *Inter-American Economic Affairs* 8 (Autumn 1954): 3-10; Aníbal Pinto, *Chile: Un Caso de Desarrollo Frustrado* (Santiago: Editorial Universitaria, 1953), p. 55, states: Chilean capital, from the Bank of Valparaiso. . .and 'other Chilean leaders, provided North and his associates, $6,000,000 to corner the market in nitrate certificates and the railroads of Tarapaca.' " The internal quote is from Francisco Encina, a venerable conservative historian.

24. Mariano Puga Vega, *El Petróleo Chileno* (Santiago: Editorial Andres Bello, 1964), p. 74.

25. Bohan and Pomeranz, *Investment in Chile,* pp. 183-87; Puga, *El Petróleo Chileno,* chaps. 5-7.

26. Bohan and Pomeranz, *Investment in Chile,* p. 181.

27. Mamalakis, *Essays,* p. 19, estimates that as much as one-fifth (on the average) of gross domestic investment was accounted for by CORFO from 1940 through 1954. No more recent figures were available to the authors.

28. Libert Ehrman, *Opportunities for Investment in Chile: A Program for Encouragement of Private Industry* (New York: Praeger, 1966), pp. 117-32.

29. Bohan and Pomeranz, *Investment in Chile,* p. 219. See also "BNAP: Una Industria Estatal al Servicio de los Monopolios," *El Siglo* (Santiago), August 28, 1966, p. 15.

30. Bain, *International Differences*, p. 102, referring to Japan, France, and Italy. Also pp. 95, 99.

31. Andrew Shonfield, *Modern Capitalism* (London: Oxford University Press, for the Royal Institute of International Affairs, 1965), referring immediately to France but indirectly to Austria, Italy and England. See pp. 109, 179, 184-86, 193. Shonfield states that, in Great Britain, "The public sector as a whole was responsible [during the 1960s] for over 40 percent of all fixed investment and for as much as 50 percent of the building work done in the country" (p. 106).

32. We do not refer here to the clear preponderance of national capital among the few large agricultural corporations, only because corporations were not the typical or decisive form of property in Chilean agriculture. The landed estates were owned by Chileans and foreign capital was of no apparent importance in agricultural production, except for cattle raising in Tierra del Fuego.

33. John M. Blair, chief economist, U.S. Senate Antitrust and Monopoly Subcommittee, made this point in his testimony before the Committee. In fact, he made "an effort to show the importance in individual industries of the 200 largest companies in manufacturing as whole" in the U.S., and considered this "something of a new contribution." *Economic Concentration: Hearings before the Subcommittee on Antitrust and Monopoly of the Committee on the Judiciary, U.S. Senate, 88th Congress,* 2nd Session, pursuant to Senate Resolution 262. Part 1: Overall and Conglomerate Aspects (Washington, D.C.: U.S.G.P.O., July 1964), pp. 211-12 (hereafter cited as *Economic Concentration: Hearings*).

34. Bain, *International Differences,* p. 68. See also Willard F. Mueller, pp. 111ff.; John M. Blair, p. 241, and M. A. Adelman, pp. 230-31, in *Economic Concentration: Hearings,* where agreement is expressed that, in Adelman's words: "The concentration ratio is a fairly crude approximation but, so far, it is the only thing we have which fits the requirements of economic theory that it [a measure] have some relevance to market behavior. Some highly refined measures have been proposed [but]...I do not think these measures have as yet proved useful."

35. Adelman, *Economic Concentration: Hearings,* p. 234. Also his statement that "as a general statistical matter, the greater the concentration, the lower the odds in favor of competitive behavior" (p. 230).

36. These are broader industry groups than are most useful to measure industrial concentration. We refer here to 3-digit rather than 4-digit,

Standard Industrial Classification categories. However, when necessary, for lack of an alternative, these have been used also by specialists. See Mueller and Blair in *Economic Concentration: Hearings,* pp. 116-20, 212-13.

37. This is about the same share (58 percent) of the estimated net capital assets controlled by the 200 largest nonfinancial corporations in the United States. See Gardiner C. Means, *Economic Concentration: Hearings,* p. 11. To the extent to which it is valid to use such "concentration ratios" to compare inter-country levels of overall concentration, this would indicate that the level of concentration was higher in Chile than in the United States. This procedure, of course, disregards the number of corporations in the different economies and the comparative proportions of the largest in the corporate populations. The top 100 nonfinancial corporations owned by Chilean investors constituted 6.2 percent of the estimated 1,611 Chilean nonfinancial corporations, compared to the 0.1 percent of the roughly 200,000 nonfinancial corporations in the United States represented by the top 200. In his study of *International Differences in Industrial Structure,* Bain uses concentration ratios for comparisons between specific industries in different countries. The same logic would appear to be applicable to comparisons of overall concentration in different countries. See also Adelman's statement that "the most important use of concentration [ratios] is in comparison: over time; or among countries, or regions, or industries at the same time." *Economic Concentration: Hearings,* p. 230.

In manufacturing, where comparisons were possible with broadly similar industrial groups in the United States, Chilean concentration ratios were all higher. In each of the 15 3-digit industrial groups compared, the proportion of net capital assets controlled by not more than the three largest (national or foreign) firms in Chile was greater than the proportion controlled by the four largest in the United States.

Bain's intercountry comparisons are based on narrower industrial groups than our data. A glance at the few industrial groups in different countries that do seem comparable suggests that Chile's was closer to (though still higher than) the level of industrial concentration in manufacturing in such countries as Japan, Sweden and Italy, than to the United States or England.

38. Bohan and Pomeranz, *Investment in Chile,* p. 14. For 1966, CORFO estimated that $35,112,759 was paid out on licensing agreements to foreign firms, principally American, Swiss and other Western European ones. It is not clear if this figure also included payments by affiliates and subsidiaries to their headquarters (or controlling interests) abroad, which was a disguised profit remittance. See Eduardo Moyano, "Notas Sobre el Pago de Licencias Industriales en Chile," *in Proceso a la Industrializacion Chilena,* ed. O. Muñoz (Santiago: Universidad Católica 1972), pp. 168-69.

39. Of course, this could have been accomplished by contract, without any minority holding.

40. All this was without reference to foreign financing—by suppliers, private banks or international lending agencies—and the role this played in the foreign control of national firms. The Chilean government estimated that between one-third and one-half of funds for investment in manufacturing consisted of foreign credits in 1965-1970. In 1965, an estimated 53 percent of private investment in manufacturing was from foreign credits, in 1966, 31 percent. *El Crédito Externo como Fuente de Financiamento del Sector Privado* (Santiago: Oficina de Planificación Nacional, March 1970), mimeographed.

41. Relevant findings on control groups are presented in the authors' (written with L. A. Ewen) forthcoming *Corporate Capital. The Large Corporation and the Capitalist Class in Chile.*

42. Between 1960 and 1969, private U.S. investment in Chile rose from $32 to $75 million, of which over half the increase came from reinvested Chilean earnings. Some of this may have been used to gain new or increase old minority holdings, but no such data have come to the author's attention. Luis Pacheco, "La Inversión Extranjera y las Corporaciones Internacionales en el Desarrollo Industrial Chilena," in *Proceso a la Industrialización Chilena,* pp. 143ff., *assumes* this, but presents no relevant evidence.

43. Sanford Rose, "The Rewarding Strategies of Multinationalism," *Fortune,* September 15, 1968, p. 104.

44. "Few companies have developed formal tools to measure foreign risks, which, though becoming less significant in the industrialized countries, is still crucially important in the less-developed world," according to Rose, in *Fortune,* September 15, 1968, p. 105. DuPont is one corporation which was making the attempt to develop a formal model of the political economy before investing. "DuPont researchers," as *Fortune* explains, "have identified fifteen to twenty interest groups per country, from small landowners to private bankers," and attempt to measure their cohesiveness and latent influence on the government's policy toward foreign investment. Other corporations, it may be assumed, with or without such models, take such social and political aspects of the "investment climate" into account in their investment decisions.

45. The tables distributing net capital assets among the large national and foreign corporations, as has been said, do not take into account the foreign shareholdings in national corporations or vice versa. If all assets are simply taken and divided by the total worth represented by shareholdings in all 182 nonfinancial corporations, the distribution scarcely differs

(though it increases the national share somewhat): 45.6 percent of the worth of the outstanding shares of the 182 nonfinancial corporations was held by foreign investors, 54.4 percent by Chilean investors. As can be seen from Table 3, the share of assets controlled by foreign-owned corporations is 48.0 percent, by national corporations, 52.0 percent, Calculated from raw data in "The Top 200 of 1966, Chile."

10
The Invisible Blockade:
The United States Reacts

Elizabeth Farnsworth, Richard Feinberg and Eric Leenson

SETTING THE STAGE

In 1970, Salvador Allende inherited a stagnating, dependent and mortgaged economy. The development policies promoted by the United States and adopted by the predecessor Christian Democratic government of Eduardo Frei had failed to promote dynamic growth.[1] This was especially significant because the United States had made Chile a "showcase" of the Alliance for Progress and Chile had received more aid per capita (under Frei), than any other nation in Latin America. The United States had poured aid into Chile to keep it safe for capitalism and to try to buy off discontented Chileans who well understood that the Chilean economy was in trouble because of its historic relationship with the developed world. The aid and the private loans that Chile courted enabled its middle class to enjoy U.S.-style consumption patterns, at the cost of a rising national indebtedness. And yet, Chile's economy continued to languish. The Unidad Popular (Popular Unity—UP) government was elected chiefly because many Chileans could no longer tolerate this situation. The UP recognized that 150 years of underdevelopment could not be overcome by one blow, but it hoped to transform the economy as swiftly as it could to serve the needs of the

Adapted by the editors from "Facing the Blockade," in *New Chile,* published by the North American Congress on Latin America, Box 226, Berkeley, Ca. 94701 and Box 57, Cathedral Station, New York, 10025. Copyright ©NACLA.

The authors wish to thank the following people for their help in compiling the data used in this chapter, which was written in January 1973: Roger Burbach, George Lawton, John Dinges, Kathy Hays, Bob High, Leslie Krebs, Ruth Needleman, Hernan Rosenberg, Rod Savoignan, Kyle Steenland and Alejandro Toledo.

majority of the people neglected in previous development efforts. UP thought it could build majority support through its short-term economic policies of income redistribution. But, in order to provide enough consumer goods to match families' rising money incomes, the government hoped to maintain at least in the short run normal trading patterns with the United States. These patterns depended on loans and credits from U.S. public and private institutions which would enable Chile to import vital parts, equipment and other inputs for its foreign-made industrial plants, as well as vehicles, food (such as corn), fertilizers, chemicals, petrochemicals and other items available chiefly in the United States.

The UP did not anticipate that a *bloqueo invisible* (invisible credit blockade) would undercut many of its programs and aid the work of the right-wing opposition, which had long benefited from dependent capitalism. In 1970, it was hard to say just what the U.S. response would be to the UP's plans to expropriate U.S. industries, particularly copper. The most recent prior case, Peru's nationalization of the properties of International Petroleum Company (IPC, a subsidiary of Standard Oil, New Jersey) provided an inconclusive precedent. Although official bilateral and multilateral aid to Peru was cut, the United States never applied the full force of its credit leverage and subsequent requests for credit were granted.[2] This easement was granted partly because Peru's acts never significantly threatened United States holdings. IPC was only one of many U.S. investments in Peru—others were left intact. Further, Peru continued to welcome large amounts of foreign investment in other areas of its economy. Chile's UP in contrast, threatened one of the largest United States investments anywhere in the Western Hemisphere. It also closed the door to any new investments in Chile, except those willing to work within UP's own more restrictive terms.

ASSUMPTIONS BEHIND U.S. POLICY

From the beginning, U.S. policy toward the Allende government was based on two key presuppositions.[3] First, foreign investments are crucial to the growth of the United States' domestic economy. Harry Magdoff, explaining why the United

States has reacted so strongly to threats on investments even in small and seemingly unimportant countries, has written: "the reality of imperialism goes far beyond the immediate interests of this or that investor: *the underlying purpose is nothing less than keeping as much as possible of the world open for trade and investment by the giant multinational corporations.*"[4] The United States has repeatedly reiterated its commitment to that goal. At a March 1972 State Department-sponsored seminar on the "Impact of Economic Nationalism on Key Mineral Resources Industries," representatives from industry and government exchanged ideas on how to protect and expand U.S. foreign investment. Lest there be any doubt about U.S. policy in this area, John M. Hennessey, deputy assistant secretary of the treasury for development finance (a man who helped shape policy toward Chile), succinctly stated the government position: "I think we assume there is a link between the availability of resources at a reasonable cost and foreign direct investment at this time. . . .At this moment, the United States has a policy of wanting to promote direct foreign investment, which is why the OPIC (Overseas Private Investment Corporation) exists." He said further, "We assume that the U.S. government *cannot* walk away from any significant expropriation."[5]

A second assumption of policymakers is that the most powerful weapon available to discourage threats to U.S. interests abroad and to insure the expansion of U.S. direct investment, except for guns, is dollars. U.S. dollars, in the form of official bilateral and multilateral aid and private loans and suppliers' credits, were, in 1970, the most important U.S. export to Chile.[6] Any hardening of U.S. policy toward Chile would raise the threat of a cutoff of these funds. This 1970s version of "dollar diplomacy" had several implications for Chile. Most importantly, it meant increasing influence for the Department of the Treasury (which is responsible for bilateral- and multilateral-aid policy[7] and which is widely considered to be the most vigorous advocate of private big business interests within the executive branch) in the determination of policy toward Chile.

These two assumptions had long underlay U.S. foreign-policy decisions, but they took on special significance with: (1) the worsening situation of the U.S. economy, especially in terms of international trade and the consequent formation of the New Economic Policy; and (2) the stronger commitment of the Nixon administration to the protection and expansion of direct U.S. investments and private financial operations overseas.

In 1970, the U.S. economy was deteriorating both at home and abroad. Domestic inflation and unemployment were high. Gold reserves were dwindling, the U.S. share in world trade was down and the balance of payments was running a deficit ($3 billion during 1970).[8] Meanwhile, the United States' partners, especially those in Japan and Western Europe, were experiencing high rates of growth in trade and industry and were expanding investment abroad. The United States was on the defensive and policy-makers confronted the threats arising out of Chilean expropriation from a perspective that magnified their importance to U.S. interests.

The New Economic Policy, announced by President Nixon in August 1971, gave notice to the world that, in order to confront the economic problems that came to a head in 1971, the United States would, henceforth, take a hard line in promoting its economic interests. Imposing the 10-percent import surcharge, cutting off gold sales and allowing the dollar to "float," were only its most visible manifestations. In recognizing Japan and Western Europe's increasing share of world trade—at the expense of the United States—U.S. policymakers essentially announced the end of what has been called "Marshall Plan liberalism"[9] and the beginning of a new era of competition between major trading blocs. This implied a new perspective on foreign relations as a whole. As presidential assistant Peter M. Flanigan described it: "In the past, economic interests were sacrificed when they came into conflict with diplomatic interests. We take the position that we can't have a strong foreign policy without a strong foreign economic policy."[10]

Or, as Assistant Secretary of the Treasury John Petty (a key figure in shaping policy towards Chile) said, "I think you'll find the U.S. less prepared to turn the other cheek. It's a new ball game with new rules."[11]

Though the implications of this new international policy were clearest for Japan and Western Europe, it obviously had profound effects on the underdeveloped world. If the United States was to meet the threats arising from the expansion of the European and Japanese economies, its government would have to be more committed than ever to the expansion and growth of its economy. This implied more support to corporations and especially more active encouragement and protection for U.S. investment in the Third World.

The people who formulated the NEP considered increasing government aid for U.S. corporations a necessity in view of similar aid provided to foreign competitors by their governments. This view came out in a report prepared by Peter G. Peterson, former president and chairman of Bell and Howell, who was then assistant to the president on international economic policy. The report, prepared for the studies that preceded the announcement of the NEP, described the decreasing competitiveness of U.S. industries vis-a-vis Japan and Western Europe and analyzed foreign-trade trends and balance-of-payments difficulties. Its most significant conclusions involved the necessity for an activist policy on the part of the government to protect and expand industry in order to increase the United States' exports and make it more competitive in the world market. Using detailed tables and graphs, the report reiterated how foreign investment benefited the United States.[12]

The report called for strong government action to expand exports and investment abroad: specifically, Peterson recommended more liberal tax treatment for exporters and foreign investors and suggested that restrictions on foreign investment abroad be dropped; he also called for special credits for exports; expanded government insurance "of certain export risks"; and the relaxing of certain antitrust laws with "inhibiting disadvantages to many potential exporters." The report lauded the Japanese example of large government-sponsored trading companies which specialized in export development.[13] Peterson's suggestions caused the *New York Times* (January 4, 1972) to editorialize that "the administration's heavy emphasis on the business-government partnership has disturbing overtones of corporate statism. . . ." Secretary of the Treasury John Connally supported the Peterson conclusions, especially in regard to the necessity of government intervention to promote exports.[14]

The importance of governmental aid to U.S. companies was a

major theme of the March 1972 State Department-sponsored seminar. Thus, C. Harry Burgess, vice-president of Kennecott, bewailed losing out to the Japanese in competition for hard minerals: "Their trading company represents a coalition or consortium with the Japanese government." Bradford Mills, president of OPIC, agreed: "Really, what American mining companies are facing today is not private competition. Mitsui is not private. . . .If we are going to have a system that continues, the U.S. government is going to have to get involved."[15]

Thus, there was a growing conviction by private businessmen and government officials alike that strong governmental action was necessary to protect U.S. economic interests around the world. It is true that the Nixon administration had not lifted the restrictions on private investment abroad that were imposed by the Johnson administration to stop the dollar outflow that contributed to the balance-of-payments deficit; and it was true that there was some negotiating going on between the Nixon administration and the multinational corporations to determine just what the administration's policy would be towards investments in the developed world.[16] But the increasingly problematic nature of economic relations with the developed world (particularly Western Europe and Japan) made U.S. investments in its traditional spheres of influence (like Latin America) more important than ever. The government was now committed to extending aid to corporations as a whole especially in those areas crucial to the growth and expansion of the U.S. economy, vis-à-vis Western Europe and Japan.[17]

The NEP also implied growing power for the Treasury Department in making foreign policy. Since foreign trade and economic advantage were seen as inextricably entwined with foreignpolicy interests, Treasury would have a great deal of clout in major foreign policy decisions.[18]

Since Treasury also made U.S. bilateral and multilateral aid policy, it would dominate policymaking towards the underdeveloped countries. Although Treasury had always been a powerful department, it had (until the advent of Connally and the NEP) shared with State the role of forming policy toward nations involved in expropriation controversies with the U.S. Thus, the State Department had been largely responsible for U.S. policies towards Peru during the IPC controversy. State took a softer line with Peru than Connally and others would have liked; and, certainly, State's position on Chile would have been softer than the credit warfare that was waged against Chile during the Allende term.[19]

The disturbing aspect of Treasury's power over the underdeveloped countries is that the people who make international economic policy in Treasury are nearly always men who have worked in high capacities in banks with important international operations or in large multinational corporations. They thus represent interests especially committed to the expansion of capitalism in the Third World.

FORMULATING POLICY TOWARD CHILE

On January 19, 1972, Nixon announced the hardline policy which would be followed in the case of Chile and any other Third World country that nationalized U.S. interests:

Thus, when a country expropriates a significant U.S. interest without making reasonable provision for such compensation to U.S. citizens, we will presume that the United States will not extend new bilateral economic benefits to the expropriating country unless and until it is determined that the country is taking reasonable steps to provide adequate compensation or that there are major factors affecting U.S. interests which require continuance of all or part of these benefits.

In the face of the expropriatory circumstances just described, we will presume that the United States Government will withhold its support from loans under consideration in multilateral development banks. Humanitarian assistance will, of course, continue to receive special consideration under such circumstances.

In order to carry out this policy effectively, I have directed that each potential expropriation case be followed closely. A special inter-agency group will be established under the Council on International Economic Policy to review such cases and recommend courses of action for the U.S. Government.

The Departments of State, Treasury, and Commerce are increasing their interchange of views with the business community on problems relating to private U.S. investment abroad in order to improve government and business awareness of each other's concerns, actions, and plans. The Department of State has set up a special office to follow expropriation cases in support of the Council on International Economic Policy.[20]

This policy was developed throughout 1971 by the Departments of State and Treasury and, peripherally, by Peterson and the staff of the Council on International Economic Policy. The way in which it was formulated demonstrates the increased power of Treasury and the big-business bias of the administration.

The administration took its first steps toward officially issuing a policy toward expropriating nations in July 1971 with the issuance of National Security Memorandum (NSSM) 131 which advocated an interagency study of current and possible future policies.[21] The issues were studied by the Council on International Economic Policy (CIEP) and by an undersecretaries' committee chaired by John N. Irwin II, undersecretary of state, and, in his absence, by Nathaniel Samuels, deputy undersecretary of state (economic affairs). Other participants in the study, according to Mark Chadwin, included: Philip H. Trezise, former assistant secretary of state (economic affairs, 1969-1971); Sidney Weintraub, deputy assistant secretary of state (international finance and development); Charls E. Walker, undersecretary of the treasury; John R. Petty, assistant secretary of the treasury (international affairs); Henry Kissinger; Peter G. Peterson; and officials from OPIC and the Export-Import Bank. To provide them with staff and to study longer-term methods of protecting U.S. investments abroad, the State Department also established a new unit under Weintraub, the Office of Investment Affairs.[22]

Though earlier expropriations than those in Chile had bothered the administration, members of the CIEP admitted that the "review" was largely to determine policy toward Chile. People spoke openly of the differing views of Peterson and Kissinger on the expropriation policy in terms of Chile. Kissinger favored a moderate stand, while Peterson proposed a harder line to discourage other governments from taking similar action.[23]

The first drafts of the official policy statement were prepared under Weintraub at State and John M. Hennessey at Treasury. Then, on October 8, 1971, National Security Decision Memorandum (NSDM) 136 assigned responsibility for handling investment and expropriation problems to the president's Council on International Economic Policy. The CIEP, working with State and Treasury, was directed to draft the public statement.

The Weintraub and Hennessey drafts were the basis of the final version. Both had expressed support for a new definition of U.S. policy, but their approaches to it varied, reflecting the traditional conflict between State and Treasury in foreign economic policy (sometimes referred to as the "soft-line" vs. the "hard-line" method).[24] According to journalist Mark Chadwin, the State Department draft was "prepared with its foreign constituencies at least as much in mind as its domestic ones. It trod lightly on the bilateral and multilateral leverage available to the government. . . ." The Treasury draft was "more blunt in style and content, asserting U.S. leverage and going into more detail about the form U.S. reactions might take in the event of future expropriations."[25]

William J. Mazzocco, the Agency for International Development (AID) representative serving on the CIEP staff, combined the two drafts, modifying somewhat the harsh language of the Treasury draft. The final statement, delivered by Nixon on January 19, 1972, supposedly contained sections from both drafts, but clearly expressed Treasury's views more than State's. As assistant secretary of Treasury, John R. Petty later said of the policy, "We hope it will make any other government contemplating such steps think twice before taking them."[26]

The long lag between the beginning (summer 1971) of inquiries into the policy and its announcement (January 1972), indicated that interest groups represented within the Nixon administration disagreed on what the policy should entail. Liberal capitalists engaged in overseas investment and trade attacked the policy. Charles W. Robinson, president of the Marcona Corporation, told a trade conference in Chicago in March 1972 that the hard-line policy towards nations expropriating U.S. interests without proper compensation was our twentieth century version of the British gunboat diplomacy of the 1800s.[27] (Marcona has interests in Peru that suffered as a result of that government's reaction to the partial U.S. blockade of development finance.) Peterson admitted to a *National Journal* reporter that, while most U.S. companies approved of the White House action, "some business groups have been less than complimentary. They are concerned that it may aggravate relations between the U.S. and the developing countries."[28]

Most of the congressional opposition centered around that portion of the policy that related to multilateral agencies. The Nixon administration had continually advocated channeling more aid through these agencies, thus lowering the U.S. profile in Latin America. Yet, as Senator Kennedy objected, this new hard-line toward nations which "unfairly" expropriate U.S. interests seemed to imply "that the World Bank and the Inter-American Bank are our tools to wield however we wish. It directly conflicts with the president's previously expressed view that we should be seeking a partnership with other nations in multilateral development efforts."[29]

Liberal criticism of the Nixon policy and the differences between the departments of State and Treasury should not be taken to indicate that there were elements of U.S. leadership which seriously questioned the importance of foreign investment to the United States. The arguments against the policy centered on the choice of strategy and tactics as to the best means of assuring the growth and expansion of the capitalist system and how best to keep as much as possible of the world free for corporate enterprise.

In fact, most of the important business groups had urged the Nixon administration to adopt the hard-line policy. This was clear from the onset of consultations between policymakers and representatives of interests affected by Chile's antiimperialist actions. In October 1971, shortly after Allende's announcement that American copper companies would not receive the compensation they expected, Secretary of State William Rogers met with representatives of Anaconda, Ford, ITT, Ralston Purina, the First National City Bank of New York and the Bank of America (all major investors in Chile) to assure them that the U.S. would "cut off aid unless she [Chile] provided prompt compensation." When asked whether this might not be interpreted as a "slap in the face" to Chile and other Latin American nations, Rogers, already reflecting the influence of Treasury's hard line, suggested that "such measures might be the only language they understand."[30]

At about the same time International Telephone and Telegraph (ITT), on its own, pressed the U.S. government for application of the "numerous justifiable leverages" available to embarrass Chile. On September 14, 1971, ITT President Harold Geneen met over lunch with Peter Peterson and Brigadier General Alexander M. Haig, Jr. (deputy assistant—under Kissinger—for national security affairs) to discuss the Chilean expropriations. Later (October 1, 1971), ITT vice-president and Washington lobbyist William R. Merriam wrote to Peterson proposing an "economic squeeze" on Chile through denial of international credit, a ban on both imports of copper and vital exports to Chile so that sufficient "economic chaos" would develop to convince the armed forces to "step in and restore order." It proposed that the Central Intelligence Agency (CIA) assist in this process.[31] The Peterson letter, like the infamous ITT "papers," indicated how close those interests felt to the Nixon administration.

Peterson actively solicited the advice of the business community during the months in which the expropriation policy was taking shape. During the Council of the Americas (the main lobby for U.S. investors in Latin America) annual meeting in Washington, in June 1971, Peterson asked for council members' ideas on protecting private investment abroad. Jose de Cubas, president of Westinghouse Electric and chairman of the Council of the Americas, responded that August with a four-page, single-spaced letter to Peterson urging that the federal government use its influence to assure that when the World Bank, or any other multilateral lending institution, rated a country's credit-worthiness, it would consider whether there was, in the country's record, any case of "insufficiently compensated nationalizations of private investment."[32] It was appropriate that the government should seek the advice of the business community, since a large proportion of the officials involved in making economic policy had previously been corporate or banking executives and would soon return to their previous roles.[33]

THE INVISIBLE BLOCKADE

Usually, import-export operations between nations are financed by credit, meaning that the importer need not pay for goods upon ordering, but rather on a pre-arranged schedule. "Short-term" credit is repaid in one to six months (generally 90 days) after the purchase is delivered; "medium-term" credit affords longer time for payment and usually covers more expensive items such as "consumer durables" (refrigerators, cars) and "capital goods" (equipment used in producing other goods).

Such credits are the grease of international trade. In their absence, great confusion arises and all transactions must be paid off in cash—a difficult, if not impossible, task in most normal business operations. The control of the world's credit mechanism is in the hands of the major capitalist nations and their banks. Their capacity to offer or withhold their "services" gives them tremendous political power. The assets of any of the major Wall Street banks surpass the annual GNP of many nations, including Chile's, and grow even faster.

Chilean private importers and state development projects had depended on credit granted by the capitalist nations—especially the United States— to import needed goods. Since World War II, the United States had provided Chile with 40 percent of its total imports and 65 percent of all its capital imports. Chief among these imports were machinery and transport equipment, manufactured goods, chemicals, food and live animals.[34] These imports were made possible by credit from the suppliers themselves (much like a charge account), by credit from private banks, by credit (or loans) from U.S. public agencies like the Export-Import Bank or by loans from the multilateral agencies such as the World Bank and Inter-American Development Bank. In fact, when the Allende government came to power, 78.4 percent of the total short-term trade credit available to Chile came from U.S. suppliers and banks.[35]

Short-term credits and longer-term credits and loans for development projects are particularly crucial to developing countries because of their chronic shortage of foreign exchange currency. Chile got around 80 percent of its foreign exchange from sales of copper. Since the price of copper fluctuated widely, the amount of foreign exchange available to Chile also fluctuated. At the same time, the prices, as well as the quantity, of goods that Chile wanted to import had increased steadily. This led to a need for more foreign exchange to cover importing, which, in turn, led to further indebtedness. This situation is often referred to as the "spiraling indebtedness" of underdeveloped countries.

Both the business community and the U.S. government clearly understood, early in 1971, that Chile was dependent on dollars in order to import needed goods. They could also guess that Chile would export less than it needed to import (largely because of the drop in the price of copper) and that it would have to borrow or dip into reserves to cover the deficit. When it couldn't borrow the dollars it needed, Chile would have to use those reserves, further impairing its "credit-worthiness." Once these means were exhausted, Chile would face an internal-adjustment process, which would mean further reductions in imports from the U.S.–which it badly needed.[36] This would, in turn, cause severe hardships, especially on Chile's middle class, which had benefited most from the imports. These groups would then withdraw support from the Allende government and provoke a crisis into which the more conservative elements, particularly the military, could move.

THE U.S. GOVERNMENT CUTS CREDIT: EXIMBANK

From 1946 to 1971, Chile received about $600 million worth of direct credits from the U.S. Export-Import Bank. These credits are actually dollar loans extended directly to borrowers outside the United States for purchases of U.S. goods and services. Chile has also benefited from Eximbank's guarantee and insurance programs. Eximbank guarantees credits granted by private banks against the commercial and political risks of nonpayment. The insurance program is administered by an Eximbank affiliate, the Foreign Credit Insurance Association (FCIA), a group of the principal U.S. maritime, casualty and property insurance companies. FCIA insurance is available to U.S. exporters, which the credit guarantees are available to bankers. The majority of the medium-term credit transactions in which commercial banks are involved are handled either by an Eximbank guarantee or with FCIA insurance.[39]

Thus, the availability of credit from the Eximbank has a great deal of impact on export financing as a whole. Any hard-line policy on the part of Eximbank would (1) cut off the disbursements of the Eximbank loans previously negotiated with Chile; (2) make it impossible to get new loans; and (3) cut off the guarantee and insurance program for commercial banks and exporters.

The Eximbank took a determined stance when it denied the Allende administration's first request for a loan—$21 million to finance the purchase of three Boeing passenger jets for the state-owned LAN-Chile airline. Chile had previously received credit for LAN-Chile purchases. At the time this request was made (early 1971), U.S. officials admitted that Chile had been scrupulous in paying its debts and a Commerce Department official admitted that Chile's "credit-worthiness" was the simplest part of the problem, implying that the question of whether to grant the request was political.[38]

That August, Eximbank President Henry Kearns finally informed Chile's ambassador in Washington that Chile could expect no loans or guarantees until the question of compensation for seized U.S. mining and other interests in Chile had been resolved. According to a *New York Times* article (August 1, 1971), the State Department indicated that the decision to block Eximbank loans to Chile was "made on the White House level" under pressure from American companies. This was the first clue that the Nixon administration would erect a credit blockade and the private banks and suppliers—experienced participants in the capitalist game—took their cue.

U.S. Aid

In the postwar years (until 1971), Chile received $540 million in "development" loans from the Agency for International Development and its predecessors. These loans flowed into Chile largely to bolster the economy and prevent the election of Allende in 1964, and then to facilitate Frei's "Revolution in Liberty." After 1967, however, AID loans to Chile decreased, partly because the Frei government, enjoying the highest copper prices in history, temporarily accumulated a positive reserve balance and, thus, made fewer requests for AID loans. In 1970, AID loaned Chile only $15 million; in the next year, Chile received no new loans from AID. Nevertheless, Chile was still saddled with a huge debt to AID: as of June 1971, Chile owed

AID about $500 million (payable in dollars) and another $30 million (payable in *escudos*).[39] Without further credit from the United States, it would be difficult for Chile to pay off these loans.

The strategy of the United States toward Chile was evident in the programs it continued to operate there. AID's "technical assistance" program continued under Allende. Under this program, the U.S. granted (not loaned) money to be used to train "selected Chileans" in urban administration, rural development and similar fields and to promote certain "small-scale, self-help projects." The program also funded labor union visits and exchanges conducted by the American Institute of Free Labor Development (AIFLD), which was basically a corporate- and labor-funded tool for infiltrating the Chilean labor movement.[40] In 1971 and 1972, Chile received $1 million in technical-assistance grants for these programs and the Nixon administration requested $805,000 for 1973.[41]

The continuation of these programs was justified on the basis that they were "humanitarian" and "people-to-people" and thus exempt from Nixon's "hard-line" policy. The truth is that the Nixon administration considered these programs and the continuing military-assistance projects important in strengthening the sources of actual and potential opposition to Allende.

U.S. foreign policymakers recognizing that the military was a crucial, if dormant, factor in Chilean social and political stability, contributed more military aid to Chile between 1950 and 1970 ($175.8 million) than to any other Latin American country except Brazil. This amounted to about 10 percent of Chile's total defense budget in the same period.[42] In 1971, the U.S. granted Chile a $5 million military credit for the acquisition of a C-130 four-engined transport aircraft and paratroop equipment. In December 1972, administration officials said that they intended to grant Chile $10 million in military aid for use in 1973.[43]

The "Multilateral" Institutions: The IDB and the World Bank

After the election of Allende, no significant loans were granted to Chile by either the World Bank or the Inter-American Development Bank (IDB), though both agencies continued to disburse loans already negotiated. The Allende government continued to pay off its loans to these banks but criticized them for becoming tools of the U.S. government. At the annual meeting of the World Bank and International Monetary Fund (September 1972) Alfonso Inostroza, president of Chile's central bank, said that, in deciding not to grant new credit, the World Bank had acted in a "manifestly precipitate and prejudiced manner. . .not as an independent multinational body at the service of the economic development of all its members, but in fact as a spokesman or instrument of private interests of one of its member countries."[44] And, in a press conference held in Washington (October 1972), Inostroza extended his criticisms to the Inter-American Development Bank.[45]

Since its founding in 1959, the IDB granted Chile 59 loans totaling $310 million (up to 1972). The flow of credit was so large that some critics charged Felipe Herrera, a Chilean and former president of IDB, with favoritism. But Herrera was not the main promoter of loans to Chile from the IDB; the United States had its own reasons for wanting aid to pour into Chile, and it is the United States, not the titular Latin leader, that controls the bank. The U.S. government supplies three-fourths of the capital for the IDB; it fully supplies the IDB's "special fund"; and it exercises a veto power over most loans.

In 1971, the Allende government asked for several new loans, some of which were considered for preliminary examination by an IDB special mission that visited Chile in June 1971. At that time, the bank's representatives and the Chilean authorities agreed to promote a petrochemical complex—a "perfect" development project, transferring technology and capable of earning foreign exchange. The loan, however, was not forthcoming, even as other well-researched and reasonable requests from Chile for electrical power and natural (liquid) gas went unfulfilled.

One excuse the bank gave for refusing the loan was Chile's unfavorable foreign-exchange position. But that difficulty was largely the result of U.S. policy. Moreover, the objective of the development bank was supposedly to help Latin nations overcome economic problems. As a Chilean working for the IDB complained, "The IDB is behaving like an umbrella that's up only when it's not raining."

Another reason why the IDB was hesitant to grant loans to Chile was that the agencies it had previously funded became dominated by Communists and Socialists under Allende. The homes built with IDB dollars in the 1960's bore Christian Democratic stickers; the Housing Agency under Allende was controlled by Communists. Likewise, the agrarian reform programs previously funded by the bank were, under Allende, administered by people who sought to create a "revolutionary worker-peasant alliance." Buildings constructed with IDB money for "adult-worker upgrading" carried posters of Che Guevara.

The IDB did make two small loans to UP Chile, for the Catholic ($7 million) and Austral ($4.6 million) universities. The Austral was dominated by Chile's conservative German population and the Catholic University was a center of anti-UP activities.

Meanwhile, Chile still continued to pay off its debt to the IDB. In 1971 and 1972, Chile paid back around $16 million and in 1973, $17.5 million was due. By January 1973, Chile was in the ironic position of being a net capital exporter to the Inter-American Development Bank.[46]

The World Bank (International Bank for Reconstruction and Development) granted Chile 18 loans totaling $234,650,000 from its founding in 1944 through 1970.[47] Two loans granted to Chile in 1970 (totaling $30.5 million) were authorized before the election of Allende. Later on, Chile requested loans for a fruit-growing project for the second stage of a cattle-breeding program (begun with the World Bank's cooperation) and for electrical power development under the National Electrical Power Company (Endesa). The electrification program had already been actively supported by the bank for 20 years.

According to representatives of the World Bank interviewed but wishing to remain anonymous, the electrification project was turned down because Chile would not agree to raise electricity rates. The Allende government had adopted a rate schedule that favored the poor and the regime simply refused to raise those rates. The same sources said that agricultural loans were delayed because of U.S. pressure. A public relations officer reiterated the World Bank's official position that failure to approve new loans for Chile was based on evidence that Chile wasn't credit-worthy. In an aside, the officer added, "Allende moved too fast—didn't he realize that the worst thing you can do is to kick an elephant?"

In the words of one of its own publications, the Bank is seen as a "safe bridge over which private capital could move into the international field."[48] To attract private capital into its projects, the Bank hinged its loans upon the availability of a favorable investment climate. Chile, however, not only expropriated the huge copper mines without compensation, but several of the Bank's previous projects were earmarked for nationalization, including the Bio-Bio Cement Company, the Lota-Schwager coal mines and the Paper and Cardboard Corporation. World Bank President Robert McNamara's former employer, Ford Motor Company, left Chile voluntarily, complaining of "impossible conditions" set up by the UP government.

McNamara, who became especially aggressive toward the Allende government stated, "The primary condition for banking lending—a soundly managed economy with a clear potential for utilizing additional funds—has not been met. The Chilean economy is in severe difficulty."[49] Such a statement, coming from the head of the World Bank, was a departure from normal diplomacy. McNamara was probably well aware of the damage such statements would do to Chile's worldwide credit rating.

THE PRIVATE BANKS FOLLOW SUIT

Bankers and suppliers grant credit to importers or national agencies that they consider to be good credit risks: a good risk is a borrower who rates well on the test of the "three C's"—capital, capacity and character.

Chile, like most Latin American nations, had little *capital,* in the sense of permanent exchange reserves. The country's *capacity* to pay had been dependent on the price of copper and on U.S. loans. Many bankers admitted in interviews in San Francisco and New York that Chile had them "worried and concerned" on several occasions, especially in the early sixties. According to one banker (who, like the others interviewed, desired to remain anonymous), "Chile had all the characteristics of underdevelopment: chronic inflation, over-valued currencies, a bad balance of payments—all in all, a reasonably inhospitable climate."

Character refers to a borrower's respect for a contract, a willingness and ability to repay loans—or from an investor's viewpoint, respect for private property. Even during the sixties, Chile's "character" was in question. An officer in a large New York bank said:

> It started with Alessandri. He would come up here and say, 'If you don't give me what I want, you'll have to deal with the Communists.' He ran a miserable government, in finance, budgeting and foreign exchange, just where you'd expect him to be good.
>
> Under Frei, there was an. . .increasing tendency to dishonor commitments. Tomic, as ambassador, left a poor impression. People thought he'd become more civilized here, but he was equally radical when he returned to run[for presidency in 1970].

In view of Chile's relatively low rating on the scale of the three C's, why was there a great increase in lending to Chile during the sixties? From 1955 to 1970, short- and medium-term bank loans to Chile rose from $50 million to over $300 million.[50] (As one banker put it, "Chileans are the world's most charming mendicants.") Banks and other lending agencies seemed willing to overlook the three C's in order to gain a foothold in Chile's expanding market; their risk was greatly lessened because U.S. aid was underwriting the Chilean economy. In effect, bilateral and multilateral aid guaranteed private bankers and suppliers that Chile would be provided the dollars needed to continue participating in the world capitalist game. What Chile lacked in terms of capital, capacity and character, the United States would make up for with loans and continuing pressures to assure that Chile respected private property and foreign investment.

But when Chile elected a Marxist president and the UP government began to act on its program to nationalize foreign-owned industries and to reclaim its natural resources, its three-C rating dropped into the lowest category. Chile no longer respected the sanctity of contracts, and did not allow free capital entry and exit; it had broken all the rules a debtor must obey. Since Chile wasn't playing by the proper rules, the United States stopped playing banker, and cut off public sources of credit, knowing that private bankers and suppliers would follow suit.

Couldn't the Allende government have anticipated this? Didn't Chile want to become less dependent on U.S. loans? The UP did not foresee that nearly all short-term bank credits would be cut. These are not really capital flows, but are the "grease" of trade and, while some U.S. bank credits are good for purchases anywhere in the world, those of other nations are not. Secondly, longer-term loans tend to have a deep effect on a nation's development that cannot be erased overnight, much less in a difficult period of political upheaval. Furthermore, Chile expected larger compensating amounts of credit from some Western European nations, as well as from socialist countries and Japan.

What the UP government failed to realize was that U.S. aid and support had, in effect, made Chile "credit-worthy" for private U.S. investors, bankers and suppliers. UP had hoped that its "legality"—won in the ballot box—would prevent the United States from setting up an economic blockade. But a *formal* blockade was not necessary. All the United States did was to pull out its props from under the Chilean economy and watch the investors scurry away from the collapse.

The bankers and exporters interviewed were quick to deny that any direct political pressure influenced their cut-back of credits to Chile. However, relations between the Treasury and the New York banks are on a day-to-day, personal basis and one banker did admit: "We are influenced to a considerable degree by the attitude of the U.S. government—it couldn't be otherwise. We deal with the USSR, with Yugoslavia and China, but not with Chile. Why? Because of the policy of the government."

Theoretically, however, no direct pressure would really have been necessary. Considering the dependent state of the Chilean economy, Chile would have become a credit risk once the support of the United States (and of the international financial agencies America controls) was withdrawn. The United States started the flight of capital from Chile—its propagating mechanism was described by one banker: "When a capital flight begins, it snowballs. Suppliers' credits to Chile were, perhaps, $300 million, in addition to another $220 million in banker's lines of credit: they were cut. Then profits are remitted faster, and cash balances held in Chile are reduced. No plot is necessary. Each one of us got scared." The effect of the capital outflow was drastic for Chile.

Chile's "current account" (a list of trade balances and profit remittances) historically had been negative, but it was partially balanced by a positive "capital account" (a record of the net dollars available from investments and loans) even after subtracting debt servicing and depreciation. This "capital account" averaged a positive $202 million from 1965-70, but was a negative $212 million in 1971, thus drastically reducing Chile's capacity to make dollar payments and forcing Chile to eat up its reserves.[51]

Thus, the United States hard-line policy toward Chile greatly influenced the decision of the private banks to cut off their credit facilities to Chile. At one time, Chile had around $220 million in short-term credit-lines from U.S. banks; in 1972, only $35 million was available. As already explained, the Eximbank position made it more difficult for bankers to lend to Chile since they no longer got guarantees for their loans. But the official U.S. position was not the only reason for cutting off loans to Chile. The institutional and financial relationship between the banks and the copper companies (whose assets were nationalized) also played a part.

Five major New York Banks—Chase Manhattan, Chemical, First National City, Manufacturers Hanover and Morgan Guarantee—had extended loans to the copper companies. The banks (Chase and Chemical) that had personal ties with Anaconda (the president of Anaconda was once an officer of Chase and a member of Chemical's international advisory board was a vice-president of Anaconda) were the most hostile toward Chile, but all five cut her credit completely.

Three other U.S. banks—Irving Trust, Bankers' Trust and the Bank of America—left open about $35 million in credit lines. Evidently, Chile was not such an absolute risk.

In interviews, the bankers justified cutting credits by referring to U.S. government policy, the copper controversy and the "run on capital" in Chile. As one New Yorker stated:

Many banks represent a financial power base for the political opposition. The Banco de Chile [until Allende, Chile's most aristocratic private bank] wasn't just that dull, grey building off Huerfanos Avenue. It was the board of directors that I

knew personally. As each bank was taken over, we c[
We didn't know if the new director would be an exp[
banker, or a political hack.

In addition, the bankers tended to believe the exaggerated U.S. press reports of "Marxist destruction" of Chile's economy.

Some bankers, especially Europeans, felt that if Allende survived for more than two years or so, some credit lines would reopen. They would rather have dealt with a capitalist regime, but working with a nationalist government was better than no business at all, which is their rationale for doing business with Eastern Europe and China. This reasoning, however, promised great difficulties during "transition" periods for any progressive Third World government.

The denial of official U.S. multilateral and private credits was the first major step in undermining Chile's economy. But, those interested in overthrowing Allende did not stop there. Additional thrusts aimed at destroying Chile's economic reputation included: (1) the U.S. government's rigid position at the Paris debt renegotiations; (2) the embargoes of Chile's New York accounts and warehouses obtained in court actions by Kennecott and Anaconda; and (3) Kennecott's aggressive actions in Europe.

THE DEBT RENEGOTIATIONS

In November 1971, Chile declared a moratorium on its debt repayments to the United States and other countries and asked for a rescheduling of its remaining 1971 debts and of the estimated $414 million due in 1972. Chile's debt repayments would have totaled around $400 million annually for the three years that followed—37 percent of anticipated foreign-exchange earnings.[52] This represented an untenable strain on Chile's already serious shortage of foreign exchange. The Frei government had won a debt postponement in 1965 and bankers admitted that, under normal circumstances, Chile would have been granted a debt consolidation and postponement. Chile's total foreign debt was nearly $4 billion, more than half of which was owed to U.S. government lending agencies and private creditors.

At the early 1972 meetings in Paris, where European and U.S. creditors met with Chilean negotiators, the U.S. sought to block renegotiation. Tactics included stalling, insisting on a formal "stand-by" arrangement that involved an orthodox monetary policy contrary to the UP program and demanding compensation for the copper companies. According to Chile's Central Bank, England and Germany tended to support the United States and France remained neutral, while Italy and Spain leaned towards Chile.[53]

The United States finally dropped its opposition to the renegotiation and the creditor nations agreed to renegotiate 70 percent of the debt, asking that Chile improve its balance of payments (which it did not) and decrease its fiscal deficit and expansion of money supply (which it did). No formal overseeing by the International Monetary Fund was included in the agreement, which Chile considered a major victory.[54]

After agreeing on the broad principles of renegotiation, Chile proceeded to work out the details bilaterally with the different countries involved. As of January 1973, the United States was the only country which had not formally signed bilateral renegotiation agreements.

To extend the debt postponement into 1973, Chile planned to return to Paris to ask that payments be reduced from 30 percent to 15 percent of the $410 million maturing debt.[55] If the U.S. could have swayed some of Chile's other creditors, Chile would have been forced either to accept a "stand-by"[56] and liquidate its revolution, or else default on its debt. The effect of this would have been to isolate Chile from the capitalist world. The United States undoubtedly assumed that this would generate an internal crisis which would force Allende's removal.

U.S. banks, however, operating with commercial motives, agreed to renegotiate approximately $300 million in loans, including $110 million incurred by the copper companies during Frei's Chileanization program. Chile meticulously met the payments due on this consolidated debt, paying $3.6 million in June and December 1972. The banks had also previously called in $180 million of short-term credits, many of which had covered materials imported during the Frei regime.

Under Allende Chile had few problems with the International

Monetary Fund (IMF). The Allende government received $148 million from the IMF for compensation due to a drop in the price of copper, and from its normal allotment of drawing rights.[57] The IMF's continuing aid to Chile was attributed to certain well-placed officials in the IMF bureaucracy who were sympathetic to UP, and to the strong European influence in the IMF as a whole. When the United States tried to oust IMF president Pierre-Paul Schweitzer, Chile rallied Latin American members to his support. However, if Chile had asked the IMF for additional funds, restrictive conditions would probably have been attached.

THE COPPER COMPANIES REACT

Kennecott Corporation joined in the economic offensive against Chile in February 1972 when it "attached" the accounts of several Chilean government agencies operating out of New York, including the Corporacion de Fomento (State Development Corporation—CORFO), and the Corporacion del Cobre (Chilean Copper Corporation—CODELCO). Kennecott did this to force Chile to pay off loans of $92 million which Chile had contracted under the 1967 Chileanization agreement. Chile had probably intended to pay this loan, but it missed the first payment (due in December 1971) because of complicated legal procedures in Chile.[58] Chile paid the installment in March and Kennecott dropped its embargoes.

Anaconda also embargoed some Chilean assets in New York (February 1972) in another attempt to force payments due under the Chileanization agreements. Since the accounts of CODELCO and CORFO were already attached, Anaconda moved against Chile's holdings in New York warehouses. This embargo was in effect for some time and it forced CODELCO to reroute its purchases through ports other than New York. Chile claimed that Anaconda should not be paid the amounts due under the agreements since they, unlike the Kennecott payment, were not reinvested in Chile.[59]

The effect of these embargoes was to further imperil Chile's credit standing in the United States. But Kennecott was still not satisfied. When the corporation was sure it would get no indemnification for its Chilean properties, it declared its own private war on Chile.

On September 30, 1972, Kennecott's threats materialized into legal action when it asked a French court to block payments to Chile for El Teniente copper sold in France. In essence, Kennecott claimed that the expropriation was not valid because there had been no compensation; therefore, Kennecott was still the rightful owner of its 49 percent share of the copper. The court was requested to embargo the proceeds of the sales until it could decide on the Kennecott claim of ownership.

To avoid having a $1,330,000 payment embargoed, French dock workers in Le Havre—in a demonstration of sympathy with Chile—refused to unload the *Birte Ollendorf*. The ship sailed to Holland where it immediately became embroiled in a new set of legal controversies which were ultimately resolved. Finally, the odyssey ended on October 21, 1972, when the ship returned to Le Havre to unload the contested cargo. Copper payments to Chile were impounded until a court rendered a decision on its competence to judge the legality of the expropriation: Chile temporarily was forced to suspend copper shipments to France. The legal battle spread across Europe when Kennecott took similar action in a Swedish court on October 30, 1972, and in German courts in mid-January 1973.

On November 29, 1972, the French court ruled that it was able to determine whether or not Chile's expropriation was illegal and, thereby, to judge Kennecott's claim of ownership. Actions were initiated for conducting a full hearing on the case. At the same time, Chile received the disputed $1.3 million payment. But the court ordered Chile to hold the money in escrow, pending further investigation of the case.[60] Thus, at that moment, Chile could sell copper to French consumers with the obligation to repay Kennecott if the court upheld Kennecott's claim. This litigation process cast a shadow over El Teniente copper.

It was no coincidence that Kennecott chose France as a testing ground for its legal actions. Not only is France a leading consumer of Chile's copper, but, more importantly, France promulgated unusually strong laws protecting private property as a result of its own Algerian experience. For the French courts to recognize the transfer of property through nationalization, CODELCO had to show that it adequately compensated Kennecott.[61]

The Pompidou government assumed a position of neutrality, noting the separation of judicial and executive activities; however, an official source added that France recalled the "correct" line followed by the U.S. when Algeria was nationalizing French oil companies.[62]

According to interviews with Chilean Embassy officials, Kennecott lawyers admitted that their strategy was aimed at pressuring Chile to enter negotiations by depriving it of copper earnings and, possibly, copper markets. They did not really expect to gain the equivalent of compensation by exacting their share of copper sales in legal actions throughout Europe. Even in their summation before the French court, Kennecott lawyers acknowledged that their actions were an exercise in "teaching Chile the political realities of life."[63]

Kennecott knew that its actions would have the following effects on Chile: short-term loss of francs; intimidation of other copper customers, jeopardy of future orders; elimination of credit possibilities based on discounting future copper sales; cutting into Chile's "credit-worthiness"; and forcing Chile to expend foreign currency on legal expenses incurred in Europe.

As of January 1973, the Kennecott strategy had achieved some success. During the previous October and November, copper sales were tied up and Chile had to suspend several shipments of copper. In addition, the Kennecott actions came at a time when Chile was negotiating new copper contracts and potential customers were hesitant to buy "complicated" copper that might end up in litigation and delay production schedules. Most damaging was the impact on negotiations of the $200 million in credit that Chile was negotiating with European banks. As a result of the embargo, those lines were never opened.[64] In addition, Dutch and Canadian credit lines were cut because Chile had become more of a risk.[65] Finally, Chile was forced to spend $150,000 to wage its legal battle against the embargo.[66]

CHILE FACES THE BLOCKADE*

A shortage of dollars was always a constraint on Chile's economy, geared as it was to importing its machines, industrial inputs and some consumer goods. In the past, the limited dollars went to fulfilling the desires of the upper and middle classes. In 1971, the UP had considerable reserves, and imports rose. But the rising consumer power of the workers allowed them to buy goods which previously had been unavailable to them. Thus, the middle classes found themselves competing for an already limited supply of food and consumer goods.

By 1972, the rising demand and the shortage of dollars together produced more serious shortages, especially in parts and replacements for U.S.-made machinery. Further, the dollar scarcity forced a reduction in nonagricultural, consumer-goods imports by 58 percent.[67] Though production was rising, money in circulation—due to rising wages and government spending—was growing faster and demand began to exceed supply for an increasing number of foodstuffs and consumer goods. This was exacerbated by a growing black market where speculators sold hoarded items at tremendous profits.

In September 1972, the Central Bank adopted differential exchange rates in order to ration dollars: food imports were set at 20 escudos to the dollar, while other consumer items were valued at 80 escudos per dollar. This made it easier to import food, which benefited everyone but made it difficult to import the items which benefited mostly the middle classes.

The lack of credit from the United States led to a drastic reduction of Chile's imports from the United States, especially in 1972. Chile had once imported around 40 percent of its total imports from the United States: in 1972, only between 13 and 20 percent of total imports (of nearly $1 billion) came from the United States.[68]

The most immediate effect of the trade reduction was production bottlenecks, caused by lack of replacements and parts for machinery of U.S. origin. Most of these imports could not be obtained elsewhere and the increasing difficulty in buying them caused serious problems in Chilean factories and mines.

In order to break its dependence on the United States, Chile had to diversify its credit and import sources. The UP government actively sought and got trade credits and medium- and long-term

*For a more detailed discussion of the effects of the blockade see the original version of this article, "Facing the Blockade," in *New Chile,* (Berkeley and New York; NACLA, 1973).

loans from many other countries. Nevertheless, most of those credits and loans were tied to purchases in the countries granting them and, as noted, Chile needed to import a substantial amount of food and machinery from the United States in order to feed people and to keep U.S.-made machines and equipment working. The impact of the U.S.-imposed credit blockade could not, in the politically crucial short-run transition period, be offset by credits from other countries. For example, in 1972, Chile paid cash ($5.5 million) for a Boeing 727, even though the USSR made credits available for buying Soviet-made *Ilyushins*. Switching to Soviet-made aircraft would have necessitated retraining Chilean crews, setting up expensive new maintenance facilities and stockpiling new parts, all of which Chile wanted to avoid.

The credit blockade reduced the amount of short-term U.S. credit to Chile from 78.4 percent of the total to around 6.6 percent. Chile partially made up for the loss by negotiating around $490 million in short-term credits from other countries, including $103 million from the USSR, $56 million from Argentina and $52 million from Italy.[69] Nevertheless, the amount did not represent a real replacement of U.S. short-term credits, because (1) many of the credits were tied to purchases in the creditor country and (2) many would not be fully utilized due to traditional dependence on U.S. imports.

Kennecott's embargo of Chilean copper in France cut off some possible credit from European countries who saw that future copper sales were endangered. In fact, Chile was not able to get the financing from European countries it had hoped. As Minister of Foreign Relations Clodomiro Almeyda said, "International capitalism shows structural solidarity. It reacts like an organism when its interests are threatened."[70] As for long-term European investments, Fiat produced trucks in a former Ford Motor plant and was to share Chile's automotive output with two other European firms. Other European investors, however, apparently shied away from a nationalist government in the "unstable" position of being in a struggle with the United States. Likewise, Japan committed nearly $50 million (primarily for mining investments), but no more.[71]

In sharp contrast to the commercial blockade erected around Cuba in the 1960s, Chile won numerous statements of support from other Latin American countries and Chile's trade with its neighbors increased significantly. Expanded imports ranged from more food from Argentina to buses and capital equipment from Brazil. Chile also negotiated $10 million in long-term credits from Brazil, $20 million from Mexico and $40 million from Peru and Argentina.

But the most significant credits came from the socialist countries, with the USSR replacing the United States as the largest lender to Chile. The following medium- and long-term credits had been negotiated with socialist countries as of November 1972 with low or, in some cases (as with China), no interest:[72]

USSR	$259 million
China	$ 55 million
Poland	$ 35 million
Bulgaria	$ 25 million
Hungary	$ 25 million
German Democratic Republic	$ 20 million
Rumania	$ 20 million
Czechoslovakia	$ 5 million
People's Democratic Republic of Korea	$ 5 million

According to a CORFO study which detailed the credits available as of June 1972 (their figures were lower than those given above), 95.2 percent of the credits granted by the socialist countries for use by CORFO had not yet been utilized, compared to 25.8 percent of the credits granted by Western European countries and the United States.[73] This was partly because the credits from socialist countries were largely long-term loans to be used for importing capital or transport equipment. Chile needed immediate credit for consumer items and for replacement parts. The middle classes continued to demand U.S.-style goods.

THE BLOCKADE AND THE MIDDLE CLASS

The economic policy of Unidad Popular had two central thrusts: (1) overcome the stagnation and dependency of the past by socializing the means of production (2) and consolidate the political support needed to undertake this construction. The election of Allende (November 1970) put the powerful executive branch in the hands of the Left, but virtually all the other centers of power—the Congress, the courts, the media, most of the means of production—stayed in opposition hands. UP wanted to use the broad powers of the executive branch to incorporate banks, farms and factories into the state sector and, simultaneously, to augment its political base. With majority backing, the Left could dissolve Congress and write a new, radical constitution that would, as Allende put it, "open the gates to socialism."

At all times, economics and politics were closely intertwined. To win political support, the economic plan of nationalization and income redistribution had to advance successfully; and, for the economic policy—especially nationalization—to proceed successfully UP needed more political support. Allende had won the three-way presidential contest with 36 percent of the vote. To complete the UP economic policy of nationalization and income redistribution, UP needed over a 50 percent plurality. This was both the strength and the weakness of the *vía chilena* (Chilean road) to socialism. If UP could win majority backing, Chile's democratic tradition allowed people to hope that real reforms could be made without much violence. But winning the approval of the majority meant, among other things, maintaining a high level of economic output and satisfaction; and no transition to socialism has occurred without short- and medium-term economic dislocations and without threatening those who had previously benefited from the unjust economic system. By early 1973 it was clear that the credit blockade was a strategy aptly adapted to fit the *vía chilena*. The financial blockade made it difficult for Chile to maintain economic growth the shortage of dollars frightened members of the middle class, who had used most of the consumer imports in the past. The UP Program did not really threaten Chile's middle class—white-collar workers, storekeepers, some professionals and so on—but scarcities of foodstuffs, consumer items and other goods did. These shortages were exacerbated by the right wing's sabotage of the economy. By 1973, economic problems had produced a situation in which the extreme right wing and its allies in the military could count on either implicit or explicit support from Chile's middle class. There is little doubt that U.S. policymakers hoped that this would happen and planned their policy towards Chile to provoke an alliance designed to put an end to Chile's experiment with "the peaceful road to socialism."

NOTES

1. For a fuller documentation see Part 1 (Chile's Dependence on Dollars) of the original version of this chapter in *New Chile*, NACLA (1973): 179-85.

2. Anibal Quijano, "Nationalism and Capitalism in Peru," *Monthly Review* 23 (July-August 1971).

3. We will not go into detail in this chapter about the early interchanges between the U.S. and UP governments. For details on this, see "Coexistence or Confrontation?" *New Chile*, NACLA (1972), and James Petras and Robert La Porte, Jr., "Chile: No" *Foreign Policy*, no. 7 (Summer 1972): 132-58. We wish to thank Petras and La Porte for supplying us with the original uncut version of that article, hereafter referred to as Petras and La Porte, original.

4. Harry Magdoff, *The Age of Imperialism* (New York: Monthly Review Press, 1969), p. 14. Emphasis ours.

5. U.S. Department of State, External Research Study, "Impact of Economic Nationalism on Key Mineral Resource Industries, Proceedings of a Conference sponsored by the Bureau of Intelligence and Research," November 10, 1971 (Study published March 20, 1972), p. 119. Emphasis ours.

6. Bilateral aid is granted by a U.S. institution to a foreign country. Multilateral aid is granted by an institution with many nations represented, like the World Bank. Suppliers' credits are credits extended by producers to foreign importers.

7. Treasury controls U.S. policy on bilateral and multilateral aid through several mechanisms. (1) It chairs the National Advisory Council, whose purpose is to "coordinate the policies and operations of the United States" on the International Monetary Fund and the World Bank and "of all agencies of the government which make or participate in making foreign

loans or which engage in foreign financial-exchange or monetary transactions." Mark L. Chadwin, "Foreign Policy Report, Nixon Administration Debates New Position Paper on Latin America," *National Journal,* January 15, 1972, 106. (2) The U.S. representatives at the Inter-American Development Bank and the executive director of the World Bank and International Development Association boards are Treasury officials, directly answerable to the secretary of the treasury.

8. See Dom Bonafede, "White House Report/Peterson Unit Helps Shape Tough International Economic Policy," *National Journal,* November 13, 1971, 2242, and Fred Block and Larry Hirschhorn, "The International Monetary Crisis," *Socialist Revolution,* September-October, 1972, 7-51. See also "The End of U.S. Hegemony," *Monthly Review,* October 1971.

9. Quoted in "The End of U.S. Hegemony," p. 3.

10. Quoted by Dom Bonafede, "White House Report/Peterson. . .," p. 2238.

11. Ibid., p. 2248.

12. Peter G. Peterson, *The United States in a Changing World Economy* (Washington: U.S. Government Printing Office, 1971), 2:41-43.

13. Ibid., 1:41-45.

14. Frank K. Fowlkes, "Economic Report/Connally Revitalizes Treasury, Assumes Stewardship of Nixon's New Economic Policy," *National Journal,* October 2, 1971, 1991.

15. U.S. Department of State External Research Study, "Impact of Economic. . .," p. 92.

16. The restrictions imposed by Johnson were at first voluntary and then mandatory after 1968. Ceilings on the amount of foreign investment allowed to a corporation varied from region to region. The ceiling was most limiting in the Western European region because it was low compared to the level of foreign investment there. In the Third World, the ceiling was high compared to the level of foreign investment and had not hindered investment from going to that part of the world.

17. We thank Fred Block for helping us clarify our ideas on these points.

18. *New York Times,* December 2, 1972.

19. On the differences between State and Treasury, see below and also Petras and La Porte, "Chile: No", pp. 22-27. State had in the past, justified its "softer" line by pointing out that it was in the U.S. national interest to get its loans to underdeveloped countries paid back. Thus, aid should have continued in sufficient amounts to cover payment. See *Yanqui Dollar*, NACLA (1971).

20. President Nixon, Policy Statement, "Economic Assistance, and Investment Security in Developing Nations," press release, January 13, 1972.

21. The discussion of the formation of the policy comes from information in Mark Chadwin, "Foreign Policy Report, Nixon Administration Debates New Position Paper on Latin America," Part 1, *National Journal*, January 15, 1972, and from Chadwin, "Nixon's Expropriations Policy Seeks to Woo the Angry Congress," Part 2, *National Journal*, January 22, 1972, 150-53. The former will hereafter be referred to as Chadwin, "Part 1," the latter as Chadwin, "Part 2."

22. Chadwin, "Part 2," pp. 150-52.

23. Bonafede, "White House Report/Peterson. . .," p. 2245.

24. See Chadwin, "Part 2," p. 152 and Petras and La Porte, "Chile: No," pp. 18-27.

25. Chadwin, "Part 2," p. 152.

26. Quoted in Chadwin, "Part 1," p. 104.

27. Quoted by Lewis H. Diuguid in *The Washington Post*, June 11, 1972, p. 36.

28. "Nixon Expropriation Warning Greeted Coolly," *National Journal*, February 12, 1972, 238.

29. Senator Edward Kennedy, "U.S. Expropriations Policy Shortsighted," *Congressional Record*, January 4, 1972, p. 5317.

30. Quoted by Benjamin Welles, *The New York Times*, October 23, 1971.

31. In *New York Times*, July 3, 1972. See also, "Secret Memos from ITT," in NACLA, *Latin American and Empire Report* (April 1972).

32. Chadwin, "Part 1," p. 101. The special case of Kennecott acting on its own to defend its interests will be considered below.

33. It is especially enlightening to note the predominance of bankers in the formation of the policy towards expropriating nations. This reflected the dominance of the Treasury Department, which was, as Representative Wright Patman (head of the House Subcommittee on Banking and Finance) decried, increasingly controlled by commercial banking interests, (in *Congressional Record,* House, January 23, 1969, p. H422). We have compiled a list of 20 men who played an important part in the development of the expropriations policy. Eight of them had been banking executives. Others were either former businessmen or lawyers with strong ties to international corporations.

34. United States Department of Commerce, "U.S. Exports by Chief Economic Categories" (1971).

35. *Chile, Dirección de presupuestos,* folleto no. 122, "Exposición sobre la política economica del gobierno y del estado de la hacienda pública," presented by Minister of Finance, Orlando Millas Correa to the *Comisión Mixta de Presupuestos* (Santiago, November 15, 1972) hereafter referred to simply as Millas, "Budget Speech."

36. For an analysis in a broader context of this process, see Magdoff, *The Age of Imperialism,* p. 91.

37. See "Financing U.S. Exports and Overseas Investment" (Washington, D.C.: 1964), Machinery and Allied Products Institute, p. 12. (The information on Eximbank operations came from various Eximbank annual reports and literature supplied by the FCIA.)

38. *Wall Street Journal,* June 4, 1971.

39. *Wall Street Journal,* October 14, 1971. The AID data is available in *New Chile,* NACLA (1972), pp. 47-49.

40. See "Leaders for Labor," *New Chile,* NACLA (1972).

41. U.S. AID, Development and Humanitarian Assistance Program, presentation to Congress FY 1973, project and program data.

42. For more on this, see "Support for your Local Police," *New Chile,* NACLA (1972).

43. Tad Szulc, *New York Times,* December 9, 1972.

44. *Washington Post,* September 29, 1972, and *New York Times,* same date.

45. *Los Angeles Times,* October 4, 1972.

46. Information on IDB operations came from interviews conducted there as well as pertinent IDB annual reports. See also *New Chile*, NACLA (1972), p. 47, and Hector Melo and Israel Yost, "Funding the Empire, Part 2 — The Multinational Strategy," NACLA *Newsletter*, vol. 4, no. 3 (May-June 1970).

47. World Bank, International Development Association (Annual Report, 1972), p. 124.

48. Quoted in *Yanqui Dollar*, NACLA (1971) from World Bank, IDA and IFC, "Policies and Operations," (Washington, June 1969), p. 3.

49. *Barron's*, October 23, 1972.

50. From an interview with an official of Manufacturers Hanover Bank, conducted December 1972.

51. Chile, Banco Central, See "Desarrollo monetario y problemas generales de intercambio," (1972).

52. See Inter-American Committee of the Alliance for Progress (CIAP) report, "Domestic Efforts and the Needs for External Financing for the Development of Chile" (April 21, 1972), p. 139. Hereafter referred to as CIAP Report.

53. From interviews carried out in the Banco Central de Chile by George Lawton, whom we thank for his help.

54. From an unpublished internal circular on the debt renegotiations by Banco Central de Chile.

55. CIAP Report, p. 144.

56. In a stand-by arrangement, a country needing IMF aid could make drawings from the fund up to a stated amount over a stated period, usually one year. Generally, governments wanting stand-by arrangements had to agree, in a "letter of intent," to achieve financial and monetary stability, as defined by the IMF.

57. *New York Times*, December 1972.

58. Kennecott had reloaned to Chile the $80 million that Chile had paid for its 51 percent interest in the El Teniente mine. This, plus interest, is what Kennecott wanted paid back in 1971. Chile was late in paying because it had determined—under the constitutional amendment nationalizing copper holdings—that it would repay only those loans which had been

usefully invested. In February 1972, Allende announced that most of the loan had been usefully invested and would be repaid.

59. The Anaconda dispute differed from Kennecott's in that it concerned the payment of promissory notes issued during the expropriation of the Anaconda properties, rather than loans. Under the scope of the nationalization of the properties, outstanding notes were to be used in the calculation for compensation and, thus, subject to deductions for excess profits. (From interviews with the legal advisor in the Chilean Embassy.)

60. Interview with Claudio Bonnefoy.

61. Ibid.

62. *Los Angeles Times,* October 17, 1972.

63. Interview at Chilean Embassy, Washington, D.C., December 6, 1972.

64. Allende U.N. Address, p. 8.

65. *Wall Street Journal,* October 12, 1972.

66. This figure includes legal fees, extra shipping costs and interest on embargoed funds. Orlando Millas detailed the costs in a speech to the budget commission of the Chile congress.

67. Millas, "Budget Speech," p. 57.

68. From interviews in the Chilean Embassy and in the New York CORFO office.

69. Millas, "Budget Speech," pp. 13-15.

70. Quoted in *Chile Hoy* (Santiago, November 3-9, 1972) p. 13.

71. From interviews at CORFO and with Japanese representatives to UNCTAD III, Santiago, 1972.

72. Millas, "Budget Speech," pp. 14-15.

73. CORFO, Gerencia de Producción Financiera, Dpto. de Créditos Externos, "Disponibilidad de recursos financieros externos para proyectos de inversión," 1972.

The Contributors

ROBERT L. AYRES is Assistant Professor of Political Science at the University of California, Berkeley. His articles on Chilean politics and Latin American development policy have appeared in *Comparative Politics*, *Studies in Comparative International Development*, *The American Political Science Review*, *The Journal of Developing Areas*, and *World Politics*. He is currently engaged in research on the politics of economic policy-making in contemporary Argentina.

PATRICIO CHAPARRO is on the faculty of the Instituto de Ciencias Políticas, Universidad Católica de Chile. He has written articles on urbanization and politics and political campaigns in Chile, and has just completed a major study of student politics in that country.

ELIZABETH FARNSWORTH has spent the past 4 years researching U.S.–Chile policy at the North American Congress on Latin America, where she is a staff member. She is an editor of NACLA's book, *New Chile*, and co-author of a new NACLA publication on U.S.–Chile policy since the coup, "Propping up the Junta," *Latin America and Empire Report*, October 1974.

374

RICHARD FEINBERG is a graduate student in economics at Stanford University, specializing in the political economy of international finance and trade. He spent two years in Chile with the Peace Corps, working in the communications division of the Department of Agriculture, during the final year of the Frei and the first year of the Allende administrations. His observations on the Chile of that period appear in his *The Triumph of Allende: Chile's Legal Revolution* (New American Library, 1972). He has published in *Latin American Perspectives*, *Kapitalistate*, and the *Rolling Stone.*

ERIC LEENSON, who graduated from Princeton University in international affairs, studied in Chile in 1970-1971 on a Fulbright scholarship. Since the coup, he has been active in the Chile solidarity movement.

BRIAN LOVEMAN is Assistant Professor of Political Science at San Diego State University. He served in the Peace Corps in Chile and returned to conduct his dissertation research on politics in rural Chile. He is the author of several articles on the general topic of agrarian reform published in Chile and the United States. His book *Struggle in the Countryside: Chile 1919-1973*, is forthcoming.

JAMES PETRAS has written widely on Chilean and Latin American topics. He is Professor of Sociology at the State University of New York at Binghamton. His publications include *Politics and Social Forces in Chilean Development*, *Politics and Social Structure in Latin America*, and *Cultivating Revolution* (with Robert Laporte).

ALEJANDRO PORTES is Professor of Sociology at Duke University. He is the author of over three dozen articles published in scholarly journals since 1968 on theoretical and Latin American topics. His research in Chile in 1969 led to a series of articles on the relationship between political radicalism and various socio-economic variables. He is currently studying, among other things, the assimilation of Latin American immigrants to the United States.

JAMES PROTHRO, Professor of Political Science and Research Professor, Institute for Research in Social Science, at the University of North Carolina in Chapel Hill, is a noted authority on United States politics. He is the coauthor of *The Politics of American Democracy* and *Negroes and the New Southern Politics*, as well as author of numerous articles and books on topics such as public opinion, political parties and voting behavior. He has lectured at the Latin American Faculty of Social Sciences (FLACSO) in Santiago, Chile and directed a Social Science Research Council project in that city in July and August 1972.

RICHARD E. RATCLIFF is on the faculty of the Department of Sociology at Washington University, St. Louis. He has done extensive research on kinship networks of the Chilean upper class and is co-author with Maurice Zeitlin and Lynda Ann Ewen of the forthcoming study *Corporate Capital: The Large Corporation and The Capitalist Class in Chile.*

PAUL SIGMUND is Professor of Politics at Princeton University. A political theorist, he is the author of *Nicholas of Cusa and Medieval Political Thought.* In addition, he has written several articles on Chilean Christian Democracy and Chilean affairs, including "The Invisible Blockade and the Overthrow of Allende," *Foreign Affairs* (January 1974) in which he takes issue with the thesis presented by Farnsworth et. al. in this volume. He is also the author of a forthcoming book on contemporary Chilean political history.

ARTURO VALENZUELA is Director of the Comparative Area Studies Program and a member of the faculty of the Department of Political Science at Duke University. He is the author of *Center-Local Linkages in Chile: Local Government in a Centralized Polity* (forthcoming, Duke University Press) and articles on Chilean politics. His extensive study on "The Breakdown of Chilean Democracy" will be published shortly in Juan Linz and Alfred Stepan, *Breakdowns and Crisis of Democratic Regimes.* An abridged version of that essay appeared in the *Rivista Italiana di Scienza Politica*, Vol. 5, No. 1 (April, 1975), pp. 83-129.

J. SAMUEL VALENZUELA, a Doctoral Candidate in Sociology at Columbia University, has written articles on Chilean society and Chilean labor, published in Chile and the United States. He has presented papers at the International Sociological Association and the Association Internationale des Sociologues de Langue Francaise. His doctoral dissertation is a comparative study of the Chilean and French labor movements.

MAURICE ZEITLIN, Professor of Sociology at the University of Wisconsin (Madison), is the author of *Revolutionary Politics and the Cuban Working Class* and the editor of *American Society, Inc.: Studies of the Social Structure and Political Economy of the United States*. The chapter in this volume is part of a forthcoming study, with Lynda Ann Ewen and Richard Earl Ratcliff, *Corporate Capital: The Large Corporation and the Capitalist Class in Chile.*

Bibliography

Selected Bibiliography of Sources in English

Alexander, Robert. *Labor Relations in Argentina, Brazil, and Chile.* New York: McGraw-Hill Book Co., 1962.

Angell, Alan. *Politics and the Labour Movement in Chile.* London: Oxford University Press, 1972.

Ayres, Robert. "Economic Stagnation and the Emergence of the Political Ideology of Chilean Underdevelopment." *World Politics* 25 (October 1972): 34-61.

Barraclough, Solon. "Agrarian Reform and Structural Change in Latin America: The Chilean Case." *Journal of Development Studies* 8 (January 1972): 163-181.

Bray, Donald W. "Chile: The Dark Side of Stability." *Studies on the Left* 4 (Fall 1964): 85-96.

Debray, Regis. *The Chilean Revolution: Conversations with Allende.* New York: Vintage Books, 1971.

Feinberg, Richard. *The Triumph of Allende: Chile's Legal*

Revolution. New York: Signet, 1972.

Frank, Andre Gunder. *Capitalism and Underdevelopment in Latin America: Historical Studies of Chile and Brazil.* New York: Monthly Review Press, 1967.

Frei, Eduardo. "Chilean Democracy in Theory and Action." In *The Ideologies of the Developing Nations*, edited by Paul E. Sigmund. New York: Frederick A. Praeger, 1964.

Galdames, Luis. *A History of Chile.* Translated and edited by Isaac J. Cox. Chapel Hill, N.C.: University of North Carolina Press, 1941.

Gil, Federico. *The Political System of Chile.* Boston: Houghton Mifflin Co., 1966.

Goldrich, Daniel; Pratt, Raymond B., and Schuller, C.R. "The Political Integration of Lower Class Urban Settlements in Chile and Peru." *Studies in Comparative International Development* 3 (1967-68): 1-22.

Gray, Richard B., and Kerwin, Frederick R. "Presidential Succession in Chile: 1877-1966." *Journal of Inter-American Studies* 11 (January 1969): 144-159.

Gregory, Peter. *Industrial Wages in Chile.* Ithaca: New York State School of Industrial and Labor Relations, Cornell University, 1967.

Halperin, Ernest. *Nationalism and Communism in Chile.* Cambridge, Mass.: MIT Press, 1964.

Herrick, Bruce H. *Urban Migration and Economic Development in Chile.* Cambridge, Mass.: MIT Press, 1965.

Hirschman, Albert. *Journeys Toward Progress.* New York: The Twentieth Century Fund, 1963.

Johnson, Dale. "Industrialization, Social Mobility, and Class Formation in Chile." *Studies in Comparative International Development* 3 (1967-68): 127-51.

380   BIBLIOGRAPHY

Johnson, Dale, ed. *The Chilean Road to Socialism.* New York: Anchor Books, 1973.

Kaufman, Robert R. *The Politics of Land Reform in Chile 1950-1970. Public Policy, Political Institutions, and Social Change.* Cambridge, Mass.: Harvard University Press, 1972.

Landsberger, Henry; Barrera, Manuel; and Toro, Abel. "The Chilean Labor Union Leader: A Preliminary Report On His Background and Attitudes," *Industrial and Labor Relations Review*[17] (April 1964): 399-420.

Mamalakis, Markos. *The Changing Structure and Roles of the Chilean Agricultural Sector.* New Haven: Economic Growth Center, Yale University, 1967.

Mamalakis, Markos, and Reynolds, Clark W. *Essays on the Chilean Economy.* Homewood, Ill.: Richard D. Irwin, 1964.

Menges, Constantine. "Public Policy and Organized Business in Chile: A Preliminary Analysis." *Journal of International Affairs* 20 (1966): 343-65.

Moran, Theodore. "The Alliance for Progress and 'The Foreign Copper Companies and Their Local Conservative Allies' in Chile 1955-1970." *Inter-American Economic Affairs* 25 (Spring 1972): 3-24.

Morris, James O. *Elites, Intellectuals, and Consensus: A Study of the Social Question and the Industrial Relations System in Chile.* Ithaca, N.Y.: Cornell University Press, 1966.

North American Congress on Latin America. *New Chile,* Rev. ed. Berkeley, Calif.: Waller Press, 1973.

North, Liisa. *Civil Military Relations in Argentina, Chile, and Peru.* Berkeley: Institute of International Studies, University of California, 1966.

Parrish, Charles J.; Lazar, Arpad J. von; and Tapia-Videla, Jorge I "Electoral Procedures and Political Parties in Chile." *Studies in Comparative International Development* (1970-71): 255-67.

Petras, James. *Politics and Social Forces in Chilean Development.* Berkeley, Calif.: University of California Press, 1969.

Petras, James. "The Transition to Socialism in Chile: Perspectives and Problems." *Monthly Review* 23 (October 1971): 43-71.

Petras, James, and Zemelman, Hugo. *Peasants in Revolt; A Chilean Case Study, 1965-1971.* Austin, Texas: University of Texas Press, 1972.

Pike, Frederick. *Chile and the United States.* Notre Dame, Ind.: University of Notre Dame Press, 1963.

Pike, Frederick. "Aspects of Class Relations in Chile, 1850-1960." *Hispanic-American Historical Review* 43 (February 1963): 14-33.

Portes, Alejandro. "Urbanization and Politics in Latin America." *Social Science Quarterly* 52 (December 1971): 697-720.

Sinding, Steven. "The Evolution of Chilean Voting Patterns: A Re-Examination of Some Old Assumptions." *Journal of Politics* 34 (August 1972):774-96.

Stevenson, John R. *The Chilean Popular Front.* Philadelphia: University of Pennsylvania Press, 1942.

Sunkel, Osvaldo. "Change and Frustration in Chile." In *Obstacles to Change in Latin America*, edited by Claudio Veliz. London: Oxford University Press, 1969.

Valenzuela, Arturo. "The Scope of the Chilean Party System." *Comparative Politics* 4 (January 1972): 179-99.

Zammit, Ann, ed. *The Chilean Way to Socialism.* Austin, Texas: University of Texas Press, 1973.

Zeitlin, Maurice. "The Social Determinants of Political Democracy in Chile." In *Latin America: Reform or Revolution?*
by James Petras and Maurice Zeitlin. Greenwich,
Conn.: Fawcett Publications, Inc., 1968.

Zemelman, Hugo, and Leon, Patricio. "Political Opposition
to the Government of Allende." *Government and Opposition*
7 (Summer 1972): 327-50.

INDEX